ST.

READINGS ON VIRTUE, LAW, AND POLITICS

EDITED BY L. JOSEPH HEBERT

Revised & Expanded Print Edition Copyright © 2018 by L. Joseph Hebert
ISBN #: 1497372305

Translation of *De Divinis Moribus* © 1995 Sophia Institute Press,
used with kind permission.

MARIÆ IMMACULATÆ - SEDI SAPIENTIÆ

TABLE OF CONTENTS

Summa Theologiæ 15
Prologue 15
First Part 15
    Question 1. The nature and extent of sacred doctrine 15
        Article 1. Whether, besides philosophy, any further doctrine is required?
.... 15
        Article 8. Whether sacred doctrine is a matter of argument? 17
    Question 2. The existence of God 18
        Article 3. Whether God exists? 18
    Question 48. The distinction of things in particular 21
        Article 1. Whether evil is a nature? 21
        Article 4. Whether evil corrupts the whole good? 23
    Question 75. Man, who is composed of a spiritual and a corporeal substance: and in the first place, concerning what belongs to the essence of the soul 25
        Article 4. Whether the soul is man? 25
    Question 83. Free-will 26
        Article 1. Whether man has free-will? 26
    Question 103. The government of things in general 28
        Article 5. Whether all things are subject to the Divine government? 28
        Article 6. Whether all things are immediately governed by God? 30
    Question 104. The special effects of the divine government 32
        Article 3. Whether God can annihilate anything? 32
        Article 4. Whether anything is annihilated? 33
First Part of the Second Part 35
    Question 1. Man's last end 35
        Article 1. Whether it belongs to man to act for an end? 35

- Article 7. Whether all men have the same last end? ... 36
- Question 5. The attainment of happiness ... 37
  - Article 3. Whether one can be happy in this life? ... 37
  - Article 5. Whether man can attain happiness by his natural powers? ... 38
  - Article 7. Whether any good works are necessary that man may receive happiness from God? ... 40
- Question 19. The goodness and malice of the interior act of the will ... 41
  - Article 3. Whether the goodness of the will depends on reason? ... 41
  - Article 5. Whether the will is evil when it is at variance with erring reason? ... 42
  - Article 6. Whether the will is good when it abides by erring reason? ... 45
- Question 21. The consequences of human actions by reason of their goodness and malice ... 47
  - Article 3. Whether a human action is meritorious or demeritorious in so far as it is good or evil? ... 47
- Question 23. How the passions differ from one another ... 48
  - Article 1. Whether the passions of the desiring part are different from those of the spirited part? ... 48
- Question 55. The virtues, as to their essence ... 50
  - Article 4. Whether virtue is suitably defined? ... 50
- Question 58. The difference between moral and intellectual virtues ... 52
  - Article 2. Whether moral virtue differs from intellectual virtue? ... 52
  - Article 4. Whether there can be moral without intellectual virtue? ... 54
  - Article 5. Whether there can be intellectual without moral virtue? ... 56
- Question 59. Moral virtue in relation to the passions ... 57
  - Article 5. Whether there can be moral virtue without passion? ... 57
- Question 61. The cardinal virtues ... 58
  - Article 3. Whether any other virtues should be called principal rather than these? ... 58
- Question 62. The theological virtues ... 60

Article 3. Whether faith, hope, and charity are fittingly reckoned as theological virtues?..60

Question 63. The cause of virtues..61

Article 2. Whether any virtue is caused in us by habituation?..................61

Question 64. The mean of virtue..63

Article 1. Whether moral virtues observe the mean?..................................63

Article 2. Whether the mean of moral virtue is the real mean, or the rational mean?..64

Article 3. Whether the intellectual virtues observe the mean?..................65

Article 4. Whether the theological virtues observe the mean?..................67

Question 65. The connection of virtues..68

Article 1. Whether the moral virtues are connected with one another?..68

Article 2. Whether moral virtues can be without charity?..................72

Article 3. Whether charity can be without moral virtue?..................73

Question 67. The duration of virtues after this life..75

Article 1. Whether the moral virtues remain after this life?..................75

Question 69. The beatitudes..76

Article 2. Whether the rewards assigned to the beatitudes refer to this life?..76

Article 3. Whether the beatitudes are suitably enumerated?..................78

Question 71. Vice and sin considered in themselves..82

Article 2. Whether vice is contrary to nature?..................82

Question 82. Original sin, as to its essence..84

Article 3. Whether original sin is desire?..................84

Question 85. The effects of sin, and, first, of the corruption of the good of nature..85

Article 1. Whether sin diminishes the good of nature?..................85

Article 2. Whether the entire good of human nature can be destroyed by sin?..87

Question 90. The essence of law..89

Article 1. Whether law is something pertaining to reason?...............89
Article 2. Whether the law is always something directed to the common good?..90
Article 3. Whether the reason of any man is competent to make laws? 92
Article 4. Whether promulgation is essential to a law?........................93

Question 91. The various kinds of law...94
Article 1. Whether there is an eternal law?..94
Article 2. Whether there is in us a natural law?....................................95
Article 3. Whether there is a human law?...96
Article 4. Whether there was any need for a Divine law?...................97

Question 92. The effects of law..99
Article 1. Whether an effect of law is to make men good?..................99

Question 94. The natural law...101
Article 2. Whether the natural law contains several precepts, or only one?..101
Article 3. Whether all acts of virtue are prescribed by the natural law? 103
Article 4. Whether the natural law is the same in all men?................104
Article 5. Whether the natural law can be changed?..........................106
Article 6. Whether the law of nature can be abolished from the heart of man?...108

Question 95. Human law..109
Article 1. Whether it was useful for laws to be framed by men?........109
Article 2. Whether every human law is derived from the natural law? 111

Question 96. The power of human law..113
Article 1. Whether human law should be framed for the community rather than for the individual?..113
Article 2. Whether it belongs to the human law to repress all vices? .114
Article 3. Whether human law prescribes acts of all the virtues?........116
Article 4. Whether human law binds a man in conscience?..............117

Table of Contents

   Article 5. Whether all are subject to the law? 118

   Article 6. Whether he who is under a law may act beside the letter of the law? 120

Question 97. Change in laws 122

   Article 1. Whether human law should be changed in any way? 122

   Article 2. Whether human law should always be changed, whenever something better occurs? 123

   Article 3. Whether custom can obtain force of law? 124

   Article 4. Whether the rulers of the people can dispense from human laws? 126

Question 100. The moral precepts of the old law 127

   Article 1. Whether all the moral precepts of the Old Law belong to the law of nature? 127

   Article 2. Whether the moral precepts of the Law are about all the acts of virtue? 129

Question 105. The reason for the judicial precepts 130

   Article 1. Whether the Old Law enjoined fitting precepts concerning rulers? 130

   Article 2. Whether the judicial precepts were suitably framed as to the relations of one man with another? 134

   Article 3. Whether the judicial precepts regarding foreigners were framed in a suitable manner? 145

   Article 4. Whether the Old Law set forth suitable precepts about the members of the household? 149

Second Part of the Second Part 155

   Question 2. The act of faith 155

   Article 7. Whether it is necessary for the salvation of all, that they should believe explicitly in the mystery of Christ? 155

   Question 4. The virtue itself of faith 157

   Article 8. Whether faith is more certain than science and the other intellectual virtues? 157

   Question 10. Unbelief in general 159

Article 1. Whether unbelief is a sin? 159

Article 8. Whether unbelievers ought to be compelled to the faith? 160

Article 10. Whether unbelievers may have authority or dominion over the faithful? 162

Article 11. Whether the rites of unbelievers ought to be tolerated? 164

Article 12. Whether the children of Jews and other unbelievers ought to be baptized against their parents' will? 165

Question 11. Heresy 168

Article 3. Whether heretics ought to be tolerated? 168

Question 23. Charity, considered in itself 170

Article 1. Whether charity is friendship? 170

Article 7. Whether any true virtue is possible without charity? 171

Question 25. The object of charity 173

Article 1. Whether the love of charity stops at God, or extends to our neighbor? 173

Article 4. Whether a man ought to love himself out of charity? 175

Article 6. Whether we ought to love sinners out of charity? 176

Article 7. Whether sinners love themselves? 178

Article 8. Whether charity requires that we should love our enemies? 179

Question 26. The order of charity 181

Article 2. Whether God ought to be loved more than our neighbor? .. 181

Article 3. Whether out of charity, man is bound to love God more than himself? 182

Article 4. Whether our of charity, man ought to love himself more than his neighbor? 183

Article 6. Whether we ought to love one neighbor more than another? 185

Article 7. Whether we ought to love those who are better more those who are more closely united us? 186

Article 13. Whether the order of charity endures in heaven? 188

Question 28. Joy 190
    Article 1. Whether joy is effected in us by 190
    charity? 190

Question 33. Fraternal correction 191
    Article 1. Whether fraternal correction is an act of charity? 191

Question 37. Discord, which is contrary to peace 193
    Article 1. Whether discord is a sin? 193

Question 40. War 195
    Article 1. Whether it is always sinful to wage war? 195

Question 47. Prudence, considered in itself 197
    Article 8. Whether command is the chief act of prudence? 197
    Article 10. Does prudence extend to the governing of many? 198
    Article 11. Whether prudence about one's own good is specifically the same as that which extends to the common good? 200
    Article 12. Whether prudence is in subjects, or only in their rulers? .. 201
    Article 15. Whether prudence is in us by nature? 202

Question 49. Each quasi-integral part of prudence 203
    Article 3. Whether docility should be accounted a part of prudence? 203
    Article 7. Whether circumspection can be a part of prudence? 204

Question 57. Right 206
    Article 1. Whether right is the object of justice? 206
    Article 2. Whether right is fittingly divided into natural right and positive right? 207
    Article 3. Whether the right of nations is the same as the natural right? 209
    Article 4. Whether paternal right and right of dominion should be distinguished as special species? 210

Question 58. Justice 212

Article 1. Whether justice is fittingly defined as being the perpetual and constant will to render to each one his right? 212

Article 3. Whether justice is a virtue? 213

Article 5. Whether justice is a general virtue? 215

Article 6. Whether justice, as a general virtue, is essentially the same as all virtue? 216

Article 7. Whether there is a particular besides a general justice? 217

Article 8. Whether particular justice has a special matter? 219

Article 12. Whether justice stands foremost among all moral virtues? 220

Question 60. Judgment 221

Article 2. Whether it is lawful to judge? 221

Article 4. Whether doubts should be 222

interpreted for the best? 222

Article 5. Whether we should always judge according to the written law? 224

Question 64. Murder 225

Article 2. Whether it is lawful to kill sinners? 225

Article 3. Whether it is lawful for a private individual to kill a man who has sinned? 227

Article 5. Whether it is lawful to kill oneself? 228

Article 6. Whether it is lawful to kill the innocent? 230

Article 7. Whether it is lawful to kill a man in self-defense? 232

Question 66. Theft and robbery 234

Article 1. Whether it is natural for man to possess external things? .. 234

Article 2. Whether it is lawful for a man to possess a thing as his own? 235

Article 7. Whether it is lawful to steal through stress of need? 236

Question 78. The sin of usury 238

Article 1. Whether it is a sin to take usury for money lent? 238

Question 104. Obedience 241

Article 5. Whether subjects are bound to obey their superiors in all things? 241

Article 6. Whether Christians are bound to obey the secular powers? 243

Question 108. Vengeance 244

Article 1. Whether vengeance is lawful? 244

Question 110. The vices opposed to truth, and first of lying 247

Article 3. Whether every lie is a sin? 247

Article 4. Whether every lie is a mortal sin? 250

Question 120. "Epikeia" or equity 252

Article 1. Whether "epikeia" is a virtue? 252

Question 123. Fortitude 254

Article 5. Whether fortitude is properly about dangers of death in battle? 254

Article 6. Whether endurance is the chief act of fortitude? 255

Article 7. Whether the brave man acts for the sake of the good of his habit? 256

Article 8. Whether the brave man delights in his act? 257

Article 10. Whether the brave man makes use of anger in his action? 259

Question 129. Magnanimity 260

Article 3. Whether magnanimity is a virtue? 260

Question 130. Presumption 263

Article 1. Whether presumption is a sin? 263

Article 2. Whether presumption is opposed to magnanimity by excess? 264

Question 131. Ambition 266

Article 1. Whether ambition is a sin? 266

Article 2. Whether ambition is opposed to 267

magnanimity by excess? 267

Question 132. Vainglory 269

Article 1. Whether the desire of glory is a sin? 269

Article 2. Whether vainglory is opposed to magnanimity?...................271
Question 133. Pusillanimity..272
   Article 1. Whether pusillanimity is a sin?..272
   Article 2. Whether pusillanimity is opposed to magnanimity?..............274
Question 141. Temperance...275
   Article 4. Whether temperance is only about desires and pleasures of touch?..275
Question 153. Lust..277
   Article 2. Whether no venereal act can be without sin?......................277
Question 154. The parts of Lust..279
   Article 1. Whether six species are fittingly assigned to lust?................279
Question 157. Clemency and meekness...281
   Article 2. Whether both clemency and meekness are virtues?............281
Question 161. Humility..283
   Article 1. Whether humility is a virtue?..283
   Article 3. Whether one ought, by humility, to subject oneself to all men?..285
Question 182. The active life in comparison with the contemplative life..286
   Article 1. Whether the active life is more excellent than the contemplative?...286
   Article 3. Whether the contemplative life is hindered by the active life?..289

Supplement to the Third Part..291
   Question 41. The sacrament of Matrimony as directed to an office of nature..291
   Article 1. Whether matrimony is of natural law?..................................291
   Question 67. The bill of divorce..293
   Article 1. Whether inseparableness of the wife is of natural law?........293
   Appendix II: Purgatory...294
   Article 1. Whether there is a Purgatory after this life?.........................294

Table of Contents

De Divinis Moribus (The Ways of God) 297
    God is unchangeable 297
    Good is pleasing to God 298
    The justice of God 299
    The rectitude of God 299
    the Longanimity of God 300
    The bounty of God 300
    God allows himself to be easily appeased 301
    The mercy of God 302
    God is perfectly balanced in his judgments 302
    the Generosity of God 303
    The discretion of God 303
    The just judgment of God 304
    The veracity of God 305
    God is no respecter of persons 306
    The care of God for creatures 307
    Nothing can disturb the serenity of God 308
    The disinterestedness of God 309
    God has done all things well 310
    The benevolence of God 311
    The soul should model itself on God 311

SUMMA THEOLOGIÆ

SECOND AND REVISED EDITION, 1920
LITERALLY TRANSLATED BY FATHERS OF THE ENGLISH DOMINICAN PROVINCE

PROLOGUE

Because the doctor of Catholic truth ought not only to teach the proficient, but also to instruct beginners (according to the Apostle: "As unto little ones in Christ, I gave you milk to drink, not meat"—1 Corinthians 3:1-2), we purpose in this book to treat of whatever belongs to the Christian religion, in such a way as may tend to the instruction of beginners. We have considered that students in this doctrine have not seldom been hampered by what they have found written by other authors, partly on account of the multiplication of useless questions, articles, and arguments, partly also because those things that are needful for them to know are not taught according to the order of the subject matter, but according as the plan of the book might require, or the occasion of the argument offer, partly, too, because frequent repetition brought weariness and confusion to the minds of readers.

Endeavoring to avoid these and other like faults, we shall try, by God's help, to set forth whatever is included in this sacred doctrine as briefly and clearly as the matter itself may allow.

FIRST PART

QUESTION 1. THE NATURE AND EXTENT OF SACRED DOCTRINE

ARTICLE 1. WHETHER, BESIDES PHILOSOPHY, ANY FURTHER DOCTRINE IS REQUIRED?

Objection 1. It seems that, besides philosophical science, we have no need of any further knowledge. For man should not seek to know what is above reason: "Seek not the things that are too high for thee" (Sirach 3:22). But whatever is not above reason is fully treated of in philosophical science. Therefore any other knowledge besides philosophical science is superfluous.

Objection 2. Further, knowledge can be concerned only with being, for nothing can be known, save what is true; and all that is, is true. But everything that is, is treated of in philosophical science—even God Himself; so that there is a part of philosophy called theology, or the divine science, as Aristotle has proved (Metaph. vi). Therefore, besides philosophical science, there is no need of any further knowledge.

On the contrary, It is written (2 Timothy 3:16): "All Scripture, inspired of God, is profitable to teach, to reprove, to correct, to instruct in justice." Now Scripture, inspired of God, is no part of philosophical science, which has been built up by human reason. Therefore it is useful that besides philosophical science, there should be other knowledge, i.e. inspired of God.

I answer that, It was necessary for man's salvation that there should be a knowledge revealed by God besides philosophical science built up by human reason. Firstly, indeed, because man is directed to God, as to an end that surpasses the grasp of his reason: "The eye hath not seen, O God, besides Thee, what things Thou hast prepared for them that wait for Thee" (Isaiah 64:4). But the end must first be known by men who are to direct their thoughts and actions to the end. Hence it was necessary for the salvation of man that certain truths which exceed human reason should be made known to him by divine revelation. Even as regards those truths about God which human reason could have discovered, it was necessary that man should be taught by a divine revelation; because the truth about God such as reason could discover, would only be known by a few, and that after a long time, and with the admixture of many errors. Whereas man's whole salvation, which is in God, depends upon the knowledge of this truth. Therefore, in order that the salvation of men might be brought about more fitly and more surely, it was necessary that they should be taught divine truths by divine revelation. It was therefore necessary that besides philosophical science built up by reason, there should be a sacred science learned through revelation.

Reply to Objection 1. Although those things which are beyond man's knowledge may not be sought for by man through his reason, nevertheless, once they are revealed by God, they must be accepted by faith. Hence the sacred text continues, "For many things are shown to thee above the understanding of man" (Sirach 3:25). And in this, the sacred science consists.

Reply to Objection 2. Sciences are differentiated according to the various means through which knowledge is obtained. For the astronomer and the physicist both may prove the same conclusion: that the earth, for instance, is round: the astronomer by means of mathematics (i.e. abstracting from matter), but the physicist by means of matter itself. Hence there is no reason why those things which may be learned from philosophical science, so far as they can be known by natural reason, may not also be taught us by another science so far as they fall within revelation. Hence theology included in sacred doctrine differs in kind from that theology which is part of philosophy.

ARTICLE 8. WHETHER SACRED DOCTRINE IS A MATTER OF ARGUMENT?

Objection 1. It seems this doctrine is not a matter of argument. For Ambrose says (De Fide 1): "Put arguments aside where faith is sought." But in this doctrine, faith especially is sought: "But these things are written that you may believe" (John 20:31). Therefore sacred doctrine is not a matter of argument.

Objection 2. Further, if it is a matter of argument, the argument is either from authority or from reason. If it is from authority, it seems unbefitting its dignity, for the proof from authority is the weakest form of proof. But if it is from reason, this is unbefitting its end, because, according to Gregory (Hom. 26), "faith has no merit in those things of which human reason brings its own experience." Therefore sacred doctrine is not a matter of argument.

On the contrary, The Scripture says that a bishop should "embrace that faithful word which is according to doctrine, that he may be able to exhort in sound doctrine and to convince the gainsayers" (Titus 1:9).

I answer that, As other sciences do not argue in proof of their principles (see glossary), but argue from their principles to demonstrate other truths in these sciences: so this doctrine does not argue in proof of its principles, which are the articles of faith, but from them it goes on to prove something else; as the Apostle from the resurrection of Christ argues in proof of the general resurrection (1 Corinthians 15). However, it is to be borne in mind, in regard to the philosophical sciences, that the inferior sciences neither prove their principles nor dispute with those who deny them, but leave this to a higher science; whereas the highest of them, viz. metaphysics, can dispute with one who denies its principles, if only the opponent will make some concession; but if he concede nothing, it can have no dispute with him, though it can answer his objections. Hence Sacred Scripture, since it has no science above itself, can dispute with one who denies its principles only if the opponent admits some at least of the truths obtained through divine revelation; thus we can argue with heretics from texts in Holy Writ, and against those who deny one article of faith, we can argue from another. If our opponent believes nothing of divine revelation, there is no longer any means of proving the articles of faith by reasoning, but only of answering his objections—if he has any—against faith. Since faith rests upon infallible truth, and since the contrary of a truth can never be demonstrated, it is clear that the arguments brought against faith cannot be demonstrations, but are difficulties that can be answered.

Reply to Objection 1. Although arguments from human reason cannot avail to prove what must be received on faith, nevertheless, this doctrine argues from articles of faith to other truths.

Reply to Objection 2. This doctrine is especially based upon arguments from authority, inasmuch as its principles are obtained by revelation: thus we ought to believe on the authority of those to whom the revelation has been made. Nor does this take away from the dignity of this doctrine, for although the argument from authority based on human reason is the weakest, yet the argument from authority based on divine revelation is the strongest. But sacred doctrine makes use even of human reason, not, indeed, to prove faith (for thereby the merit of faith would come to an end), but to make clear other things that are put forward in this doctrine. Since therefore grace does not destroy nature but perfects it, natural reason should minister to faith as the natural bent of the will ministers to charity. Hence the Apostle says: "Bringing into captivity every understanding unto the obedience of Christ" (2 Corinthians 10:5). Hence sacred doctrine makes use also of the authority of philosophers in those questions in which they were able to know the truth by natural reason, as Paul quotes a saying of Aratus: "As some also of your own poets said: For we are also His offspring" (Acts 17:28). Nevertheless, sacred doctrine makes use of these authorities as extrinsic and probable arguments; but properly uses the authority of the canonical Scriptures as an incontrovertible proof, and the authority of the doctors of the Church as one that may properly be used, yet merely as probable. For our faith rests upon the revelation made to the apostles and prophets who wrote the canonical books, and not on the revelations (if any such there are) made to other doctors. Hence Augustine says (Epis. ad Hieron. xix, 1): "Only those books of Scripture which are called canonical have I learned to hold in such honor as to believe their authors have not erred in any way in writing them. But other authors I so read as not to deem everything in their works to be true, merely on account of their having so thought and written, whatever may have been their holiness and learning."

QUESTION 2. THE EXISTENCE OF GOD

ARTICLE 3. WHETHER GOD EXISTS?

Objection 1. It seems that God does not exist; because if one of two contraries be infinite, the other would be altogether destroyed. But the word "God" means that He is infinite goodness. If, therefore, God existed, there would be no evil discoverable; but there is evil in the world. Therefore God does not exist.

Objection 2. Further, it is superfluous to suppose that what can be accounted for by a few principles has been produced by many. But it seems that everything we see in the world can be accounted for by other principles, supposing God did not exist. For all natural things can be reduced to one principle which is nature; and all voluntary things can be reduced to one principle which is human reason, or will. Therefore there is no need to suppose God's existence.

On the contrary, It is said in the person of God: "I am Who am" (Exodus 3:14).

I answer that, The existence of God can be proved in five ways.

The first and more manifest way is the argument from motion. It is certain, and evident to our senses, that in the world some things are in motion. Now whatever is in motion is put in motion by another, for nothing can be in motion except it is in potentiality to that towards which it is in motion; whereas a thing moves inasmuch as it is in act. For motion is nothing else than the reduction of something from potentiality to actuality. But nothing can be reduced from potentiality to actuality, except by something in a state of actuality. Thus that which is actually hot, as fire, makes wood, which is potentially hot, to be actually hot, and thereby moves and changes it. Now it is not possible that the same thing should be at once in actuality and potentiality in the same respect, but only in different respects. For what is actually hot cannot simultaneously be potentially hot; but it is simultaneously potentially cold. It is therefore impossible that in the same respect and in the same way a thing should be both mover and moved, i.e. that it should move itself. Therefore, whatever is in motion must be put in motion by another. If that by which it is put in motion be itself put in motion, then this also must needs be put in motion by another, and that by another again. But this cannot go on to infinity, because then there would be no first mover, and, consequently, no other mover; seeing that subsequent movers move only inasmuch as they are put in motion by the first mover; as the staff moves only because it is put in motion by the hand. Therefore it is necessary to arrive at a first mover, put in motion by no other; and this everyone understands to be God.

The second way is from the nature of the efficient cause (see glossary). In the world of sense we find there is an order of efficient causes. There is no case known (neither is it, indeed, possible) in which a thing is found to be the efficient cause of itself; for so it would be prior to itself, which is impossible. Now in efficient causes it is not possible to go on to infinity, because in all efficient causes following in order, the first is the cause of the intermediate cause, and the intermediate is the cause of the ultimate cause, whether the intermediate cause be several, or only one. Now to take away the cause is to take away the effect. Therefore, if there be no first cause among efficient causes, there will be no ultimate, nor any intermediate cause. But if in efficient causes it is possible to go on to infinity, there will be no first efficient cause, neither will there be an ultimate effect, nor any intermediate efficient causes; all of which is plainly false. Therefore it is necessary to admit a first efficient cause, to which everyone gives the name of God.

The third way is taken from possibility and necessity, and runs thus. We find in nature things that are possible to be and not to be, since they are found to be generated, and to corrupt, and consequently, they are possible to be and not to be. But it is impossible for these always to exist, for that which is possible not to be at some time is not. Therefore, if everything is possible not to be, then at one time there could have been nothing in existence. Now if this were true, even now there would be nothing in existence, because that which does not exist only begins to exist by something already existing. Therefore, if at one time nothing was in existence, it would have been impossible for anything to have begun to exist; and thus even now nothing would be in existence—which is absurd. Therefore, not all beings are merely possible, but there must exist something the existence of which is necessary. But every necessary thing either has its necessity caused by another, or not. Now it is impossible to go on to infinity in necessary things which have their necessity caused by another, as has been already proved in regard to efficient causes. Therefore we cannot but postulate the existence of some being having of itself its own necessity, and not receiving it from another, but rather causing in others their necessity. This all men speak of as God.

The fourth way is taken from the gradation to be found in things. Among beings there are some more and some less good, true, noble and the like. But "more" and "less" are predicated of different things, according as they resemble in their different ways something which is the maximum, as a thing is said to be hotter according as it more nearly resembles that which is hottest; so that there is something which is truest, something best, something noblest and, consequently, something which is uttermost being; for those things that are greatest in truth are greatest in being, as it is written in Metaph. ii. Now the maximum in any genus (see glossary) is the cause of all in that genus; as fire, which is the maximum heat, is the cause of all hot things. Therefore there must also be something which is to all beings the cause of their being, goodness, and every other perfection; and this we call God.

The fifth way is taken from the governance of the world. We see that things which lack intelligence, such as natural bodies, act for an end, and this is evident from their acting always, or nearly always, in the same way, so as to obtain the best result. Hence it is plain that not fortuitously, but designedly, do they achieve their end. Now whatever lacks intelligence cannot move towards an end, unless it be directed by some being endowed with knowledge and intelligence; as the arrow is shot to its mark by the archer. Therefore some intelligent being exists by whom all natural things are directed to their end; and this being we call God.

Reply to Objection 1. As Augustine says (Enchiridion xi): "Since God is the highest good, He would not allow any evil to exist in His works, unless His omnipotence and goodness were such as to bring good even out of evil." This is part of the infinite goodness of God, that He should allow evil to exist, and out of it produce good.

Reply to Objection 2. Since nature works for a determinate end under the direction of a higher agent, whatever is done by nature must needs be traced back to God, as to its first cause. So also whatever is done voluntarily must also be traced back to some higher cause other than human reason or will, since these can change or fail; for all things that are changeable and capable of defect must be traced back to an immovable and self-necessary first principle, as was shown in the body of the Article.

QUESTION 48. THE DISTINCTION OF THINGS IN PARTICULAR

ARTICLE 1. WHETHER EVIL IS A NATURE?

Objection 1. It would seem that evil is a nature. For every genus is a nature. But evil is a genus; for the Philosopher says (Praedic. x) that "good and evil are not in a genus, but are genera of other things." Therefore evil is a nature.

Objection 2. Further, every difference which constitutes a species (see glossary) is a nature. But evil is a difference constituting a species of morality; for a bad habit differs in species from a good habit, as liberality from illiberality. Therefore evil signifies a nature.

Objection 3. Further, each extreme of two contraries is a nature. But evil and good are not opposed as privation and habit, but as contraries, as the Philosopher shows (Praedic. x) by the fact that between good and evil there is a medium, and from evil there can be a return to good. Therefore evil signifies a nature.

Objection 4. Further, what is not, acts not. But evil acts, for it corrupts good. Therefore evil is a being and a nature.

Objection 5. Further, nothing belongs to the perfection of the universe except what is a being and a nature. But evil belongs to the perfection of the universe of things; for Augustine says (Enchir. 10,11) that the "admirable beauty of the universe is made up of all things. In which even what is called evil, well-ordered and in its place, is the eminent commendation of what is good." Therefore evil is a nature.

On the contrary, Dionysius says (Div. Nom. iv), "Evil is neither a being nor a good."

I answer that, One opposite is known through the other, as darkness is known through light. Hence also what evil is must be known from the nature of good. Now, we have said above that good is everything appetible; and thus, since every nature desires its own being and its own perfection, it must be said also that the being and the perfection of any nature is good. Hence it cannot be that evil signifies being, or any form or nature. Therefore it must be that by the name of evil is signified the absence of good. And this is what is meant by saying that "evil is neither a being nor a good." For since being, as such, is good, the absence of one implies the absence of the other.

Reply to Objection 1. Aristotle speaks there according to the opinion of Pythagoreans, who thought that evil was a kind of nature; and therefore they asserted the existence of the genus of good and evil. For Aristotle, especially in his logical works, brings forward examples that in his time were probable in the opinion of some philosophers. Or, it may be said that, as the Philosopher says (Metaph. iv, text 6), "the first kind of contrariety is habit and privation," as being verified in all contraries; since one contrary is always imperfect in relation to another, as black in relation to white, and bitter in relation to sweet. And in this way good and evil are said to be genera not simply, but in regard to contraries; because, as every form has the nature of good, so every privation, as such, has the nature of evil.

Reply to Objection 2. Good and evil are not constitutive differences except in morals, which receive their species from the end, which is the object of the will, the source of all morality. And because good has the nature of an end, therefore good and evil are specific differences in moral things; good in itself, but evil as the absence of the due end. Yet neither does the absence of the due end by itself constitute a moral species, except as it is joined to the undue end; just as we do not find the privation of the substantial form in natural things, unless it is joined to another form. Thus, therefore, the evil which is a constitutive difference in morals is a certain good joined to the privation of another good; as the end proposed by the intemperate man is not the privation of the good of reason, but the delight of sense without the order of reason. Hence evil is not a constitutive difference as such, but by reason of the good that is annexed.

Reply to Objection 3. This appears from the above. For the Philosopher speaks there of good and evil in morality. Because in that respect, between good and evil there is a medium, as good is considered as something rightly ordered, and evil as a thing not only out of right order, but also as injurious to another. Hence the Philosopher says (Ethic. iv, i) that a "prodigal man is foolish, but not evil." And from this evil in morality, there may be a return to good, but not from any sort of evil, for from blindness there is no return to sight, although blindness is an evil.

Reply to Objection 4. A thing is said to act in a threefold sense. In one way, formally, as when we say that whiteness makes white; and in that sense evil considered even as a privation is said to corrupt good, forasmuch as it is itself a corruption or privation of good. In another sense a thing is said to act effectively, as when a painter makes a wall white.

Thirdly, it is said in the sense of the final cause (see glossary), as the end is said to effect by moving the efficient cause. But in these two ways evil does not effect anything of itself, that is, as a privation, but by virtue of the good annexed to it. For every action comes from some form (see glossary); and everything which is desired as an end, is a perfection. And therefore, as Dionysius says (Div. Nom. iv): "Evil does not act, nor is it desired, except by virtue of some good joined to it: while of itself it is nothing definite, and beside the scope of our will and intention."

Reply to Objection 5. As was said above, the parts of the universe are ordered to each other, according as one acts on the other, and according as one is the end and exemplar (see glossary) of the other. But, as was said above, this can only happen to evil as joined to some good. Hence evil neither belongs to the perfection of the universe, nor does it come under the order of the same, except accidentally (see glossary), that is, by reason of some good joined to it.

ARTICLE 4. WHETHER EVIL CORRUPTS THE WHOLE GOOD?

Objection 1. It would seem that evil corrupts the whole good. For one contrary is wholly corrupted by another. But good and evil are contraries. Therefore evil corrupts the whole good.

Objection 2. Further, Augustine says (Enchiridion 12) that "evil hurts inasmuch as it takes away good." But good is all of a piece and uniform. Therefore it is wholly taken away by evil.

Objection 3. Further, evil, as long as it lasts, hurts, and takes away good. But that from which something is always being removed, is at some time consumed, unless it is infinite, which cannot be said of any created good. Therefore evil wholly consumes good.

On the contrary, Augustine says (Enchiridion 12) that "evil cannot wholly consume good."

I answer that, Evil cannot wholly consume good. To prove this we must consider that good is threefold. One kind of good is wholly destroyed by evil, and this is the good opposed to evil, as light is wholly destroyed by darkness, and sight by blindness. Another kind of good is neither wholly destroyed nor diminished by evil, and that is the good which is the subject of evil; for by darkness the substance of the air is not injured. And there is also a kind of good which is diminished by evil, but is not wholly taken away; and this good is the aptitude of a subject to some actuality.

The diminution, however, of this kind of good is not to be considered by way of subtraction, as diminution in quantity, but rather by way of remission, as diminution in qualities and forms. The remission likewise of this habitude (see glossary) is to be taken as contrary to its intensity. For this kind of aptitude receives its intensity by the dispositions whereby the matter is prepared for actuality; which the more they are multiplied in the subject the more is it fitted to receive its perfection and form; and, on the contrary, it receives its remission by contrary dispositions which, the more they are multiplied in the matter, and the more they are intensified, the more is the potentiality remitted as regards the actuality.

Therefore, if contrary dispositions cannot be multiplied and intensified to infinity, but only to a certain limit, neither is the aforesaid aptitude diminished or remitted infinitely, as appears in the active and passive qualities of the elements (see glossary); for coldness and humidity, whereby the aptitude of matter to the form of fire is diminished or remitted, cannot be infinitely multiplied. But if the contrary dispositions can be infinitely multiplied, the aforesaid aptitude is also infinitely diminished or remitted; yet, nevertheless, it is not wholly taken away, because its root always remains, which is the substance of the subject. Thus, if opaque bodies were interposed to infinity between the sun and the air, the aptitude of the air to light would be infinitely diminished, but still it would never be wholly removed while the air remained, which in its very nature is transparent. Likewise, addition in sin can be made to infinitude, whereby the aptitude of the soul to grace is more and more lessened; and these sins, indeed, are like obstacles interposed between us and God, according to Isaiah 59:2: "Our sins have divided between us and God." Yet the aforesaid aptitude of the soul is not wholly taken away, for it belongs to its very nature.

Reply to Objection 1. The good which is opposed to evil is wholly taken away; but other goods are not wholly removed, as said above.

Reply to Objection 2. The aforesaid aptitude is a medium between subject and act. Hence, where it touches act, it is diminished by evil; but where it touches the subject, it remains as it was. Therefore, although good is like to itself, yet, on account of its relation to different things, it is not wholly, but only partially taken away.

Reply to Objection 3. Some, imagining that the diminution of this kind of good is like the diminution of quantity, said that just as the continuous is infinitely divisible, if the division be made in an ever same proportion (for instance, half of half, or a third of a third), so is it in the present case. But this explanation does not avail here. For when in a division we keep the same proportion, we continue to subtract less and less; for half of half is less than half of the whole. But a second sin does not necessarily diminish the above mentioned aptitude less than a preceding sin, but perchance either equally or more.

Therefore it must be said that, although this aptitude is a finite thing, still it may be so diminished infinitely, not "per se," but accidentally; according as the contrary dispositions are also increased infinitely, as explained above.

QUESTION 75. MAN, WHO IS COMPOSED OF A SPIRITUAL AND A CORPOREAL SUBSTANCE: AND IN THE FIRST PLACE, CONCERNING WHAT BELONGS TO THE ESSENCE OF THE SOUL

ARTICLE 4. WHETHER THE SOUL IS MAN?

Objection 1. It would seem that the soul is man. For it is written (2 Corinthians 4:16): "Though our outward man is corrupted, yet the inward man is renewed day by day." But that which is within man is the soul. Therefore the soul is the inward man.

Objection 2. Further, the human soul is a substance. But it is not a universal substance. Therefore it is a particular substance. Therefore it is a "hypostasis" (see glossary) or a person; and it can only be a human person. Therefore the soul is man; for a human person is a man.

On the contrary, Augustine (De Civ. Dei xix, 3) commends Varro as holding "that man is not a mere soul, nor a mere body; but both soul and body."

I answer that, The assertion "the soul is man," can be taken in two senses. First, that man is a soul; though this particular man, Socrates, for instance, is not a soul, but composed of soul and body. I say this, forasmuch as some held that the form alone belongs to the species; while matter is part of the individual, and not the species. This cannot be true; for to the nature of the species belongs what the definition signifies; and in natural things the definition does not signify the form only, but the form and the matter. Hence in natural things the matter is part of the species; not, indeed, signate matter (see glossary), which is the principle of individuality; but the common matter. For as it belongs to the notion of this particular man to be composed of this soul, of this flesh, and of these bones; so it belongs to the notion of man to be composed of soul, flesh, and bones; for whatever belongs in common to the substance of all the individuals contained under a given species, must belong to the substance of the species.

It may also be understood in this sense, that this soul is this man; and this could be held if it were supposed that the operation of the sensitive soul were proper to it, apart from the body; because in that case all the operations which are attributed to man would belong to the soul only; and whatever performs the operations proper to a thing, is that thing; wherefore that which performs the operations of a man is man. But it has been shown above (Article 3) that sensation is not the operation of the soul only. Since, then, sensation is an operation of man, but not proper to him, it is clear that man is not a soul only, but something composed of soul and body. Plato, through supposing that sensation was proper to the soul, could maintain man to be a soul making use of the body.

Reply to Objection 1. According to the Philosopher (Ethic. ix, 8), a thing seems to be chiefly what is principal in it; thus what the governor of a city does, the city is said to do. In this way sometimes what is principle in man is said to be man; sometimes, indeed, the intellectual part which, in accordance with truth, is called the "inward" man; and sometimes the sensitive part with the body is called man in the opinion of those whose observation does not go beyond the senses. And this is called the "outward" man.

Reply to Objection 2. Not every particular substance is a hypostasis or a person, but that which has the complete nature of its species. Hence a hand, or a foot, is not called a hypostasis, or a person; nor, likewise, is the soul alone so called, since it is a part of the human species.

QUESTION 83. FREE-WILL

ARTICLE 1. WHETHER MAN HAS FREE-WILL?

Objection 1. It would seem that man has not free-will. For whoever has free-will does what he wills. But man does not what he wills; for it is written (Romans 7:19): "For the good which I will I do not, but the evil which I will not, that I do." Therefore man has not free-will.

Objection 2. Further, whoever has free-will has in his power to will or not to will, to do or not to do. But this is not in man's power: for it is written (Romans 9:16): "It is not of him that willeth"—namely, to will—"nor of him that runneth"—namely, to run. Therefore man has not free-will.

Objection 3. Further, what is "free is cause of itself," as the Philosopher says (Metaph. i, 2). Therefore what is moved by another is not free. But God moves the will, for it is written (Proverbs 21:1): "The heart of the king is in the hand of the Lord; whithersoever He will He shall turn it" and (Philippians 2:13): "It is God Who worketh in you both to will and to accomplish." Therefore man has not free-will.

Objection 4. Further, whoever has free-will is master of his own actions. But man is not master of his own actions: for it is written (Jeremiah 10:23): "The way of a man is not his: neither is it in a man to walk." Therefore man has not free-will.

Objection 5. Further, the Philosopher says (Ethic. iii, 5): "According as each one is, such does the end seem to him." But it is not in our power to be of one quality or another; for this comes to us from nature. Therefore it is natural to us to follow some particular end, and therefore we are not free in so doing.

On the contrary, It is written (Sirach 15:14): "God made man from the beginning, and left him in the hand of his own counsel"; and the gloss adds: "That is, of his free-will."

I answer that, Man has free-will: otherwise counsels, exhortations, commands, prohibitions, rewards, and punishments would be in vain. In order to make this evident, we must observe that some things act without judgment; as a stone moves downwards; and in like manner all things which lack knowledge. And some act from judgment, but not a free judgment; as brute animals. For the sheep, seeing the wolf, judges it a thing to be shunned, from a natural and not a free judgment, because it judges, not from reason, but from natural instinct. And the same thing is to be said of any judgment of brute animals. But man acts from judgment, because by his apprehensive power he judges that something should be avoided or sought. But because this judgment, in the case of some particular act, is not from a natural instinct, but from some act of comparison in the reason, therefore he acts from free judgment and retains the power of being inclined to various things. For reason in contingent matters may follow opposite courses, as we see in dialectic syllogisms (see glossary) and rhetorical arguments. Now particular operations are contingent, and therefore in such matters the judgment of reason may follow opposite courses, and is not determinate to one. And forasmuch as man is rational is it necessary that man have a free-will.

Reply to Objection 1. As we have said above (81, 3, ad 2), the sensitive appetite, though it obeys the reason, yet in a given case can resist by desiring what the reason forbids. This is therefore the good which man does not when he wishes—namely, "not to desire against reason," as Augustine says.

Reply to Objection 2. Those words of the Apostle are not to be taken as though man does not wish or does not run of his free-will, but because the free-will is not sufficient thereto unless it be moved and helped by God.

Reply to Objection 3. Free-will is the cause of its own movement, because by his free-will man moves himself to act. But it does not of necessity belong to liberty that what is free should be the first cause of itself, as neither for one thing to be cause of another need it be the first cause. God, therefore, is the first cause, Who moves causes both natural and voluntary. And just as by moving natural causes He does not prevent their acts being natural, so by moving voluntary causes He does not deprive their actions of being voluntary: but rather is He the cause of this very thing in them; for He operates in each thing according to its own nature.

Reply to Objection 4. "Man's way" is said "not to be his" in the execution of his choice, wherein he may be impeded, whether he will or not. The choice itself, however, is in us, but presupposes the help of God.

Reply to Objection 5. Quality in man is of two kinds: natural and adventitious. Now the natural quality may be in the intellectual part, or in the body and its powers. From the very fact, therefore, that man is such by virtue of a natural quality which is in the intellectual part, he naturally desires his last end, which is happiness. Which desire, indeed, is a natural desire, and is not subject to free-will, as is clear from what we have said above (82, 1, 2). But on the part of the body and its powers man may be such by virtue of a natural quality, inasmuch as he is of such a temperament or disposition due to any impression whatever produced by corporeal causes, which cannot affect the intellectual part, since it is not the act of a corporeal organ. And such as a man is by virtue of a corporeal quality, such also does his end seem to him, because from such a disposition a man is inclined to choose or reject something. But these inclinations are subject to the judgment of reason, which the lower appetite obeys, as we have said (81, 3). Wherefore this is in no way prejudicial to free-will.

The adventitious qualities are habits and passions, by virtue of which a man is inclined to one thing rather than to another. And yet even these inclinations are subject to the judgment of reason. Such qualities, too, are subject to reason, as it is in our power either to acquire them, whether by causing them or disposing ourselves to them, or to reject them. And so there is nothing in this that is repugnant to free-will.

QUESTION 103. THE GOVERNMENT OF THINGS IN GENERAL

ARTICLE 5. WHETHER ALL THINGS ARE SUBJECT TO THE DIVINE GOVERNMENT?

Objection 1. It would seem that not all things are subject to the Divine government. For it is written (Ecclesiastes 9:11): "I saw that under the sun the race is not to the swift, nor the battle to the strong, nor bread to the wise, nor riches to the learned, nor favor to the skillful, but time and chance in all." But things subject to the Divine government are not ruled by chance. Therefore those things which are under the sun are not subject to the Divine government.

Objection 2. Further, the Apostle says (1 Corinthians 9:9): "God hath no care for oxen." But he that governs has care for the things he governs. Therefore all things are not subject to the Divine government.

Objection 3. Further, what can govern itself needs not to be governed by another. But the rational creature can govern itself; since it is master of its own act, and acts of itself; and is not made to act by another, which seems proper to things which are governed. Therefore all things are not subject to the Divine government.

On the contrary, Augustine says (De Civ. Dei v, 11): "Not only heaven and earth, not only man and angel, even the bowels of the lowest animal, even the wing of the bird, the flower of the plant, the leaf of the tree, hath God endowed with every fitting detail of their nature." Therefore all things are subject to His government.

I answer that, For the same reason is God the ruler of things as He is their cause, because the same gives existence as gives perfection; and this belongs to government. Now God is the cause not indeed only of some particular kind of being, but of the whole universal being, as proved above (44, 1, 2). Wherefore, as there can be nothing which is not created by God, so there can be nothing which is not subject to His government. This can also be proved from the nature of the end of government. For a man's government extends over all those things which come under the end of his government. Now the end of the Divine government is the Divine goodness; as we have shown (2). Wherefore, as there can be nothing that is not ordered to the Divine goodness as its end, as is clear from what we have said above (44, 4; 65, 2), so it is impossible for anything to escape from the Divine government.

Foolish therefore was the opinion of those who said that the corruptible lower world, or individual things, or that even human affairs, were not subject to the Divine government. These are represented as saying, "God hath abandoned the earth" (Ezekiel 9:9).

Reply to Objection 1. Those things are said to be under the sun which are generated and corrupted according to the sun's movement. In all such things we find chance: not that everything is casual which occurs in such things; but that in each one there is an element of chance. And the very fact that an element of chance is found in those things proves that they are subject to government of some kind. For unless corruptible things were governed by a higher being, they would tend to nothing definite, especially those which possess no kind of knowledge. So nothing would happen unintentionally; which constitutes the nature of chance. Wherefore to show how things happen by chance and yet according to the ordering of a higher cause, he does not say absolutely that he observes chance in all things, but "time and chance," that is to say, that defects may be found in these things according to some order of time.

Reply to Objection 2. Government implies a certain change effected by the governor in the things governed. Now every movement is the act of a movable thing, caused by the moving principle, as is laid down Phys. iii, 3. And every act is proportionate to that of which it is an act. Consequently, various movable things must be moved variously, even as regards movement by one and the same mover. Thus by the one art of the Divine governor, various things are variously governed according to their variety. Some, according to their nature, act of themselves, having dominion over their actions; and these are governed by God, not only in this, that they are moved by God Himself, Who works in them interiorly; but also in this, that they are induced by Him to do good and to fly from evil, by precepts and prohibitions, rewards and punishments. But irrational creatures which do not act but are acted upon, are not thus governed by God. Hence, when the Apostle says that "God hath no care for oxen," he does not wholly withdraw them from the Divine government, but only as regards the way in which rational creatures are governed.

Reply to Objection 3. The rational creature governs itself by its intellect and will, both of which require to be governed and perfected by the Divine intellect and will. Therefore above the government whereby the rational creature governs itself as master of its own act, it requires to be governed by God.

ARTICLE 6. WHETHER ALL THINGS ARE IMMEDIATELY GOVERNED BY GOD?

Objection 1. It would seem that all things are governed by God immediately. For Gregory of Nyssa (Nemesius, De Nat. Hom.) reproves the opinion of Plato who divides providence into three parts. The first he ascribes to the supreme god, who watches over heavenly things and all universals; the second providence he attributes to the secondary deities, who go the round of the heavens to watch over generation and corruption; while he ascribes a third providence to certain spirits who are guardians on earth of human actions. Therefore it seems that all things are immediately governed by God.

Objection 2. Further, it is better that a thing be done by one, if possible, than by many, as the Philosopher says (Phys. viii, 6). But God can by Himself govern all things without any intermediary cause. Therefore it seems that He governs all things immediately.

Objection 3. Further, in God nothing is defective or imperfect. But it seems to be imperfect in a ruler to govern by means of others; thus an earthly king, by reason of his not being able to do everything himself, and because he cannot be everywhere at the same time, requires to govern by means of ministers. Therefore God governs all things immediately.

On the contrary, Augustine says (De Trin. iii, 4): "As the lower and grosser bodies are ruled in a certain orderly way by bodies of greater subtlety and power; so all bodies are ruled by the rational spirit of life; and the sinful and unfaithful spirit is ruled by the good and just spirit of life; and this spirit by God Himself."

I answer that, In government there are two things to be considered; the design of government, which is providence itself; and the execution of the design. As to the design of government, God governs all things immediately; whereas in its execution, He governs some things by means of others.

The reason of this is that as God is the very essence of goodness, so everything must be attributed to God in its highest degree of goodness. Now the highest degree of goodness in any practical order, design or knowledge (and such is the design of government) consists in knowing the individuals acted upon; as the best physician is not the one who can only give his attention to general principles, but who can consider the least details; and so on in other things. Therefore we must say that God has the design of the government of all things, even of the very least.

But since things which are governed should be brought to perfection by government, this government will be so much the better in the degree the things governed are brought to perfection. Now it is a greater perfection for a thing to be good in itself and also the cause of goodness in others, than only to be good in itself. Therefore God so governs things that He makes some of them to be causes of others in government; as a master, who not only imparts knowledge to his pupils, but gives also the faculty of teaching others.

Reply to Objection 1. Plato's opinion is to be rejected, because he held that God did not govern all things immediately, even in the design of government; this is clear from the fact that he divided providence, which is the design of government, into three parts.

Reply to Objection 2. If God governed alone, things would be deprived of the perfection of causality. Wherefore all that is effected by many would not be accomplished by one.

Reply to Objection 3. That an earthly king should have ministers to execute his laws is a sign not only of his being imperfect, but also of his dignity; because by the ordering of ministers the kingly power is brought into greater evidence.

QUESTION 104. THE SPECIAL EFFECTS OF THE DIVINE GOVERNMENT

ARTICLE 3. WHETHER GOD CAN ANNIHILATE ANYTHING?

Objection 1. It would seem that God cannot annihilate anything. For Augustine says (QQ. 83, qu. 21) that "God is not the cause of anything tending to non-existence." But He would be such a cause if He were to annihilate anything. Therefore He cannot annihilate anything.

Objection 2. Further, by His goodness God is the cause why things exist, since, as Augustine says (De Doctr. Christ. i, 32): "Because God is good, we exist." But God cannot cease to be good. Therefore He cannot cause things to cease to exist; which would be the case were He to annihilate anything.

Objection 3. Further, if God were to annihilate anything it would be by His action. But this cannot be; because the term of every action is existence. Hence even the action of a corrupting cause has its term in something generated; for when one thing is generated another undergoes corruption. Therefore God cannot annihilate anything.

On the contrary, It is written (Jeremiah 10:24): "Correct me, O Lord, but yet with judgment; and not in Thy fury, lest Thou bring me to nothing."

I answer that, Some have held that God, in giving existence to creatures, acted from natural necessity. Were this true, God could not annihilate anything, since His nature cannot change. But, as we have said above (Question 19, Article 4), such an opinion is entirely false, and absolutely contrary to the Catholic faith, which confesses that God created things of His own free-will, according to Psalm 134:6: "Whatsoever the Lord pleased, He hath done." Therefore that God gives existence to a creature depends on His will; nor does He preserve things in existence otherwise than by continually pouring out existence into them, as we have said. Therefore, just as before things existed, God was free not to give them existence, and not to make them; so after they are made, He is free not to continue their existence; and thus they would cease to exist; and this would be to annihilate them.

Reply to Objection 1. Non-existence has no direct cause; for nothing is a cause except inasmuch as it has existence, and a being essentially as such is a cause of something existing. Therefore God cannot cause a thing to tend to non-existence, whereas a creature has this tendency of itself, since it is produced from nothing. But indirectly God can be the cause of things being reduced to non-existence, by withdrawing His action therefrom.

Reply to Objection 2. God's goodness is the cause of things, not as though by natural necessity, because the Divine goodness does not depend on creatures; but by His free-will. Wherefore, as without prejudice to His goodness, He might not have produced things into existence, so, without prejudice to His goodness, He might not preserve things in existence.

Reply to Objection 3. If God were to annihilate anything, this would not imply an action on God's part; but a mere cessation of His action.

ARTICLE 4. WHETHER ANYTHING IS ANNIHILATED?

Objection 1. It would seem that something is annihilated. For the end corresponds to the beginning. But in the beginning there was nothing but God. Therefore all things must tend to this end, that there shall be nothing but God. Therefore creatures will be reduced to nothing.

Objection 2. Further, every creature has a finite power. But no finite power extends to the infinite. Wherefore the Philosopher proves (Phys. viii, 10) that, "a finite power cannot move in infinite time." Therefore a creature cannot last for an infinite duration; and so at some time it will be reduced to nothing.

Objection 3. Further, forms and accidents have no matter as part of themselves. But at some time they cease to exist. Therefore they are reduced to nothing.

On the contrary, It is written (Ecclesiastes 3:14): "I have learned that all the works that God hath made continue forever."

I answer that, Some of those things which God does in creatures occur in accordance with the natural course of things; others happen miraculously, and not in accordance with the natural order, as will be explained (105, 6). Now whatever God wills to do according to the natural order of things may be observed from their nature; but those things which occur miraculously, are ordered for the manifestation of grace, according to the Apostle, "To each one is given the manifestation of the Spirit, unto profit" (1 Corinthians 12:7); and subsequently he mentions, among others, the working of miracles.

Now the nature of creatures shows that none of them is annihilated. For, either they are immaterial, and therefore have no potentiality to non-existence; or they are material, and then they continue to exist, at least in matter, which is incorruptible, since it is the subject of generation and corruption. Moreover, the annihilation of things does not pertain to the manifestation of grace; since rather the power and goodness of God are manifested by the preservation of things in existence. Wherefore we must conclude by denying absolutely that anything at all will be annihilated.

Reply to Objection 1. That things are brought into existence from a state of non-existence, clearly shows the power of Him Who made them; but that they should be reduced to nothing would hinder that manifestation, since the power of God is conspicuously shown in His preserving all things in existence, according to the Apostle: "Upholding all things by the word of His power" (Hebrews 1:3).

Reply to Objection 2. A creature's potentiality to existence is merely receptive; the active power belongs to God Himself, from Whom existence is derived. Wherefore the infinite duration of things is a consequence of the infinity of the Divine power. To some things, however, is given a determinate power of duration for a certain time, so far as they may be hindered by some contrary agent from receiving the influx of existence which comes from Him Whom finite power cannot resist, for an infinite, but only for a fixed time. So things which have no contrary, although they have a finite power, continue to exist for ever.

Reply to Objection 3. Forms and accidents are not complete beings, since they do not subsist: but each one of them is something "of a being"; for it is called a being, because something is by it. Yet so far as their mode of existence is concerned, they are not entirely reduced to nothingness; not that any part of them survives, but that they remain in the potentiality of the matter, or of the subject.

FIRST PART OF THE SECOND PART

QUESTION 1. MAN'S LAST END

ARTICLE 1. WHETHER IT BELONGS TO MAN TO ACT FOR AN END?

Objection 1. It would seem that it does not belong to man to act for an end. For a cause is naturally first. But an end, in its very name, implies something that is last. Therefore an end is not a cause. But that for which a man acts, is the cause of his action; since this preposition "for" indicates a relation of causality. Therefore it does not belong to man to act for an end.

Objection 2. Further, that which is itself the last end is not for an end. But in some cases the last end is an action, as the Philosopher states (Ethic. i, 1). Therefore man does not do everything for an end.

Objection 3. Further, then does a man seem to act for an end, when he acts deliberately. But man does many things without deliberation, sometimes not even thinking of what he is doing; for instance when one moves one's foot or hand, or scratches one's beard, while intent on something else. Therefore man does not do everything for an end.

On the contrary, All things contained in a genus are derived from the principle of that genus. Now the end is the principle in human operations, as the Philosopher states (Phys. ii, 9). Therefore it belongs to man to do everything for an end.

I answer that, Of actions done by man those alone are properly called "human," which are proper to man as man. Now man differs from irrational animals in this, that he is master of his actions. Wherefore those actions alone are properly called human, of which man is master. Now man is master of his actions through his reason and will; whence, too, the free-will is defined as "the faculty and will of reason." Therefore those actions are properly called human which proceed from a deliberate will. And if any other actions are found in man, they can be called actions "of a man," but not properly "human" actions, since they are not proper to man as man. Now it is clear that whatever actions proceed from a power, are caused by that power in accordance with the nature of its object. But the object of the will is the end and the good. Therefore all human actions must be for an end.

Reply to Objection 1. Although the end be last in the order of execution, yet it is first in the order of the agent's intention. And it is this way that it is a cause.

Reply to Objection 2. If any human action be the last end, it must be voluntary, else it would not be human, as stated above. Now an action is voluntary in one of two ways: first, because it is commanded by the will, e.g. to walk, or to speak; secondly, because it is elicited by the will, for instance the very act of willing. Now it is impossible for the very act elicited by the will to be the last end. For the object of the will is the end, just as the object of sight is color: wherefore just as the first visible cannot be the act of seeing, because every act of seeing is directed to a visible object; so the first appetible, i.e. the end, cannot be the very act of willing. Consequently it follows that if a human action be the last end, it must be an action commanded by the will: so that there, some action of man, at least the act of willing, is for the end. Therefore whatever a man does, it is true to say that man acts for an end, even when he does that action in which the last end consists.

Reply to Objection 3. Such like actions are not properly human actions; since they do not proceed from deliberation of the reason, which is the proper principle of human actions. Therefore they have indeed an imaginary end, but not one that is fixed by reason.

ARTICLE 7. WHETHER ALL MEN HAVE THE SAME LAST END?

Objection 1. It would seem that all men have not the same last end. For before all else the unchangeable good seems to be the last end of man. But some turn away from the unchangeable good, by sinning. Therefore all men have not the same last end.

Objection 2. Further, man's entire life is ruled according to his last end. If, therefore, all men had the same last end, they would not have various pursuits in life. Which is evidently false.

Objection 3. Further, the end is the term of action. But actions are of individuals. Now although men agree in their specific nature, yet they differ in things pertaining to individuals. Therefore all men have not the same last end.

On the contrary, Augustine says (De Trin. xiii, 3) that all men agree in desiring the last end, which is happiness.

I answer that, We can speak of the last end in two ways: first, considering only the aspect of last end; secondly, considering the thing in which the aspect of last end is realized. So, then, as to the aspect of last end, all agree in desiring the last end: since all desire the fulfilment of their perfection, and it is precisely this fulfilment in which the last end consists, as stated above (Article 5). But as to the thing in which this aspect is realized, all men are not agreed as to their last end: since some desire riches as their consummate good; some, pleasure; others, something else. Thus to every taste the sweet is pleasant but to some, the sweetness of wine is most pleasant, to others, the sweetness of honey, or of something similar. Yet that sweet is absolutely the best of all pleasant things, in which he who has the best taste takes most pleasure. In like manner that good is most complete which the man with well disposed affections desires for his last end.

Reply to Objection 1. Those who sin turn from that in which their last end really consists: but they do not turn away from the intention of the last end, which intention they mistakenly seek in other things.

Reply to Objection 2. Various pursuits in life are found among men by reason of the various things in which men seek to find their last end.

Reply to Objection 3. Although actions are of individuals, yet their first principle of action is nature, which tends to one thing, as stated above (Article 5).

QUESTION 5. THE ATTAINMENT OF HAPPINESS

ARTICLE 3. WHETHER ONE CAN BE HAPPY IN THIS LIFE?

Objection 1. It would seem that Happiness can be had in this life. For it is written (Psalm 118:1): "Blessed are the undefiled in the way, who walk in the law of the Lord." But this happens in this life. Therefore one can be happy in this life.

Objection 2. Further, imperfect participation in the Sovereign Good does not destroy the nature of Happiness, otherwise one would not be happier than another. But men can participate in the Sovereign Good in this life, by knowing and loving God, albeit imperfectly. Therefore man can be happy in this life.

Objection 3. Further, what is said by many cannot be altogether false: since what is in many, comes, apparently, from nature; and nature does not fail altogether. Now many say that Happiness can be had in this life, as appears from Psalm 143:15: "They have called the people happy that hath these things," to wit, the good things in this life. Therefore one can be happy in this life.

On the contrary, It is written (Job 14:1): "Man born of a woman, living for a short time, is filled with many miseries." But Happiness excludes misery. Therefore man cannot be happy in this life.

I answer that, A certain participation of Happiness can be had in this life: but perfect and true Happiness cannot be had in this life. This may be seen from a twofold consideration.

First, from the general notion of happiness. For since happiness is a "perfect and sufficient good," it excludes every evil, and fulfils every desire. But in this life every evil cannot be excluded. For this present life is subject to many unavoidable evils; to ignorance on the part of the intellect; to inordinate affection on the part of the appetite, and to many penalties on the part of the body; as Augustine sets forth in De Civ. Dei xix, 4. Likewise neither can the desire for good be satiated in this life. For man naturally desires the good, which he has, to be abiding. Now the goods of the present life pass away; since life itself passes away, which we naturally desire to have, and would wish to hold abidingly, for man naturally shrinks from death. Wherefore it is impossible to have true Happiness in this life.

Secondly, from a consideration of the specific nature of Happiness, viz. the vision of the Divine Essence, which man cannot obtain in this life, as was shown in the I, 12, 11. Hence it is evident that none can attain true and perfect Happiness in this life.

Reply to Objection 1. Some are said to be happy in this life, either on account of the hope of obtaining Happiness in the life to come, according to Romans 8:24: "We are saved by hope"; or on account of a certain participation of Happiness, by reason of a kind of enjoyment of the Sovereign Good.

Reply to Objection 2. The imperfection of participated Happiness is due to one of two causes. First, on the part of the object of Happiness, which is not seen in Its Essence: and this imperfection destroys the nature of true Happiness. Secondly, the imperfection may be on the part of the participator, who indeed attains the object of Happiness, in itself, namely, God: imperfectly, however, in comparison with the way in which God enjoys Himself. This imperfection does not destroy the true nature of Happiness; because, since Happiness is an operation, as stated above (Question 3, Article 2), the true nature of Happiness is taken from the object, which specifies the act, and not from the subject.

Reply to Objection 3. Men esteem that there is some kind of happiness to be had in this life, on account of a certain likeness to true Happiness. And thus they do not fail altogether in their estimate.

ARTICLE 5. WHETHER MAN CAN ATTAIN HAPPINESS BY HIS NATURAL POWERS?

Objection 1. It would seem that man can attain Happiness by his natural powers. For nature does not fail in necessary things. But nothing is so necessary to man as that by which he attains the last end. Therefore this is not lacking to human nature. Therefore man can attain Happiness by his natural powers.

Objection 2. Further, since man is more noble than irrational creatures, it seems that he must be better equipped than they. But irrational creatures can attain their end by their natural powers. Much more therefore can man attain Happiness by his natural powers.

Objection 3. Further, Happiness is a "perfect operation," according to the Philosopher (Ethic. vii, 13). Now the beginning of a thing belongs to the same principle as the perfecting thereof. Since, therefore, the imperfect operation, which is as the beginning in human operations, is subject to man's natural power, whereby he is master of his own actions; it seems that he can attain to perfect operation, i.e. Happiness, by his natural powers.

On the contrary, Man is naturally the principle of his action, by his intellect and will. But final Happiness prepared for the saints, surpasses the intellect and will of man; for the Apostle says (1 Corinthians 2:9) "Eye hath not seen, nor ear heard, neither hath it entered into the heart of man, what things God hath prepared for them that love Him." Therefore man cannot attain Happiness by his natural powers.

I answer that, Imperfect happiness that can be had in this life, can be acquired by man by his natural powers, in the same way as virtue, in whose operation it consists: on this point we shall speak further on (63). But man's perfect Happiness, as stated above (Question 3, Article 8), consists in the vision of the Divine Essence. Now the vision of God's Essence surpasses the nature not only of man, but also of every creature, as was shown in the I, 12, 4. For the natural knowledge of every creature is in keeping with the mode of his substance: thus it is said of the intelligence (De Causis; Prop. viii) that "it knows things that are above it, and things that are below it, according to the mode of its substance." But every knowledge that is according to the mode of created substance, falls short of the vision of the Divine Essence, which infinitely surpasses all created substance. Consequently neither man, nor any creature, can attain final Happiness by his natural powers.

Reply to Objection 1. Just as nature does not fail man in necessaries, although it has not provided him with weapons and clothing, as it provided other animals, because it gave him reason and hands, with which he is able to get these things for himself; so neither did it fail man in things necessary, although it gave him not the wherewithal to attain Happiness: since this it could not do. But it did give him free-will, with which he can turn to God, that He may make him happy. "For what we do by means of our friends, is done, in a sense, by ourselves" (Ethic. iii, 3).

Reply to Objection 2. The nature that can attain perfect good, although it needs help from without in order to attain it, is of more noble condition than a nature which cannot attain perfect good, but attains some imperfect good, although it need no help from without in order to attain it, as the Philosopher says (De Coel. ii, 12). Thus he is better disposed to health who can attain perfect health, albeit by means of medicine, than he who can attain but imperfect health, without the help of medicine. And therefore the rational creature, which can attain the perfect good of happiness, but needs the Divine assistance for the purpose, is more perfect than the irrational creature, which is not capable of attaining this good, but attains some imperfect good by its natural powers.

Reply to Objection 3. When imperfect and perfect are of the same species, they can be caused by the same power. But this does not follow of necessity, if they be of different species: for not everything, that can cause the disposition of matter, can produce the final perfection. Now the imperfect operation, which is subject to man's natural power, is not of the same species as that perfect operation which is man's happiness: since operation takes its species from its object. Consequently the argument does not prove.

ARTICLE 7. WHETHER ANY GOOD WORKS ARE NECESSARY THAT MAN MAY RECEIVE HAPPINESS FROM GOD?

Objection 1. It would seem that no works of man are necessary that he may obtain Happiness from God. For since God is an agent of infinite power, He requires before acting, neither matter, nor disposition of matter, but can forthwith produce the whole effect. But man's works, since they are not required for Happiness, as the efficient cause thereof, as stated above (Article 6), can be required only as dispositions thereto. Therefore God who does not require dispositions before acting, bestows Happiness without any previous works.

Objection 2. Further, just as God is the immediate cause of Happiness, so is He the immediate cause of nature. But when God first established nature, He produced creatures without any previous disposition or action on the part of the creature, but made each one perfect forthwith in its species. Therefore it seems that He bestows Happiness on man without any previous works.

Objection 3. Further, the Apostle says (Romans 4:6) that Happiness is of the man "to whom God reputeth justice without works." Therefore no works of man are necessary for attaining Happiness.

On the contrary, It is written (John 13:17): "If you know these things, you shall be blessed if you do them." Therefore Happiness is obtained through works.

I answer that, Rectitude of the will, as stated above (Question 4, Article 4), is necessary for Happiness; since it is nothing else than the right order of the will to the last end; and it is therefore necessary for obtaining the end, just as the right disposition of matter, in order to receive the form. But this does not prove that any work of man need precede his Happiness: for God could make a will having a right tendency to the end, and at the same time attaining the end; just as sometimes He disposes matter and at the same time introduces the form. But the order of Divine wisdom demands that it should not be thus; for as is stated in De Coel. ii, 12, "of those things that have a natural capacity for the perfect good, one has it without movement, some by one movement, some by several." Now to possess the perfect good without movement, belongs to that which has it naturally: and to have Happiness naturally belongs to God alone. Therefore it belongs to God alone not to be moved towards Happiness by any previous operation. Now since Happiness surpasses every created nature, no pure creature can becomingly gain Happiness, without the movement of operation, whereby it tends thereto. But the angel, who is above man in the natural order, obtained it, according to the order of Divine wisdom, by one movement of a meritorious work, as was explained in the I, 62, 5; whereas man obtains it by many movements of works which are called merits. Wherefore also according to the Philosopher (Ethic. i, 9), happiness is the reward of works of virtue.

Reply to Objection 1. Works are necessary to man in order to gain Happiness; not on account of the insufficiency of the Divine power which bestows Happiness, but that the order in things be observed.

Reply to Objection 2. God produced the first creatures so that they are perfect forthwith, without any previous disposition or operation of the creature; because He instituted the first individuals of the various species, that through them nature might be propagated to their progeny. In like manner, because Happiness was to be bestowed on others through Christ, who is God and Man, "Who," according to Hebrews 2:10, "had brought many children into glory"; therefore, from the very beginning of His conception, His soul was happy, without any previous meritorious operation. But this is peculiar to Him: for Christ's merit avails baptized children for the gaining of Happiness, though they have no merits of their own; because by Baptism they are made members of Christ.

Reply to Objection 3. The Apostle is speaking of the Happiness of Hope, which is bestowed on us by sanctifying grace, which is not given on account of previous works. For grace is not a term of movement, as Happiness is; rather is it the principle of the movement that tends towards Happiness.

QUESTION 19. THE GOODNESS AND MALICE OF THE INTERIOR ACT OF THE WILL

ARTICLE 3. WHETHER THE GOODNESS OF THE WILL DEPENDS ON REASON?

Objection 1. It would seem that the goodness of the will does not depend on reason. For what comes first does not depend on what follows. But the good belongs to the will before it belongs to reason, as is clear from what has been said above (Question 9, Article 1). Therefore the goodness of the will does not depend on reason.

Objection 2. Further, the Philosopher says (Ethic. vi, 2) that the goodness of the practical intellect is "a truth that is in conformity with right desire." But right desire is a good will. Therefore the goodness of the practical reason depends on the goodness of the will, rather than conversely.

Objection 3. Further, the mover does not depend on that which is moved, but vice versa. But the will moves the reason and the other powers, as stated above (Question 9, Article 1). Therefore the goodness of the will does not depend on reason.

On the contrary, Hilary says (De Trin. x): "It is an unruly will that persists in its desires in opposition to reason." But the goodness of the will consists in not being unruly. Therefore the goodness of the will depends on its being subject to reason.

I answer that, As stated above (1,2), the goodness of the will depends properly on the object. Now the will's object is proposed to it by reason. Because the good understood is the proportionate object of the will; while sensitive or imaginary good is proportionate not to the will but to the sensitive appetite: since the will can tend to the universal good, which reason apprehends; whereas the sensitive appetite tends only to the particular good, apprehended by the sensitive power. Therefore the goodness of the will depends on reason, in the same way as it depends on the object.

Reply to Objection 1. The good considered as such, i.e. as appetible, pertains to the will before pertaining to the reason. But considered as true it pertains to the reason, before, under the aspect of goodness, pertaining to the will: because the will cannot desire a good that is not previously apprehended by reason.

Reply to Objection 2. The Philosopher speaks here of the practical intellect, in so far as it counsels and reasons about the means: for in this respect it is perfected by prudence. Now in regard to the means, the rectitude of the reason depends on its conformity with the desire of a due end: nevertheless the very desire of the due end presupposes on the part of reason a right apprehension of the end.

Reply to Objection 3. The will moves the reason in one way: the reason moves the will in another, viz. on the part of the object, as stated above (Question 9, Article 01).

ARTICLE 5. WHETHER THE WILL IS EVIL WHEN IT IS AT VARIANCE WITH ERRING REASON?

Objection 1. It would seem that the will is not evil when it is at variance with erring reason. Because the reason is the rule of the human will, in so far as it is derived from the eternal law, as stated above (Article 4). But erring reason is not derived from the eternal law. Therefore erring reason is not the rule of the human will. Therefore the will is not evil, if it be at variance with erring reason.

Objection 2. Further, according to Augustine, the command of a lower authority does not bind if it be contrary to the command of a higher authority: for instance, if a provincial governor command something that is forbidden by the emperor. But erring reason sometimes proposes what is against the command of a higher power, namely, God Whose power is supreme. Therefore the decision of an erring reason does not bind. Consequently the will is not evil if it be at variance with erring reason.

Objection 3. Further, every evil will is reducible to some species of malice. But the will that is at variance with erring reason is not reducible to some species of malice. For instance, if a man's reason err in telling him to commit fornication, his will in not willing to do so, cannot be reduced to any species of malice. Therefore the will is not evil when it is at variance with erring reason.

On the contrary, As stated in the I, 79, 13, conscience is nothing else than the application of knowledge to some action. Now knowledge is in the reason. Therefore when the will is at variance with erring reason, it is against conscience. But every such will is evil; for it is written (Romans 14:23): "All that is not of faith"—i.e. all that is against conscience—"is sin." Therefore the will is evil when it is at variance with erring reason.

I answer that, Since conscience is a kind of dictate of the reason (for it is an application of knowledge to action, as was stated in the I, 19, 13), to inquire whether the will is evil when it is at variance with erring reason, is the same as to inquire "whether an erring conscience binds." On this matter, some distinguished three kinds of actions: for some are good generically; some are indifferent; some are evil generically. And they say that if reason or conscience tell us to do something which is good generically, there is no error: and in like manner if it tell us not to do something which is evil generically; since it is the same reason that prescribes what is good and forbids what is evil. On the other hand if a man's reason or conscience tells him that he is bound by precept to do what is evil in itself; or that what is good in itself, is forbidden, then his reason or conscience errs. In like manner if a man's reason or conscience tell him, that what is indifferent in itself, for instance to raise a straw from the ground, is forbidden or commanded, his reason or conscience errs. They say, therefore, that reason or conscience when erring in matters of indifference, either by commanding or by forbidding them, binds: so that the will which is at variance with that erring reason is evil and sinful. But they say that when reason or conscience errs in commanding what is evil in itself, or in forbidding what is good in itself and necessary for salvation, it does not bind; wherefore in such cases the will which is at variance with erring reason or conscience is not evil.

But this is unreasonable. For in matters of indifference, the will that is at variance with erring reason or conscience, is evil in some way on account of the object, on which the goodness or malice of the will depends; not indeed on account of the object according as it is in its own nature; but according as it is accidentally apprehended by reason as something evil to do or to avoid. And since the object of the will is that which is proposed by the reason, as stated above (Article 3), from the very fact that a thing is proposed by the reason as being evil, the will by tending thereto becomes evil. And this is the case not only in indifferent matters, but also in those that are good or evil in themselves. For not only indifferent matters can received the character of goodness or malice accidentally; but also that which is good, can receive the character of evil, or that which is evil, can receive the character of goodness, on account of the reason apprehending it as such. For instance, to refrain from fornication is good: yet the will does not tend to this good except in so far as it is proposed by the reason. If, therefore, the erring reason propose it as an evil, the will tends to it as to something evil. Consequently the will is evil, because it wills evil, not indeed that which is evil in itself, but that which is evil accidentally, through being apprehended as such by the reason. In like manner, to believe in Christ is good in itself, and necessary for salvation: but the will does not tend thereto, except inasmuch as it is proposed by the reason. Consequently if it be proposed by the reason as something evil, the will tends to it as to something evil: not as if it were evil in itself, but because it is evil accidentally, through the apprehension of the reason. Hence the Philosopher says (Ethic. vii, 9) that "properly speaking the incontinent man is one who does not follow right reason; but accidentally, he is also one who does not follow false reason." We must therefore conclude that, absolutely speaking, every will at variance with reason, whether right or erring, is always evil.

Reply to Objection 1. Although the judgment of an erring reason is not derived from God, yet the erring reason puts forward its judgment as being true, and consequently as being derived from God, from Whom is all truth.

Reply to Objection 2. The saying of Augustine holds good when it is known that the inferior authority prescribes something contrary to the command of the higher authority. But if a man were to believe the command of the proconsul to be the command of the emperor, in scorning the command of the proconsul he would scorn the command of the emperor. In like manner if a man were to know that human reason was dictating something contrary to God's commandment, he would not be bound to abide by reason: but then reason would not be entirely erroneous. But when erring reason proposes something as being commanded by God, then to scorn the dictate of reason is to scorn the commandment of God.

Reply to Objection 3. Whenever reason apprehends something as evil, it apprehends it under some species of evil; for instance, as being something contrary to a divine precept, or as giving scandal, or for some such like reason. And then that evil is reduced to that species of malice.

ARTICLE 6. WHETHER THE WILL IS GOOD WHEN IT ABIDES BY ERRING REASON?

Objection 1. It would seem that the will is good when it abides by erring reason. For just as the will, when at variance with the reason, tends to that which reason judges to be evil; so, when in accord with reason, it tends to what reason judges to be good. But the will is evil when it is at variance with reason, even when erring. Therefore even when it abides by erring reason, the will is good.

Objection 2. Further, the will is always good, when it abides by the commandment of God and the eternal law. But the eternal law and God's commandment are proposed to us by the apprehension of the reason, even when it errs. Therefore the will is good, even when it abides by erring reason.

Objection 3. Further, the will is evil when it is at variance with erring reason. If, therefore, the will is evil also when it abides by erring reason, it seems that the will is always evil when in conjunction with erring reason: so that in such a case a man would be in a dilemma, and, of necessity, would sin: which is unreasonable. Therefore the will is good when it abides by erring reason.

On the contrary, The will of those who slew the apostles was evil. And yet it was in accord with the erring reason, according to John 16:2: "The hour cometh, that whosoever killeth you, will think that he doth a service to God." Therefore the will can be evil, when it abides by erring reason.

I answer that, Whereas the previous question is the same as inquiring "whether an erring conscience binds"; so this question is the same as inquiring "whether an erring conscience excuses." Now this question depends on what has been said above about ignorance. For it was said (6, 8) that ignorance sometimes causes an act to be involuntary, and sometimes not. And since moral good and evil consist in action in so far as it is voluntary, as was stated above (Article 2); it is evident that when ignorance causes an act to be involuntary, it takes away the character of moral good and evil; but not, when it does not cause the act to be involuntary. Again, it has been stated above (Question 6, Article 8) that when ignorance is in any way willed, either directly or indirectly, it does not cause the act to be involuntary. And I call that ignorance "directly" voluntary, to which the act of the will tends: and that, "indirectly" voluntary, which is due to negligence, by reason of a man not wishing to know what he ought to know, as stated above (Question 6, Article 8).

If then reason or conscience err with an error that is voluntary, either directly, or through negligence, so that one errs about what one ought to know; then such an error of reason or conscience does not excuse the will, that abides by that erring reason or conscience, from being evil. But if the error arise from ignorance of some circumstance, and without any negligence, so that it cause the act to be involuntary, then that error of reason or conscience excuses the will, that abides by that erring reason, from being evil. For instance, if erring reason tell a man that he should go to another man's wife, the will that abides by that erring reason is evil; since this error arises from ignorance of the Divine Law, which he is bound to know. But if a man's reason errs in mistaking another for his wife, and if he wish to give her her right when she asks for it, his will is excused from being evil: because this error arises from ignorance of a circumstance, which ignorance excuses, and causes the act to be involuntary.

Reply to Objection 1. As Dionysius says (Div. Nom. iv), "good results from the entire cause, evil from each particular defect." Consequently in order that the thing to which the will tends be called evil, it suffices, either that it be evil in itself, or that it be apprehended as evil. But in order for it to be good, it must be good in both ways.

Reply to Objection 2. The eternal law cannot err, but human reason can. Consequently the will that abides by human reason, is not always right, nor is it always in accord with the eternal law.

Reply to Objection 3. Just as in syllogistic arguments, granted one absurdity, others must needs follow; so in moral matters, given one absurdity, others must follow too. Thus suppose a man to seek vainglory, he will sin, whether he does his duty for vainglory or whether he omit to do it. Nor is he in a dilemma about the matter: because he can put aside his evil intention. In like manner, suppose a man's reason or conscience to err through inexcusable ignorance, then evil must needs result in the will. Nor is this man in a dilemma: because he can lay aside his error, since his ignorance is vincible and voluntary.

QUESTION 21. THE CONSEQUENCES OF HUMAN ACTIONS BY REASON OF THEIR GOODNESS AND MALICE

ARTICLE 3. WHETHER A HUMAN ACTION IS MERITORIOUS OR DEMERITORIOUS IN SO FAR AS IT IS GOOD OR EVIL?

Objection 1. It would seem that a human action is not meritorious or demeritorious on account of its goodness or malice. For we speak of merit or demerit in relation to retribution, which has no place save in matters relating to another person. But good or evil actions are not all related to another person, for some are related to the person of the agent. Therefore not every good or evil human action is meritorious or demeritorious.

Objection 2. Further, no one deserves punishment or reward for doing as he chooses with that of which he is master: thus if a man destroys what belongs to him, he is not punished, as if he had destroyed what belongs to another. But man is master of his own actions. Therefore a man does not merit punishment or reward, through putting his action to a good or evil purpose.

Objection 3. Further, if a man acquire some good for himself, he does not on that account deserve to be benefited by another man: and the same applies to evil. Now a good action is itself a kind of good and perfection of the agent: while an inordinate action is his evil. Therefore a man does not merit or demerit, from the fact that he does a good or an evil deed.

On the contrary, It is written (Isaiah 3:10-11): "Say to the just man that it is well; for he shall eat the fruit of his doings. Woe to the wicked unto evil; for the reward of his hands shall be given him."

I answer that, We speak of merit and demerit, in relation to retribution, rendered according to justice. Now, retribution according to justice is rendered to a man, by reason of his having done something to another's advantage or hurt. It must, moreover, be observed that every individual member of a society is, in a fashion, a part and member of the whole society. Wherefore, any good or evil, done to the member of a society, redounds on the whole society: thus, who hurts the hand, hurts the man. When, therefore, anyone does good or evil to another individual, there is a twofold measure of merit or demerit in his action: first, in respect of the retribution owed to him by the individual to whom he has done good or harm; secondly, in respect of the retribution owed to him by the whole of society. Now when a man ordains his action directly for the good or evil of the whole society, retribution is owed to him, before and above all, by the whole society; secondarily, by all the parts of society. Whereas when a man does that which conduces to his own benefit or disadvantage, then again is retribution owed to him, in so far as this too affects the community, forasmuch as he is a part of society: although retribution is not due to him, in so far as it conduces to the good or harm of an individual, who is identical with the agent: unless, perchance, he owe retribution to himself, by a sort of resemblance, in so far as man is said to be just to himself.

It is therefore evident that a good or evil action deserves praise or blame, in so far as it is in the power of the will: that it is right or sinful, according as it is ordained to the end; and that its merit or demerit depends on the recompense for justice or injustice towards another.

Reply to Objection 1. A man's good or evil actions, although not ordained to the good or evil of another individual, are nevertheless ordained to the good or evil of another, i.e. the community.

Reply to Objection 2. Man is master of his actions; and yet, in so far as he belongs to another, i.e. the community, of which he forms part, he merits or demerits, inasmuch as he disposes his actions well or ill: just as if he were to dispense well or ill other belongings of his, in respect of which he is bound to serve the community.

Reply to Objection 3. This very good or evil, which a man does to himself by his action, redounds to the community, as stated above.

QUESTION 23. HOW THE PASSIONS DIFFER FROM ONE ANOTHER

ARTICLE 1. WHETHER THE PASSIONS OF THE DESIRING PART ARE DIFFERENT FROM THOSE OF THE SPIRITED PART?

Objection 1. It would seem that the same passions are in the spirited and desiring parts. For the Philosopher says (Ethic. ii, 5) that the passions of the soul are those emotions "which are followed by joy or sorrow." But joy and sorrow are in the desiring part. Therefore all the passions are in the desiring part, and not some in the spirited, others in the desiring part.

Objection 2. Further, on the words of Matthew 13:33, "The kingdom of heaven is like to leaven," etc., Jerome's gloss says: "We should have prudence in the reason; hatred of vice in the spirited faculty; desire of virtue, in the desiring part." But hatred is in the desiring faculty, as also is love, of which it is the contrary, as is stated in Topic. ii, 7. Therefore the same passion is in the desiring and spirited faculties.

Objection 3. Further, passions and actions differ specifically according to their objects. But the objects of the spirited and desiring passions are the same, viz. good and evil. Therefore the same passions are in the spirited and desiring faculties.

On the contrary, The acts of the different powers differ in species; for instance, to see, and to hear. But the spirited and the desiring are two powers into which the sensitive appetite is divided, as stated in the I, 81, 2. Therefore, since the passions are movements of the sensitive appetite, as stated above (Question 22, Article 3), the passions of the spirited faculty are specifically distinct from those of the desiring part.

I answer that, The passions of the spirited part differ in species from those of the desiring faculty. For since different powers have different objects, as stated in the I, 77, 3, the passions of different powers must of necessity be referred to different objects. Much more, therefore, do the passions of different faculties differ in species; since a greater difference in the object is required to diversify the species of the powers, than to diversify the species of passions or actions. For just as in the physical order, diversity of genus arises from diversity in the potentiality of matter, while diversity of species arises from diversity of form in the same matter; so in the acts of the soul, those that belong to different powers, differ not only in species but also in genus, while acts and passions regarding different specific objects, included under the one common object of a single power, differ as the species of that genus.

In order, therefore, to discern which passions are in the spirited, and which in the desiring, we must take the object of each of these powers. For we have stated in the I, 81, 2, that the object of the desiring power is sensible good or evil, simply apprehended as such, which causes pleasure or pain. But, since the soul must, of necessity, experience difficulty or struggle at times, in acquiring some such good, or in avoiding some such evil, in so far as such good or evil is more than our animal nature can easily acquire or avoid; therefore this very good or evil, inasmuch as it is of an arduous or difficult nature, is the object of the spirited faculty. Therefore whatever passions regard good or evil absolutely, belong to the desiring power; for instance, joy, sorrow, love, hatred, and such like: whereas those passions which regard good or bad as arduous, through being difficult to obtain or avoid, belong to the spirited faculty; such are daring, fear, hope and the like.

Reply to Objection 1. As stated in the I, 81, 2, the spirited faculty is bestowed on animals, in order to remove the obstacles that hinder the desiring power from tending towards its object, either by making some good difficult to obtain, or by making some evil hard to avoid. The result is that all the spirited passions terminate in the desiring passions: and thus it is that even the passions which are in the spirited faculty are followed by joy and sadness which are in the desiring faculty.

Reply to Objection 2. Jerome ascribes hatred of vice to the spirited faculty, not by reason of hatred, which is properly a desiring passion; but on account of the struggle, which belongs to the spirited power.

Reply to Objection 3. Good, inasmuch as it is delightful, moves the desiring power. But if it prove difficult to obtain, from this very fact it has a certain contrariety to the desiring power: and hence the need of another power tending to that good. The same applies to evil. And this power is the spirited faculty. Consequently the desiring passions are specifically different from the spirited passions.

QUESTION 55. THE VIRTUES, AS TO THEIR ESSENCE

ARTICLE 4. WHETHER VIRTUE IS SUITABLY DEFINED?

Objection 1. It would seem that the definition, usually given, of virtue, is not suitable, to wit: "Virtue is a good quality of the mind, by which we live righteously, of which no one can make bad use, which God works in us, without us." For virtue is man's goodness, since virtue it is that makes its subject good. But goodness does not seem to be good, as neither is whiteness white. It is therefore unsuitable to describe virtue as a "good quality."

Objection 2. Further, no difference is more common than its genus; since it is that which divides the genus. But good is more common than quality, since it is convertible with being. Therefore "good" should not be put in the definition of virtue, as a difference of quality.

Objection 3. Further, as Augustine says (De Trin. xii, 3): "When we come across anything that is not common to us and the beasts of the field, it is something appertaining to the mind." But there are virtues even of the irrational parts; as the Philosopher says (Ethic. iii, 10). Every virtue, therefore, is not a good quality "of the mind."

Objection 4. Further, righteousness seems to belong to justice; whence the righteous are called just. But justice is a species of virtue. It is therefore unsuitable to put "righteous" in the definition of virtue, when we say that virtue is that "by which we live righteously."

Objection 5. Further, whoever is proud of a thing, makes bad use of it. But many are proud of virtue, for Augustine says in his Rule, that "pride lies in wait for good works in order to slay them." It is untrue, therefore, "that no one can make bad use of virtue."

Objection 6. Further, man is justified by virtue. But Augustine commenting on John 15:11: "He shall do greater things than these," says [Tract. xxvii in Joan.: Serm. xv de Verb. Ap. 11: "He who created thee without thee, will not justify thee without thee." It is therefore unsuitable to say that "God works virtue in us, without us."

On the contrary, We have the authority of Augustine from whose words this definition is gathered, and principally in De Libero Arbitrio ii, 19.

I answer that, This definition comprises perfectly the whole essential notion of virtue. For the perfect essential notion of anything is gathered from all its causes. Now the above definition comprises all the causes of virtue. For the formal cause of virtue, as of everything, is gathered from its genus and difference, when it is defined as "a good quality": for "quality" is the genus of virtue, and the difference, "good." But the definition would be more suitable if for "quality" we substitute "habit," which is the proximate genus.

Now virtue has no matter "out of which" it is formed, as neither has any other accident; but it has matter "about which" it is concerned, and matter "in which" it exits, namely, the subject. The matter about which virtue is concerned is its object, and this could not be included in the above definition, because the object fixes the virtue to a certain species, and here we are giving the definition of virtue in general. And so for material cause we have the subject, which is mentioned when we say that virtue is a good quality "of the mind."

The end of virtue, since it is an operative habit, is operation. But it must be observed that some operative habits are always referred to evil, as vicious habits: others are sometimes referred to good, sometimes to evil; for instance, opinion is referred both to the true and to the untrue: whereas virtue is a habit which is always referred to good: and so the distinction of virtue from those habits which are always referred to evil, is expressed in the words "by which we live righteously": and its distinction from those habits which are sometimes directed unto good, sometimes unto evil, in the words, "of which no one makes bad use."

Lastly, God is the efficient cause of infused virtue, to which this definition applies; and this is expressed in the words "which God works in us without us." If we omit this phrase, the remainder of the definition will apply to all virtues in general, whether acquired or infused.

Reply to Objection 1. That which is first seized by the intellect is being: wherefore everything that we apprehend we consider as being, and consequently as gone, and as good, which are convertible with being. Wherefore we say that essence is being and is one and is good; and that oneness is being and one and good: and in like manner goodness. But this is not the case with specific forms, as whiteness and health; for everything that we apprehend, is not apprehended with the notion of white and healthy. We must, however, observe that, as accidents and non-subsistent forms are called beings, not as if they themselves had being, but because things are by them; so also are they called good or one, not by some distinct goodness or oneness, but because by them something is good or one. So also is virtue called good, because by it something is good.

Reply to Objection 2. Good, which is put in the definition of virtue, is not good in general which is convertible with being, and which extends further than quality, but the good as fixed by reason, with regard to which Dionysius says (Div. Nom. iv) "that the good of the soul is to be in accord with reason."

Reply to Objection 3. Virtue cannot be in the irrational part of the soul, except in so far as this participates in the reason (Ethic. i, 13). And therefore reason, or the mind, is the proper subject of virtue.

Reply to Objection 4. Justice has a righteousness of its own by which it puts those outward things right which come into human use, and are the proper matter of justice, as we shall show further on (60, 2; II-II, 58, 8). But the righteousness which denotes order to a due end and to the Divine law, which is the rule of the human will, as stated above (Question 19, Article 4), is common to all virtues.

Reply to Objection 5. One can make bad use of a virtue objectively, for instance by having evil thoughts about a virtue, e.g. by hating it, or by being proud of it: but one cannot make bad use of virtue as principle of action, so that an act of virtue be evil.

Reply to Objection 6. Infused virtue is caused in us by God without any action on our part, but not without our consent. This is the sense of the words, "which God works in us without us." As to those things which are done by us, God causes them in us, yet not without action on our part, for He works in every will and in every nature.

QUESTION 58. THE DIFFERENCE BETWEEN MORAL AND INTELLECTUAL VIRTUES

ARTICLE 2. WHETHER MORAL VIRTUE DIFFERS FROM INTELLECTUAL VIRTUE?

Objection 1. It would seem that moral virtue does not differ from intellectual virtue. For Augustine says (De Civ. Dei iv, 21) "that virtue is the art of right conduct." But art is an intellectual virtue. Therefore moral and intellectual virtue do not differ.

Objection 2. Further, some authors put science in the definition of virtues: thus some define perseverance as a "science or habit regarding those things to which we should hold or not hold"; and holiness as "a science which makes man to be faithful and to do his duty to God." Now science is an intellectual virtue. Therefore moral virtue should not be distinguished from intellectual virtue.

Objection 3. Further, Augustine says (Soliloq. i, 6) that "virtue is the rectitude and perfection of reason." But this belongs to the intellectual virtues, as stated in Ethic. vi, 13. Therefore moral virtue does not differ from intellectual.

Objection 4. Further, a thing does not differ from that which is included in its definition. But intellectual virtue is included in the definition of moral virtue: for the Philosopher says (Ethic. ii, 6) that "moral virtue is a habit of choosing the mean appointed by reason as a prudent man would appoint it." Now this right reason that fixes the mean of moral virtue, belongs to an intellectual virtue, as stated in Ethic. vi, 13. Therefore moral virtue does not differ from intellectual.

On the contrary, It is stated in Ethic. i, 13 that "there are two kinds of virtue: some we call intellectual; some moral."

I answer that, Reason is the first principle of all human acts; and whatever other principles of human acts may be found, they obey reason somewhat, but in various ways. For some obey reason blindly and without any contradiction whatever: such are the limbs of the body, provided they be in a healthy condition, for as soon as reason commands, the hand or the foot proceeds to action. Hence the Philosopher says (Polit. i, 3) that "the soul rules the body like a despot," i.e. as a master rules his slave, who has no right to rebel. Accordingly some held that all the active principles in man are subordinate to reason in this way. If this were true, for man to act well it would suffice that his reason be perfect. Consequently, since virtue is a habit perfecting man in view of his doing good actions, it would follow that it is only in the reason, so that there would be none but intellectual virtues. This was the opinion of Socrates, who said "every virtue is a kind of prudence," as stated in Ethic. vi, 13. Hence he maintained that as long as man is in possession of knowledge, he cannot sin; and that everyone who sins, does so through ignorance.

Now this is based on a false supposition. Because the appetitive faculty obeys the reason, not blindly, but with a certain power of opposition; wherefore the Philosopher says (Polit. i, 3) that "reason commands the appetitive faculty by a politic power," whereby a man rules over subjects that are free, having a certain right of opposition. Hence Augustine says on Psalm 118 (Serm. 8) that "sometimes we understand [what is right] while desire is slow, or follows not at all," in so far as the habits or passions of the appetitive faculty cause the use of reason to be impeded in some particular action. And in this way, there is some truth in the saying of Socrates that so long as a man is in possession of knowledge he does not sin: provided, however, that this knowledge is made to include the use of reason in this individual act of choice.

Accordingly for a man to do a good deed, it is requisite not only that his reason be well disposed by means of a habit of intellectual virtue; but also that his appetite be well disposed by means of a habit of moral virtue. And so moral differs from intellectual virtue, even as the appetite differs from the reason. Hence just as the appetite is the principle of human acts, in so far as it partakes of reason, so are moral habits to be considered virtues in so far as they are in conformity with reason.

Reply to Objection 1. Augustine usually applies the term "art" to any form of right reason; in which sense art includes prudence which is the right reason about things to be done, even as art is the right reason about things to be made. Accordingly, when he says that "virtue is the art of right conduct," this applies to prudence essentially; but to other virtues, by participation, for as much as they are directed by prudence.

Reply to Objection 2. All such definitions, by whomsoever given, were based on the Socratic theory, and should be explained according to what we have said about art (ad 1).

The same applies to the Third Objection.

Reply to Objection 4. Right reason which is in accord with prudence is included in the definition of moral virtue, not as part of its essence, but as something belonging by way of participation to all the moral virtues, in so far as they are all under the direction of prudence.

ARTICLE 4. WHETHER THERE CAN BE MORAL WITHOUT INTELLECTUAL VIRTUE?

Objection 1. It would seem that moral can be without intellectual virtue. Because moral virtue, as Cicero says (De Invent. Rhet. ii) is "a habit like a second nature in accord with reason." Now though nature may be in accord with some sovereign reason that moves it, there is no need for that reason to be united to nature in the same subject, as is evident of natural things devoid of knowledge. Therefore in a man there may be a moral virtue like a second nature, inclining him to consent to his reason, without his reason being perfected by an intellectual virtue.

Objection 2. Further, by means of intellectual virtue man obtains perfect use of reason. But it happens at times that men are virtuous and acceptable to God, without being vigorous in the use of reason. Therefore it seems that moral virtue can be without intellectual.

Objection 3. Further moral virtue makes us inclined to do good works. But some, without depending on the judgment of reason, have a natural inclination to do good works. Therefore moral virtues can be without intellectual virtues.

On the contrary, Gregory says (Moral. xxii) that "the other virtues, unless we do prudently what we desire to do, cannot be real virtues." But prudence is an intellectual virtue, as stated above (Question 57, Article 5). Therefore moral virtues cannot be without intellectual virtues.

I answer that, Moral virtue can be without some of the intellectual virtues, viz. wisdom, science, and art; but not without understanding and prudence. Moral virtue cannot be without prudence, because it is a habit of choosing, i.e. making us choose well. Now in order that a choice be good, two things are required. First, that the intention be directed to a due end; and this is done by moral virtue, which inclines the appetitive faculty to the good that is in accord with reason, which is a due end. Secondly, that man take rightly those things which have reference to the end: and this he cannot do unless his reason counsel, judge and command aright, which is the function of prudence and the virtues annexed to it, as stated above (57, A5,6). Wherefore there can be no moral virtue without prudence: and consequently neither can there be without understanding. For it is by the virtue of understanding that we know self-evident principles both in speculative and in practical matters. Consequently just as right reason in speculative matters, in so far as it proceeds from naturally known principles, presupposes the understanding of those principles, so also does prudence, which is the right reason about things to be done.

Reply to Objection 1. The inclination of nature in things devoid of reason is without choice: wherefore such an inclination does not of necessity require reason. But the inclination of moral virtue is with choice: and consequently in order that it may be perfect it requires that reason be perfected by intellectual virtue.

Reply to Objection 2. A man may be virtuous without having full use of reason as to everything, provided he have it with regard to those things which have to be done virtuously. In this way all virtuous men have full use of reason. Hence those who seem to be simple, through lack of worldly cunning, may possibly be prudent, according to Matthew 10:16: "Be ye therefore prudent [Douay: 'wise'] as serpents, and simple as doves."

Reply to Objection 3. The natural inclination to a good of virtue is a kind of beginning of virtue, but is not perfect virtue. For the stronger this inclination is, the more perilous may it prove to be, unless it be accompanied by right reason, which rectifies the choice of fitting means towards the due end. Thus if a running horse be blind, the faster it runs the more heavily will it fall, and the more grievously will it be hurt. And consequently, although moral virtue be not right reason, as Socrates held, yet not only is it "according to right reason," in so far as it inclines man to that which is, according to right reason, as the Platonists maintained [Cf. Plato, Meno xli.]; but also it needs to be "joined with right reason," as Aristotle declares (Ethic. vi, 13).

ARTICLE 5. WHETHER THERE CAN BE INTELLECTUAL WITHOUT MORAL VIRTUE?

Objection 1. It would seem that there can be intellectual without moral virtue. Because perfection of what precedes does not depend on the perfection of what follows. Now reason precedes and moves the sensitive appetite. Therefore intellectual virtue, which is a perfection of the reason, does not depend on moral virtue, which is a perfection of the appetitive faculty; and can be without it.

Objection 2. Further, morals are the matter of prudence, even as things makeable are the matter of art. Now art can be without its proper matter, as a smith without iron. Therefore prudence can be without the moral virtue, although of all the intellectual virtues, it seems most akin to the moral virtues.

Objection 3. Further, prudence is "a virtue whereby we are of good counsel" (Ethic. vi, 9). Now many are of good counsel without having the moral virtues. Therefore prudence can be without a moral virtue.

On the contrary, To wish to do evil is directly opposed to moral virtue; and yet it is not opposed to anything that can be without moral virtue. Now it is contrary to prudence "to sin willingly" (Ethic. vi, 5). Therefore prudence cannot be without moral virtue.

I answer that, Other intellectual virtues can, but prudence cannot, be without moral virtue. The reason for this is that prudence is the right reason about things to be done (and this, not merely in general, but also in particular); about which things actions are. Now right reason demands principles from which reason proceeds to argue. And when reason argues about particular cases, it needs not only universal but also particular principles. As to universal principles of action, man is rightly disposed by the natural understanding of principles, whereby he understands that he should do no evil; or again by some practical science. But this is not enough in order that man may reason aright about particular cases. For it happens sometimes that the aforesaid universal principle, known by means of understanding or science, is destroyed in a particular case by a passion: thus to one who is swayed by desire, when he is overcome thereby, the object of his desire seems good, although it is opposed to the universal judgment of his reason. Consequently, as by the habit of natural understanding or of science, man is made to be rightly disposed in regard to the universal principles of action; so, in order that he be rightly disposed with regard to the particular principles of action, viz. the ends, he needs to be perfected by certain habits, whereby it becomes connatural, as it were, to man to judge aright to the end. This is done by moral virtue: for the virtuous man judges aright of the end of virtue, because "such a man is, such does the end seem to him" (Ethic. iii, 5). Consequently the right reason about things to be done, viz. prudence, requires man to have moral virtue.

Reply to Objection 1. Reason, as apprehending the end, precedes the appetite for the end: but appetite for the end precedes the reason, as arguing about the choice of the means, which is the concern of prudence. Even so, in speculative matters the understanding of principles is the foundation on which the syllogism of the reason is based.

Reply to Objection 2. It does not depend on the disposition of our appetite whether we judge well or ill of the principles of art, as it does, when we judge of the end which is the principle in moral matters: in the former case our judgment depends on reason alone. Hence art does not require a virtue perfecting the appetite, as prudence does.

Reply to Objection 3. Prudence not only helps us to be of good counsel, but also to judge and command well. This is not possible unless the impediment of the passions, destroying the judgment and command of prudence, be removed; and this is done by moral virtue.

QUESTION 59. MORAL VIRTUE IN RELATION TO THE PASSIONS

ARTICLE 5. WHETHER THERE CAN BE MORAL VIRTUE WITHOUT PASSION?

Objection 1. It would seem that moral virtue can be without passion. For the more perfect moral virtue is, the more does it overcome the passions. Therefore at its highest point of perfection it is altogether without passion.

Objection 2. Further, then is a thing perfect, when it is removed from its contrary and from whatever inclines to its contrary. Now the passions incline us to sin which is contrary to virtue: hence (Romans 7:5) they are called "passions of sins." Therefore perfect virtue is altogether without passion.

Objection 3. Further, it is by virtue that we are conformed to God, as Augustine declares (De Moribus Eccl. vi, xi, xiii). But God does all things without passion at all. Therefore the most perfect virtue is without any passion.

On the contrary, "No man is just who rejoices not in his deeds," as stated in Ethic. i, 8. But joy is a passion. Therefore justice cannot be without passion; and still less can the other virtues be.

I answer that, If we take the passions as being inordinate emotions, as the Stoics did, it is evident that in this sense perfect virtue is without the passions. But if by passions we understand any movement of the sensitive appetite, it is plain that moral virtues, which are about the passions as about their proper matter, cannot be without passions. The reason for this is that otherwise it would follow that moral virtue makes the sensitive appetite altogether idle: whereas it is not the function of virtue to deprive the powers subordinate to reason of their proper activities, but to make them execute the commands of reason, by exercising their proper acts. Wherefore just as virtue directs the bodily limbs to their due external acts, so does it direct the sensitive appetite to its proper regulated movements.

Those moral virtues, however, which are not about the passions, but about operations, can be without passions. Such a virtue is justice: because it applies the will to its proper act, which is not a passion. Nevertheless, joy results from the act of justice; at least in the will, in which case it is not a passion. And if this joy be increased through the perfection of justice, it will overflow into the sensitive appetite; in so far as the lower powers follow the movement of the higher, as stated above (17, 7; 24, 3). Wherefore by reason of this kind of overflow, the more perfect a virtue is, the more does it cause passion.

Reply to Objection 1. Virtue overcomes inordinate passion; it produces ordinate passion.

Reply to Objection 2. It is inordinate, not ordinate, passion that leads to sin.

Reply to Objection 3. The good of anything depends on the condition of its nature. Now there is no sensitive appetite in God and the angels, as there is in man. Consequently good operation in God and the angels is altogether without passion, as it is without a body: whereas the good operation of man is with passion, even as it is produced with the body's help.

QUESTION 61. THE CARDINAL VIRTUES

ARTICLE 3. WHETHER ANY OTHER VIRTUES SHOULD BE CALLED PRINCIPAL RATHER THAN THESE?

Objection 1. It would seem that other virtues should be called principal rather than these. For, seemingly, the greatest is the principal in any genus. Now "magnanimity has a great influence on all the virtues" (Ethic. iv, 3). Therefore magnanimity should more than any be called a principal virtue.

Objection 2. Further, that which strengthens the other virtues should above all be called a principal virtue. But such is humility: for Gregory says (Hom. iv in Ev.) that "he who gathers the other virtues without humility is as one who carries straw against the wind." Therefore humility seems above all to be a principal virtue.

Objection 3. Further, that which is most perfect seems to be principal. But this applies to patience, according to James 1:4: "Patience hath a perfect work." Therefore patience should be reckoned a principal virtue.

On the contrary, Cicero reduces all other virtues to these four (De Invent. Rhet. ii).

I answer that, As stated above (Article 2), these four are reckoned as cardinal virtues, in respect of the four formal principles of virtue as we understand it now. These principles are found chiefly in certain acts and passions. Thus the good which exists in the act of reason, is found chiefly in reason's command, but not in its counsel or its judgment, as stated above (Question 57, Article 6). Again, good as defined by reason and put into our operations as something right and due, is found chiefly in commutations and distributions in respect of another person, and on a basis of equality. The good of curbing the passions is found chiefly in those passions which are most difficult to curb, viz. in the pleasures of touch. The good of being firm in holding to the good defined by reason, against the impulse of passion, is found chiefly in perils of death, which are most difficult to withstand.

Accordingly the above four virtues may be considered in two ways. First, in respect of their common formal principles. In this way they are called principal, being general, as it were, in comparison with all the virtues: so that, for instance, any virtue that causes good in reason's act of consideration, may be called prudence; every virtue that causes the good of right and due in operation, be called justice; every virtue that curbs and represses the passions, be called temperance; and every virtue that strengthens the mind against any passions whatever, be called fortitude. Many, both holy doctors, as also philosophers, speak about these virtues in this sense: and in this way the other virtues are contained under them. Wherefore all the objections fail.

Secondly, they may be considered in point of their being denominated, each one from that which is foremost in its respective matter, and thus they are specific virtues, condivided with the others. Yet they are called principal in comparison with the other virtues, on account of the importance of their matter: so that prudence is the virtue which commands; justice, the virtue which is about due actions between equals; temperance, the virtue which suppresses desires for the pleasures of touch; and fortitude, the virtue which strengthens against dangers of death. Thus again do the objections fail: because the other virtues may be principal in some other way, but these are called principal by reason of their matter, as stated above.

QUESTION 62. THE THEOLOGICAL VIRTUES

ARTICLE 3. WHETHER FAITH, HOPE, AND CHARITY ARE FITTINGLY RECKONED AS THEOLOGICAL VIRTUES?

Objection 1. It would seem that faith, hope, and charity are not fittingly reckoned as three theological virtues. For the theological virtues are in relation to Divine happiness, what the natural inclination is in relation to the connatural end. Now among the virtues directed to the connatural end there is but one natural virtue, viz. the understanding of principles. Therefore there should be but one theological virtue.

Objection 2. Further, the theological virtues are more perfect than the intellectual and moral virtues. Now faith is not reckoned among the intellectual virtues, but is something less than a virtue, since it is imperfect knowledge. Likewise hope is not reckoned among the moral virtues, but is something less than a virtue, since it is a passion. Much less therefore should they be reckoned as theological virtues.

Objection 3. Further, the theological virtues direct man's soul to God. Now man's soul cannot be directed to God, save through the intellective part, wherein are the intellect and will. Therefore there should be only two theological virtues, one perfecting the intellect, the other, the will.

On the contrary, The Apostle says (1 Corinthians 13:13): "Now there remain faith, hope, charity, these three."

I answer that, As stated above (Article 1), the theological virtues direct man to supernatural happiness in the same way as by the natural inclination man is directed to his connatural end. Now the latter happens in respect of two things. First, in respect of the reason or intellect, in so far as it contains the first universal principles which are known to us by the natural light of the intellect, and which are reason's starting-point, both in speculative and in practical matters. Secondly, through the rectitude of the will which tends naturally to good as defined by reason.

But these two fall short of the order of supernatural happiness, according to 1 Corinthians 2:9: "The eye hath not seen, nor ear heard, neither hath it entered into the heart of man, what things God hath prepared for them that love Him." Consequently in respect of both the above things man needed to receive in addition something supernatural to direct him to a supernatural end. First, as regards the intellect, man receives certain supernatural principles, which are held by means of a Divine light: these are the articles of faith, about which is faith. Secondly, the will is directed to this end, both as to that end as something attainable—and this pertains to hope—and as to a certain spiritual union, whereby the will is, so to speak, transformed into that end—and this belongs to charity. For the appetite of a thing is moved and tends towards its connatural end naturally; and this movement is due to a certain conformity of the thing with its end.

Reply to Objection 1. The intellect requires intelligible species whereby to understand: consequently there is need of a natural habit in addition to the power. But the very nature of the will suffices for it to be directed naturally to the end, both as to the intention of the end and as to its conformity with the end. But the nature of the power is insufficient in either of these respects, for the will to be directed to things that are above its nature. Consequently there was need for an additional supernatural habit in both respects.

Reply to Objection 2. Faith and hope imply a certain imperfection: since faith is of things unseen, and hope, of things not possessed. Hence faith and hope, in things that are subject to human power, fall short of the notion of virtue. But faith and hope in things which are above the capacity of human nature surpass all virtue that is in proportion to man, according to 1 Corinthians 1:25: "The weakness of God is stronger than men."

Reply to Objection 3. Two things pertain to the appetite, viz. movement to the end, and conformity with the end by means of love. Hence there must needs be two theological virtues in the human appetite, namely, hope and charity.

QUESTION 63. THE CAUSE OF VIRTUES

ARTICLE 2. WHETHER ANY VIRTUE IS CAUSED IN US BY HABITUATION?

Objection 1. It would seem that virtues can not be caused in us by habituation. Because a gloss of Augustine [Cf. Lib. Sentent. Prosperi cvi.] commenting on Romans 14:23, "All that is not of faith is sin," says: "The whole life of an unbeliever is a sin: and there is no good without the Sovereign Good. Where knowledge of the truth is lacking, virtue is a mockery even in the best behaved people." Now faith cannot be acquired by means of works, but is caused in us by God, according to Ephesians 2:8: "By grace you are saved through faith." Therefore no acquired virtue can be in us by habituation.

Objection 2. Further, sin and virtue are contraries, so that they are incompatible. Now man cannot avoid sin except by the grace of God, according to Wisdom 8:21: "I knew that I could not otherwise be continent, except God gave it." Therefore neither can any virtues be caused in us by habituation, but only by the gift of God.

Objection 3. Further, actions which lead toward virtue, lack the perfection of virtue. But an effect cannot be more perfect than its cause. Therefore a virtue cannot be caused by actions that precede it.

On the contrary, Dionysius says (Div. Nom. iv) that good is more efficacious than evil. But vicious habits are caused by evil acts. Much more, therefore, can virtuous habits be caused by good acts.

I answer that, We have spoken above (51, A2,3) in a general way about the production of habits from acts; and speaking now in a special way of this matter in relation to virtue, we must take note that, as stated above (55, A3,4), man's virtue perfects him in relation to good. Now since the notion of good consists in "mode, species, and order," as Augustine states (De Nat. Boni. iii) or in "number, weight, and measure," as expressed in Wisdom 11:21, man's good must needs be appraised with respect to some rule. Now this rule is twofold, as stated above (19, A3,4), viz. human reason and Divine Law. And since Divine Law is the higher rule, it extends to more things, so that whatever is ruled by human reason, is ruled by the Divine Law too; but the converse does not hold.

It follows that human virtue directed to the good which is defined according to the rule of human reason can be caused by human acts: inasmuch as such acts proceed from reason, by whose power and rule the aforesaid good is established. On the other hand, virtue which directs man to good as defined by the Divine Law, and not by human reason, cannot be caused by human acts, the principle of which is reason, but is produced in us by the Divine operation alone. Hence Augustine in giving the definition of the latter virtue inserts the words, "which God works in us without us" (Super Ps. 118, Serm. xxvi). It is also of these virtues that the First Objection holds good.

Reply to Objection 2. Mortal sin is incompatible with divinely infused virtue, especially if this be considered in its perfect state. But actual sin, even mortal, is compatible with humanly acquired virtue; because the use of a habit in us is subject to our will, as stated above (Question 49, Article 3): and one sinful act does not destroy a habit of acquired virtue, since it is not an act but a habit, that is directly contrary to a habit. Wherefore, though man cannot avoid mortal sin without grace, so as never to sin mortally, yet he is not hindered from acquiring a habit of virtue, whereby he may abstain from evil in the majority of cases, and chiefly in matters most opposed to reason. There are also certain mortal sins which man can nowise avoid without grace, those, namely, which are directly opposed to the theological virtues, which are in us through the gift of grace. This, however, will be more fully explained later (109, 4).

Reply to Objection 3. As stated above (1; 51, 1), certain seeds or principles of acquired virtue pre-exist in us by nature. These principles are more excellent than the virtues acquired through them: thus the understanding of speculative principles is more excellent than the science of conclusions, and the natural rectitude of the reason is more excellent than the rectification of the appetite which results through the appetite partaking of reason, which rectification belongs to moral virtue. Accordingly human acts, in so far as they proceed from higher principles, can cause acquired human virtues.

QUESTION 64. THE MEAN OF VIRTUE

ARTICLE 1. WHETHER MORAL VIRTUES OBSERVE THE MEAN?

Objection 1. It would seem that moral virtue does not observe the mean. For the nature of a mean is incompatible with that which is extreme. Now the nature of virtue is to be something extreme; for it is stated in De Coelo i that "virtue is the limit of power." Therefore moral virtue does not observe the mean.

Objection 2. Further, the maximum is not a mean. Now some moral virtues tend to a maximum: for instance, magnanimity to very great honors, and magnificence to very large expenditure, as stated in Ethic. iv, 2,3. Therefore not every moral virtue observes the mean.

Objection 3. Further, if it is essential to a moral virtue to observe the mean, it follows that a moral virtue is not perfected, but the contrary corrupted, through tending to something extreme. Now some moral virtues are perfected by tending to something extreme; thus virginity, which abstains from all sexual pleasure, observes the extreme, and is the most perfect chastity: and to give all to the poor is the most perfect mercy or liberality. Therefore it seems that it is not essential to moral virtue that it should observe the mean.

On the contrary, The Philosopher says (Ethic. ii, 6) that "moral virtue is a habit of choosing the mean."

I answer that, As already explained (55, 3), the nature of virtue is that it should direct man to good. Now moral virtue is properly a perfection of the appetitive part of the soul in regard to some determinate matter: and the measure or rule of the appetitive movement in respect of appetible objects is the reason. But the good of that which is measured or ruled consists in its conformity with its rule: thus the good things made by art is that they follow the rule of art. Consequently, in things of this sort, evil consists in discordance from their rule or measure. Now this may happen either by their exceeding the measure or by their falling short of it; as is clearly the case in all things ruled or measured. Hence it is evident that the good of moral virtue consists in conformity with the rule of reason. Now it is clear that between excess and deficiency the mean is equality or conformity. Therefore it is evident that moral virtue observes the mean.

Reply to Objection 1. Moral virtue derives goodness from the rule of reason, while its matter consists in passions or operations. If therefore we compare moral virtue to reason, then, if we look at that which it has of reason, it holds the position of one extreme, viz. conformity; while excess and defect take the position of the other extreme, viz. deformity. But if we consider moral virtue in respect of its matter, then it holds the position of mean, in so far as it makes the passion conform to the rule of reason. Hence the Philosopher says (Ethic. ii, 6) that "virtue, as to its essence, is a mean state," in so far as the rule of virtue is imposed on its proper matter: "but it is an extreme in reference to the 'best' and the 'excellent,'" viz. as to its conformity with reason.

Reply to Objection 2. In actions and passions the mean and the extremes depend on various circumstances: hence nothing hinders something from being extreme in a particular virtue as to one circumstance, while the same thing is a mean in respect of other circumstances, through being in conformity with reason. This is the case with magnanimity and magnificence. For if we look at the absolute quantity of the respective objects of these virtues, we shall call it an extreme and a maximum: but if we consider the quantity in relation to other circumstances, then it has the character of a mean: since these virtues tend to this maximum in accordance with the rule of reason, i.e. "where" it is right, "when" it is right, and for an "end" that is right. There will be excess, if one tends to this maximum "when" it is not right, or "where" it is not right, or for an undue "end"; and there will be deficiency if one fails to tend thereto "where" one ought, and "when" one aught. This agrees with the saying of the Philosopher (Ethic. iv, 3) that the "magnanimous man observes the extreme in quantity, but the mean in the right mode of his action."

Reply to Objection 3. The same is to be said of virginity and poverty as of magnanimity. For virginity abstains from all sexual matters, and poverty from all wealth, for a right end, and in a right manner, i.e. according to God's word, and for the sake of eternal life. But if this be done in an undue manner, i.e. out of unlawful superstition, or again for vainglory, it will be in excess. And if it be not done when it ought to be done, or as it ought to be done, it is a vice by deficiency: for instance, in those who break their vows of virginity or poverty.

ARTICLE 2. WHETHER THE MEAN OF MORAL VIRTUE IS THE REAL MEAN, OR THE RATIONAL MEAN?

Objection 1. It would seem that the mean of moral virtue is not the rational mean, but the real mean. For the good of moral virtue consists in its observing the mean. Now, good, as stated in Metaph. ii, text. 8, is in things themselves. Therefore the mean of moral virtue is a real mean.

Objection 2. Further, the reason is a power of apprehension. But moral virtue does not observe a mean between apprehensions, but rather a mean between operations or passions. Therefore the mean of moral virtue is not the rational, but the real mean.

Objection 3. Further, a mean that is observed according to arithmetical or geometrical proportion is a real mean. Now such is the mean of justice, as stated in Ethic. v, 3. Therefore the mean of moral virtue is not the rational, but the real mean.

On the contrary, The Philosopher says (Ethic. ii, 6) that "moral virtue observes the mean fixed, in our regard, by reason."

I answer that, The rational mean can be understood in two ways. First, according as the mean is observed in the act itself of reason, as though the very act of reason were made to observe the mean: in this sense, since moral virtue perfects not the act of reason, but the act of the appetitive power, the mean of moral virtue is not the rational mean. Secondly, the mean of reason may be considered as that which the reason puts into some particular matter. In this sense every mean of moral virtue is a rational mean, since, as above stated (1), moral virtue is said to observe the mean, through conformity with right reason.

But it happens sometimes that the rational mean is also the real mean: in which case the mean of moral virtue is the real mean, for instance, in justice. On the other hand, sometimes the rational mean is not the real mean, but is considered in relation to us: and such is the mean in all the other moral virtues. The reason for this is that justice is about operations, which deal with external things, wherein the right has to be established simply and absolutely, as stated above (Question 60, Article 2): wherefore the rational mean in justice is the same as the real mean, in so far, to wit as justice gives to each one his due, neither more nor less. But the other moral virtues deal with interior passions wherein the right cannot be established in the same way, since men are variously situated in relation to their passions; hence the rectitude of reason has to be established in the passions, with due regard to us, who are moved in respect of the passions.

This suffices for the Replies to the Objections. For the first two arguments take the rational mean as being in the very act of reason, while the third argues from the mean of justice.

ARTICLE 3. WHETHER THE INTELLECTUAL VIRTUES OBSERVE THE MEAN?

Objection 1. It would seem that the intellectual virtues do not observe the mean. Because moral virtue observes the mean by conforming to the rule of reason. But the intellectual virtues are in reason itself, so that they seem to have no higher rule. Therefore the intellectual virtues do not observe the mean.

Objection 2. Further, the mean of moral virtue is fixed by an intellectual virtue: for it is stated in Ethic. ii, 6, that "virtue observes the mean appointed by reason, as a prudent man would appoint it." If therefore intellectual virtue also observe the mean, this mean will have to be appointed for them by another virtue, so that there would be an indefinite series of virtues.

Objection 3. Further, a mean is, properly speaking, between contraries, as the Philosopher explains (Metaph. x, text. 22,23). But there seems to be no contrariety in the intellect; since contraries themselves, as they are in the intellect, are not in opposition to one another, but are understood together, as white and black, healthy and sick. Therefore there is no mean in the intellectual virtues.

On the contrary, Art is an intellectual virtue; and yet there is a mean in art (Ethic. ii, 6). Therefore also intellectual virtue observes the mean.

I answer that, The good of anything consists in its observing the mean, by conforming with a rule or measure in respect of which it may happen to be excessive or deficient, as stated above (Article 1). Now intellectual virtue, like moral virtue, is directed to the good, as stated above (Question 56, Article 3). Hence the good of an intellectual virtue consists in observing the mean, in so far as it is subject to a measure. Now the good of intellectual virtue is the true; in the case of contemplative virtue, it is the true taken absolutely (Ethic. vi, 2); in the case of practical virtue, it is the true in conformity with a right appetite.

Now truth apprehended by our intellect, if we consider it absolutely, is measured by things; since things are the measure of our intellect, as stated in Metaph. x, text. 5; because there is truth in what we think or say, according as the thing is so or not. Accordingly the good of speculative intellectual virtue consists in a certain mean, by way of conformity with things themselves, in so far as the intellect expresses them as being what they are, or as not being what they are not: and it is in this that the nature of truth consists. There will be excess if something false is affirmed, as though something were, which in reality it is not: and there will be deficiency if something is falsely denied, and declared not to be, whereas in reality it is.

The truth of practical intellectual virtue, if we consider it in relation to things, is by way of that which is measured; so that both in practical and in speculative intellectual virtues, the mean consists in conformity with things. But if we consider it in relation to the appetite, it has the character of a rule and measure. Consequently the rectitude of reason is the mean of moral virtue, and also the mean of prudence—of prudence as ruling and measuring, of moral virtue, as ruled and measured by that mean. In like manner the difference between excess and deficiency is to be applied in both cases.

Reply to Objection 1. Intellectual virtues also have their measure, as stated, and they observe the mean according as they conform to that measure.

Reply to Objection 2. There is no need for an indefinite series of virtues: because the measure and rule of intellectual virtue is not another kind of virtue, but things themselves.

Reply to Objection 3. The things themselves that are contrary have no contrariety in the mind, because one is the reason for knowing the other: nevertheless there is in the intellect contrariety of affirmation and negation, which are contraries, as stated at the end of Peri Hermenias. For though "to be" and "not to be" are not in contrary, but in contradictory opposition to one another, so long as we consider their signification in things themselves, for on the one hand we have "being" and on the other we have simply "non-being"; yet if we refer them to the act of the mind, there is something positive in both cases. Hence "to be" and "not to be" are contradictory: but the opinion stating that "good is good" is contrary to the opinion stating that "good is not good": and between two such contraries intellectual virtue observes the mean.

ARTICLE 4. WHETHER THE THEOLOGICAL VIRTUES OBSERVE THE MEAN?

Objection 1. It would seem that theological virtue observes the mean. For the good of other virtues consists in their observing the mean. Now the theological virtues surpass the others in goodness. Therefore much more does theological virtue observe the mean.

Objection 2. Further, the mean of moral virtue depends on the appetite being ruled by reason; while the mean of intellectual virtue consists in the intellect being measured by things. Now theological virtue perfects both intellect and appetite, as stated above (Question 62, Article 3). Therefore theological virtue also observes the mean.

Objection 3. Further, hope, which is a theological virtue, is a mean between despair and presumption. Likewise faith holds a middle course between contrary heresies, as Boethius states (De Duab. Natur. vii): thus, by confessing one Person and two natures in Christ, we observe the mean between the heresy of Nestorius, who maintained the existence of two persons and two natures, and the heresy of Eutyches, who held to one person and one nature. Therefore theological virtue observes the mean.

On the contrary, Wherever virtue observes the mean it is possible to sin by excess as well as by deficiency. But there is no sinning by excess against God, Who is the object of theological virtue: for it is written (Sirach 43:33): "Blessing the Lord, exalt Him as much as you can: for He is above all praise." Therefore theological virtue does not observe the mean.

I answer that, As stated above (Article 1), the mean of virtue depends on conformity with virtue's rule or measure, in so far as one may exceed or fall short of that rule. Now the measure of theological virtue may be twofold. One is taken from the very nature of virtue, and thus the measure and rule of theological virtue is God Himself: because our faith is ruled according to Divine truth; charity, according to His goodness; hope, according to the immensity of His omnipotence and loving kindness. This measure surpasses all human power: so that never can we love God as much as He ought to be loved, nor believe and hope in Him as much as we should. Much less therefore can there be excess in such things. Accordingly the good of such virtues does not consist in a mean, but increases the more we approach to the summit.

The other rule or measure of theological virtue is by comparison with us: for although we cannot be borne towards God as much as we ought, yet we should approach to Him by believing, hoping and loving, according to the measure of our condition. Consequently it is possible to find a mean and extremes in theological virtue, accidentally and in reference to us.

Reply to Objection 1. The good of intellectual and moral virtues consists in a mean of reason by conformity with a measure that may be exceeded: whereas this is not so in the case of theological virtue, considered in itself, as stated above.

Reply to Objection 2. Moral and intellectual virtues perfect our intellect and appetite in relation to a created measure and rule; whereas the theological virtues perfect them in relation to an uncreated rule and measure. Wherefore the comparison fails.

Reply to Objection 3. Hope observes the mean between presumption and despair, in relation to us, in so far, to wit, as a man is said to be presumptuous, through hoping to receive from God a good in excess of his condition; or to despair through failing to hope for that which according to his condition he might hope for. But there can be no excess of hope in comparison with God, Whose goodness is infinite. In like manner faith holds a middle course between contrary heresies, not by comparison with its object, which is God, in Whom we cannot believe too much; but in so far as human opinion itself takes a middle position between contrary opinions, as was explained above.

QUESTION 65. THE CONNECTION OF VIRTUES

ARTICLE 1. WHETHER THE MORAL VIRTUES ARE CONNECTED WITH ONE ANOTHER?

Objection 1. It would seem that the moral virtues are not connected with one another. Because moral virtues are sometimes caused by the exercise of acts, as is proved in Ethic. ii, 1,2. But man can exercise himself in the acts of one virtue, without exercising himself in the acts of some other virtue. Therefore it is possible to have one moral virtue without another.

Objection 2. Further, magnificence and magnanimity are moral virtues. Now a man may have other moral virtues without having magnificence or magnanimity: for the Philosopher says (Ethic. iv, 2,3) that "a poor man cannot be magnificent," and yet he may have other virtues; and (Ethic. iv) that "he who is worthy of small things, and so accounts his worth, is modest, but not magnanimous." Therefore the moral virtues are not connected with one another.

Objection 3. Further, as the moral virtues perfect the appetitive part of the soul, so do the intellectual virtues perfect the intellective part. But the intellectual virtues are not mutually connected: since we may have one science, without having another. Neither, therefore, are the moral virtues connected with one another.

Objection 4. Further, if the moral virtues are mutually connected, this can only be because they are united together in prudence. But this does not suffice to connect the moral virtues together. For, seemingly, one may be prudent about things to be done in relation to one virtue, without being prudent in those that concern another virtue: even as one may have the art of making certain things, without the art of making certain others. Now prudence is right reason about things to be done. Therefore the moral virtues are not necessarily connected with one another.

On the contrary, Ambrose says on Luke 6:20: "The virtues are connected and linked together, so that whoever has one, is seen to have several": and Augustine says (De Trin. vi, 4) that "the virtues that reside in the human mind are quite inseparable from one another": and Gregory says (Moral. xxii, 1) that "one virtue without the other is either of no account whatever, or very imperfect": and Cicero says (Quaest. Tusc. ii): "If you confess to not having one particular virtue, it must needs be that you have none at all."

I answer that, Moral virtue may be considered either as perfect or as imperfect. An imperfect moral virtue, temperance for instance, or fortitude, is nothing but an inclination in us to do some kind of good deed, whether such inclination be in us by nature or by habituation. If we take the moral virtues in this way, they are not connected: since we find men who, by natural temperament or by being accustomed, are prompt in doing deeds of liberality, but are not prompt in doing deeds of chastity.

But the perfect moral virtue is a habit that inclines us to do a good deed well; and if we take moral virtues in this way, we must say that they are connected, as nearly as all are agreed in saying. For this two reasons are given, corresponding to the different ways of assigning the distinction of the cardinal virtues. For, as we stated above (61, A3,4), some distinguish them according to certain general properties of the virtues: for instance, by saying that discretion belongs to prudence, rectitude to justice, moderation to temperance, and strength of mind to fortitude, in whatever matter we consider these properties to be. In this way the reason for the connection is evident: for strength of mind is not commended as virtuous, if it be without moderation or rectitude or discretion: and so forth. This, too, is the reason assigned for the connection by Gregory, who says (Moral. xxii, 1) that "a virtue cannot be perfect" as a virtue, "if isolated from the others: for there can be no true prudence without temperance, justice and fortitude": and he continues to speak in like manner of the other virtues (cf. 61, 4, Objection 1). Augustine also gives the same reason (De Trin. vi, 4).

Others, however, differentiate these virtues in respect of their matters, and it is in this way that Aristotle assigns the reason for their connection (Ethic. vi, 13). Because, as stated above (Question 58, Article 4), no moral virtue can be without prudence; since it is proper to moral virtue to make a right choice, for it is an elective habit. Now right choice requires not only the inclination to a due end, which inclination is the direct outcome of moral virtue, but also correct choice of things conducive to the end, which choice is made by prudence, that counsels, judges, and commands in those things that are directed to the end. In like manner one cannot have prudence unless one has the moral virtues: since prudence is "right reason about things to be done," and the starting point of reason is the end of the thing to be done, to which end man is rightly disposed by moral virtue. Hence, just as we cannot have speculative science unless we have the understanding of the principles, so neither can we have prudence without the moral virtues: and from this it follows clearly that the moral virtues are connected with one another.

Reply to Objection 1. Some moral virtues perfect man as regards his general state, in other words, with regard to those things which have to be done in every kind of human life. Hence man needs to exercise himself at the same time in the matters of all moral virtues. And if he exercise himself, by good deeds, in all such matters, he will acquire the habits of all the moral virtues. But if he exercise himself by good deeds in regard to one matter, but not in regard to another, for instance, by behaving well in matters of anger, but not in matters of desire; he will indeed acquire a certain habit of restraining his anger; but this habit will lack the nature of virtue, through the absence of prudence, which is wanting in matters of desire. In the same way, natural inclinations fail to have the complete character of virtue, if prudence be lacking.

But there are some moral virtues which perfect man with regard to some eminent state, such as magnificence and magnanimity; and since it does not happen to all in common to be exercised in the matter of such virtues, it is possible for a man to have the other moral virtues, without actually having the habits of these virtues—provided we speak of acquired virtue. Nevertheless, when once a man has acquired those other virtues he possesses these in proximate potentiality. Because when, by practice, a man has acquired liberality in small gifts and expenditure, if he were to come in for a large sum of money, he would acquire the habit of magnificence with but little practice: even as a geometrician, by dint of little study, acquires scientific knowledge about some conclusion which had never been presented to his mind before. Now we speak of having a thing when we are on the point of having it, according to the saying of the Philosopher (Phys. ii, text. 56): "That which is scarcely lacking is not lacking at all."

This suffices for the Reply to the Second Objection.

Reply to Objection 3. The intellectual virtues are about divers matters having no relation to one another, as is clearly the case with the various sciences and arts. Hence we do not observe in them the connection that is to be found among the moral virtues, which are about passions and operations, that are clearly related to one another. For all the passions have their rise in certain initial passions, viz. love and hatred, and terminate in certain others, viz. pleasure and sorrow. In like manner all the operations that are the matter of moral virtue are related to one another, and to the passions. Hence the whole matter of moral virtues falls under the one rule of prudence.

Nevertheless, all intelligible things are related to first principles. And in this way, all the intellectual virtues depend on the understanding of principles; even as prudence depends on the moral virtues, as stated. On the other hand, the universal principles which are the object of the virtue of understanding of principles, do not depend on the conclusions, which are the objects of the other intellectual virtues, as do the moral virtues depend on prudence, because the appetite, in a fashion, moves the reason, and the reason the appetite, as stated above (9, 1; 58, 5, ad 1).

Reply to Objection 4. Those things to which the moral virtues incline, are as the principles of prudence: whereas the products of art are not the principles, but the matter of art. Now it is evident that, though reason may be right in one part of the matter, and not in another, yet in no way can it be called right reason, if it be deficient in any principle whatever. Thus, if a man be wrong about the principle, "A whole is greater than its part," he cannot acquire the science of geometry, because he must necessarily wander from the truth in his conclusion. Moreover, things "done" are related to one another, but not things "made," as stated above (ad 3). Consequently the lack of prudence in one department of things to be done, would result in a deficiency affecting other things to be done: whereas this does not occur in things to be made.

ARTICLE 2. WHETHER MORAL VIRTUES CAN BE WITHOUT CHARITY?

Objection 1. It would seem that moral virtues can be without charity. For it is stated in the Liber Sentent. Prosperi vii, that "every virtue save charity may be common to the good and bad." But "charity can be in none except the good," as stated in the same book. Therefore the other virtues can be had without charity.

Objection 2. Further, moral virtues can be acquired by means of human acts, as stated in Ethic. ii, 1,2, whereas charity cannot be had otherwise than by infusion, according to Romans 5:5: "The charity of God is poured forth in our hearts by the Holy Ghost Who is given to us." Therefore it is possible to have the other virtues without charity.

Objection 3. Further, the moral virtues are connected together, through depending on prudence. But charity does not depend on prudence; indeed, it surpasses prudence, according to Ephesians 3:19: "The charity of Christ, which surpasseth all knowledge." Therefore the moral virtues are not connected with charity, and can be without it.

On the contrary, It is written (1 John 3:14): "He that loveth not, abideth in death." Now the spiritual life is perfected by the virtues, since it is "by them" that "we lead a good life," as Augustine states (De Lib. Arb. ii, 17,19). Therefore they cannot be without the love of charity.

I answer that, As stated above (Question 63, Article 2), it is possible by means of human works to acquire moral virtues, in so far as they produce good works that are directed to an end not surpassing the natural power of man: and when they are acquired thus, they can be without charity, even as they were in many of the Gentiles. But in so far as they produce good works in proportion to a supernatural last end, thus they have the character of virtue, truly and perfectly; and cannot be acquired by human acts, but are infused by God. Such like moral virtues cannot be without charity. For it has been stated above (1; 58, A4,5) that the other moral virtues cannot be without prudence; and that prudence cannot be without the moral virtues, because these latter make man well-disposed to certain ends, which are the starting-point of the procedure of prudence. Now for prudence to proceed aright, it is much more necessary that man be well disposed towards his ultimate end, which is the effect of charity, than that he be well disposed in respect of other ends, which is the effect of moral virtue: just as in speculative matters right reason has greatest need of the first indemonstrable principle, that "contradictories cannot both be true at the same time." It is therefore evident that neither can infused prudence be without charity; nor, consequently, the other moral virtues, since they cannot be without prudence.

It is therefore clear from what has been said that only the infused virtues are perfect, and deserve to be called virtues simply: since they direct man well to the ultimate end. But the other virtues, those, namely, that are acquired, are virtues in a restricted sense, but not simply: for they direct man well in respect of the last end in some particular genus of action, but not in respect of the last end simply. Hence a gloss of Augustine [Cf. Lib. Sentent. Prosperi cvi.] on the words, "All that is not of faith is sin" (Romans 14:23), says: "He that fails to acknowledge the truth, has no true virtue, even if his conduct be good."

Reply to Objection 1. Virtue, in the words quoted, denotes imperfect virtue. Else if we take moral virtue in its perfect state, "it makes its possessor good," and consequently cannot be in the wicked.

Reply to Objection 2. This argument holds good of virtue in the sense of acquired virtue.

Reply to Objection 3. Though charity surpasses science and prudence, yet prudence depends on charity, as stated: and consequently so do all the infused moral virtues.

ARTICLE 3. WHETHER CHARITY CAN BE WITHOUT MORAL VIRTUE?

Objection 1. It would seem possible to have charity without the moral virtues. For when one thing suffices for a certain purpose, it is superfluous to employ others. Now charity alone suffices for the fulfilment of all the works of virtue, as is clear from 1 Corinthians 13:4, seqq.: "Charity is patient, is kind," etc. Therefore it seems that if one has charity, other virtues are superfluous.

Objection 2. Further, he that has a habit of virtue easily performs the works of that virtue, and those works are pleasing to him for their own sake: hence "pleasure taken in a work is a sign of habit" (Ethic. ii, 3). Now many have charity, being free from mortal sin, and yet they find it difficult to do works of virtue; nor are these works pleasing to them for their own sake, but only for the sake of charity. Therefore many have charity without the other virtues.

Objection 3. Further, charity is to be found in every saint: and yet there are some saints who are without certain virtues. For Bede says (on Luke 17:10) that the saints are more humbled on account of their not having certain virtues, than rejoiced at the virtues they have. Therefore, if a man has charity, it does not follow of necessity that he has all the moral virtues.

On the contrary, The whole Law is fulfilled through charity, for it is written (Romans 13:8): "He that loveth his neighbor, hath fulfilled the Law." Now it is not possible to fulfil the whole Law, without having all the moral virtues: since the law contains precepts about all acts of virtue, as stated in Ethic. v, 1,2. Therefore he that has charity, has all the moral virtues. Moreover, Augustine says in a letter (Epis. clxvii) [Cf. Serm. xxxix and xlvi de Temp.] that charity contains all the cardinal virtues.

I answer that, All the moral virtues are infused together with charity. The reason for this is that God operates no less perfectly in works of grace than in works of nature. Now, in the works of nature, we find that whenever a thing contains a principle of certain works, it has also whatever is necessary for their execution: thus animals are provided with organs whereby to perform the actions that their souls empower them to do. Now it is evident that charity, inasmuch as it directs man to his last end, is the principle of all the good works that are referable to his last end. Wherefore all the moral virtues must needs be infused together with charity, since it is through them that man performs each different kind of good work.

It is therefore clear that the infused moral virtues are connected, not only through prudence, but also on account of charity: and, again, that whoever loses charity through mortal sin, forfeits all the infused moral virtues.

Reply to Objection 1. In order that the act of a lower power be perfect, not only must there be perfection in the higher, but also in the lower power: for if the principal agent were well disposed, perfect action would not follow, if the instrument also were not well disposed. Consequently, in order that man work well in things referred to the end, he needs not only a virtue disposing him well to the end, but also those virtues which dispose him well to whatever is referred to the end: for the virtue which regards the end is the chief and moving principle in respect of those things that are referred to the end. Therefore it is necessary to have the moral virtues together with charity.

Reply to Objection 2. It happens sometimes that a man who has a habit, finds it difficult to act in accordance with the habit, and consequently feels no pleasure and complacency in the act, on account of some impediment supervening from without: thus a man who has a habit of science, finds it difficult to understand, through being sleepy or unwell. In like manner sometimes the habits of moral virtue experience difficulty in their works, by reason of certain ordinary dispositions remaining from previous acts. This difficulty does not occur in respect of acquired moral virtue: because the repeated acts by which they are acquired, remove also the contrary dispositions.

Reply to Objection 3. Certain saints are said not to have certain virtues, in so far as they experience difficulty in the acts of those virtues, for the reason stated; although they have the habits of all the virtues.

QUESTION 67. THE DURATION OF VIRTUES AFTER THIS LIFE

ARTICLE 1. WHETHER THE MORAL VIRTUES REMAIN AFTER THIS LIFE?

Objection 1. It would seem that the moral virtues do not remain after this life. For in the future state of glory men will be like angels, according to Matthew 22:30. But it is absurd to put moral virtues in the angels ["Whatever relates to moral action is petty, and unworthy of the gods" (Ethic. x, 8)], as stated in Ethic. x, 8. Therefore neither in man will there be moral virtues after this life.

Objection 2. Further, moral virtues perfect man in the active life. But the active life does not remain after this life: for Gregory says (Moral. iv, 18): "The works of the active life pass away from the body." Therefore moral virtues do not remain after this life.

Objection 3. Further, temperance and fortitude, which are moral virtues, are in the irrational parts of the soul, as the Philosopher states (Ethic. iii, 10). Now the irrational parts of the soul are corrupted, when the body is corrupted: since they are acts of bodily organs. Therefore it seems that the moral virtues do not remain after this life.

On the contrary, It is written (Wisdom 1:15) that "justice is perpetual and immortal."

I answer that, As Augustine says (De Trin. xiv, 9), Cicero held that the cardinal virtues do not remain after this life; and that, as Augustine says (De Trin. xiv, 9), "in the other life men are made happy by the mere knowledge of that nature, than which nothing is better or more lovable, that Nature, to wit, which created all others." Afterwards he concludes that these four virtues remain in the future life, but after a different manner.

In order to make this evident, we must note that in these virtues there is a formal element, and a quasi-material element. The material element in these virtues is a certain inclination of the appetitive part to the passions and operations according to a certain mode: and since this mode is fixed by reason, the formal element is precisely this order of reason.

Accordingly we must say that these moral virtues do not remain in the future life, as regards their material element. For in the future life there will be no desires and pleasures in matters of food and sex; nor fear and daring about dangers of death; nor distributions and commutations of things employed in this present life. But, as regards the formal element, they will remain most perfect, after this life, in the Blessed, in as much as each one's reason will have most perfect rectitude in regard to things concerning him in respect of that state of life: and his appetitive power will be moved entirely according to the order of reason, in things pertaining to that same state. Hence Augustine says (De Trin. xiv, 9) that "prudence will be there without any danger of error; fortitude, without the anxiety of bearing with evil; temperance, without the rebellion of the desires: so that prudence will neither prefer nor equal any good to God; fortitude will adhere to Him most steadfastly; and temperance will delight in Him Who knows no imperfection." As to justice, it is yet more evident what will be its act in that life, viz. "to be subject to God": because even in this life subjection to a superior is part of justice.

Reply to Objection 1. The Philosopher is speaking there of these moral virtues, as to their material element; thus he speaks of justice, as regards "commutations and distributions"; of fortitude, as to "matters of terror and danger"; of temperance, in respect of "lewd desires."

The same applies to the Second Objection. For those things that concern the active life, belong to the material element of the virtues.

Reply to Objection 3. There is a twofold state after this life; one before the resurrection, during which the soul will be separate from the body; the other, after the resurrection, when the souls will be reunited to their bodies. In this state of resurrection, the irrational powers will be in the bodily organs, just as they now are. Hence it will be possible for fortitude to be in the spirited, and temperance in the desiring part, in so far as each power will be perfectly disposed to obey the reason. But in the state preceding the resurrection, the irrational parts will not be in the soul actually, but only radically in its essence, as stated in the I, 77, 8. Wherefore neither will these virtues be actually, but only in their root, i.e. in the reason and will, wherein are certain nurseries of these virtues, as stated above (Question 63, Article 1). Justice, however, will remain because it is in the will. Hence of justice it is specially said that it is "perpetual and immortal"; both by reason of its subject, since the will is incorruptible; and because its act will not change, as stated.

QUESTION 69. THE BEATITUDES

ARTICLE 2. WHETHER THE REWARDS ASSIGNED TO THE BEATITUDES REFER TO THIS LIFE?

Objection 1. It would seem that the rewards assigned to the beatitudes do not refer to this life. Because some are said to be happy because they hope for a reward, as stated above (Article 1). Now the object of hope is future happiness. Therefore these rewards refer to the life to come.

Objection 2. Further, certain punishments are set down in opposition to the beatitudes, Luke 6:25, where we read: "Woe to you that are filled; for you shall hunger. Woe to you that now laugh, for you shall mourn and weep." Now these punishments do not refer to this life, because frequently men are not punished in this life, according to Job 21:13: "They spend their days in wealth." Therefore neither do the rewards of the beatitudes refer to this life.

Objection 3. Further, the kingdom of heaven which is set down as the reward of poverty is the happiness of heaven, as Augustine says (De Civ. Dei xix) [Cf. De Serm. Dom. in Monte i, 1. Again, abundant fullness is not to be had save in the life to come, according to Psalm 16:15: "I shall be filled [Douay: 'satisfied'] when Thy glory shall appear." Again, it is only in the future life that we shall see God, and that our Divine sonship will be made manifest, according to 1 John 3:2: "We are now the sons of God; and it hath not yet appeared what we shall be. We know that, when He shall appear, we shall be like to Him, because we shall see Him as He is." Therefore these rewards refer to the future life.

On the contrary, Augustine says (De Serm. Dom. in Monte i, 4): "These promises can be fulfilled in this life, as we believe them to have been fulfilled in the apostles. For no words can express that complete change into the likeness even of an angel, which is promised to us after this life."

I answer that, Expounders of Holy Writ are not agreed in speaking of these rewards. For some, with Ambrose (Super Luc. v), hold that all these rewards refer to the life to come; while Augustine (De Serm. Dom. in Monte i, 4) holds them to refer to the present life; and Chrysostom in his homilies (In Matth. xv) says that some refer to the future, and some to the present life.

In order to make the matter clear we must take note that hope of future happiness may be in us for two reasons. First, by reason of our having a preparation for, or a disposition to future happiness; and this is by way of merit; secondly, by a kind of imperfect inchoation of future happiness in holy men, even in this life. For it is one thing to hope that the tree will bear fruit, when the leaves begin to appear, and another, when we see the first signs of the fruit.

Accordingly, those things which are set down as merits in the beatitudes, are a kind of preparation for, or disposition to happiness, either perfect or inchoate: while those that are assigned as rewards, may be either perfect happiness, so as to refer to the future life, or some beginning of happiness, such as is found in those who have attained perfection, in which case they refer to the present life. Because when a man begins to make progress in the acts of the virtues and gifts, it is to be hoped that he will arrive at perfection, both as a wayfarer, and as a citizen of the heavenly kingdom.

Reply to Objection 1. Hope regards future happiness as the last end: yet it may also regard the assistance of grace as that which leads to that end, according to Psalm 27:7: "In Him hath my heart hoped, and I have been helped."

Reply to Objection 2. Although sometimes the wicked do not undergo temporal punishment in this life, yet they suffer spiritual punishment. Hence Augustine says (Confess. i): "Thou hast decreed, and it is so, Lord—that the disordered mind should be its own punishment." The Philosopher, too, says of the wicked (Ethic. ix, 4) that "their soul is divided against itself . . . one part pulls this way, another that"; and afterwards he concludes, saying: "If wickedness makes a man so miserable, he should strain every nerve to avoid vice." In like manner, although, on the other hand, the good sometimes do not receive material rewards in this life, yet they never lack spiritual rewards, even in this life, according to Matthew 19:29, and Mark 10:30: "Ye shall receive a hundred times as much" even "in this time."

Reply to Objection 3. All these rewards will be fully consummated in the life to come: but meanwhile they are, in a manner, begun, even in this life. Because the "kingdom of heaven," as Augustine says (De Civ. Dei xiv; Cf. De Serm. Dom. in Monte, i, 1), can denote the beginning of perfect wisdom, in so far as "the spirit" begins to reign in men. The "possession" of the land denotes the well-ordered affections of the soul that rests, by its desire, on the solid foundation of the eternal inheritance, signified by "the land." They are "comforted" in this life, by receiving the Holy Ghost, Who is called the "Paraclete," i.e. the Comforter. They "have their fill," even in this life, of that food of which Our Lord said (John 4:34): "My meat is to do the will of Him that sent Me." Again, in this life, men "obtain" God's "Mercy." Again, the eye being cleansed by the gift of understanding, we can, so to speak, "see God." Likewise, in this life, those who are the "peacemakers" of their own movements, approach to likeness to God, and are called "the children of God." Nevertheless these things will be more perfectly fulfilled in heaven.

ARTICLE 3. WHETHER THE BEATITUDES ARE SUITABLY ENUMERATED?

Objection 1. It would seem that the beatitudes are unsuitably enumerated. For the beatitudes are assigned to the gifts, as stated above (1, ad 1). Now some of the gifts, viz. wisdom and understanding, belong to the contemplative life: yet no beatitude is assigned to the act of contemplation, for all are assigned to matters connected with the active life. Therefore the beatitudes are insufficiently enumerated.

Objection 2. Further, not only do the executive gifts belong to the active life, but also some of the directive gifts, e.g. knowledge and counsel: yet none of the beatitudes seems to be directly connected with the acts of knowledge or counsel. Therefore the beatitudes are insufficiently indicated.

Objection 3. Further, among the executive gifts connected with the active life, fear is said to be connected with poverty, while piety seems to correspond to the beatitude of mercy: yet nothing is included directly connected with justice. Therefore the beatitudes are insufficiently enumerated.

Objection 4. Further, many other beatitudes are mentioned in Holy Writ. Thus, it is written (Job 5:17): "Blessed is the man whom God correcteth"; and (Psalm 1:1): "Blessed is the man who hath not walked in the counsel of the ungodly"; and (Proverbs 3:13): "Blessed is the man that findeth wisdom." Therefore the beatitudes are insufficiently enumerated.

Objection 5. On the other hand, it seems that too many are mentioned. For there are seven gifts of the Holy Ghost: whereas eight beatitudes are indicated.

Objection 6. Further, only four beatitudes are indicated in Luke 6. Therefore the seven or eight mentioned in Matthew 5 are too many.

I answer that, These beatitudes are most suitably enumerated. To make this evident it must be observed that beatitude has been held to consist in one of three things: for some have ascribed it to a sensual life, some, to an active life, and some, to a contemplative life [See 3]. Now these three kinds of happiness stand in different relations to future beatitude, by hoping for which we are said to be happy. Because sensual happiness, being false and contrary to reason, is an obstacle to future beatitude; while happiness of the active life is a disposition of future beatitude; and contemplative happiness, if perfect, is the very essence of future beatitude, and, if imperfect, is a beginning thereof.

And so Our Lord, in the first place, indicated certain beatitudes as removing the obstacle of sensual happiness. For a life of pleasure consists of two things. First, in the affluence of external goods, whether riches or honors; from which man is withdrawn—by a virtue so that he uses them in moderation—and by a gift, in a more excellent way, so that he despises them altogether. Hence the first beatitude is: "Blessed are the poor in spirit," which may refer either to the contempt of riches, or to the contempt of honors, which results from humility. Secondly, the sensual life consists in following the bent of one's passions, whether spirited or concupiscible. From following the spirited passions man is withdrawn—by a virtue, so that they are kept within the bounds appointed by the ruling of reason—and by a gift, in a more excellent manner, so that man, according to God's will, is altogether undisturbed by them: hence the second beatitude is: "Blessed are the meek." From following the desiring passions, man is withdrawn—by a virtue, so that man uses these passions in moderation—and by gift, so that, if necessary, he casts them aside altogether; nay more, so that, if need be, he makes a deliberate choice of sorrow [Cf. 35, 3]; hence the third beatitude is: "Blessed are they that mourn."

Active life consists chiefly in man's relations with his neighbor, either by way of duty or by way of spontaneous gratuity. To the former we are disposed—by a virtue, so that we do not refuse to do our duty to our neighbor, which pertains to justice—and by a gift, so that we do the same much more heartily, by accomplishing works of justice with an ardent desire, even as a hungry and thirsty man eats and drinks with eager appetite. Hence the fourth beatitude is: "Blessed are they that hunger and thirst after justice." With regard to spontaneous favors we are perfected—by a virtue, so that we give where reason dictates we should give, e.g. to our friends or others united to us; which pertains to the virtue of liberality—and by a gift, so that, through reverence for God, we consider only the needs of those on whom we bestow our gratuitous bounty: hence it is written (Luke 14:12-13): "When thou makest a dinner or supper, call not thy friends, nor thy brethren," etc. . . "but . . . call the poor, the maimed," etc.; which, properly, is to have mercy: hence the fifth beatitude is: "Blessed are the merciful."

Those things which concern the contemplative life, are either final beatitude itself, or some beginning thereof: wherefore they are included in the beatitudes, not as merits, but as rewards. Yet the effects of the active life, which dispose man for the contemplative life, are included in the beatitudes. Now the effect of the active life, as regards those virtues and gifts whereby man is perfected in himself, is the cleansing of man's heart, so that it is not defiled by the passions: hence the sixth beatitude is: "Blessed are the clean of heart." But as regards the virtues and gifts whereby man is perfected in relation to his neighbor, the effect of the active life is peace, according to Isaiah 32:17: "The work of justice shall be peace": hence the seventh beatitude is "Blessed are the peacemakers."

Reply to Objection 1. The acts of the gifts which belong to the active life are indicated in the merits: but the acts of the gifts pertaining to the contemplative life are indicated in the rewards, for the reason given above. Because to "see God" corresponds to the gift of understanding; and to be like God by being adoptive "children of God," corresponds to the gift of wisdom.

Reply to Objection 2. In things pertaining to the active life, knowledge is not sought for its own sake, but for the sake of operation, as even the Philosopher states (Ethic. ii, 2). And therefore, since beatitude implies something ultimate, the beatitudes do not include the acts of those gifts which direct man in the active life, such acts, to wit, as are elicited by those gifts, as, e.g. to counsel is the act of counsel, and to judge, the act of knowledge: but, on the other hand, they include those operative acts of which the gifts have the direction, as, e.g. mourning in respect of knowledge, and mercy in respect of counsel.

Reply to Objection 3. In applying the beatitudes to the gifts we may consider two things. One is likeness of matter. In this way all the first five beatitudes may be assigned to knowledge and counsel as to their directing principles: whereas they must be distributed among the executive gifts: so that, to wit, hunger and thirst for justice, and mercy too, correspond to piety, which perfects man in his relations to others; meekness to fortitude, for Ambrose says on Luke 6:22: "It is the business of fortitude to conquer anger, and to curb indignation," fortitude being about the spirited passions: poverty and mourning to the gift of fear, whereby man withdraws from the lusts and pleasures of the world.

Secondly, we may consider the motives of the beatitudes: and, in this way, some of them will have to be assigned differently. Because the principal motive for meekness is reverence for God, which belongs to piety. The chief motive for mourning is knowledge, whereby man knows his failings and those of worldly things, according to Ecclesiastes 1:18: "He that addeth knowledge, addeth also sorrow [Vulgate: labor]." The principal motive for hungering after the works of justice is fortitude of the soul: and the chief motive for being merciful is God's counsel, according to Daniel 4:24: "Let my counsel be acceptable to the king [Vulgate: to thee, O king]: and redeem thou thy sins with alms, and thy iniquities with works of mercy to the poor." It is thus that Augustine assigns them (De Serm. Dom. in Monte i, 4).

Reply to Objection 4. All the beatitudes mentioned in Holy Writ must be reduced to these, either as to the merits or as to the rewards: because they must all belong either to the active or to the contemplative life. Accordingly, when we read, "Blessed is the man whom the Lord correcteth," we must refer this to the beatitude of mourning: when we read, "Blessed is the man that hath not walked in the counsel of the ungodly," we must refer it to cleanness of heart: and when we read, "Blessed is the man that findeth wisdom," this must be referred to the reward of the seventh beatitude. The same applies to all others that can be adduced.

Reply to Objection 5. The eighth beatitude is a confirmation and declaration of all those that precede. Because from the very fact that a man is confirmed in poverty of spirit, meekness, and the rest, it follows that no persecution will induce him to renounce them. Hence the eighth beatitude corresponds, in a way, to all the preceding seven.

Reply to Objection 6. Luke relates Our Lord's sermon as addressed to the multitude (Luke 6:17). Hence he sets down the beatitudes according to the capacity of the multitude, who know no other happiness than pleasure, temporal and earthly: wherefore by these four beatitudes Our Lord excludes four things which seem to belong to such happiness. The first of these is abundance of external goods, which he sets aside by saying: "Blessed are ye poor." The second is that man be well off as to his body, in food and drink, and so forth; this he excludes by saying in the second place: "Blessed are ye that hunger." The third is that it should be well with man as to joyfulness of heart, and this he puts aside by saying: "Blessed are ye that weep now." The fourth is the outward favor of man; and this he excludes, saying, fourthly: "Blessed shall you be, when men shall hate you." And as Ambrose says on Luke 6:20, "poverty corresponds to temperance, which is unmoved by delights; hunger, to justice, since who hungers is compassionate and, through compassion gives; mourning, to prudence, which deplores perishable things; endurance of men's hatred belongs to fortitude."

QUESTION 71. VICE AND SIN CONSIDERED IN THEMSELVES

ARTICLE 2. WHETHER VICE IS CONTRARY TO NATURE?

Objection 1. It would seem that vice is not contrary to nature. Because vice is contrary to virtue, as stated above (Article 1). Now virtue is in us, not by nature but by infusion or habituation, as stated above (63, A1,2,3). Therefore vice is not contrary to nature.

Objection 2. Further, it is impossible to become habituated to that which is contrary to nature: thus "a stone never becomes habituated to upward movement" (Ethic. ii, 1). But some men become habituated to vice. Therefore vice is not contrary to nature.

Objection 3. Further, anything contrary to a nature, is not found in the greater number of individuals possessed of that nature. Now vice is found in the greater number of men; for it is written (Matthew 7:13): "Broad is the way that leadeth to destruction, and many there are who go in thereat." Therefore vice is not contrary to nature.

Objection 4. Further, sin is compared to vice, as act to habit, as stated above (Article 1). Now sin is defined as "a word, deed, or desire, contrary to the Law of God," as Augustine shows (Contra Faust. xxii, 27). But the Law of God is above nature. Therefore we should say that vice is contrary to the Law, rather than to nature.

On the contrary, Augustine says (De Lib. Arb. iii, 13): "Every vice, simply because it is a vice, is contrary to nature."

I answer that, As stated above (Article 1), vice is contrary to virtue. Now the virtue of a thing consists in its being well disposed in a manner befitting its nature, as stated above (Article 1). Hence the vice of any thing consists in its being disposed in a manner not befitting its nature, and for this reason is that thing "vituperated," which word is derived from "vice" according to Augustine (De Lib. Arb. iii, 14).

But it must be observed that the nature of a thing is chiefly the form from which that thing derives its species. Now man derives his species from his rational soul: and consequently whatever is contrary to the order of reason is, properly speaking, contrary to the nature of man, as man; while whatever is in accord with reason, is in accord with the nature of man, as man. Now "man's good is to be in accord with reason, and his evil is to be against reason," as Dionysius states (Div. Nom. iv). Therefore human virtue, which makes a man good, and his work good, is in accord with man's nature, for as much as it accords with his reason: while vice is contrary to man's nature, in so far as it is contrary to the order of reason.

Reply to Objection 1. Although the virtues are not caused by nature as regards their perfection of being, yet they incline us to that which accords with reason, i.e. with the order of reason. For Cicero says (De Inv. Rhet. ii) that "virtue is a habit in accord with reason, like a second nature": and it is in this sense that virtue is said to be in accord with nature, and on the other hand that vice is contrary to nature.

Reply to Objection 2. The Philosopher is speaking there of a thing being against nature, in so far as "being against nature" is contrary to "being from nature": and not in so far as "being against nature" is contrary to "being in accord with nature," in which latter sense virtues are said to be in accord with nature, in as much as they incline us to that which is suitable to nature.

Reply to Objection 3. There is a twofold nature in man, rational nature, and the sensitive nature. And since it is through the operation of his senses that man accomplishes acts of reason, hence there are more who follow the inclinations of the sensitive nature, than who follow the order of reason: because more reach the beginning of a business than achieve its completion. Now the presence of vices and sins in man is owing to the fact that he follows the inclination of his sensitive nature against the order of his reason.

Reply to Objection 4. Whatever is irregular in a work of art, is unnatural to the art which produced that work. Now the eternal law is compared to the order of human reason, as art to a work of art. Therefore it amounts to the same that vice and sin are against the order of human reason, and that they are contrary to the eternal law. Hence Augustine says (De Lib. Arb. iii, 6) that "every nature, as such, is from God; and is a vicious nature, in so far as it fails from the Divine art whereby it was made."

QUESTION 82. ORIGINAL SIN, AS TO ITS ESSENCE

ARTICLE 3. WHETHER ORIGINAL SIN IS DESIRE?

Objection 1. It would seem that original sin is not desire. For every sin is contrary to nature, according to Damascene (De Fide Orth. ii, 4,30). But desire is in accordance with nature, since it is the proper act of the desiring faculty which is a natural power. Therefore desire is not original sin.

Objection 2. Further, through original sin "the passions of sins" are in us, according to the Apostle (Romans 7:5). Now there are several other passions besides desire, as stated above (Question 23, Article 4). Therefore original sin is not desire any more than another passion.

Objection 3. Further, by original sin, all the parts of the soul are disordered, as stated above (2, Objection 3). But the intellect is the highest of the soul's parts, as the Philosopher states (Ethic. x, 7). Therefore original sin is ignorance rather than desire.

On the contrary, Augustine says (Retract. i, 15): "Desire is the guilt of original sin."

I answer that, Everything takes its species from its form: and it has been stated (2) that the species of original sin is taken from its cause. Consequently the formal element of original sin must be considered in respect of the cause of original sin. But contraries have contrary causes. Therefore the cause of original sin must be considered with respect to the cause of original justice, which is opposed to it. Now the whole order of original justice consists in man's will being subject to God: which subjection, first and chiefly, was in the will, whose function it is to move all the other parts to the end, as stated above (Question 9, Article 1), so that the will being turned away from God, all the other powers of the soul become inordinate. Accordingly the privation of original justice, whereby the will was made subject to God, is the formal element in original sin; while every other disorder of the soul's powers, is a kind of material element in respect of original sin. Now the inordinateness of the other powers of the soul consists chiefly in their turning inordinately to mutable good; which inordinateness may be called by the general name of desire. Hence original sin is desire, materially, but privation of original justice, formally.

Reply to Objection 1. Since, in man, the desiring power is naturally governed by reason, the act of desire is so far natural to man, as it is in accord with the order of reason; while, in so far as it trespasses beyond the bounds of reason, it is, for a man, contrary to reason. Such is the desire of original sin.

Reply to Objection 2. As stated above (Question 25, Article 1), all the spirited passions are reducible to desiring passions, as holding the principle place: and of these, desire is the most impetuous in moving, and is felt most, as stated above (25, 2, ad 1). Therefore original sin is ascribed to desire, as being the chief passion, and as including all the others, in a fashion.

Reply to Objection 3. As, in good things, the intellect and reason stand first, so conversely in evil things, the lower part of the soul is found to take precedence, for it clouds and draws the reason, as stated above (77, A1,2; 80, 2). Hence original sin is called desire rather than ignorance, although ignorance is comprised among the material defects of original sin.

QUESTION 85. THE EFFECTS OF SIN, AND, FIRST, OF THE CORRUPTION OF THE GOOD OF NATURE

ARTICLE 1. WHETHER SIN DIMINISHES THE GOOD OF NATURE?

Objection 1. It would seem that sin does not diminish the good of nature. For man's sin is no worse than the devil's. But natural good remains unimpaired in devils after sin, as Dionysius states (Div. Nom. iv). Therefore neither does sin diminish the good of human nature.

Objection 2. Further, when that which follows is changed, that which precedes remains unchanged, since substance remains the same when its accidents are changed. But nature exists before the voluntary action. Therefore, when sin has caused a disorder in a voluntary act, nature is not changed on that account, so that the good of nature be diminished.

Objection 3. Further, sin is an action, while diminution is a passion. Now no agent is passive by the very reason of its acting, although it is possible for it to act on one thing, and to be passive as regards another. Therefore he who sins, does not, by his sin, diminish the good of his nature.

Objection 4. Further, no accident acts on its subject: because that which is patient is a potential being, while that which is subjected to an accident, is already an actual being as regards that accident. But sin is in the good of nature as an accident in a subject. Therefore sin does not diminish the good of nature, since to diminish is to act.

On the contrary, "A certain man going down from Jerusalem to Jericho (Luke 10:30), i.e. to the corruption of sin, was stripped of his gifts, and wounded in his nature," as Bede [the quotation is from the Glossa Ordinaria of Strabo] expounds the passage. Therefore sin diminishes the good of nature.

I answer that, The good of human nature is threefold. First, there are the principles of which nature is constituted, and the properties that flow from them, such as the powers of the soul, and so forth. Secondly, since man has from nature an inclination to virtue, as stated above (60, 1; 63, 1), this inclination to virtue is a good of nature. Thirdly, the gift of original justice, conferred on the whole of human nature in the person of the first man, may be called a good of nature.

Accordingly, the first-mentioned good of nature is neither destroyed nor diminished by sin. The third good of nature was entirely destroyed through the sin of our first parent. But the second good of nature, viz. the natural inclination to virtue, is diminished by sin. Because human acts produce an inclination to like acts, as stated above (Question 50, Article 1). Now from the very fact that thing becomes inclined to one of two contraries, its inclination to the other contrary must needs be diminished. Wherefore as sin is opposed to virtue, from the very fact that a man sins, there results a diminution of that good of nature, which is the inclination to virtue.

Reply to Objection 1. Dionysius is speaking of the first-mentioned good of nature, which consists in "being, living and understanding," as anyone may see who reads the context.

Reply to Objection 2. Although nature precedes the voluntary action, it has an inclination to a certain voluntary action. Wherefore nature is not changed in itself, through a change in the voluntary action: it is the inclination that is changed in so far as it is directed to its term.

Reply to Objection 3. A voluntary action proceeds from various powers, active and passive. The result is that through voluntary actions something is caused or taken away in the man who acts, as we have stated when treating of the production of habits (51, 2).

Reply to Objection 4. An accident does not act effectively on its subject, but it acts on it formally, in the same sense as when we say that whiteness makes a thing white. In this way there is nothing to hinder sin from diminishing the good of nature; but only in so far as sin is itself a diminution of the good of nature, through being an inordinateness of action. But as regards the inordinateness of the agent, we must say that such like inordinateness is caused by the fact that in the acts of the soul, there is an active, and a passive element: thus the sensible object moves the sensitive appetite, and the sensitive appetite inclines the reason and will, as stated above (77, A1, 2). The result of this is the inordinateness, not as though an accident acted on its own subject, but in so far as the object acts on the power, and one power acts on another and puts it out of order.

ARTICLE 2. WHETHER THE ENTIRE GOOD OF HUMAN NATURE CAN BE DESTROYED BY SIN?

Objection 1. It would seem that the entire good of human nature can be destroyed by sin. For the good of human nature is finite, since human nature itself is finite. Now any finite thing is entirely taken away, if the subtraction be continuous. Since therefore the good of nature can be continually diminished by sin, it seems that in the end it can be entirely taken away.

Objection 2. Further, in a thing of one nature, the whole and the parts are uniform, as is evidently the case with air, water, flesh and all bodies with similar parts. But the good of nature is wholly uniform. Since therefore a part thereof can be taken away by sin, it seems that the whole can also be taken away by sin.

Objection 3. Further, the good of nature, that is weakened by sin, is aptitude for virtue. Now this aptitude is destroyed entirely in some on account of sin: thus the lost cannot be restored to virtue any more than the blind can to sight. Therefore sin can take away the good of nature entirely.

On the contrary, Augustine says (Enchiridion xiv) that "evil does not exist except in some good." But the evil of sin cannot be in the good of virtue or of grace, because they are contrary to it. Therefore it must be in the good of nature, and consequently it does not destroy it entirely.

I answer that, As stated above (Article 1), the good of nature, that is diminished by sin, is the natural inclination to virtue, which is befitting to man from the very fact that he is a rational being; for it is due to this that he performs actions in accord with reason, which is to act virtuously. Now sin cannot entirely take away from man the fact that he is a rational being, for then he would no longer be capable of sin. Wherefore it is not possible for this good of nature to be destroyed entirely.

Since, however, this same good of nature may be continually diminished by sin, some, in order to illustrate this, have made use of the example of a finite thing being diminished indefinitely, without being entirely destroyed. For the Philosopher says (Phys. i, text. 37) that if from a finite magnitude a continual subtraction be made in the same quantity, it will at last be entirely destroyed, for instance if from any finite length I continue to subtract the length of a span. If, however, the subtraction be made each time in the same proportion, and not in the same quantity, it may go on indefinitely, as, for instance, if a quantity be halved, and one half be diminished by half, it will be possible to go on thus indefinitely, provided that what is subtracted in each case be less than what was subtracted before. But this does not apply to the question at issue, since a subsequent sin does not diminish the good of nature less than a previous sin, but perhaps more, if it be a more grievous sin.

We must, therefore, explain the matter otherwise by saying that the aforesaid inclination is to be considered as a middle term between two others: for it is based on the rational nature as on its root, and tends to the good of virtue, as to its term and end. Consequently its diminution may be understood in two ways: first, on the part of its rood, secondly, on the part of its term. In the first way, it is not diminished by sin, because sin does not diminish nature, as stated above (Article 1). But it is diminished in the second way, in so far as an obstacle is placed against its attaining its term. Now if it were diminished in the first way, it would needs be entirely destroyed at last by the rational nature being entirely destroyed. Since, however, it is diminished on the part of the obstacle which is place against its attaining its term, it is evident that it can be diminished indefinitely, because obstacles can be placed indefinitely, inasmuch as man can go on indefinitely adding sin to sin: and yet it cannot be destroyed entirely, because the root of this inclination always remains. An example of this may be seen in a transparent body, which has an inclination to receive light, from the very fact that it is transparent; yet this inclination or aptitude is diminished on the part of supervening clouds, although it always remains rooted in the nature of the body.

Reply to Objection 1. This objection avails when diminution is made by subtraction. But here the diminution is made by raising obstacles, and this neither diminishes nor destroys the root of the inclination, as stated above.

Reply to Objection 2. The natural inclination is indeed wholly uniform: nevertheless it stands in relation both to its principle and to its term, in respect of which diversity of relation, it is diminished on the one hand, and not on the other.

Reply to Objection 3. Even in the lost the natural inclination to virtue remains, else they would have no remorse of conscience. That it is not reduced to act is owing to their being deprived of grace by Divine justice. Thus even in a blind man the aptitude to see remains in the very root of his nature, inasmuch as he is an animal naturally endowed with sight: yet this aptitude is not reduced to act, for the lack of a cause capable of reducing it, by forming the organ requisite for sight.

QUESTION 90. THE ESSENCE OF LAW

ARTICLE 1. WHETHER LAW IS SOMETHING PERTAINING TO REASON?

Objection 1. It would seem that law is not something pertaining to reason. For the Apostle says (Romans 7:23): "I see another law in my members," etc. But nothing pertaining to reason is in the members; since the reason does not make use of a bodily organ. Therefore law is not something pertaining to reason.

Objection 2. Further, in the reason there is nothing else but power, habit, and act. But law is not the power itself of reason. In like manner, neither is it a habit of reason: because the habits of reason are the intellectual virtues of which we have spoken above (Article 57). Nor again is it an act of reason: because then law would cease, when the act of reason ceases, for instance, while we are asleep. Therefore law is nothing pertaining to reason.

Objection 3. Further, the law moves those who are subject to it to act aright. But it belongs properly to the will to move to act, as is evident from what has been said above (Question 9, Article 1). Therefore law pertains, not to the reason, but to the will; according to the words of the Jurist (Lib. i, ff., De Const. Prin. leg. i): "Whatsoever pleaseth the sovereign, has force of law."

On the contrary, It belongs to the law to command and to forbid. But it belongs to reason to command, as stated above (Question 17, Article 1). Therefore law is something pertaining to reason.

I answer that, Law is a rule and measure of acts, whereby man is induced to act or is restrained from acting: for "lex" [law] is derived from "ligare" [to bind], because it binds one to act. Now the rule and measure of human acts is the reason, which is the first principle of human acts, as is evident from what has been stated above (1, 1, ad 3); since it belongs to the reason to direct to the end, which is the first principle in all matters of action, according to the Philosopher (Phys. ii). Now that which is the principle in any genus, is the rule and measure of that genus: for instance, unity in the genus of numbers, and the first movement in the genus of movements. Consequently it follows that law is something pertaining to reason.

Reply to Objection 1. Since law is a kind of rule and measure, it may be in something in two ways. First, as in that which measures and rules: and since this is proper to reason, it follows that, in this way, law is in the reason alone. Secondly, as in that which is measured and ruled. In this way, law is in all those things that are inclined to something by reason of some law: so that any inclination arising from a law, may be called a law, not essentially but by participation as it were. And thus the inclination of the members to desire is called "the law of the members."

Reply to Objection 2. Just as, in external action, we may consider the work and the work done, for instance the work of building and the house built; so in the acts of reason, we may consider the act itself of reason, i.e. to understand and to reason, and something produced by this act. With regard to the speculative reason, this is first of all the definition; secondly, the proposition; thirdly, the syllogism or argument. And since also the practical reason makes use of a syllogism in respect of the work to be done, as stated above (13, 3; 76, 1) and since as the Philosopher teaches (Ethic. vii, 3); hence we find in the practical reason something that holds the same position in regard to operations, as, in the speculative intellect, the proposition holds in regard to conclusions. Such like universal propositions of the practical intellect that are directed to actions have the nature of law. And these propositions are sometimes under our actual consideration, while sometimes they are retained in the reason by means of a habit.

Reply to Objection 3. Reason has its power of moving from the will, as stated above (Question 17, Article 1): for it is due to the fact that one wills the end, that the reason issues its commands as regards things ordained to the end. But in order that the volition of what is commanded may have the nature of law, it needs to be in accord with some rule of reason. And in this sense is to be understood the saying that the will of the sovereign has the force of law; otherwise the sovereign's will would savor of lawlessness rather than of law.

ARTICLE 2. WHETHER THE LAW IS ALWAYS SOMETHING DIRECTED TO THE COMMON GOOD?

Objection 1. It would seem that the law is not always directed to the common good as to its end. For it belongs to law to command and to forbid. But commands are directed to certain individual goods. Therefore the end of the law is not always the common good.

Objection 2. Further, the law directs man in his actions. But human actions are concerned with particular matters. Therefore the law is directed to some particular good.

Objection 3. Further, Isidore says (Etym. v, 3): "If the law is based on reason, whatever is based on reason will be a law." But reason is the foundation not only of what is ordained to the common good, but also of that which is directed private good. Therefore the law is not only directed to the good of all, but also to the private good of an individual.

On the contrary, Isidore says (Etym. v, 21) that "laws are enacted for no private profit, but for the common benefit of the citizens."

I answer that, As stated above (Article 1), the law belongs to that which is a principle of human acts, because it is their rule and measure. Now as reason is a principle of human acts, so in reason itself there is something which is the principle in respect of all the rest: wherefore to this principle chiefly and mainly law must needs be referred. Now the first principle in practical matters, which are the object of the practical reason, is the last end: and the last end of human life is bliss or happiness, as stated above (2, 7; 3, 1). Consequently the law must needs regard principally the relationship to happiness. Moreover, since every part is ordained to the whole, as imperfect to perfect; and since one man is a part of the perfect community, the law must needs regard properly the relationship to universal happiness. Wherefore the Philosopher, in the above definition of legal matters mentions both happiness and the body politic: for he says (Ethic. v, 1) that we call those legal matters "just, which are adapted to produce and preserve happiness and its parts for the body politic": since the city is a perfect community, as he says in Polit. i, 1.

Now in every genus, that which belongs to it chiefly is the principle of the others, and the others belong to that genus in subordination to that thing: thus fire, which is chief among hot things, is the cause of heat in mixed bodies, and these are said to be hot in so far as they have a share of fire. Consequently, since the law is chiefly ordained to the common good, any other precept in regard to some individual work, must needs be devoid of the nature of a law, save in so far as it regards the common good. Therefore every law is ordained to the common good.

Reply to Objection 1. A command denotes an application of a law to matters regulated by the law. Now the order to the common good, at which the law aims, is applicable to particular ends. And in this way commands are given even concerning particular matters.

Reply to Objection 2. Actions are indeed concerned with particular matters: but those particular matters are referable to the common good, not as to a common genus or species, but as to a common final cause, according as the common good is said to be the common end.

Reply to Objection 3. Just as nothing stands firm with regard to the speculative reason except that which is traced back to the first indemonstrable principles, so nothing stands firm with regard to the practical reason, unless it be directed to the last end which is the common good: and whatever stands to reason in this sense, has the nature of a law.

ARTICLE 3. WHETHER THE REASON OF ANY MAN IS COMPETENT TO MAKE LAWS?

Objection 1. It would seem that the reason of any man is competent to make laws. For the Apostle says (Romans 2:14) that "when the Gentiles, who have not the law, do by nature those things that are of the law, . . . they are a law to themselves." Now he says this of all in general. Therefore anyone can make a law for himself.

Objection 2. Further, as the Philosopher says (Ethic. ii. 1), "the intention of the lawgiver is to lead men to virtue." But every man can lead another to virtue. Therefore the reason of any man is competent to make laws.

Objection 3. Further, just as the sovereign of a city governs the city, so every father of a family governs his household. But the sovereign of a city can make laws for the city. Therefore every father of a family can make laws for his household.

On the contrary, Isidore says (Etym. v. 10): "A law is an ordinance of the people, whereby something is sanctioned by the Elders together with the Commonalty."

I answer that, A law, properly speaking, regards first and foremost the order to the common good. Now to order anything to the common good, belongs either to the whole people, or to someone who is the viceregent of the whole people. And therefore the making of a law belongs either to the whole people or to a public personage who has care of the whole people: since in all other matters the directing of anything to the end concerns him to whom the end belongs.

Reply to Objection 1. As stated above (A. 1 ad 1), a law is in a person not only as in one that rules, but also by participation as in one that is ruled. In the latter way each one is a law to himself, in so far as he shares the direction that he receives from one who rules him. Hence the same text goes on: "Who shows the work of the law written in their hearts."

Reply to Objection 2. A private person cannot lead another to virtue efficaciously: for he can only advise, and if his advice be not taken, it has no coercive power, such as the law should have, in order to prove an efficacious inducement to virtue, as the Philosopher says (Ethic. x. 9). But this coercive power is vested in the whole people or in some public personage, to whom it belongs to inflict penalties, as we shall state further on (Q. 92, A. 2 ad 3; II-II, Q. 64, A. 3). Wherefore the framing of laws belongs to him alone.

Reply to Objection 3. As one man is a part of the household, so a household is a part of the city: and the city is a perfect community, according to Polit. i. 1. And therefore, as the good of one man is not the last end, but is ordained to the common good; so too the good of one household is ordained to the good of a single city, which is a perfect community. Consequently he that governs a family, can indeed make certain commands or ordinances, but not such as to have properly the force of law.

ARTICLE 4. WHETHER PROMULGATION IS ESSENTIAL TO A LAW?

Objection 1. It would seem that promulgation is not essential to a law. For the natural law above all has the character of law. But the natural law needs no promulgation. Therefore it is not essential to a law that it be promulgated.

Objection 2. Further, it belongs properly to a law to bind one to do or not to do something. But the obligation of fulfilling a law touches not only those in whose presence it is promulgated, but also others. Therefore promulgation is not essential to a law.

Objection 3. Further, the binding force of a law extends even to the future, since "laws are binding in matters of the future," as the jurists say (Cod. 1, tit. De lege et constit. leg. vii). But promulgation concerns those who are present. Therefore it is not essential to a law.

On the contrary, It is laid down in the Decretals, dist. 4, that "laws are established when they are promulgated."

I answer that, As stated above (Article 1), a law is imposed on others by way of a rule and measure. Now a rule or measure is imposed by being applied to those who are to be ruled and measured by it. Wherefore, in order that a law obtain the binding force which is proper to a law, it must needs be applied to the men who have to be ruled by it. Such application is made by its being notified to them by promulgation. Wherefore promulgation is necessary for the law to obtain its force.

Thus from the four preceding articles, the definition of law may be gathered; and it is nothing else than an ordinance of reason for the common good, made by him who has care of the community, and promulgated.

Reply to Objection 1. The natural law is promulgated by the very fact that God instilled it into man's mind so as to be known by him naturally.

Reply to Objection 2. Those who are not present when a law is promulgated, are bound to observe the law, in so far as it is notified or can be notified to them by others, after it has been promulgated.

Reply to Objection 3. The promulgation that takes place now, extends to future time by reason of the durability of written characters, by which means it is continually promulgated. Hence Isidore says (Etym. v, 3; ii, 10) that "lex [law] is derived from legere [to read] because it is written."

QUESTION 91. THE VARIOUS KINDS OF LAW

ARTICLE 1. WHETHER THERE IS AN ETERNAL LAW?

Objection 1. It would seem that there is no eternal law. Because every law is imposed on someone. But there was not someone from eternity on whom a law could be imposed: since God alone was from eternity. Therefore no law is eternal.

Objection 2. Further, promulgation is essential to law. But promulgation could not be from eternity: because there was no one to whom it could be promulgated from eternity. Therefore no law can be eternal.

Objection 3. Further, a law implies order to an end. But nothing ordained to an end is eternal: for the last end alone is eternal. Therefore no law is eternal.

On the contrary, Augustine says (De Lib. Arb. i, 6): "That Law which is the Supreme Reason cannot be understood to be otherwise than unchangeable and eternal."

I answer that, As stated above (90, 1, ad 2; A3,4), a law is nothing else but a dictate of practical reason emanating from the ruler who governs a perfect community. Now it is evident, granted that the world is ruled by Divine Providence, as was stated in the I, 22, A1,2, that the whole community of the universe is governed by Divine Reason. Wherefore the very Idea of the government of things in God the Ruler of the universe, has the nature of a law. And since the Divine Reason's conception of things is not subject to time but is eternal, according to Proverbs 8:23, therefore it is that this kind of law must be called eternal.

Reply to Objection 1. Those things that are not in themselves, exist with God, inasmuch as they are foreknown and preordained by Him, according to Romans 4:17: "Who calls those things that are not, as those that are." Accordingly the eternal concept of the Divine law bears the character of an eternal law, in so far as it is ordained by God to the government of things foreknown by Him.

Reply to Objection 2. Promulgation is made by word of mouth or in writing; and in both ways the eternal law is promulgated: because both the Divine Word and the writing of the Book of Life are eternal. But the promulgation cannot be from eternity on the part of the creature that hears or reads.

Reply to Objection 3. The law implies order to the end actively, in so far as it directs certain things to the end; but not passively—that is to say, the law itself is not ordained to the end—except accidentally, in a governor whose end is extrinsic to him, and to which end his law must needs be ordained. But the end of the Divine government is God Himself, and His law is not distinct from Himself. Wherefore the eternal law is not ordained to another end.

ARTICLE 2. WHETHER THERE IS IN US A NATURAL LAW?

Objection 1. It would seem that there is no natural law in us. Because man is governed sufficiently by the eternal law: for Augustine says (De Lib. Arb. i) that "the eternal law is that by which it is right that all things should be most orderly." But nature does not abound in superfluities as neither does she fail in necessaries. Therefore no law is natural to man.

Objection 2. Further, by the law man is directed, in his acts, to the end, as stated above (Question 90, Article 2). But the directing of human acts to their end is not a function of nature, as is the case in irrational creatures, which act for an end solely by their natural appetite; whereas man acts for an end by his reason and will. Therefore no law is natural to man.

Objection 3. Further, the more a man is free, the less is he under the law. But man is freer than all the animals, on account of his free-will, with which he is endowed above all other animals. Since therefore other animals are not subject to a natural law, neither is man subject to a natural law.

On the contrary, A gloss on Romans 2:14: "When the Gentiles, who have not the law, do by nature those things that are of the law," comments as follows: "Although they have no written law, yet they have the natural law, whereby each one knows, and is conscious of, what is good and what is evil."

I answer that, As stated above (90, 1, ad 1), law, being a rule and measure, can be in a person in two ways: in one way, as in him that rules and measures; in another way, as in that which is ruled and measured, since a thing is ruled and measured, in so far as it partakes of the rule or measure. Wherefore, since all things subject to Divine providence are ruled and measured by the eternal law, as was stated above (Article 1); it is evident that all things partake somewhat of the eternal law, in so far as, namely, from its being imprinted on them, they derive their respective inclinations to their proper acts and ends. Now among all others, the rational creature is subject to Divine providence in the most excellent way, in so far as it partakes of a share of providence, by being provident both for itself and for others. Wherefore it has a share of the Eternal Reason, whereby it has a natural inclination to its proper act and end: and this participation of the eternal law in the rational creature is called the natural law. Hence the Psalmist after saying (Psalm 4:6): "Offer up the sacrifice of justice," as though someone asked what the works of justice are, adds: "Many say, Who showeth us good things?" in answer to which question he says: "The light of Thy countenance, O Lord, is signed upon us": thus implying that the light of natural reason, whereby we discern what is good and what is evil, which is the function of the natural law, is nothing else than an imprint on us of the Divine light. It is therefore evident that the natural law is nothing else than the rational creature's participation of the eternal law.

Reply to Objection 1. This argument would hold, if the natural law were something different from the eternal law: whereas it is nothing but a participation thereof, as stated above.

Reply to Objection 2. Every act of reason and will in us is based on that which is according to nature, as stated above (Question 10, Article 1): for every act of reasoning is based on principles that are known naturally, and every act of appetite in respect of the means is derived from the natural appetite in respect of the last end. Accordingly the first direction of our acts to their end must needs be in virtue of the natural law.

Reply to Objection 3. Even irrational animals partake in their own way of the Eternal Reason, just as the rational creature does. But because the rational creature partakes thereof in an intellectual and rational manner, therefore the participation of the eternal law in the rational creature is properly called a law, since a law is something pertaining to reason, as stated above (Question 90, Article 1). Irrational creatures, however, do not partake thereof in a rational manner, wherefore there is no participation of the eternal law in them, except by way of similitude.

ARTICLE 3. WHETHER THERE IS A HUMAN LAW?

Objection 1. It would seem that there is not a human law. For the natural law is a participation of the eternal law, as stated above (Article 2). Now through the eternal law "all things are most orderly," as Augustine states (De Lib. Arb. i, 6). Therefore the natural law suffices for the ordering of all human affairs. Consequently there is no need for a human law.

Objection 2. Further, a law bears the character of a measure, as stated above (Question 90, Article 1). But human reason is not a measure of things, but vice versa, as stated in Metaph. x, text. 5. Therefore no law can emanate from human reason.

Objection 3. Further, a measure should be most certain, as stated in Metaph. x, text. 3. But the dictates of human reason in matters of conduct are uncertain, according to Wisdom 9:14: "The thoughts of mortal men are fearful, and our counsels uncertain." Therefore no law can emanate from human reason.

On the contrary, Augustine (De Lib. Arb. i, 6) distinguishes two kinds of law, the one eternal, the other temporal, which he calls human.

I answer that, As stated above (90, 1, ad 2), a law is a dictate of the practical reason. Now it is to be observed that the same procedure takes place in the practical and in the speculative reason: for each proceeds from principles to conclusions, as stated above (De Lib. Arb. i, 6). Accordingly we conclude that just as, in the speculative reason, from naturally known indemonstrable principles, we draw the conclusions of the various sciences, the knowledge of which is not imparted to us by nature, but acquired by the efforts of reason, so too it is from the precepts of the natural law, as from general and indemonstrable principles, that the human reason needs to proceed to the more particular determination of certain matters. These particular determinations, devised by human reason, are called human laws, provided the other essential conditions of law be observed, as stated above (90, A2,3,4). Wherefore Tully says in his Rhetoric (De Invent. Rhet. ii) that "justice has its source in nature; thence certain things came into custom by reason of their utility; afterwards these things which emanated from nature and were approved by custom, were sanctioned by fear and reverence for the law."

Reply to Objection 1. The human reason cannot have a full participation of the dictate of the Divine Reason, but according to its own mode, and imperfectly. Consequently, as on the part of the speculative reason, by a natural participation of Divine Wisdom, there is in us the knowledge of certain general principles, but not proper knowledge of each single truth, such as that contained in the Divine Wisdom; so too, on the part of the practical reason, man has a natural participation of the eternal law, according to certain general principles, but not as regards the particular determinations of individual cases, which are, however, contained in the eternal law. Hence the need for human reason to proceed further to sanction them by law.

Reply to Objection 2. Human reason is not, of itself, the rule of things: but the principles impressed on it by nature, are general rules and measures of all things relating to human conduct, whereof the natural reason is the rule and measure, although it is not the measure of things that are from nature.

Reply to Objection 3. The practical reason is concerned with practical matters, which are singular and contingent: but not with necessary things, with which the speculative reason is concerned. Wherefore human laws cannot have that inerrancy that belongs to the demonstrated conclusions of sciences. Nor is it necessary for every measure to be altogether unerring and certain, but according as it is possible in its own particular genus.

ARTICLE 4. WHETHER THERE WAS ANY NEED FOR A DIVINE LAW?

Objection 1. It would seem that there was no need for a Divine law. Because, as stated above (Article 2), the natural law is a participation in us of the eternal law. But the eternal law is a Divine law, as stated above (Article 1). Therefore there was no need for a Divine law in addition to the natural law, and human laws derived therefrom.

Objection 2. Further, it is written (Sirach 15:14) that "God left man in the hand of his own counsel." Now counsel is an act of reason, as stated above (Question 14, Article 1). Therefore man was left to the direction of his reason. But a dictate of human reason is a human law as stated above (Article 3). Therefore there is no need for man to be governed also by a Divine law.

Objection 3. Further, human nature is more self-sufficing than irrational creatures. But irrational creatures have no Divine law besides the natural inclination impressed on them. Much less, therefore, should the rational creature have a Divine law in addition to the natural law.

On the contrary, David prayed God to set His law before him, saying (Psalm 118:33): "Set before me for a law the way of Thy justifications, O Lord."

I answer that, Besides the natural and the human law it was necessary for the directing of human conduct to have a Divine law. And this for four reasons. First, because it is by law that man is directed how to perform his proper acts in view of his last end. And indeed if man were ordained to no other end than that which is proportionate to his natural faculty, there would be no need for man to have any further direction of the part of his reason, besides the natural law and human law which is derived from it. But since man is ordained to an end of eternal happiness which is inproportionate to man's natural faculty, as stated above (Question 5, Article 5), therefore it was necessary that, besides the natural and the human law, man should be directed to his end by a law given by God.

Secondly, because, on account of the uncertainty of human judgment, especially on contingent and particular matters, different people form different judgments on human acts; whence also different and contrary laws result. In order, therefore, that man may know without any doubt what he ought to do and what he ought to avoid, it was necessary for man to be directed in his proper acts by a law given by God, for it is certain that such a law cannot err.

Thirdly, because man can make laws in those matters of which he is competent to judge. But man is not competent to judge of interior movements, that are hidden, but only of exterior acts which appear: and yet for the perfection of virtue it is necessary for man to conduct himself aright in both kinds of acts. Consequently human law could not sufficiently curb and direct interior acts; and it was necessary for this purpose that a Divine law should supervene.

Fourthly, because, as Augustine says (De Lib. Arb. i, 5,6), human law cannot punish or forbid all evil deeds: since while aiming at doing away with all evils, it would do away with many good things, and would hinder the advance of the common good, which is necessary for human intercourse. In order, therefore, that no evil might remain unforbidden and unpunished, it was necessary for the Divine law to supervene, whereby all sins are forbidden.

And these four causes are touched upon in Psalm 118:8, where it is said: "The law of the Lord is unspotted," i.e. allowing no foulness of sin; "converting souls," because it directs not only exterior, but also interior acts; "the testimony of the Lord is faithful," because of the certainty of what is true and right; "giving wisdom to little ones," by directing man to an end supernatural and Divine.

Reply to Objection 1. By the natural law the eternal law is participated proportionately to the capacity of human nature. But to his supernatural end man needs to be directed in a yet higher way. Hence the additional law given by God, whereby man shares more perfectly in the eternal law.

Reply to Objection 2. Counsel is a kind of inquiry: hence it must proceed from some principles. Nor is it enough for it to proceed from principles imparted by nature, which are the precepts of the natural law, for the reasons given above: but there is need for certain additional principles, namely, the precepts of the Divine law.

Reply to Objection 3. Irrational creatures are not ordained to an end higher than that which is proportionate to their natural powers: consequently the comparison fails.

QUESTION 92. THE EFFECTS OF LAW

ARTICLE 1. WHETHER AN EFFECT OF LAW IS TO MAKE MEN GOOD?

Objection 1. It seems that it is not an effect of law to make men good. For men are good through virtue, since virtue, as stated in Ethic. ii, 6 is "that which makes its subject good." But virtue is in man from God alone, because He it is Who "works it in us without us," as we stated above (Question 55, Article 4) in giving the definition of virtue. Therefore the law does not make men good.

Objection 2. Further, Law does not profit a man unless he obeys it. But the very fact that a man obeys a law is due to his being good. Therefore in man goodness is presupposed to the law. Therefore the law does not make men good.

Objection 3. Further, Law is ordained to the common good, as stated above (Question 90, Article 2). But some behave well in things regarding the community, who behave ill in things regarding themselves. Therefore it is not the business of the law to make men good.

Objection 4. Further, some laws are tyrannical, as the Philosopher says (Polit. iii, 6). But a tyrant does not intend the good of his subjects, but considers only his own profit. Therefore law does not make men good.

On the contrary, The Philosopher says (Ethic. ii, 1) that the "intention of every lawgiver is to make good citizens."

I answer that, as stated above (90, 1, ad 2; A3,4), a law is nothing else than a dictate of reason in the ruler by whom his subjects are governed. Now the virtue of any subordinate thing consists in its being well subordinated to that by which it is regulated: thus we see that the virtue of the spirited and desiring faculties consists in their being obedient to reason; and accordingly "the virtue of every subject consists in his being well subjected to his ruler," as the Philosopher says (Polit. i). But every law aims at being obeyed by those who are subject to it. Consequently it is evident that the proper effect of law is to lead its subjects to their proper virtue: and since virtue is "that which makes its subject good," it follows that the proper effect of law is to make those to whom it is given, good, either simply or in some particular respect. For if the intention of the lawgiver is fixed on true good, which is the common good regulated according to Divine justice, it follows that the effect of the law is to make men good simply. If, however, the intention of the lawgiver is fixed on that which is not simply good, but useful or pleasurable to himself, or in opposition to Divine justice; then the law does not make men good simply, but in respect to that particular government. In this way good is found even in things that are bad of themselves: thus a man is called a good robber, because he works in a way that is adapted to his end.

Reply to Objection 1. Virtue is twofold, as explained above (Question 63, Article 2), viz. acquired and infused. Now the fact of being accustomed to an action contributes to both, but in different ways; for it causes the acquired virtue; while it disposes to infused virtue, and preserves and fosters it when it already exists. And since law is given for the purpose of directing human acts; as far as human acts conduce to virtue, so far does law make men good. Wherefore the Philosopher says in the second book of the Politics (Ethic. ii) that "lawgivers make men good by habituating them to good works."

Reply to Objection 2. It is not always through perfect goodness of virtue that one obeys the law, but sometimes it is through fear of punishment, and sometimes from the mere dictates of reason, which is a beginning of virtue, as stated above (Question 63, Article 1).

Reply to Objection 3. The goodness of any part is considered in comparison with the whole; hence Augustine says (Confess. iii) that "unseemly is the part that harmonizes not with the whole." Since then every man is a part of the city, it is impossible that a man be good, unless he be well proportionate to the common good: nor can the whole be well consistent unless its parts be proportionate to it. Consequently the common good of the city cannot flourish, unless the citizens be virtuous, at least those whose business it is to govern. But it is enough for the good of the community, that the other citizens be so far virtuous that they obey the commands of their rulers. Hence the Philosopher says (Polit. ii, 2) that "the virtue of a sovereign is the same as that of a good man, but the virtue of any common citizen is not the same as that of a good man."

Reply to Objection 4. A tyrannical law, through not being according to reason, is not a law, absolutely speaking, but rather a perversion of law; and yet in so far as it is something in the nature of a law, it aims at the citizens' being good. For all it has in the nature of a law consists in its being an ordinance made by a superior to his subjects, and aims at being obeyed by them, which is to make them good, not simply, but with respect to that particular government.

QUESTION 94. THE NATURAL LAW

ARTICLE 2. WHETHER THE NATURAL LAW CONTAINS SEVERAL PRECEPTS, OR ONLY ONE?

Objection 1. It would seem that the natural law contains, not several precepts, but one only. For law is a kind of precept, as stated above (Question 92, Article 2). If therefore there were many precepts of the natural law, it would follow that there are also many natural laws.

Objection 2. Further, the natural law is consequent to human nature. But human nature, as a whole, is one; though, as to its parts, it is manifold. Therefore, either there is but one precept of the law of nature, on account of the unity of nature as a whole; or there are many, by reason of the number of parts of human nature. The result would be that even things relating to the inclination of the desiring faculty belong to the natural law.

Objection 3. Further, law is something pertaining to reason, as stated above (Question 90, Article 1). Now reason is but one in man. Therefore there is only one precept of the natural law.

On the contrary, The precepts of the natural law in man stand in relation to practical matters, as the first principles to matters of demonstration. But there are several first indemonstrable principles. Therefore there are also several precepts of the natural law.

I answer that, As stated above (Question 91, Article 3), the precepts of the natural law are to the practical reason, what the first principles of demonstrations are to the speculative reason; because both are self-evident principles. Now a thing is said to be self-evident in two ways: first, in itself; secondly, in relation to us. Any proposition is said to be self-evident in itself, if its predicate is contained in the notion of the subject: although, to one who knows not the definition of the subject, it happens that such a proposition is not self-evident. For instance, this proposition, "Man is a rational being," is, in its very nature, self-evident, since who says "man," says "a rational being": and yet to one who knows not what a man is, this proposition is not self-evident. Hence it is that, as Boethius says (De Hebdom.), certain axioms or propositions are universally self-evident to all; and such are those propositions whose terms are known to all, as, "Every whole is greater than its part," and, "Things equal to one and the same are equal to one another." But some propositions are self-evident only to the wise, who understand the meaning of the terms of such propositions: thus to one who understands that an angel is not a body, it is self-evident that an angel is not circumscriptively in a place: but this is not evident to the unlearned, for they cannot grasp it.

Now a certain order is to be found in those things that are apprehended universally. For that which, before aught else, falls under apprehension, is "being," the notion of which is included in all things whatsoever a man apprehends. Wherefore the first indemonstrable principle is that "the same thing cannot be affirmed and denied at the same time," which is based on the notion of "being" and "not-being": and on this principle all others are based, as is stated in Metaph. iv, text. 9. Now as "being" is the first thing that falls under the apprehension simply, so "good" is the first thing that falls under the apprehension of the practical reason, which is directed to action: since every agent acts for an end under the aspect of good. Consequently the first principle of practical reason is one founded on the notion of good, viz. that "good is that which all things seek after." Hence this is the first precept of law, that "good is to be done and pursued, and evil is to be avoided." All other precepts of the natural law are based upon this: so that whatever the practical reason naturally apprehends as man's good (or evil) belongs to the precepts of the natural law as something to be done or avoided.

Since, however, good has the nature of an end, and evil, the nature of a contrary, hence it is that all those things to which man has a natural inclination, are naturally apprehended by reason as being good, and consequently as objects of pursuit, and their contraries as evil, and objects of avoidance. Wherefore according to the order of natural inclinations, is the order of the precepts of the natural law. Because in man there is first of all an inclination to good in accordance with the nature which he has in common with all substances: inasmuch as every substance seeks the preservation of its own being, according to its nature: and by reason of this inclination, whatever is a means of preserving human life, and of warding off its obstacles, belongs to the natural law.

Secondly, there is in man an inclination to things that pertain to him more specially, according to that nature which he has in common with other animals: and in virtue of this inclination, those things are said to belong to the natural law, "which nature has taught to all animals" [Pandect. Just. I, tit. i], such as sexual intercourse, education of offspring and so forth. Thirdly, there is in man an inclination to good, according to the nature of his reason, which nature is proper to him: thus man has a natural inclination to know the truth about God, and to live in society: and in this respect, whatever pertains to this inclination belongs to the natural law; for instance, to shun ignorance, to avoid offending those among whom one has to live, and other such things regarding the above inclination.

Reply to Objection 1. All these precepts of the law of nature have the character of one natural law, inasmuch as they flow from one first precept.

Reply to Objection 2. All the inclinations of any parts whatsoever of human nature, e.g. of the desiring and spirited parts, in so far as they are ruled by reason, belong to the natural law, and are reduced to one first precept, as stated above: so that the precepts of the natural law are many in themselves, but are based on one common foundation.

Reply to Objection 3. Although reason is one in itself, yet it directs all things regarding man; so that whatever can be ruled by reason, is contained under the law of reason.

ARTICLE 3. WHETHER ALL ACTS OF VIRTUE ARE PRESCRIBED BY THE NATURAL LAW?

Objection 1. It would seem that not all acts of virtue are prescribed by the natural law. Because, as stated above (Question 90, Article 2) it is essential to a law that it be ordained to the common good. But some acts of virtue are ordained to the private good of the individual, as is evident especially in regards to acts of temperance. Therefore not all acts of virtue are the subject of natural law.

Objection 2. Further, every sin is opposed to some virtuous act. If therefore all acts of virtue are prescribed by the natural law, it seems to follow that all sins are against nature: whereas this applies to certain special sins.

Objection 3. Further, those things which are according to nature are common to all. But acts of virtue are not common to all: since a thing is virtuous in one, and vicious in another. Therefore not all acts of virtue are prescribed by the natural law.

On the contrary, Damascene says (De Fide Orth. iii, 4) that "virtues are natural." Therefore virtuous acts also are a subject of the natural law.

I answer that, We may speak of virtuous acts in two ways: first, under the aspect of virtuous; secondly, as such and such acts considered in their proper species. If then we speak of acts of virtue, considered as virtuous, thus all virtuous acts belong to the natural law. For it has been stated (2) that to the natural law belongs everything to which a man is inclined according to his nature. Now each thing is inclined naturally to an operation that is suitable to it according to its form: thus fire is inclined to give heat. Wherefore, since the rational soul is the proper form of man, there is in every man a natural inclination to act according to reason: and this is to act according to virtue. Consequently, considered thus, all acts of virtue are prescribed by the natural law: since each one's reason naturally dictates to him to act virtuously. But if we speak of virtuous acts, considered in themselves, i.e. in their proper species, thus not all virtuous acts are prescribed by the natural law: for many things are done virtuously, to which nature does not incline at first; but which, through the inquiry of reason, have been found by men to be conducive to well-living.

Reply to Objection 1. Temperance is about the natural desires of food, drink and sexual matters, which are indeed ordained to the natural common good, just as other matters of law are ordained to the moral common good.

Reply to Objection 2. By human nature we may mean either that which is proper to man—and in this sense all sins, as being against reason, are also against nature, as Damascene states (De Fide Orth. ii, 30): or we may mean that nature which is common to man and other animals; and in this sense, certain special sins are said to be against nature; thus contrary to sexual intercourse, which is natural to all animals, is unisexual lust, which has received the special name of the unnatural crime.

Reply to Objection 3. This argument considers acts in themselves. For it is owing to the various conditions of men, that certain acts are virtuous for some, as being proportionate and becoming to them, while they are vicious for others, as being out of proportion to them.

ARTICLE 4. WHETHER THE NATURAL LAW IS THE SAME IN ALL MEN?

Objection 1. It would seem that the natural law is not the same in all. For it is stated in the Decretals (Dist. i) that "the natural law is that which is contained in the Law and the Gospel." But this is not common to all men; because, as it is written (Romans 10:16), "all do not obey the gospel." Therefore the natural law is not the same in all men.

Objection 2. Further, "Things which are according to the law are said to be just," as stated in Ethic. v. But it is stated in the same book that nothing is so universally just as not to be subject to change in regard to some men. Therefore even the natural law is not the same in all men.

Objection 3. Further, as stated above (2,3), to the natural law belongs everything to which a man is inclined according to his nature. Now different men are naturally inclined to different things; some to the desire of pleasures, others to the desire of honors, and other men to other things. Therefore there is not one natural law for all.

On the contrary, Isidore says (Etym. v, 4): "The natural law is common to all nations."

I answer that, As stated above (2,3), to the natural law belongs those things to which a man is inclined naturally: and among these it is proper to man to be inclined to act according to reason. Now the process of reason is from the common to the proper, as stated in Phys. i. The speculative reason, however, is differently situated in this matter, from the practical reason. For, since the speculative reason is busied chiefly with the necessary things, which cannot be otherwise than they are, its proper conclusions, like the universal principles, contain the truth without fail. The practical reason, on the other hand, is busied with contingent matters, about which human actions are concerned: and consequently, although there is necessity in the general principles, the more we descend to matters of detail, the more frequently we encounter defects. Accordingly then in speculative matters truth is the same in all men, both as to principles and as to conclusions: although the truth is not known to all as regards the conclusions, but only as regards the principles which are called common notions. But in matters of action, truth or practical rectitude is not the same for all, as to matters of detail, but only as to the general principles: and where there is the same rectitude in matters of detail, it is not equally known to all.

It is therefore evident that, as regards the general principles whether of speculative or of practical reason, truth or rectitude is the same for all, and is equally known by all. As to the proper conclusions of the speculative reason, the truth is the same for all, but is not equally known to all: thus it is true for all that the three angles of a triangle are together equal to two right angles, although it is not known to all. But as to the proper conclusions of the practical reason, neither is the truth or rectitude the same for all, nor, where it is the same, is it equally known by all. Thus it is right and true for all to act according to reason: and from this principle it follows as a proper conclusion, that goods entrusted to another should be restored to their owner. Now this is true for the majority of cases: but it may happen in a particular case that it would be injurious, and therefore unreasonable, to restore goods held in trust; for instance, if they are claimed for the purpose of fighting against one's country. And this principle will be found to fail the more, according as we descend further into detail, e.g. if one were to say that goods held in trust should be restored with such and such a guarantee, or in such and such a way; because the greater the number of conditions added, the greater the number of ways in which the principle may fail, so that it be not right to restore or not to restore.

Consequently we must say that the natural law, as to general principles, is the same for all, both as to rectitude and as to knowledge. But as to certain matters of detail, which are conclusions, as it were, of those general principles, it is the same for all in the majority of cases, both as to rectitude and as to knowledge; and yet in some few cases it may fail, both as to rectitude, by reason of certain obstacles (just as natures subject to generation and corruption fail in some few cases on account of some obstacle), and as to knowledge, since in some the reason is perverted by passion, or evil habit, or an evil disposition of nature; thus formerly, theft, although it is expressly contrary to the natural law, was not considered wrong among the Germans, as Julius Caesar relates (De Bello Gall. vi).

Reply to Objection 1. The meaning of the sentence quoted is not that whatever is contained in the Law and the Gospel belongs to the natural law, since they contain many things that are above nature; but that whatever belongs to the natural law is fully contained in them. Wherefore Gratian, after saying that "the natural law is what is contained in the Law and the Gospel," adds at once, by way of example, "by which everyone is commanded to do to others as he would be done by."

Reply to Objection 2. The saying of the Philosopher is to be understood of things that are naturally just, not as general principles, but as conclusions drawn from them, having rectitude in the majority of cases, but failing in a few.

Reply to Objection 3. As, in man, reason rules and commands the other powers, so all the natural inclinations belonging to the other powers must needs be directed according to reason. Wherefore it is universally right for all men, that all their inclinations should be directed according to reason.

ARTICLE 5. WHETHER THE NATURAL LAW CAN BE CHANGED?

Objection 1. It would seem that the natural law can be changed. Because on Sirach 17:9, "He gave them instructions, and the law of life," the gloss says: "He wished the law of the letter to be written, in order to correct the law of nature." But that which is corrected is changed. Therefore the natural law can be changed.

Objection 2. Further, the slaying of the innocent, adultery, and theft are against the natural law. But we find these things changed by God: as when God commanded Abraham to slay his innocent son (Genesis 22:2); and when he ordered the Jews to borrow and purloin the vessels of the Egyptians (Exodus 12:35); and when He commanded Osee to take to himself "a wife of fornications" (Hosea 1:2). Therefore the natural law can be changed.

Objection 3. Further, Isidore says (Etym. 5:4) that "the possession of all things in common, and universal freedom, are matters of natural law." But these things are seen to be changed by human laws. Therefore it seems that the natural law is subject to change.

On the contrary, It is said in the Decretals (Dist. v): "The natural law dates from the creation of the rational creature. It does not vary according to time, but remains unchangeable."

I answer that, A change in the natural law may be understood in two ways. First, by way of addition. In this sense nothing hinders the natural law from being changed: since many things for the benefit of human life have been added over and above the natural law, both by the Divine law and by human laws.

Secondly, a change in the natural law may be understood by way of subtraction, so that what previously was according to the natural law, ceases to be so. In this sense, the natural law is altogether unchangeable in its first principles: but in its secondary principles, which, as we have said (4), are certain detailed proximate conclusions drawn from the first principles, the natural law is not changed so that what it prescribes be not right in most cases. But it may be changed in some particular cases of rare occurrence, through some special causes hindering the observance of such precepts, as stated above (Article 4).

Reply to Objection 1. The written law is said to be given for the correction of the natural law, either because it supplies what was wanting to the natural law; or because the natural law was perverted in the hearts of some men, as to certain matters, so that they esteemed those things good which are naturally evil; which perversion stood in need of correction.

Reply to Objection 2. All men alike, both guilty and innocent, die the death of nature: which death of nature is inflicted by the power of God on account of original sin, according to 1 Samuel 2:6: "The Lord killeth and maketh alive." Consequently, by the command of God, death can be inflicted on any man, guilty or innocent, without any injustice whatever. In like manner adultery is intercourse with another's wife; who is allotted to him by the law emanating from God. Consequently intercourse with any woman, by the command of God, is neither adultery nor fornication. The same applies to theft, which is the taking of another's property. For whatever is taken by the command of God, to

Whom all things belong, is not taken against the will of its owner, whereas it is in this that theft consists. Nor is it only in human things, that whatever is commanded by God is right; but also in natural things, whatever is done by God, is, in some way, natural, as stated in the I, 105, 6, ad 1.

Reply to Objection 3. A thing is said to belong to the natural law in two ways. First, because nature inclines thereto: e.g. that one should not do harm to another. Secondly, because nature did not bring in the contrary: thus we might say that for man to be naked is of the natural law, because nature did not give him clothes, but art invented them. In this sense, "the possession of all things in common and universal freedom" are said to be of the natural law, because, to wit, the distinction of possessions and slavery were not brought in by nature, but devised by human reason for the benefit of human life. Accordingly the law of nature was not changed in this respect, except by addition.

ARTICLE 6. WHETHER THE LAW OF NATURE CAN BE ABOLISHED FROM THE HEART OF MAN?

Objection 1. It would seem that the natural law can be abolished from the heart of man. Because on Romans 2:14, "When the Gentiles who have not the law," etc. a gloss says that "the law of righteousness, which sin had blotted out, is graven on the heart of man when he is restored by grace." But the law of righteousness is the law of nature. Therefore the law of nature can be blotted out.

Objection 2. Further, the law of grace is more efficacious than the law of nature. But the law of grace is blotted out by sin. Much more therefore can the law of nature be blotted out.

Objection 3. Further, that which is established by law is made just. But many things are enacted by men, which are contrary to the law of nature. Therefore the law of nature can be abolished from the heart of man.

On the contrary, Augustine says (Confess. ii): "Thy law is written in the hearts of men, which iniquity itself effaces not." But the law which is written in men's hearts is the natural law. Therefore the natural law cannot be blotted out.

I answer that, As stated above (4,5), there belong to the natural law, first, certain most general precepts, that are known to all; and secondly, certain secondary and more detailed precepts, which are, as it were, conclusions following closely from first principles. As to those general principles, the natural law, in the abstract, can nowise be blotted out from men's hearts. But it is blotted out in the case of a particular action, in so far as reason is hindered from applying the general principle to a particular point of practice, on account of desire or some other passion, as stated above (Question 77, Article 2). But as to the other, i.e. the secondary precepts, the natural law can be blotted out from the human heart, either by evil persuasions, just as in speculative matters errors occur in respect of necessary conclusions; or by vicious customs and corrupt habits, as among some men, theft, and even unnatural vices, as the Apostle states (Romans 1), were not esteemed sinful.

Reply to Objection 1. Sin blots out the law of nature in particular cases, not universally, except perchance in regard to the secondary precepts of the natural law, in the way stated above.

Reply to Objection 2. Although grace is more efficacious than nature, yet nature is more essential to man, and therefore more enduring.

Reply to Objection 3. This argument is true of the secondary precepts of the natural law, against which some legislators have framed certain enactments which are unjust.

QUESTION 95. HUMAN LAW

ARTICLE 1. WHETHER IT WAS USEFUL FOR LAWS TO BE FRAMED BY MEN?

Objection 1. It would seem that it was not useful for laws to be framed by men. Because the purpose of every law is that man be made good thereby, as stated above (Question 92, Article 1). But men are more to be induced to be good willingly by means of admonitions, than against their will, by means of laws. Therefore there was no need to frame laws.

Objection 2. Further, As the Philosopher says (Ethic. v, 4), "men have recourse to a judge as to animate justice." But animate justice is better than inanimate justice, which contained in laws. Therefore it would have been better for the execution of justice to be entrusted to the decision of judges, than to frame laws in addition.

Objection 3. Further, every law is framed for the direction of human actions, as is evident from what has been stated above (90, A1,2). But since human actions are about singulars, which are infinite in number, matter pertaining to the direction of human actions cannot be taken into sufficient consideration except by a wise man, who looks into each one of them. Therefore it would have been better for human acts to be directed by the judgment of wise men, than by the framing of laws. Therefore there was no need of human laws.

On the contrary, Isidore says (Etym. v, 20): "Laws were made that in fear thereof human audacity might be held in check, that innocence might be safeguarded in the midst of wickedness, and that the dread of punishment might prevent the wicked from doing harm." But these things are most necessary to mankind. Therefore it was necessary that human laws should be made.

I answer that, As stated above (63, 1; 94, 3), man has a natural aptitude for virtue; but the perfection of virtue must be acquired by man by means of some kind of training. Thus we observe that man is helped by industry in his necessities, for instance, in food and clothing. Certain beginnings of these he has from nature, viz. his reason and his hands; but he has not the full complement, as other animals have, to whom nature has given sufficiency of clothing and food. Now it is difficult to see how man could suffice for himself in the matter of this training: since the perfection of virtue consists chiefly in withdrawing man from undue pleasures, to which above all man is inclined, and especially the young, who are more capable of being trained. Consequently a man needs to receive this training from another, whereby to arrive at the perfection of virtue. And as to those young people who are inclined to acts of virtue, by their good natural disposition, or by custom, or rather by the gift of God, paternal training suffices, which is by admonitions. But since some are found to be depraved, and prone to vice, and not easily amenable to words, it was necessary for such to be restrained from evil by force and fear, in order that, at least, they might desist from evil-doing, and leave others in peace, and that they themselves, by being habituated in this way, might be brought to do willingly what hitherto they did from fear, and thus become virtuous. Now this kind of training, which compels through fear of punishment, is the discipline of laws. Therefore in order that man might have peace and virtue, it was necessary for laws to be framed: for, as the Philosopher says (Polit. i, 2), "as man is the most noble of animals if he be perfect in virtue, so is he the lowest of all, if he be severed from law and righteousness"; because man can use his reason to devise means of satisfying his lusts and evil passions, which other animals are unable to do.

Reply to Objection 1. Men who are well disposed are led willingly to virtue by being admonished better than by coercion: but men who are evilly disposed are not led to virtue unless they are compelled.

Reply to Objection 2. As the Philosopher says (Rhet. i, 1), "it is better that all things be regulated by law, than left to be decided by judges": and this for three reasons. First, because it is easier to find a few wise men competent to frame right laws, than to find the many who would be necessary to judge aright of each single case. Secondly, because those who make laws consider long beforehand what laws to make; whereas judgment on each single case has to be pronounced as soon as it arises: and it is easier for man to see what is right, by taking many instances into consideration, than by considering one solitary fact. Thirdly, because lawgivers judge in the abstract and of future events; whereas those who sit in judgment of things present, towards which they are affected by love, hatred, or some kind of cupidity; wherefore their judgment is perverted.

Since then the animated justice of the judge is not found in every man, and since it can be deflected, therefore it was necessary, whenever possible, for the law to determine how to judge, and for very few matters to be left to the decision of men.

Reply to Objection 3. Certain individual facts which cannot be covered by the law "have necessarily to be committed to judges," as the Philosopher says in the same passage: for instance, "concerning something that has happened or not happened," and the like.

ARTICLE 2. WHETHER EVERY HUMAN LAW IS DERIVED FROM THE NATURAL LAW?

Objection 1. It would seem that not every human law is derived from the natural law. For the Philosopher says (Ethic. v, 7) that "the legal just is that which originally was a matter of indifference." But those things which arise from the natural law are not matters of indifference. Therefore the enactments of human laws are not derived from the natural law.

Objection 2. Further, positive law is contrasted with natural law, as stated by Isidore (Etym. v, 4) and the Philosopher (Ethic. v, 7). But those things which flow as conclusions from the general principles of the natural law belong to the natural law, as stated above (Question 94, Article 4). Therefore that which is established by human law does not belong to the natural law.

Objection 3. Further, the law of nature is the same for all; since the Philosopher says (Ethic. v, 7) that "the natural just is that which is equally valid everywhere." If therefore human laws were derived from the natural law, it would follow that they too are the same for all: which is clearly false.

Objection 4. Further, it is possible to give a reason for things which are derived from the natural law. But "it is not possible to give the reason for all the legal enactments of the lawgivers," as the jurist says [Pandect. Justin. lib. i, ff, tit. iii, v; De Leg. et Senat.]. Therefore not all human laws are derived from the natural law.

On the contrary, Tully says (Rhet. ii): "Things which emanated from nature and were approved by custom, were sanctioned by fear and reverence for the laws."

I answer that, As Augustine says (De Lib. Arb. i, 5) "that which is not just seems to be no law at all": wherefore the force of a law depends on the extent of its justice. Now in human affairs a thing is said to be just, from being right, according to the rule of reason. But the first rule of reason is the law of nature, as is clear from what has been stated above (91, 2, ad 2). Consequently every human law has just so much of the nature of law, as it is derived from the law of nature. But if in any point it deflects from the law of nature, it is no longer a law but a perversion of law.

But it must be noted that something may be derived from the natural law in two ways: first, as a conclusion from premises, secondly, by way of determination of certain generalities. The first way is like to that by which, in sciences, demonstrated conclusions are drawn from the principles: while the second mode is likened to that whereby, in the arts, general forms are particularized as to details: thus the craftsman needs to determine the general form of a house to some particular shape. Some things are therefore derived from the general principles of the natural law, by way of conclusions; e.g. that "one must not kill" may be derived as a conclusion from the principle that "one should do harm to no man": while some are derived therefrom by way of determination; e.g. the law of nature has it that the evil-doer should be punished; but that he be punished in this or that way, is a determination of the law of nature.

Accordingly both modes of derivation are found in the human law. But those things which are derived in the first way, are contained in human law not as emanating therefrom exclusively, but have some force from the natural law also. But those things which are derived in the second way, have no other force than that of human law.

Reply to Objection 1. The Philosopher is speaking of those enactments which are by way of determination or specification of the precepts of the natural law.

Reply to Objection 2. This argument avails for those things that are derived from the natural law, by way of conclusions.

Reply to Objection 3. The general principles of the natural law cannot be applied to all men in the same way on account of the great variety of human affairs: and hence arises the diversity of positive laws among various people.

Reply to Objection 4. These words of the Jurist are to be understood as referring to decisions of rulers in determining particular points of the natural law: on which determinations the judgment of expert and prudent men is based as on its principles; in so far, to wit, as they see at once what is the best thing to decide.

Hence the Philosopher says (Ethic. vi, 11) that in such matters, "we ought to pay as much attention to the undemonstrated sayings and opinions of persons who surpass us in experience, age and prudence, as to their demonstrations."

QUESTION 96. THE POWER OF HUMAN LAW

ARTICLE 1. WHETHER HUMAN LAW SHOULD BE FRAMED FOR THE COMMUNITY RATHER THAN FOR THE INDIVIDUAL?

Objection 1. It would seem that human law should be framed not for the community, but rather for the individual. For the Philosopher says (Ethic. v, 7) that "the legal just . . . includes all particular acts of legislation . . . and all those matters which are the subject of decrees," which are also individual matters, since decrees are framed about individual actions. Therefore law is framed not only for the community, but also for the individual.

Objection 2. Further, law is the director of human acts, as stated above (90, A1,2). But human acts are about individual matters. Therefore human laws should be framed, not for the community, but rather for the individual.

Objection 3. Further, law is a rule and measure of human acts, as stated above (90, A1,2). But a measure should be most certain, as stated in Metaph. x. Since therefore in human acts no general proposition can be so certain as not to fail in some individual cases, it seems that laws should be framed not in general but for individual cases.

On the contrary, The jurist says (Pandect. Justin. lib. i, tit. iii, art. ii; De legibus, etc.) that "laws should be made to suit the majority of instances; and they are not framed according to what may possibly happen in an individual case."

I answer that, Whatever is for an end should be proportionate to that end. Now the end of law is the common good; because, as Isidore says (Etym. v, 21) that "law should be framed, not for any private benefit, but for the common good of all the citizens." Hence human laws should be proportionate to the common good. Now the common good comprises many things. Wherefore law should take account of many things, as to persons, as to matters, and as to times. Because the community of the city is composed of many persons; and its good is procured by many actions; nor is it established to endure for only a short time, but to last for all time by the citizens succeeding one another, as Augustine says (De Civ. Dei ii, 21; xxii, 6).

Reply to Objection 1. The Philosopher (Ethic. v, 7) divides the legal just, i.e. positive law, into three parts. For some things are laid down simply in a general way: and these are the general laws. Of these he says that "the legal is that which originally was a matter of indifference, but which, when enacted, is so no longer": as the fixing of the ransom of a captive. Some things affect the community in one respect, and individuals in another. These are called "privileges," i.e. "private laws," as it were, because they regard private persons, although their power extends to many matters; and in regard to these, he adds, "and further, all particular acts of legislation." Other matters are legal, not through being laws, but through being applications of general laws to particular cases: such are decrees which have the force of law; and in regard to these, he adds "all matters subject to decrees."

Reply to Objection 2. A principle of direction should be applicable to many; wherefore (Metaph. x, text. 4) the Philosopher says that all things belonging to one genus, are measured by one, which is the principle in that genus. For if there were as many rules or measures as there are things measured or ruled, they would cease to be of use, since their use consists in being applicable to many things. Hence law would be of no use, if it did not extend further than to one single act, because the decrees of prudent men are made for the purpose of directing individual actions; whereas law is a general precept, as stated above (92, 2, Objection 2).

Reply to Objection 3. "We must not seek the same degree of certainty in all things" (Ethic. i, 3). Consequently in contingent matters, such as natural and human things, it is enough for a thing to be certain, as being true in the greater number of instances, though at times and less frequently it fail.

ARTICLE 2. WHETHER IT BELONGS TO THE HUMAN LAW TO REPRESS ALL VICES?

Objection 1. It would seem that it belongs to human law to repress all vices. For Isidore says (Etym. v, 20) that "laws were made in order that, in fear thereof, man's audacity might be held in check." But it would not be held in check sufficiently, unless all evils were repressed by law. Therefore human laws should repress all evils.

Objection 2. Further, the intention of the lawgiver is to make the citizens virtuous. But a man cannot be virtuous unless he forbear from all kinds of vice. Therefore it belongs to human law to repress all vices.

Objection 3. Further, human law is derived from the natural law, as stated above (Question 95, Article 2). But all vices are contrary to the law of nature. Therefore human law should repress all vices.

On the contrary, We read in De Lib. Arb. i, 5: [where Evodius, not Augustine, remarks that] "It seems to me that the law which is written for the governing of the people rightly permits these things [killing in self-defense], and that Divine providence punishes them." But Divine providence punishes nothing but vices. Therefore human law rightly allows some vices, by not repressing them.

I answer that, As stated above (90, A1,2), law is framed as a rule or measure of human acts. Now a measure should be homogeneous with that which it measures, as stated in Metaph. x, text. 3,4, since different things are measured by different measures. Wherefore laws imposed on men should also be in keeping with their condition, for, as Isidore says (Etym. v, 21), law should be "possible both according to nature, and according to the customs of the country." Now possibility or faculty of action is due to an interior habit or disposition: since the same thing is not possible to one who has not a virtuous habit, as is possible to one who has. Thus the same is not possible to a child as to a full-grown man: for which reason the law for children is not the same as for adults, since many things are permitted to children, which in an adult are punished by law or at any rate are open to blame. In like manner many things are permissible to men not perfect in virtue, which would be intolerable in a virtuous man.

Now human law is framed for a number of human beings, the majority of whom are not perfect in virtue. Wherefore human laws do not forbid all vices, from which the virtuous abstain, but only the more grievous vices, from which it is possible for the majority to abstain; and chiefly those that are to the hurt of others, without the prohibition of which human society could not be maintained: thus human law prohibits murder, theft and such like.

Reply to Objection 1. Audacity seems to refer to the assailing of others. Consequently it belongs to those sins chiefly whereby one's neighbor is injured: and these sins are forbidden by human law, as stated.

Reply to Objection 2. The purpose of human law is to lead men to virtue, not suddenly, but gradually. Wherefore it does not lay upon the multitude of imperfect men the burdens of those who are already virtuous, viz. that they should abstain from all evil. Otherwise these imperfect ones, being unable to bear such precepts, would break out into yet greater evils: thus it is written (Prov. 30:33): "He that violently bloweth his nose, bringeth out blood"; and (Matthew 9:17) that if "new wine," i.e. precepts of a perfect life, "is put into old bottles," i.e. into imperfect men, "the bottles break, and the wine runneth out," i.e. the precepts are despised, and those men, from contempt, break into evils worse still.

Reply to Objection 3. The natural law is a participation in us of the eternal law: while human law falls short of the eternal law. Now Augustine says (De Lib. Arb. i, 5): "The law which is framed for the government of states, allows and leaves unpunished many things that are punished by Divine providence. Nor, if this law does not attempt to do everything, is this a reason why it should be blamed for what it does." Wherefore, too, human law does not prohibit everything that is forbidden by the natural law.

ARTICLE 3. WHETHER HUMAN LAW PRESCRIBES ACTS OF ALL THE VIRTUES?

Objection 1. It would seem that human law does not prescribe acts of all the virtues. For vicious acts are contrary to acts of virtue. But human law does not prohibit all vices, as stated above (Article 2). Therefore neither does it prescribe all acts of virtue.

Objection 2. Further, a virtuous act proceeds from a virtue. But virtue is the end of law; so that whatever is from a virtue, cannot come under a precept of law. Therefore human law does not prescribe all acts of virtue.

Objection 3. Further, law is ordained to the common good, as stated above (Question 90, Article 2). But some acts of virtue are ordained, not to the common good, but to private good. Therefore the law does not prescribe all acts of virtue.

On the contrary, The Philosopher says (Ethic. v, 1) that the law "prescribes the performance of the acts of a brave man . . . and the acts of the temperate man . . . and the acts of the meek man: and in like manner as regards the other virtues and vices, prescribing the former, forbidding the latter."

I answer that, The species of virtues are distinguished by their objects, as explained above (54, 2; 60, 1; 62, 2). Now all the objects of virtues can be referred either to the private good of an individual, or to the common good of the multitude: thus matters of fortitude may be achieved either for the preservation of the city, or for upholding the rights of a friend, and in like manner with the other virtues. But law, as stated above (Question 90, Article 2) is ordained to the common good. Wherefore there is no virtue whose acts cannot be prescribed by the law. Nevertheless human law does not prescribe concerning all the acts of every virtue: but only in regard to those that are ordainable to the common good—either immediately, as when certain things are done directly for the common good—or mediately, as when a lawgiver prescribes certain things pertaining to good order, whereby the citizens are directed in the upholding of the common good of justice and peace.

Reply to Objection 1. Human law does not forbid all vicious acts, by the obligation of a precept, as neither does it prescribe all acts of virtue. But it forbids certain acts of each vice, just as it prescribes some acts of each virtue.

Reply to Objection 2. An act is said to be an act of virtue in two ways. First, from the fact that a man does something virtuous; thus the act of justice is to do what is right, and an act of fortitude is to do brave things: and in this way law prescribes certain acts of virtue. Secondly an act of virtue is when a man does a virtuous thing in a way in which a virtuous man does it. Such an act always proceeds from virtue: and it does not come under a precept of law, but is the end at which every lawgiver aims.

Reply to Objection 3. There is no virtue whose act is not ordainable to the common good, as stated above, either mediately or immediately.

ARTICLE 4. WHETHER HUMAN LAW BINDS A MAN IN CONSCIENCE?

Objection 1. It would seem that human law does not bind man in conscience. For an inferior power has no jurisdiction in a court of higher power. But the power of man, which frames human law, is beneath the Divine power. Therefore human law cannot impose its precept in a Divine court, such as is the court of conscience.

Objection 2. Further, the judgment of conscience depends chiefly on the commandments of God. But sometimes God's commandments are made void by human laws, according to Matthew 15:6: "You have made void the commandment of God for your tradition." Therefore human law does not bind a man in conscience.

Objection 3. Further, human laws often bring loss of character and injury on man, according to Isaiah 10:1 et seqq.: "Woe to them that make wicked laws, and when they write, write injustice; to oppress the poor in judgment, and do violence to the cause of the humble of My people." But it is lawful for anyone to avoid oppression and violence. Therefore human laws do not bind man in conscience.

On the contrary, It is written (1 Peter 2:19): "This is thankworthy, if for conscience . . . a man endure sorrows, suffering wrongfully."

I answer that, Laws framed by man are either just or unjust. If they be just, they have the power of binding in conscience, from the eternal law whence they are derived, according to Proverbs 8:15: "By Me kings reign, and lawgivers decree just things." Now laws are said to be just, both from the end, when, to wit, they are ordained to the common good—and from their author, that is to say, when the law that is made does not exceed the power of the lawgiver—and from their form, when, to wit, burdens are laid on the subjects, according to an equality of proportion and with a view to the common good. For, since one man is a part of the community, each man in all that he is and has, belongs to the community; just as a part, in all that it is, belongs to the whole; wherefore nature inflicts a loss on the part, in order to save the whole: so that on this account, such laws as these, which impose proportionate burdens, are just and binding in conscience, and are legal laws.

On the other hand laws may be unjust in two ways: first, by being contrary to human good, through being opposed to the things mentioned above—either in respect of the end, as when an authority imposes on his subjects burdensome laws, conducive, not to the common good, but rather to his own cupidity or vainglory—or in respect of the author, as when a man makes a law that goes beyond the power committed to him—or in respect of the form, as when burdens are imposed unequally on the community, although with a view to the common good. The like are acts of violence rather than laws; because, as Augustine says (De Lib. Arb. i, 5), "a law that is not just, seems to be no law at all." Wherefore such laws do not bind in conscience, except perhaps in order to avoid scandal or disturbance, for which cause a man should even yield his right, according to Matthew 5:40-41: "If a man . . . take away thy coat, let go thy cloak also unto him; and whosoever will force thee one mile, go with him other two."

Secondly, laws may be unjust through being opposed to the Divine good: such are the laws of tyrants inducing to idolatry, or to anything else contrary to the Divine law: and laws of this kind must nowise be observed, because, as stated in Acts 5:29, "we ought to obey God rather than man."

Reply to Objection 1. As the Apostle says (Romans 13:1-2), all human power is from God . . . "therefore he that resisteth the power," in matters that are within its scope, "resisteth the ordinance of God"; so that he becomes guilty according to his conscience.

Reply to Objection 2. This argument is true of laws that are contrary to the commandments of God, which is beyond the scope of (human) power. Wherefore in such matters human law should not be obeyed.

Reply to Objection 3. This argument is true of a law that inflicts unjust hurt on its subjects. The power that man holds from God does not extend to this: wherefore neither in such matters is man bound to obey the law, provided he avoid giving scandal or inflicting a more grievous hurt.

ARTICLE 5. WHETHER ALL ARE SUBJECT TO THE LAW?

Objection 1. It would seem that not all are subject to the law. For those alone are subject to a law for whom a law is made. But the Apostle says (1 Timothy 1:9): "The law is not made for the just man." Therefore the just are not subject to the law.

Objection 2. Further, Pope Urban says [Decretals. caus. xix, qu. 2]: "He that is guided by a private law need not for any reason be bound by the public law." Now all spiritual men are led by the private law of the Holy Ghost, for they are the sons of God, of whom it is said (Romans 8:14): "Whosoever are led by the Spirit of God, they are the sons of God." Therefore not all men are subject to human law.

Objection 3. Further, the jurist says [Pandect. Justin. i, ff., tit. 3, De Leg. et Senat.] that "the sovereign is exempt from the laws." But he that is exempt from the law is not bound thereby. Therefore not all are subject to the law.

On the contrary, The Apostle says (Romans 13:1): "Let every soul be subject to the higher powers." But subjection to a power seems to imply subjection to the laws framed by that power. Therefore all men should be subject to human law.

I answer that, As stated above (90, A1,2; 3, ad 2), the notion of law contains two things: first, that it is a rule of human acts; secondly, that it has coercive power. Wherefore a man may be subject to law in two ways. First, as the regulated is subject to the regulator: and, in this way, whoever is subject to a power, is subject to the law framed by that power. But it may happen in two ways that one is not subject to a power. In one way, by being altogether free from its authority: hence the subjects of one city or kingdom are not bound by the laws of the sovereign of another city or kingdom, since they are not subject to his authority. In another way, by being under a yet higher law; thus the subject of a proconsul should be ruled by his command, but not in those matters in which the subject receives his orders from the emperor: for in these matters, he is not bound by the mandate of the lower authority, since he is directed by that of a higher. In this way, one who is simply subject to a law, may not be a subject thereto in certain matters, in respect of which he is ruled by a higher law.

Secondly, a man is said to be subject to a law as the coerced is subject to the coercer. In this way the virtuous and righteous are not subject to the law, but only the wicked. Because coercion and violence are contrary to the will: but the will of the good is in harmony with the law, whereas the will of the wicked is discordant from it. Wherefore in this sense the good are not subject to the law, but only the wicked.

Reply to Objection 1. This argument is true of subjection by way of coercion: for, in this way, "the law is not made for the just men": because "they are a law to themselves," since they "show the work of the law written in their hearts," as the Apostle says (Romans 2:14-15). Consequently the law does not enforce itself upon them as it does on the wicked.

Reply to Objection 2. The law of the Holy Ghost is above all law framed by man: and therefore spiritual men, in so far as they are led by the law of the Holy Ghost, are not subject to the law in those matters that are inconsistent with the guidance of the Holy Ghost. Nevertheless the very fact that spiritual men are subject to law, is due to the leading of the Holy Ghost, according to 1 Peter 2:13: "Be ye subject . . . to every human creature for God's sake."

Reply to Objection 3. The sovereign is said to be "exempt from the law," as to its coercive power; since, properly speaking, no man is coerced by himself, and law has no coercive power save from the authority of the sovereign. Thus then is the sovereign said to be exempt from the law, because none is competent to pass sentence on him, if he acts against the law. Wherefore on Psalm 50:6: "To Thee only have I sinned," a gloss says that "there is no man who can judge the deeds of a king." But as to the directive force of law, the sovereign is subject to the law by his own will, according to the statement (Extra, De Constit. cap. Cum omnes) that "whatever law a man makes for another, he should keep himself. And a wise authority [Dionysius Cato, Dist. de Moribus] says: 'Obey the law that thou makest thyself.'" Moreover the Lord reproaches those who "say and do not"; and who "bind heavy burdens and lay them on men's shoulders, but with a finger of their own they will not move them" (Matthew 23:3-4). Hence, in the judgment of God, the sovereign is not exempt from the law, as to its directive force; but he should fulfil it to his own free-will and not of constraint. Again the sovereign is above the law, in so far as, when it is expedient, he can change the law, and dispense in it according to time and place.

ARTICLE 6. WHETHER HE WHO IS UNDER A LAW MAY ACT BESIDE THE LETTER OF THE LAW?

Objection 1. It seems that he who is subject to a law may not act beside the letter of the law. For Augustine says (De Vera Relig. 31): "Although men judge about temporal laws when they make them, yet when once they are made they must pass judgment not on them, but according to them." But if anyone disregard the letter of the law, saying that he observes the intention of the lawgiver, he seems to pass judgment on the law. Therefore it is not right for one who is under the law to disregard the letter of the law, in order to observe the intention of the lawgiver.

Objection 2. Further, he alone is competent to interpret the law who can make the law. But those who are subject to the law cannot make the law. Therefore they have no right to interpret the intention of the lawgiver, but should always act according to the letter of the law.

Objection 3. Further, every wise man knows how to explain his intention by words. But those who framed the laws should be reckoned wise: for Wisdom says (Proverbs 8:15): "By Me kings reign, and lawgivers decree just things." Therefore we should not judge of the intention of the lawgiver otherwise than by the words of the law.

On the contrary, Hilary says (De Trin. iv): "The meaning of what is said is according to the motive for saying it: because things are not subject to speech, but speech to things." Therefore we should take account of the motive of the lawgiver, rather than of his very words.

I answer that, As stated above (Article 4), every law is directed to the common weal of men, and derives the force and nature of law accordingly. Hence the jurist says [Pandect. Justin. lib. i, ff., tit. 3, De Leg. et Senat.]: "By no reason of law, or favor of equity, is it allowable for us to interpret harshly, and render burdensome, those useful measures which have been enacted for the welfare of man." Now it happens often that the observance of some point of law conduces to the common weal in the majority of instances, and yet, in some cases, is very hurtful. Since then the lawgiver cannot have in view every single case, he shapes the law according to what happens most frequently, by directing his attention to the common good. Wherefore if a case arise wherein the observance of that law would be hurtful to the general welfare, it should not be observed. For instance, suppose that in a besieged city it be an established law that the gates of the city are to be kept closed, this is good for public welfare as a general rule: but, it were to happen that the enemy are in pursuit of certain citizens, who are defenders of the city, it would be a great loss to the city, if the gates were not opened to them: and so in that case the gates ought to be opened, contrary to the letter of the law, in order to maintain the common weal, which the lawgiver had in view.

Nevertheless it must be noted, that if the observance of the law according to the letter does not involve any sudden risk needing instant remedy, it is not competent for everyone to expound what is useful and what is not useful to the city: those alone can do this who are in authority, and who, on account of such like cases, have the power to dispense from the laws. If, however, the peril be so sudden as not to allow of the delay involved by referring the matter to authority, the mere necessity brings with it a dispensation, since necessity knows no law.

Reply to Objection 1. He who in a case of necessity acts beside the letter of the law, does not judge the law; but of a particular case in which he sees that the letter of the law is not to be observed.

Reply to Objection 2. He who follows the intention of the lawgiver, does not interpret the law simply; but in a case in which it is evident, by reason of the manifest harm, that the lawgiver intended otherwise. For if it be a matter of doubt, he must either act according to the letter of the law, or consult those in power.

Reply to Objection 3. No man is so wise as to be able to take account of every single case; wherefore he is not able sufficiently to express in words all those things that are suitable for the end he has in view. And even if a lawgiver were able to take all the cases into consideration, he ought not to mention them all, in order to avoid confusion: but should frame the law according to that which is of most common occurrence.

QUESTION 97. CHANGE IN LAWS

ARTICLE 1. WHETHER HUMAN LAW SHOULD BE CHANGED IN ANY WAY?

Objection 1. It would seem that human law should not be changed in any way at all. Because human law is derived from the natural law, as stated above (Question 95, Article 2). But the natural law endures unchangeably. Therefore human law should also remain without any change.

Objection 2. Further, as the Philosopher says (Ethic. v, 5), a measure should be absolutely stable. But human law is the measure of human acts, as stated above (90, A1,2). Therefore it should remain without change.

Objection 3. Further, it is of the essence of law to be just and right, as stated above (Question 95, Article 2). But that which is right once is right always. Therefore that which is law once, should be always law.

On the contrary, Augustine says (De Lib. Arb. i, 6): "A temporal law, however just, may be justly changed in course of time."

I answer that, As stated above (Question 91, Article 3), human law is a dictate of reason, whereby human acts are directed. Thus there may be two causes for the just change of human law: one on the part of reason; the other on the part of man whose acts are regulated by law. The cause on the part of reason is that it seems natural to human reason to advance gradually from the imperfect to the perfect. Hence, in speculative sciences, we see that the teaching of the early philosophers was imperfect, and that it was afterwards perfected by those who succeeded them. So also in practical matters: for those who first endeavored to discover something useful for the human community, not being able by themselves to take everything into consideration, set up certain institutions which were deficient in many ways; and these were changed by subsequent lawgivers who made institutions that might prove less frequently deficient in respect of the common weal.

On the part of man, whose acts are regulated by law, the law can be rightly changed on account of the changed condition of man, to whom different things are expedient according to the difference of his condition. An example is proposed by Augustine (De Lib. Arb. i, 6): "If the people have a sense of moderation and responsibility, and are most careful guardians of the common weal, it is right to enact a law allowing such a people to choose their own magistrates for the government of the commonwealth. But if, as time goes on, the same people become so corrupt as to sell their votes, and entrust the government to scoundrels and criminals; then the right of appointing their public officials is rightly forfeit to such a people, and the choice devolves to a few good men."

Reply to Objection 1. The natural law is a participation of the eternal law, as stated above (Question 91, Article 2), and therefore endures without change, owing to the unchangeableness and perfection of the Divine Reason, the Author of nature. But the reason of man is changeable and imperfect: wherefore his law is subject to change. Moreover the natural law contains certain universal precepts, which are everlasting: whereas human law contains certain particular precepts, according to various emergencies.

Reply to Objection 2. A measure should be as enduring as possible. But nothing can be absolutely unchangeable in things that are subject to change. And therefore human law cannot be altogether unchangeable.

Reply to Objection 3. In corporal things, right is predicated absolutely: and therefore, as far as itself is concerned, always remains right. But right is predicated of law with reference to the common weal, to which one and the same thing is not always adapted, as stated above: wherefore rectitude of this kind is subject to change.

ARTICLE 2. WHETHER HUMAN LAW SHOULD ALWAYS BE CHANGED, WHENEVER SOMETHING BETTER OCCURS?

Objection 1. It would seem that human law should be changed, whenever something better occurs. Because human laws are devised by human reason, like other arts. But in the other arts, the tenets of former times give place to others, if something better occurs. Therefore the same should apply to human laws.

Objection 2. Further, by taking note of the past we can provide for the future. Now unless human laws had been changed when it was found possible to improve them, considerable inconvenience would have ensued; because the laws of old were crude in many points. Therefore it seems that laws should be changed, whenever anything better occurs to be enacted.

Objection 3. Further, human laws are enacted about single acts of man. But we cannot acquire perfect knowledge in singular matters, except by experience, which "requires time," as stated in Ethic. ii. Therefore it seems that as time goes on it is possible for something better to occur for legislation.

On the contrary, It is stated in the Decretals (Dist. xii, 5): "It is absurd, and a detestable shame, that we should suffer those traditions to be changed which we have received from the fathers of old."

I answer that, As stated above (Article 1), human law is rightly changed, in so far as such change is conducive to the common weal. But, to a certain extent, the mere change of law is of itself prejudicial to the common good: because custom avails much for the observance of laws, seeing that what is done contrary to general custom, even in slight matters, is looked upon as grave. Consequently, when a law is changed, the binding power of the law is diminished, in so far as custom is abolished. Wherefore human law should never be changed, unless, in some way or other, the common weal be compensated according to the extent of the harm done in this respect. Such compensation may arise either from some very great and every evident benefit conferred by the new enactment; or from the extreme urgency of the case, due to the fact that either the existing law is clearly unjust, or its observance extremely harmful. Wherefore the jurist says [Pandect. Justin. lib. i, ff., tit. 4, De Constit. Princip.] that "in establishing new laws, there should be evidence of the benefit to be derived, before departing from a law which has long been considered just."

Reply to Objection 1. Rules of art derive their force from reason alone: and therefore whenever something better occurs, the rule followed hitherto should be changed. But "laws derive very great force from custom," as the Philosopher states (Polit. ii, 5): consequently they should not be quickly changed.

Reply to Objection 2. This argument proves that laws ought to be changed: not in view of any improvement, but for the sake of a great benefit or in a case of great urgency, as stated above. This answer applies also to the Third Objection.

ARTICLE 3. WHETHER CUSTOM CAN OBTAIN FORCE OF LAW?

Objection 1. It would seem that custom cannot obtain force of law, nor abolish a law. Because human law is derived from the natural law and from the Divine law, as stated above (93, 3; 95, 2). But human custom cannot change either the law of nature or the Divine law. Therefore neither can it change human law.

Objection 2. Further, many evils cannot make one good. But he who first acted against the law, did evil. Therefore by multiplying such acts, nothing good is the result. Now a law is something good; since it is a rule of human acts. Therefore law is not abolished by custom, so that the mere custom should obtain force of law.

Objection 3. Further, the framing of laws belongs to those public men whose business it is to govern the community; wherefore private individuals cannot make laws. But custom grows by the acts of private individuals. Therefore custom cannot obtain force of law, so as to abolish the law.

On the contrary, Augustine says (Ep. ad Casulan. xxxvi): "The customs of God's people and the institutions of our ancestors are to be considered as laws.

And those who throw contempt on the customs of the Church ought to be punished as those who disobey the law of God."

I answer that, All law proceeds from the reason and will of the lawgiver; the Divine and natural laws from the reasonable will of God; the human law from the will of man, regulated by reason. Now just as human reason and will, in practical matters, may be made manifest by speech, so may they be made known by deeds: since seemingly a man chooses as good that which he carries into execution. But it is evident that by human speech, law can be both changed and expounded, in so far as it manifests the interior movement and thought of human reason. Wherefore by actions also, especially if they be repeated, so as to make a custom, law can be changed and expounded; and also something can be established which obtains force of law, in so far as by repeated external actions, the inward movement of the will, and concepts of reason are most effectually declared; for when a thing is done again and again, it seems to proceed from a deliberate judgment of reason. Accordingly, custom has the force of a law, abolishes law, and is the interpreter of law.

Reply to Objection 1. The natural and Divine laws proceed from the Divine will, as stated above. Wherefore they cannot be changed by a custom proceeding from the will of man, but only by Divine authority. Hence it is that no custom can prevail over the Divine or natural laws: for Isidore says (Synon. ii, 16): "Let custom yield to authority: evil customs should be eradicated by law and reason."

Reply to Objection 2. As stated above (Question 96, Article 6), human laws fail in some cases: wherefore it is possible sometimes to act beside the law; namely, in a case where the law fails; yet the act will not be evil. And when such cases are multiplied, by reason of some change in man, then custom shows that the law is no longer useful: just as it might be declared by the verbal promulgation of a law to the contrary. If, however, the same reason remains, for which the law was useful hitherto, then it is not the custom that prevails against the law, but the law that overcomes the custom: unless perhaps the sole reason for the law seeming useless, be that it is not "possible according to the custom of the country" [95, 3], which has been stated to be one of the conditions of law. For it is not easy to set aside the custom of a whole people.

Reply to Objection 3. The people among whom a custom is introduced may be of two conditions. For if they are free, and able to make their own laws, the consent of the whole people expressed by a custom counts far more in favor of a particular observance, that does the authority of the sovereign, who has not the power to frame laws, except as representing the people. Wherefore although each individual cannot make laws, yet the whole people can. If however the people have not the free power to make their own laws, or to abolish a law made by a higher authority; nevertheless with such a people a prevailing custom obtains force of law, in so far as it is tolerated by those to whom it belongs to make laws for that people: because by the very fact that they tolerate it they seem to approve of that which is introduced by custom.

ARTICLE 4. WHETHER THE RULERS OF THE PEOPLE CAN DISPENSE FROM HUMAN LAWS?

Objection 1. It would seem that the rulers of the people cannot dispense from human laws. For the law is established for the "common weal," as Isidore says (Etym. v, 21). But the common good should not be set aside for the private convenience of an individual: because, as the Philosopher says (Ethic. i, 2), "the good of the nation is more godlike than the good of one man." Therefore it seems that a man should not be dispensed from acting in compliance with the general law.

Objection 2. Further, those who are placed over others are commanded as follows (Deuteronomy 1:17): "You shall hear the little as well as the great; neither shall you respect any man's person, because it is the judgment of God." But to allow one man to do that which is equally forbidden to all, seems to be respect of persons. Therefore the rulers of a community cannot grant such dispensations, since this is against a precept of the Divine law.

Objection 3. Further, human law, in order to be just, should accord with the natural and Divine laws: else it would not "foster religion," nor be "helpful to discipline," which is requisite to the nature of law, as laid down by Isidore (Etym. v, 3). But no man can dispense from the Divine and natural laws. Neither, therefore, can he dispense from the human law.

On the contrary, The Apostle says (1 Corinthians 9:17): "A dispensation is committed to me."

I answer that, Dispensation, properly speaking, denotes a measuring out to individuals of some common goods: thus the head of a household is called a dispenser, because to each member of the household he distributes work and necessaries of life in due weight and measure. Accordingly in every community a man is said to dispense, from the very fact that he directs how some general precept is to be fulfilled by each individual. Now it happens at times that a precept, which is conducive to the common weal as a general rule, is not good for a particular individual, or in some particular case, either because it would hinder some greater good, or because it would be the occasion of some evil, as explained above (Question 96, Article 6). But it would be dangerous to leave this to the discretion of each individual, except perhaps by reason of an evident and sudden emergency, as stated above (Question 96, Article 6). Consequently he who is placed over a community is empowered to dispense in a human law that rests upon his authority, so that, when the law fails in its application to persons or circumstances, he may allow the precept of the law not to be observed. If however he grant this permission without any such reason, and of his mere will, he will be an unfaithful or an imprudent dispenser: unfaithful, if he has not the common good in view; imprudent, if he ignores the reasons for granting dispensations. Hence Our Lord says (Luke 12:42): "Who, thinkest thou, is the faithful and wise dispenser [Douay: steward], whom his lord setteth over his family?"

Reply to Objection 1. When a person is dispensed from observing the general law, this should not be done to the prejudice of, but with the intention of benefiting, the common good.

Reply to Objection 2. It is not respect of persons if unequal measures are served out to those who are themselves unequal. Wherefore when the condition of any person requires that he should reasonably receive special treatment, it is not respect of persons if he be the object of special favor.

Reply to Objection 3. Natural law, so far as it contains general precepts, which never fail, does not allow of dispensations. In other precepts, however, which are as conclusions of the general precepts, man sometimes grants a dispensation: for instance, that a loan should not be paid back to the betrayer of his country, or something similar. But to the Divine law each man stands as a private person to the public law to which he is subject. Wherefore just as none can dispense from public human law, except the man from whom the law derives its authority, or his delegate; so, in the precepts of the Divine law, which are from God, none can dispense but God, or the man to whom He may give special power for that purpose.

QUESTION 100. THE MORAL PRECEPTS OF THE OLD LAW

ARTICLE 1. WHETHER ALL THE MORAL PRECEPTS OF THE OLD LAW BELONG TO THE LAW OF NATURE?

Objection 1. It would seem that not all the moral precepts belong to the law of nature. For it is written (Sirach 17:9): "Moreover He gave them instructions, and the law of life for an inheritance." But instruction is in contradistinction to the law of nature; since the law of nature is not learnt, but instilled by natural instinct. Therefore not all the moral precepts belong to the natural law.

Objection 2. Further, the Divine law is more perfect than human law. But human law adds certain things concerning good morals, to those that belong to the law of nature: as is evidenced by the fact that the natural law is the same in all men, while these moral institutions are various for various people. Much more reason therefore was there why the Divine law should add to the law of nature, ordinances pertaining to good morals.

Objection 3. Further, just as natural reason leads to good morals in certain matters, so does faith: hence it is written (Galatians 5:6) that faith "worketh by charity." But faith is not included in the law of nature; since that which is of faith is above nature. Therefore not all the moral precepts of the Divine law belong to the law of nature.

On the contrary, The Apostle says (Romans 2:14) that "the Gentiles, who have not the Law, do by nature those things that are of the Law": which must be understood of things pertaining to good morals. Therefore all the moral precepts of the Law belong to the law of nature.

I answer that, The moral precepts, distinct from the ceremonial and judicial precepts, are about things pertaining of their very nature to good morals. Now since human morals depend on their relation to reason, which is the proper principle of human acts, those morals are called good which accord with reason, and those are called bad which are discordant from reason. And as every judgment of speculative reason proceeds from the natural knowledge of first principles, so every judgment of practical reason proceeds from principles known naturally, as stated above (94, A2,4): from which principles one may proceed in various ways to judge of various matters. For some matters connected with human actions are so evident, that after very little consideration one is able at once to approve or disapprove of them by means of these general first principles: while some matters cannot be the subject of judgment without much consideration of the various circumstances, which all are not competent to do carefully, but only those who are wise: just as it is not possible for all to consider the particular conclusions of sciences, but only for those who are versed in philosophy: and lastly there are some matters of which man cannot judge unless he be helped by Divine instruction; such as the articles of faith.

It is therefore evident that since the moral precepts are about matters which concern good morals; and since good morals are those which are in accord with reason; and since also every judgment of human reason must needs by derived in some way from natural reason; it follows, of necessity, that all the moral precepts belong to the law of nature; but not all in the same way. For there are certain things which the natural reason of every man, of its own accord and at once, judges to be done or not to be done: e.g. "Honor thy father and thy mother," and "Thou shalt not kill, Thou shalt not steal": and these belong to the law of nature absolutely. And there are certain things which, after a more careful consideration, wise men deem obligatory. Such belong to the law of nature, yet so that they need to be inculcated, the wiser teaching the less wise: e.g. "Rise up before the hoary head, and honor the person of the aged man," and the like. And there are some things, to judge of which, human reason needs Divine instruction, whereby we are taught about the things of God: e.g. "Thou shalt not make to thyself a graven thing, nor the likeness of anything; Thou shalt not take the name of the Lord thy God in vain."

This suffices for the Replies to the Objections.

ARTICLE 2. WHETHER THE MORAL PRECEPTS OF THE LAW ARE ABOUT ALL THE ACTS OF VIRTUE?

Objection 1. It would seem that the moral precepts of the Law are not about all the acts of virtue. For observance of the precepts of the Old Law is called justification, according to Psalm 118:8: "I will keep Thy justifications." But justification is the execution of justice. Therefore the moral precepts are only about acts of justice.

Objection 2. Further, that which comes under a precept has the character of a duty. But the character of duty belongs to justice alone and to none of the other virtues, for the proper act of justice consists in rendering to each one his due. Therefore the precepts of the moral law are not about the acts of the other virtues, but only about the acts of justice.

Objection 3. Further, every law is made for the common good, as Isidore says (Etym. v, 21). But of all the virtues justice alone regards the common good, as the Philosopher says (Ethic. v, 1). Therefore the moral precepts are only about the acts of justice.

On the contrary, Ambrose says (De Paradiso viii) that "a sin is a transgression of the Divine law, and a disobedience to the commandments of heaven." But there are sins contrary to all the acts of virtue. Therefore it belongs to Divine law to direct all the acts of virtue.

I answer that, Since the precepts of the Law are ordained to the common good, as stated above (Question 90, Article 2), the precepts of the Law must needs be diversified according to the various kinds of community: hence the Philosopher (Polit. iv, 1) teaches that the laws which are made in a city which is ruled by a king must be different from the laws of a city which is ruled by the people, or by a few powerful men in the city. Now human law is ordained for one kind of community, and the Divine law for another kind. Because human law is ordained for the civil community, implying mutual duties of man and his fellows: and men are ordained to one another by outward acts, whereby men live in communion with one another. This life in common of man with man pertains to justice, whose proper function consists in directing the human community. Wherefore human law makes precepts only about acts of justice; and if it commands acts of other virtues, this is only in so far as they assume the nature of justice, as the Philosopher explains (Ethic. v, 1).

But the community for which the Divine law is ordained, is that of men in relation to God, either in this life or in the life to come. And therefore the Divine law proposes precepts about all those matters whereby men are well ordered in their relations to God. Now man is united to God by his reason or mind, in which is God's image. Wherefore the Divine law proposes precepts about all those matters whereby human reason is well ordered. But this is effected by the acts of all the virtues: since the intellectual virtues set in good order the acts of the reason in themselves: while the moral virtues set in good order the acts of the reason in reference to the interior passions and exterior actions. It is therefore evident that the Divine law fittingly proposes precepts about the acts of all the virtues: yet so that certain matters, without which the order of virtue, which is the order of reason, cannot even exist, come under an obligation of precept; while other matters, which pertain to the well-being of perfect virtue, come under an admonition of counsel.

Reply to Objection 1. The fulfilment of the commandments of the Law, even of those which are about the acts of the other virtues, has the character of justification, inasmuch as it is just that man should obey God: or again, inasmuch as it is just that all that belongs to man should be subject to reason.

Reply to Objection 2. Justice properly so called regards the duty of one man to another: but all the other virtues regard the duty of the lower powers to reason. It is in relation to this latter duty that the Philosopher speaks (Ethic. v, 11) of a kind of metaphorical justice.

The Reply to the Third Objection is clear from what has been said about the different kinds of community.

QUESTION 105. THE REASON FOR THE JUDICIAL PRECEPTS

ARTICLE 1. WHETHER THE OLD LAW ENJOINED FITTING PRECEPTS CONCERNING RULERS?

Objection 1. It would seem that the Old Law made unfitting precepts concerning rulers. Because, as the Philosopher says (Polit. iii, 4), "the ordering of the people depends mostly on the chief ruler." But the Law contains no precept relating to the institution of the chief ruler; and yet we find therein prescriptions concerning the inferior rulers: firstly (Exodus 18:21): "Provide out of all the people wise [Vulgate: 'able'] men," etc.; again (Numbers 11:16): "Gather unto Me seventy men of the ancients of Israel"; and again (Deuteronomy 1:13): "Let Me have from among you wise and understanding men," etc. Therefore the Law provided insufficiently in regard to the rulers of the people.

Objection 2. Further, "The best gives of the best," as Plato states (Tim. ii). Now the best ordering of a city or of any nation is to be ruled by a king: because this kind of government approaches nearest in resemblance to the Divine government, whereby God rules the world from the beginning. Therefore the Law should have set a king over the people, and they should not have been allowed a choice in the matter, as indeed they were allowed (Deuteronomy 17:14-15): "When thou . . . shalt say: I will set a king over me . . . thou shalt set him," etc.

Objection 3. Further, according to Matthew 12:25: "Every kingdom divided against itself shall be made desolate": a saying which was verified in the Jewish people, whose destruction was brought about by the division of the kingdom. But the Law should aim chiefly at things pertaining to the general well-being of the people. Therefore it should have forbidden the kingdom to be divided under two kings: nor should this have been introduced even by Divine authority; as we read of its being introduced by the authority of the prophet Ahias the Silonite (1 Kings 11:29, seqq.).

Objection 4. Further, just as priests are instituted for the benefit of the people in things concerning God, as stated in Hebrews 5:1; so are rulers set up for the benefit of the people in human affairs. But certain things were allotted as a means of livelihood for the priests and Levites of the Law: such as the tithes and first-fruits, and many like things. Therefore in like manner certain things should have been determined for the livelihood of the rulers of the people: the more that they were forbidden to accept presents, as is clearly stated in Exodus 23:8: "You shall not [Vulgate: 'Neither shalt thou'] take bribes, which even blind the wise, and pervert the words of the just."

Objection 5. Further, as a kingdom is the best form of government, so is tyranny the most corrupt. But when the Lord appointed the king, He established a tyrannical law; for it is written (1 Samuel 8:11): "This will be the right of the king, that shall reign over you: He will take your sons," etc. Therefore the Law made unfitting provision with regard to the institution of rulers.

On the contrary, The people of Israel is commended for the beauty of its order (Numbers 24:5): "How beautiful are thy tabernacles, O Jacob, and thy tents." But the beautiful ordering of a people depends on the right establishment of its rulers. Therefore the Law made right provision for the people with regard to its rulers.

I answer that, Two points are to be observed concerning the right ordering of rulers in a city or nation. One is that all should take some share in the government: for this form of constitution ensures peace among the people, commends itself to all, and is most enduring, as stated in Polit. ii, 6. The other point is to be observed in respect of the kinds of government, or the different ways in which the constitutions are established. For whereas these differ in kind, as the Philosopher states (Polit. iii, 5), nevertheless the first place is held by the "kingdom," where the power of government is vested in one; and "aristocracy," which signifies government by the best, where the power of government is vested in a few. Accordingly, the best form of government is in a city or kingdom, where one is given the power to preside over all; while under him are others having governing powers: and yet a government of this kind is shared by all, both because all are eligible to govern, and because the rules are chosen by all. For this is the best form of polity, being partly kingdom, since there is one at the head of all; partly aristocracy, in so far as a number of persons are set in authority; partly democracy, i.e. government by the people, in so far as the rulers can be chosen from the people, and the people have the right to choose their rulers.

Such was the form of government established by the Divine Law. For Moses and his successors governed the people in such a way that each of them was ruler over all; so that there was a kind of kingdom. Moreover, seventy-two men were chosen, who were elders in virtue: for it is written (Deuteronomy 1:15): "I took out of your tribes wise and honorable, and appointed them rulers": so that there was an element of aristocracy. But it was a democratical government in so far as the rulers were chosen from all the people; for it is written (Exodus 18:21): "Provide out of all the people wise [Vulgate: 'able'] men," etc.; and, again, in so far as they were chosen by the people; wherefore it is written (Deuteronomy 1:13): "Let me have from among you wise [Vulgate: 'able'] men," etc. Consequently it is evident that the ordering of the rulers was well provided for by the Law.

Reply to Objection 1. This people was governed under the special care of God: wherefore it is written (Deuteronomy 7:6): "The Lord thy God hath chosen thee to be His peculiar people": and this is why the Lord reserved to Himself the institution of the chief ruler. For this too did Moses pray (Numbers 27:16): "May the Lord the God of the spirits of all the flesh provide a man, that may be over this multitude." Thus by God's orders Josue was set at the head in place of Moses; and we read about each of the judges who succeeded Josue that God "raised . . . up a savior" for the people, and that "the spirit of the Lord was" in them (Judges 3:9-15). Hence the Lord did not leave the choice of a king to the people; but reserved this to Himself, as appears from Deuteronomy 17:15: "Thou shalt set him whom the Lord thy God shall choose."

Reply to Objection 2. A kingdom is the best form of government of the people, so long as it is not corrupt. But since the power granted to a king is so great, it easily degenerates into tyranny, unless he to whom this power is given be a very virtuous man: for it is only the virtuous man that conducts himself well in the midst of prosperity, as the Philosopher observes (Ethic. iv, 3). Now perfect virtue is to be found in few: and especially were the Jews inclined to cruelty and avarice, which vices above all turn men into tyrants. Hence from the very first the Lord did not set up the kingly authority with full power, but gave them judges and governors to rule them. But afterwards when the people asked Him to do so, being indignant with them, so to speak, He granted them a king, as is clear from His words to Samuel (1 Samuel 8:7): "They have not rejected thee, but Me, that I should not reign over them."

Nevertheless, as regards the appointment of a king, He did establish the manner of election from the very beginning (Deuteronomy 17:14, seqq.): and then He determined two points: first, that in choosing a king they should wait for the Lord's decision; and that they should not make a man of another nation king, because such kings are wont to take little interest in the people they are set over, and consequently to have no care for their welfare: secondly, He prescribed how the king after his appointment should behave, in regard to himself; namely, that he should not accumulate chariots and horses, nor wives, nor immense wealth: because through craving for such things princes become tyrants and forsake justice. He also appointed the manner in which they were to conduct themselves towards God: namely, that they should continually read and ponder on God's Law, and should ever fear and obey God. Moreover, He decided how they should behave towards their subjects: namely, that they should not proudly despise them, or ill-treat them, and that they should not depart from the paths of justice.

Reply to Objection 3. The division of the kingdom, and a number of kings, was rather a punishment inflicted on that people for their many dissensions, especially against the just rule of David, than a benefit conferred on them for their profit. Hence it is written (Hosea 13:11): "I will give thee a king in My wrath"; and (Hosea 8:4): "They have reigned, but not by Me: they have been princes, and I knew not."

Reply to Objection 4. The priestly office was bequeathed by succession from father to son: and this, in order that it might be held in greater respect, if not any man from the people could become a priest: since honor was given to them out of reverence for the divine worship. Hence it was necessary to put aside certain things for them both as to tithes and as to first-fruits, and, again, as to oblations and sacrifices, that they might be afforded a means of livelihood. On the other hand, the rulers, as stated above, were chosen from the whole people; wherefore they had their own possessions, from which to derive a living: and so much the more, since the Lord forbade even a king to have superabundant wealth to make too much show of magnificence: both because he could scarcely avoid the excesses of pride and tyranny, arising from such things, and because, if the rulers were not very rich, and if their office involved much work and anxiety, it would not tempt the ambition of the common people; and would not become an occasion of sedition.

Reply to Objection 5. That right was not given to the king by Divine institution: rather was it foretold that kings would usurp that right, by framing unjust laws, and by degenerating into tyrants who preyed on their subjects. This is clear from the context that follows: "And you shall be his slaves [Douay: 'servants']": which is significative of tyranny, since a tyrant rules is subjects as though they were his slaves. Hence Samuel spoke these words to deter them from asking for a king; since the narrative continues: "But the people would not hear the voice of Samuel." It may happen, however, that even a good king, without being a tyrant, may take away the sons, and make them tribunes and centurions; and may take many things from his subjects in order to secure the common weal.

ARTICLE 2. WHETHER THE JUDICIAL PRECEPTS WERE SUITABLY FRAMED AS TO THE RELATIONS OF ONE MAN WITH ANOTHER?

Objection 1. It would seem that the judicial precepts were not suitably framed as regards the relations of one man with another. Because men cannot live together in peace, if one man takes what belongs to another. But this seems to have been approved by the Law: since it is written (Deuteronomy 23:24): "Going into thy neighbor's vineyard, thou mayest eat as many grapes as thou pleasest." Therefore the Old Law did not make suitable provisions for man's peace.

Objection 2. Further, one of the chief causes of the downfall of states has been the holding of property by women, as the Philosopher says (Polit. ii, 6). But this was introduced by the Old Law; for it is written (Numbers 27:8): "When a man dieth without a son, his inheritance shall pass to his daughter." Therefore the Law made unsuitable provision for the welfare of the people.

Objection 3. Further, it is most conducive to the preservation of human society that men may provide themselves with necessaries by buying and selling, as stated in Polit. i. But the Old Law took away the force of sales; since it prescribes that in the 50th year of the jubilee all that is sold shall return to the vendor (Leviticus 25:28). Therefore in this matter the Law gave the people an unfitting command.

Objection 4. Further, man's needs require that men should be ready to lend: which readiness ceases if the creditors do not return the pledges: hence it is written (Sirach 29:10): "Many have refused to lend, not out of wickedness, but they were afraid to be defrauded without cause." And yet this was encouraged by the Law. First, because it prescribed (Deuteronomy 15:2): "He to whom any thing is owing from his friend or neighbor or brother, cannot demand it again, because it is the year of remission of the Lord"; and (Exodus 22:15) it is stated that if a borrowed animal should die while the owner is present, the borrower is not bound to make restitution. Secondly, because the security acquired through the pledge is lost: for it is written (Deuteronomy 24:10): "When thou shalt demand of thy neighbor any thing that he oweth thee, thou shalt not go into his house to take away a pledge"; and again (Deuteronomy 24:12-13): "The pledge shall not lodge with thee that night, but thou shalt restore it to him presently." Therefore the Law made insufficient provision in the matter of loans.

Objection 5. Further, considerable risk attaches to goods deposited with a fraudulent depositary: wherefore great caution should be observed in such matters: hence it is stated in 2 Maccabees 3:15 that "the priests . . . called upon Him from heaven, Who made the law concerning things given to be kept, that He would preserve them safe, for them that had deposited them." But the precepts of the Old Law observed little caution in regard to deposits: since it is prescribed (Exodus 22:10-11) that when goods deposited are lost, the owner is to stand by the oath of the depositary. Therefore the Law made unsuitable provision in this matter.

Objection 6. Further, just as a workman offers his work for hire, so do men let houses and so forth. But there is no need for the tenant to pay his rent as soon as he takes a house. Therefore it seems an unnecessarily hard prescription (Leviticus 19:13) that "the wages of him that hath been hired by thee shall not abide with thee until morning."

Objection 7. Further, since there is often pressing need for a judge, it should be easy to gain access to one. It was therefore unfitting that the Law (Deuteronomy 17:8-9) should command them to go to a fixed place to ask for judgment on doubtful matters.

Objection 8. Further, it is possible that not only two, but three or more, should agree to tell a lie. Therefore it is unreasonably stated (Deuteronomy 19:15) that "in the mouth of two or three witnesses every word shall stand."

Objection 9. Further, punishment should be fixed according to the gravity of the fault: for which reason also it is written (Deuteronomy 25:2): "According to the measure of the sin, shall the measure also of the stripes be." Yet the Law fixed unequal punishments for certain faults: for it is written (Exodus 22:1) that the thief "shall restore five oxen for one ox, and four sheep for one sheep." Moreover, certain slight offenses are severely punished: thus (Numbers 15:32, seqq.) a man is stoned for gathering sticks on the sabbath day: and (Deuteronomy 21:18, seqq.) the unruly son is commanded to be stoned on account of certain small transgressions, viz. because "he gave himself to revelling . . . and banquetings." Therefore the Law prescribed punishments in an unreasonable manner.

Objection 10. Further, as Augustine says (De Civ. Dei xxi, 11), "Tully writes that the laws recognize eight forms of punishment, indemnity, prison, stripes, retaliation, public disgrace, exile, death, slavery." Now some of these were prescribed by the Law. "Indemnity," as when a thief was condemned to make restitution fivefold or fourfold. "Prison," as when (Numbers 15:34) a certain man is ordered to be imprisoned. "Stripes"; thus (Deuteronomy 25:2), "if they see that the offender be worthy of stripes; they shall lay him down, and shall cause him to be beaten before them." "Public disgrace" was brought on to him who refused to take to himself the wife of his deceased brother, for she took "off his shoe from his foot, and" did "spit in his face" (Deuteronomy 25:9). It prescribed the "death" penalty, as is clear from (Leviticus 20:9): "He that curseth his father, or mother, dying let him die." The Law also recognized the "lex talionis," by prescribing (Exodus 21:24): "Eye for eye, tooth for tooth." Therefore it seems unreasonable that the Law should not have inflicted the two other punishments, viz. "exile" and "slavery."

Objection 11. Further, no punishment is due except for a fault. But dumb animals cannot commit a fault. Therefore the Law is unreasonable in punishing them (Exodus 21:29): "If the ox ... shall kill a man or a woman," it "shall be stoned": and (Leviticus 20:16): "The woman that shall lie under any beast, shall be killed together with the same." Therefore it seems that matters pertaining to the relations of one man with another were unsuitably regulated by the Law.

Objection 12. Further, the Lord commanded (Exodus 21:12) a murderer to be punished with death. But the death of a dumb animal is reckoned of much less account than the slaying of a man. Hence murder cannot be sufficiently punished by the slaying of a dumb animal. Therefore it is unfittingly prescribed (Deuteronomy 21:1-4) that "when there shall be found ... the corpse of a man slain, and it is not known who is guilty of the murder ... the ancients" of the nearest city "shall take a heifer of the herd, that hath not drawn in the yoke, nor ploughed the ground, and they shall bring her into a rough and stony valley, that never was ploughed, nor sown; and there they shall strike off the head of the heifer."

On the contrary, It is recalled as a special blessing (Psalm 147:20) that "He hath not done in like manner to every nation; and His judgments He hath not made manifest to them."

I answer that, As Augustine says (De Civ. Dei ii, 21), quoting Tully, "a nation is a body of men united together by consent to the law and by community of welfare." Consequently it is of the essence of a nation that the mutual relations of the citizens be ordered by just laws. Now the relations of one man with another are twofold: some are effected under the guidance of those in authority: others are effected by the will of private individuals. And since whatever is subject to the power of an individual can be disposed of according to his will, hence it is that the decision of matters between one man and another, and the punishment of evildoers, depend on the direction of those in authority, to whom men are subject. On the other hand, the power of private persons is exercised over the things they possess: and consequently their dealings with one another, as regards such things, depend on their own will, for instance in buying, selling, giving, and so forth. Now the Law provided sufficiently in respect of each of these relations between one man and another. For it established judges, as is clearly indicated in Deuteronomy 16:18: "Thou shalt appoint judges and magistrates in all its [Vulgate: 'thy'] gates . . . that they may judge the people with just judgment." It is also directed the manner of pronouncing just judgments, according to Deuteronomy 1:16-17: "Judge that which is just, whether he be one of your own country or a stranger: there shall be no difference of persons." It also removed an occasion of pronouncing unjust judgment, by forbidding judges to accept bribes (Exodus 23:8; Deuteronomy 16:19). It prescribed the number of witnesses, viz. two or three: and it appointed certain punishments to certain crimes, as we shall state farther on (ad 10).

But with regard to possessions, it is a very good thing, says the Philosopher (Polit. ii, 2) that the things possessed should be distinct, and the use thereof should be partly common, and partly granted to others by the will of the possessors. These three points were provided for by the Law. Because, in the first place, the possessions themselves were divided among individuals: for it is written (Numbers 33:53-54): "I have given you" the land "for a possession: and you shall divide it among you by lot." And since many states have been ruined through want of regulations in the matter of possessions, as the Philosopher observes (Polit. ii, 6); therefore the Law provided a threefold remedy against the regularity of possessions. The first was that they should be divided equally, wherefore it is written (Numbers 33:54): "To the more you shall give a larger part, and to the fewer, a lesser." A second remedy was that possessions could not be alienated forever, but after a certain lapse of time should return to their former owner, so as to avoid confusion of possessions (cf. ad 3). The third remedy aimed at the removal of this confusion, and provided that the dead should be succeeded by their next of kin: in the first place, the son; secondly, the daughter; thirdly, the brother; fourthly, the father's brother; fifthly, any other next of kin. Furthermore, in order to preserve the distinction of property, the Law enacted that heiresses should marry within their own tribe, as recorded in Numbers 36:6.

Secondly, the Law commanded that, in some respects, the use of things should belong to all in common. Firstly, as regards the care of them; for it was prescribed (Deuteronomy 22:1-4): "Thou shalt not pass by, if thou seest thy brother's ox or his sheep go astray; but thou shalt bring them back to thy brother," and in like manner as to other things. Secondly, as regards fruits. For all alike were allowed on entering a friend's vineyard to eat of the fruit, but not to take any away. And, specially, with respect to the poor, it was prescribed that the forgotten sheaves, and the bunches of grapes and fruit, should be left behind for them (Leviticus 19:9; Deuteronomy 24:19). Moreover, whatever grew in the seventh year was common property, as stated in Exodus 23:11 and Leviticus 25:4.

Thirdly, the law recognized the transference of goods by the owner. There was a purely gratuitous transfer: thus it is written (Deuteronomy 14:28-29): "The third day thou shalt separate another tithe . . . and the Levite . . . and the stranger, and the fatherless, and the widow . . . shall come and shall eat and be filled." And there was a transfer for a consideration, for instance, by selling and buying, by letting out and hiring, by loan and also by deposit, concerning all of which we find that the Law made ample provision. Consequently it is clear that the Old Law provided sufficiently concerning the mutual relations of one man with another.

Reply to Objection 1. As the Apostle says (Romans 13:8), "he that loveth his neighbor hath fulfilled the Law": because, to wit, all the precepts of the Law, chiefly those concerning our neighbor, seem to aim at the end that men should love one another. Now it is an effect of love that men give their own goods to others: because, as stated in 1 John 3:17: "He that . . . shall see his brother in need, and shall shut up his bowels from him: how doth the charity of God abide in him?" Hence the purpose of the Law was to accustom men to give of their own to others readily: thus the Apostle (1 Timothy 6:18) commands the rich "to give easily and to communicate to others." Now a man does not give easily to others if he will not suffer another man to take some little thing from him without any great injury to him. And so the Law laid down that it should be lawful for a man, on entering his neighbor's vineyard, to eat of the fruit there: but not to carry any away, lest this should lead to the infliction of a grievous harm, and cause a disturbance of the peace: for among well-behaved people, the taking of a little does not disturb the peace; in fact, it rather strengthens friendship and accustoms men to give things to one another.

Reply to Objection 2. The Law did not prescribe that women should succeed to their father's estate except in default of male issue: failing which it was necessary that succession should be granted to the female line in order to comfort the father, who would have been sad to think that his estate would pass to strangers. Nevertheless the Law observed due caution in the matter, by providing that those women who succeeded to their father's estate, should marry within their own tribe, in order to avoid confusion of tribal possessions, as stated in Numbers 36:7-8.

Reply to Objection 3. As the Philosopher says (Polit. ii, 4), the regulation of possessions conduces much to the preservation of a city or nation. Consequently, as he himself observes, it was forbidden by the law in some of the heathen states, "that anyone should sell his possessions, except to avoid a manifest loss." For if possessions were to be sold indiscriminately, they might happen to come into the hands of a few: so that it might become necessary for a city or country to become void of inhabitants. Hence the Old Law, in order to remove this danger, ordered things in such a way that while provision was made for men's needs, by allowing the sale of possessions to avail for a certain period, at the same time the said danger was removed, by prescribing the return of those possessions after that period had elapsed. The reason for this law was to prevent confusion of possessions, and to ensure the continuance of a definite distinction among the tribes.

But as the town houses were not allotted to distinct estates, therefore the Law allowed them to be sold in perpetuity, like movable goods. Because the number of houses in a town was not fixed, whereas there was a fixed limit to the amount of estates, which could not be exceeded, while the number of houses in a town could be increased. On the other hand, houses situated not in a town, but "in a village that hath no walls," could not be sold in perpetuity: because such houses are built merely with a view to the cultivation and care of possessions; wherefore the Law rightly made the same prescription in regard to both (Leviticus 25).

Reply to Objection 4. As stated above (ad 1), the purpose of the Law was to accustom men to its precepts, so as to be ready to come to one another's assistance: because this is a very great incentive to friendship. The Law granted these facilities for helping others in the matter not only of gratuitous and absolute donations, but also of mutual transfers: because the latter kind of succor is more frequent and benefits the greater number: and it granted facilities for this purpose in many ways. First of all by prescribing that men should be ready to lend, and that they should not be less inclined to do so as the year of remission drew nigh, as stated in Deuteronomy 15:7, seqq. Secondly, by forbidding them to burden a man to whom they might grant a loan, either by exacting usury, or by accepting necessities of life in security; and by prescribing that when this had been done they should be restored at once. For it is written (Deuteronomy 23:19): "Thou shalt not lend to thy brother money to usury": and (Deuteronomy 24:6): "Thou shalt not take the nether nor the upper millstone to pledge; for he hath pledged his life to thee": and (Exodus 22:26): "If thou take of thy neighbor a garment in pledge, thou shalt give it him again before sunset." Thirdly, by forbidding them to be importunate in exacting payment. Hence it is written (Exodus 22:25): "If thou lend money to any of my people that is poor that dwelleth with thee, thou shalt not be hard upon them as an extortioner." For this reason, too, it is enacted (Deuteronomy 24:10-11): "When thou shalt demand of thy neighbor anything that he oweth thee, thou shalt not go into his house to take away a pledge, but thou shalt stand without, and he shall bring out to thee what he hath": both because a man's house is his surest refuge, wherefore it is offensive to a man to be set upon in his own house; and because the Law does not allow the creditor to take away whatever he likes in security, but rather permits the debtor to give what he needs least. Fourthly, the Law prescribed that debts should cease together after the lapse of seven years. For it was probable that those who could conveniently pay their debts, would do so before the seventh year, and would not defraud the lender without cause. But if they were altogether insolvent, there was the same reason for remitting the debt from love for them, as there was for renewing the loan on account of their need.

As regards animals granted in loan, the Law enacted that if, through the neglect of the person to whom they were lent, they perished or deteriorated in his absence, he was bound to make restitution. But if they perished or deteriorated while he was present and taking proper care of them, he was not bound to make restitution, especially if they were hired for a consideration: because they might have died or deteriorated in the same way if they had remained in possession of the lender, so that if the animal had been saved through being lent, the lender would have gained something by the loan which would no longer have been gratuitous. And especially was this to be observed when animals were hired for a consideration: because then the owner received a certain price for the use of the animals; wherefore he had no right to any profit, by receiving indemnity for the animal, unless the person who had charge of it were negligent. In the case, however, of animals not hired for a consideration, equity demanded that he should receive something by way of restitution at least to the value of the hire of the animal that had perished or deteriorated.

Reply to Objection 5. The difference between a loan and a deposit is that a loan is in respect of goods transferred for the use of the person to whom they are transferred, whereas a deposit is for the benefit of the depositor. Hence in certain cases there was a stricter obligation of returning a loan than of restoring goods held in deposit. Because the latter might be lost in two ways. First, unavoidably: i.e. either through a natural cause, for instance if an animal held in deposit were to die or depreciate in value; or through an extrinsic cause, for instance, if it were taken by an enemy, or devoured by a beast (in which case, however, a man was bound to restore to the owner what was left of the animal thus slain): whereas in the other cases mentioned above, he was not bound to make restitution; but only to take an oath in order to clear himself of suspicion. Secondly, the goods deposited might be lost through an avoidable cause, for instance by theft: and then the depositary was bound to restitution on account of his neglect. But, as stated above (ad 4), he who held an animal on loan, was bound to restitution, even if he were absent when it depreciated or died: because he was held responsible for less negligence than a depositary, who was only held responsible in case of theft.

Reply to Objection 6. Workmen who offer their labor for hire, are poor men who toil for their daily bread: and therefore the Law commanded wisely that they should be paid at once, lest they should lack food. But they who offer other commodities for hire, are wont to be rich: nor are they in such need of their price in order to gain a livelihood: and consequently the comparison does not hold.

Reply to Objection 7. The purpose for which judges are appointed among men, is that they may decide doubtful points in matters of justice. Now a matter may be doubtful in two ways. First, among simple-minded people: and in order to remove doubts of this kind, it was prescribed (Deuteronomy 16:18) that "judges and magistrates" should be appointed in each tribe, "to judge the people with just judgment." Secondly, a matter may be doubtful even among experts: and therefore, in order to remove doubts of this kind, the Law prescribed that all should foregather in some chief place chosen by God, where there would be both the high-priest, who would decide doubtful matters relating to the ceremonies of divine worship; and the chief judge of the people, who would decide matters relating to the judgments of men: just as even now cases are taken from a lower to a higher court either by appeal or by consultation. Hence it is written (Deuteronomy 17:8-9): "If thou perceive that there be among you a hard and doubtful matter in judgment . . . and thou see that the words of the judges within thy gates do vary; arise and go up to the place, which the Lord thy God shall choose; and thou shalt come to the priests of the Levitical race, and to the judge that shall be at that time." But such like doubtful matters did not often occur for judgment: wherefore the people were not burdened on this account.

Reply to Objection 8. In the business affairs of men, there is no such thing as demonstrative and infallible proof, and we must be content with a certain conjectural probability, such as that which an orator employs to persuade. Consequently, although it is quite possible for two or three witnesses to agree to a falsehood, yet it is neither easy nor probable that they succeed in so doing:

wherefore their testimony is taken as being true, especially if they do not waver in giving it, or are not otherwise suspect. Moreover, in order that witnesses might not easily depart from the truth, the Law commanded that they should be most carefully examined, and that those who were found untruthful should be severely punished, as stated in Deuteronomy 19:16, seqq.

There was, however, a reason for fixing on this particular number, in token of the unerring truth of the Divine Persons, Who are sometimes mentioned as two, because the Holy Ghost is the bond of the other two Persons; and sometimes as three: as Augustine observes on John 8:17: "In your law it is written that the testimony of two men is true."

Reply to Objection 9. A severe punishment is inflicted not only on account of the gravity of a fault, but also for other reasons. First, on account of the greatness of the sin, because a greater sin, other things being equal, deserves a greater punishment. Secondly, on account of a habitual sin, since men are not easily cured of habitual sin except by severe punishments. Thirdly, on account of a great desire for or a great pleasure in the sin: for men are not easily deterred from such sins unless they be severely punished. Fourthly, on account of the facility of committing a sin and of concealing it: for such like sins, when discovered, should be more severely punished in order to deter others from committing them.

Again, with regard to the greatness of a sin, four degrees may be observed, even in respect of one single deed. The first is when a sin is committed unwillingly; because then, if the sin be altogether involuntary, man is altogether excused from punishment; for it is written (Deuteronomy 22:25, seqq.) that a damsel who suffers violence in a field is not guilty of death, because "she cried, and there was no man to help her." But if a man sinned in any way voluntarily, and yet through weakness, as for instance when a man sins from passion, the sin is diminished: and the punishment, according to true judgment, should be diminished also; unless perchance the common weal requires that the sin be severely punished in order to deter others from committing such sins, as stated above. The second degree is when a man sins through ignorance: and then he was held to be guilty to a certain extent, on account of his negligence in acquiring knowledge: yet he was not punished by the judges but expiated his sin by sacrifices. Hence it is written (Leviticus 4:2): "The soul that sinneth through ignorance," etc. This is, however, to be taken as applying to ignorance of fact; and not to ignorance of the Divine precept, which all were bound to know. The third degree was when a man sinned from pride, i.e. through deliberate choice or malice: and then he was punished according to the greatness of the sin [Cf. Deuteronomy 25:2]. The fourth degree was when a man sinned from stubbornness or obstinacy: and then he was to be utterly cut off as a rebel and a destroyer of the commandment of the Law [Cf. Numbers 15:30-31].

Accordingly we must say that, in appointing the punishment for theft, the Law considered what would be likely to happen most frequently (Exodus 22:1-9): wherefore, as regards theft of other things which can easily be safeguarded from a thief, the thief restored only twice their value. But sheep cannot be easily safeguarded from a thief, because they graze in the fields: wherefore it happened more frequently that sheep were stolen in the fields. Consequently the Law inflicted a heavier penalty, by ordering four sheep to be restored for the theft of one. As to cattle, they were yet more difficult to safeguard, because they are kept in the fields, and do not graze in flocks as sheep do; wherefore a yet more heavy penalty was inflicted in their regard, so that five oxen were to be restored for one ox. And this I say, unless perchance the animal itself were discovered in the thief's possession: because in that case he had to restore only twice the number, as in the case of other thefts: for there was reason to presume that he intended to restore the animal, since he kept it alive. Again, we might say, according to a gloss, that "a cow is useful in five ways: it may be used for sacrifice, for ploughing, for food, for milk, and its hide is employed for various purposes": and therefore for one cow five had to be restored. But the sheep was useful in four ways: "for sacrifice, for meat, for milk, and for its wool." The unruly son was slain, not because he ate and drank: but on account of his stubbornness and rebellion, which was always punished by death, as stated above. As to the man who gathered sticks on the sabbath, he was stoned as a breaker of the Law, which commanded the sabbath to be observed, to testify the belief in the newness of the world, as stated above (Question 100, Article 5): wherefore he was slain as an unbeliever.

Reply to Objection 10. The Old Law inflicted the death penalty for the more grievous crimes, viz. for those which are committed against God, and for murder, for stealing a man, irreverence towards one's parents, adultery and incest. In the case of thief of other things it inflicted punishment by indemnification: while in the case of blows and mutilation it authorized punishment by retaliation; and likewise for the sin of bearing false witness. In other faults of less degree it prescribed the punishment of stripes or of public disgrace.

The punishment of slavery was prescribed by the Law in two cases. First, in the case of a slave who was unwilling to avail himself of the privilege granted by the Law, whereby he was free to depart in the seventh year of remission: wherefore he was punished by remaining a slave for ever. Secondly, in the case of a thief, who had not wherewith to make restitution, as stated in Exodus 22:3.

The punishment of absolute exile was not prescribed by the Law: because God was worshipped by that people alone, whereas all other nations were given to idolatry: wherefore if any man were exiled from that people absolutely, he would be in danger of falling into idolatry. For this reason it is related (1 Samuel 26:19) that David said to Saul: "They are cursed in the sight of the Lord, who have cast me out this day, that I should not dwell in the inheritance of the Lord, saying: Go, serve strange gods." There was, however, a restricted sort of exile: for it is written in Deuteronomy 19:4 [Cf. Numbers 35:25] that "he that striketh [Vulgate: 'killeth'] his neighbor ignorantly, and is proved to have had no hatred against him, shall flee to one of the cities" of refuge and "abide there until the death of the high-priest." For then it became lawful for him to return home, because when the whole people thus suffered a loss they forgot their private quarrels, so that the next of kin of the slain were not so eager to kill the slayer.

Reply to Objection 11. Dumb animals were ordered to be slain, not on account of any fault of theirs; but as a punishment to their owners, who had not safeguarded their beasts from these offenses. Hence the owner was more severely punished if his ox had butted anyone "yesterday or the day before" (in which case steps might have been taken to butting suddenly). Or again, the animal was slain in detestation of the sin; and lest men should be horrified at the sight thereof.

Reply to Objection 12. The literal reason for this commandment, as Rabbi Moses declares (Doct. Perplex. iii), was because the slayer was frequently from the nearest city: wherefore the slaying of the calf was a means of investigating the hidden murder. This was brought about in three ways. In the first place the elders of the city swore that they had taken every measure for safeguarding the roads. Secondly, the owner of the heifer was indemnified for the slaying of his beast, and if the murder was previously discovered, the beast was not slain. Thirdly, the place, where the heifer was slain, remained uncultivated. Wherefore, in order to avoid this twofold loss, the men of the city would readily make known the murderer, if they knew who he was: and it would seldom happen but that some word or sign would escape about the matter. Or again, this was done in order to frighten people, in detestation of murder. Because the slaying of a heifer, which is a useful animal and full of strength, especially before it has been put under the yoke, signified that whoever committed murder, however useful and strong he might be, was to forfeit his life; and that, by a cruel death, which was implied by the striking off of its head; and that the murderer, as vile and abject, was to be cut off from the fellowship of men, which was betokened by the fact that the heifer after being slain was left to rot in a rough and uncultivated place.

Mystically, the heifer taken from the herd signifies the flesh of Christ; which had not drawn a yoke, since it had done no sin; nor did it plough the ground, i.e. it never knew the stain of revolt. The fact of the heifer being killed in an uncultivated valley signified the despised death of Christ, whereby all sins are washed away, and the devil is shown to be the arch-murderer.

ARTICLE 3. WHETHER THE JUDICIAL PRECEPTS REGARDING FOREIGNERS WERE FRAMED IN A SUITABLE MANNER?

Objection 1. It would seem that the judicial precepts regarding foreigners were not suitably framed. For Peter said (Acts 10:34-35): "In very deed I perceive that God is not a respecter of persons, but in every nation, he that feareth Him and worketh justice is acceptable to Him." But those who are acceptable to God should not be excluded from the Church of God. Therefore it is unsuitably commanded (Deuteronomy 23:3) that "the Ammonite and the Moabite, even after the tenth generation, shall not enter into the church of the Lord forever": whereas, on the other hand, it is prescribed (Deuteronomy 23:7) to be observed with regard to certain other nations: "Thou shalt not abhor the Edomite, because he is thy brother; nor the Egyptian because thou wast a stranger in his land."

Objection 2. Further, we do not deserve to be punished for those things which are not in our power. But it is not in man's power to be an eunuch, or born of a prostitute. Therefore it is unsuitably commanded (Deuteronomy 23:1-2) that "an eunuch and one born of a prostitute shalt not enter into the church of the Lord."

Objection 3. Further, the Old Law mercifully forbade strangers to be molested: for it is written (Exodus 22:21): "Thou shalt not molest a stranger, nor afflict him; for yourselves also were strangers in the land of Egypt": and (Exodus 23:9): "Thou shalt not molest a stranger, for you know the hearts of strangers, for you also were strangers in the land of Egypt." But it is an affliction to be burdened with usury. Therefore the Law unsuitably permitted them (Deuteronomy 23:19-20) to lend money to the stranger for usury.

Objection 4. Further, men are much more akin to us than trees. But we should show greater care and love for these things that are nearest to us, according to Sirach 13:19: "Every beast loveth its like: so also every man him that is nearest to himself." Therefore the Lord unsuitably commanded (Deuteronomy 20:13-19) that all the inhabitants of a captured hostile city were to be slain, but that the fruit-trees should not be cut down.

Objection 5. Further, everyone should prefer the common good of virtue to the good of the individual. But the common good is sought in a war which men fight against their enemies. Therefore it is unsuitably commanded

(Deuteronomy 20:5-7) that certain men should be sent home, for instance a man that had built a new house, or who had planted a vineyard, or who had married a wife.

Objection 6. Further, no man should profit by his own fault. But it is a man's fault if he be timid or faint-hearted: since this is contrary to the virtue of fortitude. Therefore the timid and faint-hearted are unfittingly excused from the toil of battle (Deuteronomy 20:8).

On the contrary, Divine Wisdom declares (Proverbs 8:8): "All my words are just, there is nothing wicked nor perverse in them."

I answer that, Man's relations with foreigners are twofold: peaceful, and hostile: and in directing both kinds of relation the Law contained suitable precepts. For the Jews were offered three opportunities of peaceful relations with foreigners. First, when foreigners passed through their land as travelers. Secondly, when they came to dwell in their land as newcomers. And in both these respects the Law made kind provision in its precepts: for it is written (Exodus 22:21): "Thou shalt not molest a stranger [advenam]"; and again (Exodus 22:9): "Thou shalt not molest a stranger [peregrino]." Thirdly, when any foreigners wished to be admitted entirely to their fellowship and mode of worship. With regard to these a certain order was observed. For they were not at once admitted to citizenship: just as it was law with some nations that no one was deemed a citizen except after two or three generations, as the Philosopher says (Polit. iii, 1). The reason for this was that if foreigners were allowed to meddle with the affairs of a nation as soon as they settled down in its midst, many dangers might occur, since the foreigners not yet having the common good firmly at heart might attempt something hurtful to the people. Hence it was that the Law prescribed in respect of certain nations that had close relations with the Jews (viz., the Egyptians among whom they were born and educated, and the Idumeans, the children of Esau, Jacob's brother), that they should be admitted to the fellowship of the people after the third generation; whereas others (with whom their relations had been hostile, such as the Ammonites and Moabites) were never to be admitted to citizenship; while the Amalekites, who were yet more hostile to them, and had no fellowship of kindred with them, were to be held as foes in perpetuity: for it is written (Exodus 17:16): "The war of the Lord shall be against Amalec from generation to generation."

In like manner with regard to hostile relations with foreigners, the Law contained suitable precepts. For, in the first place, it commanded that war should be declared for a just cause: thus it is commanded (Deuteronomy 20:10) that when they advanced to besiege a city, they should at first make an offer of peace. Secondly, it enjoined that when once they had entered on a war they should undauntedly persevere in it, putting their trust in God. And in order that they might be the more heedful of this command, it ordered that on the approach of battle the priest should hearten them by promising them God's aid. Thirdly, it prescribed the removal of whatever might prove an obstacle to the fight, and that certain men, who might be in the way, should be sent home. Fourthly, it enjoined that they should use moderation in pursuing the advantage of victory, by sparing women and children, and by not cutting down fruit-trees of that country.

Reply to Objection 1. The Law excluded the men of no nation from the worship of God and from things pertaining to the welfare of the soul: for it is written (Exodus 12:48): "If any stranger be willing to dwell among you, and to keep the Phase of the Lord; all his males shall first be circumcised, and then shall he celebrate it according to the manner, and he shall be as that which is born in the land." But in temporal matters concerning the public life of the people, admission was not granted to everyone at once, for the reason given above: but to some, i.e. the Egyptians and Idumeans, in the third generation; while others were excluded in perpetuity, in detestation of their past offense, i.e. the peoples of Moab, Ammon, and Amalec. For just as one man is punished for a sin committed by him, in order that others seeing this may be deterred and refrain from sinning; so too may one nation or city be punished for a crime, that others may refrain from similar crimes.

Nevertheless it was possible by dispensation for a man to be admitted to citizenship on account of some act of virtue: thus it is related (Judith 14:6) that Achior, the captain of the children of Ammon, "was joined to the people of Israel, with all the succession of his kindred." The same applies to Ruth the Moabite who was "a virtuous woman" (Ruth 3:11): although it may be said that this prohibition regarded men and not women, who are not competent to be citizens absolutely speaking.

Reply to Objection 2. As the Philosopher says (Polit. iii, 3), a man is said to be a citizen in two ways: first, simply; secondly, in a restricted sense. A man is a citizen simply if he has all the rights of citizenship, for instance, the right of debating or voting in the popular assembly. On the other hand, any man may be called citizen, only in a restricted sense, if he dwells within the city, even common people or children or old men, who are not fit to enjoy power in matters pertaining to the common weal. For this reason bastards, by reason of their base origin, were excluded from the "ecclesia," i.e. from the popular assembly, down to the tenth generation. The same applies to eunuchs, who were not competent to receive the honor due to a father, especially among the Jews, where the divine worship was continued through carnal generation: for even among the heathens, those who had many children were marked with special honor, as the Philosopher remarks (Polit. ii, 6). Nevertheless, in matters pertaining to the grace of God, eunuchs were not discriminated from others, as neither were strangers, as already stated: for it is written (Isaiah 56:3): "Let not the son of the stranger that adhereth to the Lord speak, saying: The Lord will divide and separate me from His people. And let not the eunuch say: Behold I am a dry tree."

Reply to Objection 3. It was not the intention of the Law to sanction the acceptance of usury from strangers, but only to tolerate it on account of the proneness of the Jews to avarice; and in order to promote an amicable feeling towards those out of whom they made a profit.

Reply to Objection 4. A distinction was observed with regard to hostile cities. For some of them were far distant, and were not among those which had been promised to them. When they had taken these cities, they killed all the men who had fought against God's people; whereas the women and children were spared. But in the neighboring cities which had been promised to them, all were ordered to be slain, on account of their former crimes, to punish which God sent the Israelites as executor of Divine justice: for it is written (Deuteronomy 9:5) "because they have done wickedly, they are destroyed at thy coming in." The fruit-trees were commanded to be left untouched, for the use of the people themselves, to whom the city with its territory was destined to be subjected.

Reply to Objection 5. The builder of a new house, the planter of a vineyard, the newly married husband, were excluded from fighting, for two reasons. First, because man is wont to give all his affection to those things which he has lately acquired, or is on the point of having, and consequently he is apt to dread the loss of these above other things. Wherefore it was likely enough that on account of this affection they would fear death all the more, and be so much the less brave in battle. Secondly, because, as the Philosopher says (Phys. ii, 5), "it is a misfortune for a man if he is prevented from obtaining something good when it is within his grasp." And so lest the surviving relations should be the more grieved at the death of these men who had not entered into the possession of the good things prepared for them; and also lest the people should be horror-stricken at the sight of their misfortune: these men were taken away from the danger of death by being removed from the battle.

Reply to Objection 6. The timid were sent back home, not that they might be the gainers thereby; but lest the people might be the losers by their presence, since their timidity and flight might cause others to be afraid and run away.

ARTICLE 4. WHETHER THE OLD LAW SET FORTH SUITABLE PRECEPTS ABOUT THE MEMBERS OF THE HOUSEHOLD?

Objection 1. It would seem that the Old Law set forth unsuitable precepts about the members of the household. For a slave "is in every respect his master's property," as the Philosopher states (Polit. i, 2). But that which is a man's property should be his always. Therefore it was unfitting for the Law to command (Exodus 21:2) that slaves should "go out free" in the seventh year.

Objection 2. Further, a slave is his master's property, just as an animal, e.g. an ass or an ox. But it is commanded (Deuteronomy 22:1-3) with regard to animals, that they should be brought back to the owner if they be found going astray. Therefore it was unsuitably commanded (Deuteronomy 23:15): "Thou shalt not deliver to his master the servant that is fled to thee."

Objection 3. Further, the Divine Law should encourage mercy more even than the human law. But according to human laws those who ill-treat their servants and maidservants are severely punished: and the worse treatment of all seems to be that which results in death. Therefore it is unfittingly commanded (Exodus 21:20-21) that "he that striketh his bondman or bondwoman with a rod, and they die under his hands . . . if the party remain alive a day . . . he shall not be subject to the punishment, because it is his money."

Objection 4. Further, the dominion of a master over his slave differs from that of the father over his son (Polit. i, 3). But the dominion of master over slave gives the former the right to sell his servant or maidservant. Therefore it was unfitting for the Law to allow a man to sell his daughter to be a servant or handmaid (Exodus 21:7).

Objection 5. Further, a father has power over his son. But he who has power over the sinner has the right to punish him for his offenses. Therefore it is unfittingly commanded (Deuteronomy 21:18, seqq.) that a father should bring his son to the ancients of the city for punishment.

Objection 6. Further, the Lord forbade them (Deuteronomy 7:3, seqq.) to make marriages with strange nations; and commanded the dissolution of such as had been contracted (Ezra 10). Therefore it was unfitting to allow them to marry captive women from strange nations (Deuteronomy 21:10, seqq.).

Objection 7. Further, the Lord forbade them to marry within certain degrees of consanguinity and affinity, according to Leviticus 18. Therefore it was unsuitably commanded (Deuteronomy 25:5) that if any man died without issue, his brother should marry his wife.

Objection 8. Further, as there is the greatest familiarity between man and wife, so should there be the staunchest fidelity. But this is impossible if the marriage bond can be sundered. Therefore it was unfitting for the Lord to allow (Deuteronomy 24:1-4) a man to put his wife away, by writing a bill of divorce; and besides, that he could not take her again to wife.

Objection 9. Further, just as a wife can be faithless to her husband, so can a slave be to his master, and a son to his father. But the Law did not command any sacrifice to be offered in order to investigate the injury done by a servant to his master, or by a son to his father. Therefore it seems to have been superfluous for the Law to prescribe the "sacrifice of jealousy" in order to investigate a wife's adultery (Numbers 5:12, seqq.). Consequently it seems that the Law put forth unsuitable judicial precepts about the members of the household.

On the contrary, It is written (Psalm 18:10): "The judgments of the Lord are true, justified in themselves."

I answer that, The mutual relations of the members of a household regard everyday actions directed to the necessities of life, as the Philosopher states (Polit. i, 1). Now the preservation of man's life may be considered from two points of view. First, from the point of view of the individual, i.e. in so far as man preserves his individuality: and for the purpose of the preservation of life, considered from this standpoint, man has at his service external goods, by means of which he provides himself with food and clothing and other such necessaries of life: in the handling of which he has need of servants. Secondly man's life is preserved from the point of view of the species, by means of generation, for which purpose man needs a wife, that she may bear him children. Accordingly the mutual relations of the members of a household admit of a threefold combination: viz. those of master and servant, those of husband and wife, and those of father and son: and in respect of all these relationships the Old Law contained fitting precepts. Thus, with regard to servants, it commanded them to be treated with moderation—both as to their work, lest, to wit, they should be burdened with excessive labor, wherefore the Lord commanded (Deuteronomy 5:14) that on the Sabbath day "thy manservant and thy maidservant" should "rest even as thyself"—and also as to the infliction of punishment, for it ordered those who maimed their servants, to set them free (Exodus 21:26-27). Similar provision was made in favor of a maidservant when married to anyone (Exodus 21:7, seqq.). Moreover, with regard to those servants in particular who were taken from among the people, the Law prescribed that they should go out free in the seventh year taking whatever they brought with them, even their clothes (Exodus 21:2, seqq.): and furthermore it was commanded (Deuteronomy 15:13) that they should be given provision for the journey.

With regard to wives the Law made certain prescriptions as to those who were to be taken in marriage: for instance, that they should marry a wife from their own tribe (Numbers 36:6): and this lest confusion should ensue in the property of various tribes. Also that a man should marry the wife of his deceased brother when the latter died without issue, as prescribed in Deuteronomy 25:5-6: and this in order that he who could not have successors according to carnal origin, might at least have them by a kind of adoption, and that thus the deceased might not be entirely forgotten. It also forbade them to marry certain women; to wit, women of strange nations, through fear of their losing their faith; and those of their near kindred, on account of the natural respect due to them. Furthermore it prescribed in what way wives were to be treated after marriage. To wit, that they should not be slandered without grave reason: wherefore it ordered punishment to be inflicted on the man who falsely accused his wife of a crime (Deuteronomy 22:13, seqq.). Also that a man's hatred of his wife should not be detrimental to his son (Deuteronomy 21:15, seqq.). Again, that a man should not ill-use his wife through hatred of her, but rather that he should write a bill of divorce and send her away (Deuteronomy 24:1). Furthermore, in order to foster conjugal love from the very outset, it was prescribed that no public duties should be laid on a recently married man, so that he might be free to rejoice with his wife.

With regard to children, the Law commanded parents to educate them by instructing them in the faith: hence it is written (Exodus 12:26, seqq.): "When your children shall say to you: What is the meaning of this service? You shall say to them: It is the victim of the passage of the Lord." Moreover, they are commanded to teach them the rules of right conduct: wherefore it is written (Deuteronomy 21:20) that the parents had to say: "He slighteth hearing our admonitions, he giveth himself to revelling and to debauchery."

Reply to Objection 1. As the children of Israel had been delivered by the Lord from slavery, and for this reason were bound to the service of God, He did not wish them to be slaves in perpetuity. Hence it is written (Leviticus 25:39, seqq.): "If thy brother, constrained by poverty, sell himself to thee, thou shalt not oppress him with the service of bondservants: but he shall be as a hireling and a sojourner . . . for they are My servants, and I brought them out of the land of Egypt: let them not be sold as bondmen": and consequently, since they were slaves, not absolutely but in a restricted sense, after a lapse of time they were set free.

Reply to Objection 2. This commandment is to be understood as referring to a servant whom his master seeks to kill, or to help him in committing some sin.

Reply to Objection 3. With regard to the ill-treatment of servants, the Law seems to have taken into consideration whether it was certain or not: since if it were certain, the Law fixed a penalty: for maiming, the penalty was forfeiture of the servant, who was ordered to be given his liberty: while for slaying, the punishment was that of a murderer, when the slave died under the blow of his master. If, however, the hurt was not certain, but only probable, the Law did not impose any penalty as regards a man's own servant: for instance if the servant did not die at once after being struck, but after some days: for it would be uncertain whether he died as a result of the blows he received. For when a man struck a free man, yet so that he did not die at once, but "walked abroad again upon his staff," he that struck him was quit of murder, even though afterwards he died. Nevertheless he was bound to pay the doctor's fees incurred by the victim of his assault. But this was not the case if a man killed his own servant: because whatever the servant had, even his very person, was the property of his master. Hence the reason for his not being subject to a pecuniary penalty is set down as being "because it is his money."

Reply to Objection 4. As stated above (ad 1), no Jew could own a Jew as a slave absolutely: but only in a restricted sense, as a hireling for a fixed time. And in this way the Law permitted that through stress of poverty a man might sell his son or daughter. This is shown by the very words of the Law, where we read: "If any man sell his daughter to be a servant, she shall not go out as bondwomen are wont to go out." Moreover, in this way a man might sell not only his son, but even himself, rather as a hireling than as a slave, according to Leviticus 25:39-40: "If thy brother, constrained by poverty, sell himself to thee, thou shalt not oppress him with the service of bondservants: but he shall be as a hireling and a sojourner."

Reply to Objection 5. As the Philosopher says (Ethic. x, 9), the paternal authority has the power only of admonition; but not that of coercion, whereby rebellious and headstrong persons can be compelled. Hence in this case the Lord commanded the stubborn son to be punished by the rulers of the city.

Reply to Objection 6. The Lord forbade them to marry strange women on account of the danger of seduction, lest they should be led astray into idolatry. And specially did this prohibition apply with respect to those nations who dwelt near them, because it was more probable that they would adopt their religious practices. When, however, the woman was willing to renounce idolatry, and become an adherent of the Law, it was lawful to take her in marriage: as was the case with Ruth whom Booz married. Wherefore she said to her mother-in-law (Ruth 1:16): "Thy people shall be my people, and thy God my God." Accordingly it was not permitted to marry a captive woman unless she first shaved her hair, and pared her nails, and put off the raiment wherein she was taken, and mourned for her father and mother, in token that she renounced idolatry forever.

Reply to Objection 7. As Chrysostom says (Hom. xlviii super Matth.), "because death was an unmitigated evil for the Jews, who did everything with a view to the present life, it was ordained that children should be born to the dead man through his brother: thus affording a certain mitigation to his death. It was not, however, ordained that any other than his brother or one next of kin should marry the wife of the deceased, because" the offspring of this union "would not be looked upon as that of the deceased: and moreover, a stranger would not be under the obligation to support the household of the deceased, as his brother would be bound to do from motives of justice on account of his relationship." Hence it is evident that in marrying the wife of his dead brother, he took his dead brother's place.

Reply to Objection 8. The Law permitted a wife to be divorced, not as though it were just absolutely speaking, but on account of the Jews' hardness of heart, as Our Lord declared (Matthew 19:8). Of this, however, we must speak more fully in the treatise on Matrimony (SP, 67).

Reply to Objection 9. Wives break their conjugal faith by adultery, both easily, for motives of pleasure, and hiddenly, since "the eye of the adulterer observeth darkness" (Job 24:15). But this does not apply to a son in respect of his father, or to a servant in respect of his master: because the latter infidelity is not the result of the lust of pleasure, but rather of malice: nor can it remain hidden like the infidelity of an adulterous woman.

SECOND PART OF THE SECOND PART

QUESTION 2. THE ACT OF FAITH

ARTICLE 7. WHETHER IT IS NECESSARY FOR THE SALVATION OF ALL, THAT THEY SHOULD BELIEVE EXPLICITLY IN THE MYSTERY OF CHRIST?

Objection 1. It would seem that it is not necessary for the salvation of all that they should believe explicitly in the mystery of Christ. For man is not bound to believe explicitly what the angels are ignorant about: since the unfolding of faith is the result of Divine revelation, which reaches man by means of the angels, as stated above (6; I, 111, 1). Now even the angels were in ignorance of the mystery of the Incarnation: hence, according to the commentary of Dionysius (Coel. Hier. vii), it is they who ask (Psalm 23:8): "Who is this king of glory?" and (Isaiah 63:1): "Who is this that cometh from Edom?" Therefore men were not bound to believe explicitly in the mystery of Christ's Incarnation.

Objection 2. Further, it is evident that John the Baptist was one of the teachers, and most nigh to Christ, Who said of him (Matthew 11:11) that "there hath not risen among them that are born of women, a greater than" he. Now John the Baptist does not appear to have known the mystery of Christ explicitly, since he asked Christ (Matthew 11:3): "Art Thou He that art to come, or look we for another?" Therefore even the teachers were not bound to explicit faith in Christ.

Objection 3. Further, many gentiles obtained salvation through the ministry of the angels, as Dionysius states (Coel. Hier. ix). Now it would seem that the gentiles had neither explicit nor implicit faith in Christ, since they received no revelation. Therefore it seems that it was not necessary for the salvation of all to believe explicitly in the mystery of Christ.

On the contrary, Augustine says (De Corr. et Gratia vii; Ep. cxc): "Our faith is sound if we believe that no man, old or young is delivered from the contagion of death and the bonds of sin, except by the one Mediator of God and men, Jesus Christ."

I answer that, As stated above (5; 1, 8), the object of faith includes, properly and directly, that thing through which man obtains beatitude. Now the mystery of Christ's Incarnation and Passion is the way by which men obtain beatitude; for it is written (Acts 4:12): "There is no other name under heaven given to men, whereby we must be saved." Therefore belief of some kind in the mystery of Christ's Incarnation was necessary at all times and for all persons, but this belief differed according to differences of times and persons. The reason of this is that before the state of sin, man believed, explicitly in Christ's Incarnation, in so far as it was intended for the consummation of glory, but not as it was intended to deliver man from sin by the Passion and Resurrection, since man had no foreknowledge of his future sin. He does, however, seem to have had foreknowledge of the Incarnation of Christ, from the fact that he said (Genesis 2:24): "Wherefore a man shall leave father and mother, and shall cleave to his wife," of which the Apostle says (Ephesians 5:32) that "this is a great sacrament . . . in Christ and the Church," and it is incredible that the first man was ignorant about this sacrament.

But after sin, man believed explicitly in Christ, not only as to the Incarnation, but also as to the Passion and Resurrection, whereby the human race is delivered from sin and death: for they would not, else, have foreshadowed Christ's Passion by certain sacrifices both before and after the Law, the meaning of which sacrifices was known by the learned explicitly, while the simple folk, under the veil of those sacrifices, believed them to be ordained by God in reference to Christ's coming, and thus their knowledge was covered with a veil, so to speak. And, as stated above (Question 1, Article 7), the nearer they were to Christ, the more distinct was their knowledge of Christ's mysteries.

After grace had been revealed, both learned and simple folk are bound to explicit faith in the mysteries of Christ, chiefly as regards those which are observed throughout the Church, and publicly proclaimed, such as the articles which refer to the Incarnation, of which we have spoken above (Question 1, Article 8). As to other minute points in reference to the articles of the Incarnation, men have been bound to believe them more or less explicitly according to each one's state and office.

Reply to Objection 1. The mystery of the Kingdom of God was not entirely hidden from the angels, as Augustine observes (Gen. ad lit. v, 19), yet certain aspects thereof were better known to them when Christ revealed them to them.

Reply to Objection 2. It was not through ignorance that John the Baptist inquired of Christ's advent in the flesh, since he had clearly professed his belief therein, saying: "I saw, and I gave testimony, that this is the Son of God" (John 1:34). Hence he did not say: "Art Thou He that hast come?" but "Art Thou He that art to come?" thus saying about the future, not about the past. Likewise it is not to be believed that he was ignorant of Christ's future Passion, for he had already said (John 1:39): "Behold the Lamb of God, behold Him who taketh away the sins [Vulgate: 'sin'] of the world," thus foretelling His future immolation; and since other prophets had foretold it, as may be seen especially in Isaias 53. We may therefore say with Gregory (Hom. xxvi in Evang.) that he asked this question, being in ignorance as to whether Christ would descend into hell in His own Person. But he did not ignore the fact that the power of

Christ's Passion would be extended to those who were detained in Limbo, according to Zechariah 9:11: "Thou also, by the blood of Thy testament hast sent forth Thy prisoners out of the pit, wherein there is no water"; nor was he bound to believe explicitly, before its fulfilment, that Christ was to descend thither Himself.

It may also be replied that, as Ambrose observes in his commentary on Luke 7:19, he made this inquiry, not from doubt or ignorance but from devotion: or again, with Chrysostom (Hom. xxxvi in Matth.), that he inquired, not as though ignorant himself, but because he wished his disciples to be satisfied on that point, through Christ: hence the latter framed His answer so as to instruct the disciples, by pointing to the signs of His works.

Reply to Objection 3. Many of the gentiles received revelations of Christ, as is clear from their predictions. Thus we read (Job 19:25): "I know that my Redeemer liveth." The Sibyl too foretold certain things about Christ, as Augustine states (Contra Faust. xiii, 15). Moreover, we read in the history of the Romans, that at the time of Constantine Augustus and his mother Irene a tomb was discovered, wherein lay a man on whose breast was a golden plate with the inscription: "Christ shall be born of a virgin, and in Him, I believe. O sun, during the lifetime of Irene and Constantine, thou shalt see me again" [Cf. Baron, Annal., A.D. 780. If, however, some were saved without receiving any revelation, they were not saved without faith in a Mediator, for, though they did not believe in Him explicitly, they did, nevertheless, have implicit faith through believing in Divine providence, since they believed that God would deliver mankind in whatever way was pleasing to Him, and according to the revelation of the Spirit to those who knew the truth, as stated in Job 35:11: "Who teacheth us more than the beasts of the earth."

QUESTION 4. THE VIRTUE ITSELF OF FAITH

ARTICLE 8. WHETHER FAITH IS MORE CERTAIN THAN SCIENCE AND THE OTHER INTELLECTUAL VIRTUES?

Objection 1. It would seem that faith is not more certain than science and the other intellectual virtues. For doubt is opposed to certitude, wherefore a thing would seem to be the more certain, through being less doubtful, just as a thing is the whiter, the less it has of an admixture of black. Now understanding, science and also wisdom are free of any doubt about their objects; whereas the believer may sometimes suffer a movement of doubt, and doubt about matters of faith. Therefore faith is no more certain than the intellectual virtues.

Objection 2. Further, sight is more certain than hearing. But "faith is through hearing" according to Romans 10:17; whereas understanding, science and wisdom imply some kind of intellectual sight. Therefore science and understanding are more certain than faith.

Further, in matters concerning the intellect, the more perfect is the more certain. Now understanding is more perfect than faith, since faith is the way to understanding, according to another version [the Septuagint] of Isaiah 7:9: "If you will not believe, you shall not understand [Vulgate: 'continue']": and Augustine says (De Trin. xiv, 1) that "faith is strengthened by science." Therefore it seems that science or understanding is more certain than faith.

On the contrary, The Apostle says (1 Thessalonians 2:15): "When you had received of us the word of the hearing," i.e. by faith . . . "you received it not as the word of men, but, as it is indeed, the word of God." Now nothing is more certain than the word of God. Therefore science is not more certain than faith; nor is anything else.

I answer that, As stated above (I-II, 57, 4, ad 2) two of the intellectual virtues are about contingent matter, viz. prudence and art; to which faith is preferable in point of certitude, by reason of its matter, since it is about eternal things, which never change, whereas the other three intellectual virtues, viz. wisdom, science [In English the corresponding 'gift' is called knowledge] and understanding, are about necessary things, as stated above (I-II, 57, 5, ad 3). But it must be observed that wisdom, science and understanding may be taken in two ways: first, as intellectual virtues, according to the Philosopher (Ethic. vi, 2,3); secondly, for the gifts of the Holy Ghost. If we consider them in the first way, we must note that certitude can be looked at in two ways. First, on the part of its cause, and thus a thing which has a more certain cause, is itself more certain. In this way faith is more certain than those three virtues, because it is founded on the Divine truth, whereas the aforesaid three virtues are based on human reason. Secondly, certitude may be considered on the part of the subject, and thus the more a man's intellect lays hold of a thing, the more certain it is. In this way, faith is less certain, because matters of faith are above the human intellect, whereas the objects of the aforesaid three virtues are not. Since, however, a thing is judged simply with regard to its cause, but relatively, with respect to a disposition on the part of the subject, it follows that faith is more certain simply, while the others are more certain relatively, i.e. for us. Likewise if these three be taken as gifts received in this present life, they are related to faith as to their principle which they presuppose: so that again, in this way, faith is more certain.

Reply to Objection 1. This doubt is not on the side of the cause of faith, but on our side, in so far as we do not fully grasp matters of faith with our intellect.

Reply to Objection 2. Other things being equal sight is more certain than hearing; but if (the authority of) the person from whom we hear greatly surpasses that of the seer's sight, hearing is more certain than sight: thus a man of little science is more certain about what he hears on the authority of an expert in science, than about what is apparent to him according to his own reason: and much more is a man certain about what he hears from God, Who cannot be deceived, than about what he sees with his own reason, which can be mistaken.

Reply to Objection 3. The gifts of understanding and knowledge are more perfect than the knowledge of faith in the point of their greater clearness, but not in regard to more certain adhesion: because the whole certitude of the gifts of understanding and knowledge, arises from the certitude of faith, even as the certitude of the knowledge of conclusions arises from the certitude of premisses. But in so far as science, wisdom and understanding are intellectual virtues, they are based upon the natural light of reason, which falls short of the certitude of God's word, on which faith is founded.

QUESTION 10. UNBELIEF IN GENERAL

ARTICLE 1. WHETHER UNBELIEF IS A SIN?

Objection 1. It would seem that unbelief is not a sin. For every sin is contrary to nature, as Damascene proves (De Fide Orth. ii, 4). Now unbelief seems not to be contrary to nature; for Augustine says (De Praedest. Sanct. v) that "to be capable to having faith, just as to be capable of having charity, is natural to all men; whereas to have faith, even as to have charity, belongs to the grace of the faithful." Therefore not to have faith, which is to be an unbeliever, is not a sin.

Objection 2. Further, no one sins that which he cannot avoid, since every sin is voluntary. Now it is not in a man's power to avoid unbelief, for he cannot avoid it unless he have faith, because the Apostle says (Romans 10:14): "How shall they believe in Him, of Whom they have not heard? And how shall they hear without a preacher?" Therefore unbelief does not seem to be a sin.

Objection 3. Further, as stated above (I-II, 84, 4), there are seven capital sins, to which all sins are reduced. But unbelief does not seem to be comprised under any of them. Therefore unbelief is not a sin.

On the contrary, Vice is opposed to virtue. Now faith is a virtue, and unbelief is opposed to it. Therefore unbelief is a sin.

I answer that, Unbelief may be taken in two ways: first, by way of pure negation, so that a man be called an unbeliever, merely because he has not the faith. Secondly, unbelief may be taken by way of opposition to the faith; in which sense a man refuses to hear the faith, or despises it, according to Isaiah

53:1: "Who hath believed our report?" It is this that completes the notion of unbelief, and it is in this sense that unbelief is a sin.

If, however, we take it by way of pure negation, as we find it in those who have heard nothing about the faith, it bears the character, not of sin, but of punishment, because such like ignorance of Divine things is a result of the sin of our first parent. If such like unbelievers are damned, it is on account of other sins, which cannot be taken away without faith, but not on account of their sin of unbelief. Hence Our Lord said (John 15:22) "If I had not come, and spoken to them, they would not have sin"; which Augustine expounds (Tract. lxxxix in Joan.) as "referring to the sin whereby they believed not in Christ."

Reply to Objection 1. To have the faith is not part of human nature, but it is part of human nature that man's mind should not thwart his inner instinct, and the outward preaching of the truth. Hence, in this way, unbelief is contrary to nature.

Reply to Objection 2. This argument takes unbelief as denoting a pure negation.

Reply to Objection 3. Unbelief, in so far as it is a sin, arises from pride, through which man is unwilling to subject his intellect to the rules of faith, and to the sound interpretation of the Fathers. Hence Gregory says (Moral. xxxi, 45) that "presumptuous innovations arise from vainglory."

It might also be replied that just as the theological virtues are not reduced to the cardinal virtues, but precede them, so too, the vices opposed to the theological virtues are not reduced to the capital vices.

ARTICLE 8. WHETHER UNBELIEVERS OUGHT TO BE COMPELLED TO THE FAITH?

Objection 1. It would seem that unbelievers ought by no means to be compelled to the faith. For it is written (Matthew 13:28) that the servants of the householder, in whose field cockle had been sown, asked him: "Wilt thou that we go and gather it up?" and that he answered: "No, lest perhaps gathering up the cockle, you root up the wheat also together with it": on which passage Chrysostom says (Hom. xlvi in Matth.): "Our Lord says this so as to forbid the slaying of men. For it is not right to slay heretics, because if you do you will necessarily slay many innocent persons." Therefore it seems that for the same reason unbelievers ought not to be compelled to the faith.

Objection 2. Further, we read in the Decretals (Dist. xlv can., De Judaeis): "The holy synod prescribes, with regard to the Jews, that for the future, none are to be compelled to believe." Therefore, in like manner, neither should unbelievers be compelled to the faith.

Objection 3. Further, Augustine says (Tract. xxvi in Joan.) that "it is possible for a man to do other things against his will, but he cannot believe unless he is willing." Therefore it seems that unbelievers ought not to be compelled to the faith.

Objection 4. It is said in God's person (Ezekiel 18:32 [Ezekiel 33:11]): "I desire not the death of the sinner [Vulgate: 'of him that dieth']." Now we ought to conform our will to the Divine will, as stated above (I-II, 19, A9,10). Therefore we should not even wish unbelievers to be put to death.

On the contrary, It is written (Luke 14:23): "Go out into the highways and hedges; and compel them to come in." Now men enter into the house of God, i.e. into Holy Church, by faith. Therefore some ought to be compelled to the faith.

I answer that, Among unbelievers there are some who have never received the faith, such as the heathens and the Jews: and these are by no means to be compelled to the faith, in order that they may believe, because to believe depends on the will: nevertheless they should be compelled by the faithful, if it be possible to do so, so that they do not hinder the faith, by their blasphemies, or by their evil persuasions, or even by their open persecutions. It is for this reason that Christ's faithful often wage war with unbelievers, not indeed for the purpose of forcing them to believe, because even if they were to conquer them, and take them prisoners, they should still leave them free to believe, if they will, but in order to prevent them from hindering the faith of Christ.

On the other hand, there are unbelievers who at some time have accepted the faith, and professed it, such as heretics and all apostates: such should be submitted even to bodily compulsion, that they may fulfil what they have promised, and hold what they, at one time, received.

Reply to Objection 1. Some have understood the authority quoted to forbid, not the excommunication but the slaying of heretics, as appears from the words of Chrysostom. Augustine too, says (Ep. ad Vincent. xciii) of himself: "It was once my opinion that none should be compelled to union with Christ, that we should deal in words, and fight with arguments. However this opinion of mine is undone, not by words of contradiction, but by convincing examples. Because fear of the law was so profitable, that many say: Thanks be to the Lord Who has broken our chains asunder." Accordingly the meaning of Our Lord's words, "Suffer both to grow until the harvest," must be gathered from those which precede, "lest perhaps gathering up the cockle, you root the wheat also together with it." For, Augustine says (Contra Ep. Parmen. iii, 2) "these words show that when this is not to be feared, that is to say, when a man's crime is so publicly known, and so hateful to all, that he has no defenders, or none such as might cause a schism, the severity of discipline should not slacken."

Reply to Objection 2. Those Jews who have in no way received the faith, ought not by no means to be compelled to the faith: if, however, they have received it, they ought to be compelled to keep it, as is stated in the same chapter.

Reply to Objection 3. Just as taking a vow is a matter of will, and keeping a vow, a matter of obligation, so acceptance of the faith is a matter of the will, whereas keeping the faith, when once one has received it, is a matter of obligation. Wherefore heretics should be compelled to keep the faith. Thus Augustine says to the Count Boniface (Ep. clxxxv): "What do these people mean by crying out continually: 'We may believe or not believe just as we choose. Whom did Christ compel?' They should remember that Christ at first compelled Paul and afterwards taught Him."

Reply to Objection 4. As Augustine says in the same letter, "none of us wishes any heretic to perish. But the house of David did not deserve to have peace, unless his son Absalom had been killed in the war which he had raised against his father. Thus if the Catholic Church gathers together some of the perdition of others, she heals the sorrow of her maternal heart by the delivery of so many nations."

ARTICLE 10. WHETHER UNBELIEVERS MAY HAVE AUTHORITY OR DOMINION OVER THE FAITHFUL?

Objection 1. It would seem that unbelievers may have authority or dominion over the faithful. For the Apostle says (1 Timothy 6:1): "Whosoever are servants under the yoke, let them count their masters worthy of all honor": and it is clear that he is speaking of unbelievers, since he adds (1 Timothy 6:2): "But they that have believing masters, let them not despise them." Moreover it is written (1 Peter 2:18): "Servants be subject to your masters with all fear, not only to the good and gentle, but also to the froward." Now this command would not be contained in the apostolic teaching unless unbelievers could have authority over the faithful. Therefore it seems that unbelievers can have authority over the faithful.

Objection 2. Further, all the members of a prince's household are his subjects. Now some of the faithful were members of unbelieving princes' households, for we read in the Epistle to the Philippians (4:22): "All the saints salute you, especially they that are of Caesar's household," referring to Nero, who was an unbeliever. Therefore unbelievers can have authority over the faithful.

Objection 3. Further, according to the Philosopher (Polit. i, 2) a slave is his master's instrument in matters concerning everyday life, even as a craftsman's laborer is his instrument in matters concerning the working of his art. Now, in such matters, a believer can be subject to an unbeliever, for he may work on an unbeliever's farm. Therefore unbelievers may have authority over the faithful even as to dominion.

On the contrary, Those who are in authority can pronounce judgment on those over whom they are placed. But unbelievers cannot pronounce judgment on the faithful, for the Apostle says (1 Corinthians 6:1): "Dare any of you, having a matter against another, go to be judged before the unjust," i.e. unbelievers, "and not before the saints?" Therefore it seems that unbelievers cannot have authority over the faithful.

I answer that, That this question may be considered in two ways. First, we may speak of dominion or authority of unbelievers over the faithful as of a thing to be established for the first time. This ought by no means to be allowed, since it would provoke scandal and endanger the faith, for subjects are easily influenced by their superiors to comply with their commands, unless the subjects are of great virtue: moreover unbelievers hold the faith in contempt, if they see the faithful fall away. Hence the Apostle forbade the faithful to go to law before an unbelieving judge. And so the Church altogether forbids unbelievers to acquire dominion over believers, or to have authority over them in any capacity whatever.

Secondly, we may speak of dominion or authority, as already in force: and here we must observe that dominion and authority are institutions of human law, while the distinction between faithful and unbelievers arises from the Divine law. Now the Divine law which is the law of grace, does not do away with human law which is the law of natural reason. Wherefore the distinction between faithful and unbelievers, considered in itself, does not do away with dominion and authority of unbelievers over the faithful.

Nevertheless this right of dominion or authority can be justly done away with by the sentence or ordination of the Church who has the authority of God: since unbelievers in virtue of their unbelief deserve to forfeit their power over the faithful who are converted into children of God.

This the Church does sometimes, and sometimes not. For among those unbelievers who are subject, even in temporal matters, to the Church and her members, the Church made the law that if the slave of a Jew became a Christian, he should forthwith receive his freedom, without paying any price, if he should be a "vernaculus," i.e. born in slavery; and likewise if, when yet an unbeliever, he had been bought for his service: if, however, he had been bought for sale, then he should be offered for sale within three months. Nor does the Church harm them in this, because since those Jews themselves are subject to the Church, she can dispose of their possessions, even as secular princes have enacted many laws to be observed by their subjects, in favor of liberty. On the other hand, the Church has not applied the above law to those unbelievers who are not subject to her or her members, in temporal matters, although she has the right to do so: and this, in order to avoid scandal, for as Our Lord showed (Matthew 17:25-26) that He could be excused from paying the tribute, because "the children are free," yet He ordered the tribute to be paid in order to avoid giving scandal. Thus Paul too, after saying that servants should honor their masters, adds, "lest the name of the Lord and His doctrine be blasphemed."

This suffices for the Reply to the First Objection.

Reply to Objection 2. The authority of Caesar preceded the distinction of faithful from unbelievers. Hence it was not cancelled by the conversion of some to the faith. Moreover it was a good thing that there should be a few of the faithful in the emperor's household, that they might defend the rest of the faithful. Thus the Blessed Sebastian encouraged those whom he saw faltering under torture, and, the while, remained hidden under the military cloak in the palace of Diocletian.

Reply to Objection 3. Slaves are subject to their masters for their whole lifetime, and are subject to their overseers in everything: whereas the craftsman's laborer is subject to him for certain special works. Hence it would be more dangerous for unbelievers to have dominion or authority over the faithful, than that they should be allowed to employ them in some craft. Wherefore the Church permits Christians to work on the land of Jews, because this does not entail their living together with them. Thus Solomon besought the King of Tyre to send master workmen to hew the trees, as related in 1 Kings 5:6. Yet, if there be reason to fear that the faithful will be perverted by such communications and dealings, they should be absolutely forbidden.

ARTICLE 11. WHETHER THE RITES OF UNBELIEVERS OUGHT TO BE TOLERATED?

Objection 1. It would seem that rites of unbelievers ought not to be tolerated. For it is evident that unbelievers sin in observing their rites: and not to prevent a sin, when one can, seems to imply consent therein, as a gloss observes on Romans 1:32: "Not only they that do them, but they also that consent to them that do them." Therefore it is a sin to tolerate their rites.

Objection 2. Further, the rites of the Jews are compared to idolatry, because a gloss on Galatians 5:1, "Be not held again under the yoke of bondage," says: "The bondage of that law was not lighter than that of idolatry." But it would not be allowable for anyone to observe the rites of idolatry, in fact Christian princes at first caused the temples of idols to be closed, and afterwards, to be destroyed, as Augustine relates (De Civ. Dei xviii, 54). Therefore it follows that even the rites of Jews ought not to be tolerated.

Objection 3. Further, unbelief is the greatest of sins, as stated above (Article 3). Now other sins such as adultery, theft and the like, are not tolerated, but are punishable by law. Therefore neither ought the rites of unbelievers to be tolerated.

On the contrary, Gregory [Regist. xi, Ep. 15: cf. Decret., dist. xlv, can., Qui sincera] says, speaking of the Jews: "They should be allowed to observe all their feasts, just as hitherto they and their fathers have for ages observed them."

I answer that, Human government is derived from the Divine government, and should imitate it. Now although God is all-powerful and supremely good, nevertheless He allows certain evils to take place in the universe, which He might prevent, lest, without them, greater goods might be forfeited, or greater evils ensue. Accordingly in human government also, those who are in authority, rightly tolerate certain evils, lest certain goods be lost, or certain greater evils be incurred: thus Augustine says (De Ordine ii, 4): "If you do away with harlots, the world will be convulsed with lust." Hence, though unbelievers sin in their rites, they may be tolerated, either on account of some good that ensues therefrom, or because of some evil avoided. Thus from the fact that the Jews observe their rites, which, of old, foreshadowed the truth of the faith which we hold, there follows this good—that our very enemies bear witness to our faith, and that our faith is represented in a figure, so to speak. For this reason they are tolerated in the observance of their rites.

On the other hand, the rites of other unbelievers, which are neither truthful nor profitable are by no means to be tolerated, except perchance in order to avoid an evil, e.g. the scandal or disturbance that might ensue, or some hindrance to the salvation of those who if they were unmolested might gradually be converted to the faith. For this reason the Church, at times, has tolerated the rites even of heretics and pagans, when unbelievers were very numerous.

This suffices for the Replies to the Objections.

ARTICLE 12. WHETHER THE CHILDREN OF JEWS AND OTHER UNBELIEVERS OUGHT TO BE BAPTIZED AGAINST THEIR PARENTS' WILL?

Objection 1. It would seem that the children of Jews and of other unbelievers ought to be baptized against their parents' will. For the bond of marriage is stronger than the right of parental authority over children, since the right of parental authority can be made to cease, when a son is set at liberty; whereas the marriage bond cannot be severed by man, according to Matthew 19:6: "What . . . God hath joined together let no man put asunder." And yet the marriage bond is broken on account of unbelief: for the Apostle says (1 Corinthians 7:15): "If the unbeliever depart, let him depart. For a brother or sister is not under servitude in such cases": and a canon [Can. Uxor legitima, and Idololatria, qu. i] says that "if the unbelieving partner is unwilling to abide with the other, without insult to their Creator, then the other partner is not bound to cohabitation." Much more, therefore, does unbelief abrogate the right of unbelieving parents' authority over their children: and consequently their children may be baptized against their parents' will.

Objection 2. Further, one is more bound to succor a man who is in danger of everlasting death, than one who is in danger of temporal death. Now it would be a sin, if one saw a man in danger of temporal death and failed to go to his aid. Since, then, the children of Jews and other unbelievers are in danger of everlasting death, should they be left to their parents who would imbue them with their unbelief, it seems that they ought to be taken away from them and baptized, and instructed in the faith.

Objection 3. Further, the children of a bondsman are themselves bondsmen, and under the power of his master. Now the Jews are bondsmen of kings and princes: therefore their children are also. Consequently kings and princes have the power to do what they will with Jewish children. Therefore no injustice is committed if they baptize them against their parents' wishes.

Objection 4. Further, every man belongs more to God, from Whom he has his soul, than to his carnal father, from whom he has his body. Therefore it is not unjust if Jewish children be taken away from their parents, and consecrated to God in Baptism.

Objection 5. Further, Baptism avails for salvation more than preaching does, since Baptism removes forthwith the stain of sin and the debt of punishment, and opens the gate of heaven. Now if danger ensue through not preaching, it is imputed to him who omitted to preach, according to the words of Ezekiel 33:6 about the man who "sees the sword coming and sounds not the trumpet." Much more therefore, if Jewish children are lost through not being baptized are they accounted guilty of sin, who could have baptized them and did not.

On the contrary, Injustice should be done to no man. Now it would be an injustice to Jews if their children were to be baptized against their will, since they would lose the rights of parental authority over their children as soon as these were Christians. Therefore these should not be baptized against their parents' will.

I answer that, The custom of the Church has very great authority and ought to be jealously observed in all things, since the very doctrine of catholic doctors derives its authority from the Church. Hence we ought to abide by the authority of the Church rather than by that of an Augustine or a Jerome or of any doctor whatever. Now it was never the custom of the Church to baptize the children of the Jews against the will of their parents, although at times past there have been many very powerful catholic princes like Constantine and Theodosius, with whom most holy bishops have been on most friendly terms, as Sylvester with Constantine, and Ambrose with Theodosius, who would certainly not have failed to obtain this favor from them if it had been at all reasonable. It seems therefore hazardous to repeat this assertion, that the children of Jews should be baptized against their parents' wishes, in contradiction to the Church's custom observed hitherto.

There are two reasons for this custom. One is on account of the danger to the faith. For children baptized before coming to the use of reason, afterwards when they come to perfect age, might easily be persuaded by their parents to renounce what they had unknowingly embraced; and this would be detrimental to the faith.

The other reason is that it is against natural justice. For a child is by nature part of its father: thus, at first, it is not distinct from its parents as to its body, so long as it is enfolded within its mother's womb; and later on after birth, and before it has the use of its free-will, it is enfolded in the care of its parents, which is like a spiritual womb, for so long as man has not the use of reason, he differs not from an irrational animal; so that even as an ox or a horse belongs to someone who, according to the civil law, can use them when he likes, as his own instrument, so, according to the natural law, a son, before coming to the use of reason, is under his father's care. Hence it would be contrary to natural justice, if a child, before coming to the use of reason, were to be taken away from its parents' custody, or anything done to it against its parents' wish. As soon, however, as it begins to have the use of its free-will, it begins to belong to itself, and is able to look after itself, in matters concerning the Divine or the natural law, and then it should be induced, not by compulsion but by persuasion, to embrace the faith: it can then consent to the faith, and be baptized, even against its parents' wish; but not before it comes to the use of reason. Hence it is said of the children of the fathers of old that they were saved in the faith of their parents; whereby we are given to understand that it is the parents' duty to look after the salvation of their children, especially before they come to the use of reason.

Reply to Objection 1. In the marriage bond, both husband and wife have the use of the free-will, and each can assent to the faith without the other's consent. But this does not apply to a child before it comes to the use of reason: yet the comparison holds good after the child has come to the use of reason, if it is willing to be converted.

Reply to Objection 2. No one should be snatched from natural death against the order of civil law: for instance, if a man were condemned by the judge to temporal death, nobody ought to rescue him by violence: hence no one ought to break the order of the natural law, whereby a child is in the custody of its father, in order to rescue it from the danger of everlasting death.

Reply to Objection 3. Jews are bondsmen of princes by civil bondage, which does not exclude the order of natural or Divine law.

Reply to Objection 4. Man is directed to God by his reason, whereby he can know Him. Hence a child before coming to the use of reason, in the natural order of things, is directed to God by its parents' reason, under whose care it lies by nature: and it is for them to dispose of the child in all matters relating to God.

Reply to Objection 5. The peril that ensues from the omission of preaching, threatens only those who are entrusted with the duty of preaching. Hence it had already been said (Ezekiel 3:17): "I have made thee a watchman to the children [Vulgate: 'house'] of Israel." On the other hand, to provide the sacraments of salvation for the children of unbelievers is the duty of their parents. Hence it is they whom the danger threatens, if through being deprived of the sacraments their children fail to obtain salvation.

QUESTION 11. HERESY

ARTICLE 3. WHETHER HERETICS OUGHT TO BE TOLERATED?

Objection 1. It seems that heretics ought to be tolerated. For the Apostle says (2 Timothy 2:24-25): "The servant of the Lord must not wrangle . . . with modesty admonishing them that resist the truth, if peradventure God may give them repentance to know the truth, and they may recover themselves from the snares of the devil." Now if heretics are not tolerated but put to death, they lose the opportunity of repentance. Therefore it seems contrary to the Apostle's command.

Objection 2. Further, whatever is necessary in the Church should be tolerated. Now heresies are necessary in the Church, since the Apostle says (1 Corinthians 11:19): "There must be . . . heresies, that they . . . who are reproved, may be manifest among you." Therefore it seems that heretics should be tolerated.

Objection 3. Further, the Master commanded his servants (Matthew 13:30) to suffer the cockle "to grow until the harvest," i.e. the end of the world, as a gloss explains it. Now holy men explain that the cockle denotes heretics. Therefore heretics should be tolerated.

On the contrary, The Apostle says (Titus 3:10-11): "A man that is a heretic, after the first and second admonition, avoid: knowing that he, that is such an one, is subverted."

I answer that, With regard to heretics two points must be observed: one, on their own side; the other, on the side of the Church. On their own side there is the sin, whereby they deserve not only to be separated from the Church by excommunication, but also to be severed from the world by death. For it is a much graver matter to corrupt the faith which quickens the soul, than to forge money, which supports temporal life. Wherefore if forgers of money and other evil-doers are forthwith condemned to death by the secular authority, much more reason is there for heretics, as soon as they are convicted of heresy, to be not only excommunicated but even put to death.

On the part of the Church, however, there is mercy which looks to the conversion of the wanderer, wherefore she condemns not at once, but "after the first and second admonition," as the Apostle directs: after that, if he is yet stubborn, the Church no longer hoping for his conversion, looks to the salvation of others, by excommunicating him and separating him from the Church, and furthermore delivers him to the secular tribunal to be exterminated thereby from the world by death. For Jerome commenting on Galatians 5:9, "A little leaven," says: "Cut off the decayed flesh, expel the mangy sheep from the fold, lest the whole house, the whole paste, the whole body, the whole flock, burn, perish, rot, die. Arius was but one spark in Alexandria, but as that spark was not at once put out, the whole earth was laid waste by its flame."

Reply to Objection 1. This very modesty demands that the heretic should be admonished a first and second time: and if he be unwilling to retract, he must be reckoned as already "subverted," as we may gather from the words of the Apostle quoted above.

Reply to Objection 2. The profit that ensues from heresy is beside the intention of heretics, for it consists in the constancy of the faithful being put to the test, and "makes us shake off our sluggishness, and search the Scriptures more carefully," as Augustine states (De Gen. cont. Manich. i, 1). What they really intend is the corruption of the faith, which is to inflict very great harm indeed. Consequently we should consider what they directly intend, and expel them, rather than what is beside their intention, and so, tolerate them.

Reply to Objection 3. According to Decret. (xxiv, qu. iii, can. Notandum), "to be excommunicated is not to be uprooted." A man is excommunicated, as the Apostle says (1 Corinthians 5:5) that his "spirit may be saved in the day of Our Lord." Yet if heretics be altogether uprooted by death, this is not contrary to Our Lord's command, which is to be understood as referring to the case when the cockle cannot be plucked up without plucking up the wheat, as we explained above (10, 8, ad 1), when treating of unbelievers in general.

QUESTION 23. CHARITY, CONSIDERED IN ITSELF

ARTICLE 1. WHETHER CHARITY IS FRIENDSHIP?

Objection 1. It would seem that charity is not friendship. For nothing is so appropriate to friendship as to dwell with one's friend, according to the Philosopher (Ethic. viii, 5). Now charity is of man towards God and the angels, "whose dwelling [Douay: 'conversation'] is not with men" (Daniel 2:11). Therefore charity is not friendship.

Objection 2. Further, there is no friendship without return of love (Ethic. viii, 2). But charity extends even to one's enemies, according to Matthew 5:44: "Love your enemies." Therefore charity is not friendship.

Objection 3. Further, according to the Philosopher (Ethic. viii, 3) there are three kinds of friendship, directed respectively towards the delightful, the useful, or the virtuous. Now charity is not the friendship for the useful or delightful; for Jerome says in his letter to Paulinus which is to be found at the beginning of the Bible: "True friendship cemented by Christ, is where men are drawn together, not by household interests, not by mere bodily presence, not by crafty and cajoling flattery, but by the fear of God, and the study of the Divine Scriptures." No more is it friendship for the virtuous, since by charity we love even sinners, whereas friendship based on the virtuous is only for virtuous men (Ethic. viii). Therefore charity is not friendship.

On the contrary, It is written (John 15:15): "I will not now call you servants ... but My friends." Now this was said to them by reason of nothing else than charity. Therefore charity is friendship.

I answer that, According to the Philosopher (Ethic. viii, 2,3) not every love has the character of friendship, but that love which is together with benevolence, when, to wit, we love someone so as to wish good to him. If, however, we do not wish good to what we love, but wish its good for ourselves, (thus we are said to love wine, or a horse, or the like), it is love not of friendship, but of a kind of desire. For it would be absurd to speak of having friendship for wine or for a horse.

Yet neither does well-wishing suffice for friendship, for a certain mutual love is requisite, since friendship is between friend and friend: and this well-wishing is founded on some kind of communication.

Accordingly, since there is a communication between man and God, inasmuch as He communicates His happiness to us, some kind of friendship must needs be based on this same communication, of which it is written (1

Corinthians 1:9): "God is faithful: by Whom you are called unto the fellowship of His Son." The love which is based on this communication, is charity: wherefore it is evident that charity is the friendship of man for God.

Reply to Objection 1. Man's life is twofold. There is his outward life in respect of his sensitive and corporeal nature: and with regard to this life there is no communication or fellowship between us and God or the angels. The other is man's spiritual life in respect of his mind, and with regard to this life there is fellowship between us and both God and the angels, imperfectly indeed in this present state of life, wherefore it is written (Philippians 3:20): "Our conversation is in heaven." But this "conversation" will be perfected in heaven, when "His servants shall serve Him, and they shall see His face" (Apocalypse 22:3-4). Therefore charity is imperfect here, but will be perfected in heaven.

Reply to Objection 2. Friendship extends to a person in two ways: first in respect of himself, and in this way friendship never extends but to one's friends: secondly, it extends to someone in respect of another, as, when a man has friendship for a certain person, for his sake he loves all belonging to him, be they children, servants, or connected with him in any way. Ondeed so much do we love our friends, that for their sake we love all who belong to them, even if they hurt or hate us; so that, in this way, the friendship of charity extends even to our enemies, whom we love out of charity in relation to God, to Whom the friendship of charity is chiefly directed.

Reply to Objection 3. The friendship that is based on the virtuous is directed to none but a virtuous man as the principal person, but for his sake we love those who belong to him, even though they be not virtuous: in this way charity, which above all is friendship based on the virtuous, extends to sinners, whom, out of charity, we love for God's sake.

ARTICLE 7. WHETHER ANY TRUE VIRTUE IS POSSIBLE WITHOUT CHARITY?

Objection 1. It would seem that there can be true virtue without charity. For it is proper to virtue to produce a good act. Now those who have not charity, do some good actions, as when they clothe the naked, or feed the hungry and so forth. Therefore true virtue is possible without charity.

Objection 2. Further, charity is not possible without faith, since it comes of "an unfeigned faith," as the Apostle says (1 Timothy 1:5). Now, in unbelievers, there can be true chastity, if they curb their desires, and true justice, if they judge rightly. Therefore true virtue is possible without charity.

Objection 3. Further, science and art are virtues, according to Ethic. vi. But they are to be found in sinners who lack charity. Therefore true virtue can be without charity.

On the contrary, The Apostle says (1 Corinthians 13:3): "If I should distribute all my goods to the poor, and if I should deliver my body to be burned, and have not charity, it profiteth me nothing." And yet true virtue is very profitable, according to Wisdom 8:7: "She teacheth temperance, and prudence, and justice, and fortitude, which are such things as men can have nothing more profitable in life." Therefore no true virtue is possible without charity.

I answer that, Virtue is ordered to the good, as stated above (I-II, 55, 4). Now the good is chiefly an end, for things directed to the end are not said to be good except in relation to the end. Accordingly, just as the end is twofold, the last end, and the proximate end, so also, is good twofold, one, the ultimate and universal good, the other proximate and particular. The ultimate and principal good of man is the enjoyment of God, according to Psalm 72:28: "It is good for me to adhere to God," and to this good man is ordered by charity. Man's secondary and, as it were, particular good may be twofold: one is truly good, because, considered in itself, it can be directed to the principal good, which is the last end; while the other is good apparently and not truly, because it leads us away from the final good. Accordingly it is evident that simply true virtue is that which is directed to man's principal good; thus also the Philosopher says (Phys. vii, text. 17) that "virtue is the disposition of a perfect thing to that which is best": and in this way no true virtue is possible without charity.

If, however, we take virtue as being ordered to some particular end, then we speak of virtue being where there is no charity, in so far as it is directed to some particular good. But if this particular good is not a true, but an apparent good, it is not a true virtue that is ordered to such a good, but a counterfeit virtue. Even so, as Augustine says (Contra Julian. iv, 3), "the prudence of the miser, whereby he devises various roads to gain, is no true virtue; nor the miser's justice, whereby he scorns the property of another through fear of severe punishment; nor the miser's temperance, whereby he curbs his desire for expensive pleasures; nor the miser's fortitude, whereby as Horace, says, 'he braves the sea, he crosses mountains, he goes through fire, in order to avoid poverty'" (Epis. lib, 1; Ep. i, 45). If, on the other hand, this particular good be a true good, for instance the welfare of the city, or the like, it will indeed be a true virtue, imperfect, however, unless it be referred to the final and perfect good. Accordingly no strictly true virtue is possible without charity.

Reply to Objection 1. The act of one lacking charity may be of two kinds; one is in accordance with his lack of charity, as when he does something that is referred to that whereby he lacks charity. Such an act is always evil: thus Augustine says (Contra Julian. iv, 3) that the actions which an unbeliever performs as an unbeliever, are always sinful, even when he clothes the naked, or does any like thing, and directs it to his unbelief as end.

There is, however, another act of one lacking charity, not in accordance with his lack of charity, but in accordance with his possession of some other gift of God, whether faith, or hope, or even his natural good, which is not completely taken away by sin, as stated above (10, 4; I-II, 85, 2). On this way it is possible for an act, without charity, to be generically good, but not perfectly good, because it lacks its due order to the last end.

Reply to Objection 2. Since the end is in practical matters, what the principle is in speculative matters, just as there can be no strictly true science, if a right estimate of the first indemonstrable principle be lacking, so, there can be no strictly true justice, or chastity, without that due ordering to the end, which is effected by charity, however rightly a man may be affected about other matters.

Reply to Objection 3. Science and art of their very nature imply a relation to some particular good, and not to the ultimate good of human life, as do the moral virtues, which make man good simply, as stated above (I-II, 56, 3). Hence the comparison fails.

QUESTION 25. THE OBJECT OF CHARITY

ARTICLE 1. WHETHER THE LOVE OF CHARITY STOPS AT GOD, OR EXTENDS TO OUR NEIGHBOR?

Objection 1. It would seem that the love of charity stops at God and does not extend to our neighbor. For as we owe God love, so do we owe Him fear, according Deuteronomy 10:12: "And now Israel, what doth the Lord thy God require of thee, but that thou fear . . . and love Him?" Now the fear with which we fear man, and which is called human fear, is distinct from the fear with which we fear God, and which is either servile or filial, as is evident from what has been stated above (Question 10, Article 2). Therefore also the love with which we love God, is distinct from the love with which we love our neighbor.

Objection 2. Further, the Philosopher says (Ethic. viii, 8) that "to be loved is to be honored." Now the honor due to God, which is known as "latria", is distinct from the honor due to a creature, and known as "dulia." Therefore again the love wherewith we love God, is distinct from that with which we love our neighbor.

Objection 3. Further, hope begets charity, as a gloss states on Matthew 1:2. Now hope is so due to God that it is reprehensible to hope in man, according to Jeremiah 17:5: "Cursed be the man that trusteth in man." Therefore charity is so due to God, as not to extend to our neighbor.

On the contrary, It is written (1 John 4:21): "This commandment we have from God, that he, who loveth God, love also his brother."

I answer that, As stated above (17, 6; 19, 3; I-II, 54, 3) habits are not differentiated except their acts be of different species. For every act of the one species belongs to the same habit. Now since the species of an act is derived from its object, considered under its formal aspect, it follows of necessity that it is specifically the same act that tends to an aspect of the object, and that tends to the object under that aspect: thus it is specifically the same visual act whereby we see the light, and whereby we see the color under the aspect of light.

Now the aspect under which our neighbor is to be loved, is God, since what we ought to love in our neighbor is that he may be in God. Hence it is clear that it is specifically the same act whereby we love God, and whereby we love our neighbor. Consequently the habit of charity extends not only to the love of God, but also to the love of our neighbor.

Reply to Objection 1. We may fear our neighbor, even as we may love him, in two ways: first, on account of something that is proper to him, as when a man fears a tyrant on account of his cruelty, or loves him by reason of his own desire to get something from him. Such like human fear is distinct from the fear of God, and the same applies to love. Secondly, we fear a man, or love him on account of what he has of God; as when we fear the secular power by reason of its exercising the ministry of God for the punishment of evildoers, and love it for its justice: such like fear of man is not distinct from fear of God, as neither is such like love.

Reply to Objection 2. Love regards good in general, whereas honor regards the honored person's own good, for it is given to a person in recognition of his own virtue. Hence love is not differentiated specifically on account of the various degrees of goodness in various persons, so long as it is referred to one good common to all, whereas honor is distinguished according to the good belonging to individuals. Consequently we love all our neighbors with the same love of charity, in so far as they are referred to one good common to them all, which is God; whereas we give various honors to various people, according to each one's own virtue, and likewise to God we give the singular honor of latria on account of His singular virtue.

Reply to Objection 3. It is wrong to hope in man as though he were the principal author of salvation, but not, to hope in man as helping us ministerially under God. On like manner it would be wrong if a man loved his neighbor as though he were his last end, but not, if he loved him for God's sake; and this is what charity does.

ARTICLE 4. WHETHER A MAN OUGHT TO LOVE HIMSELF OUT OF CHARITY?

Objection 1. It would seem that a man is not bound to love himself out of charity. For Gregory says in a homily (In Evang. xvii) that there "can be no charity between less than two." Therefore no man has charity towards himself.

Objection 2. Further, friendship, by its very nature, implies mutual love and equality (Ethic. viii, 2,7), which cannot be of one man towards himself. But charity is a kind of friendship, as stated above (Question 23, Article 1). Therefore a man cannot have charity towards himself.

Objection 3. Further, anything relating to charity cannot be blameworthy, since charity "dealeth not perversely" (1 Corinthians 13:4). Now a man deserves to be blamed for loving himself, since it is written (2 Timothy 3:1-2): "In the last days shall come dangerous times, men shall be lovers of themselves." Therefore a man cannot love himself out of charity.

On the contrary, It is written (Leviticus 19:18): "Thou shalt love thy friend as thyself." Now we love our friends out of charity. Therefore we should love ourselves too out of charity.

I answer that, Since charity is a kind of friendship, as stated above (Question 23, Article 1), we may consider charity from two standpoints: first, under the general notion of friendship, and in this way we must hold that, properly speaking, a man is not a friend to himself, but something more than a friend, since friendship implies union, for Dionysius says (Div. Nom. iv) that "love is a unitive force," whereas a man is one with himself which is more than being united to another. Hence, just as unity is the principle of union, so the love with which a man loves himself is the form and root of friendship. For if we have friendship with others it is because we do unto them as we do unto ourselves, hence we read in Ethic. ix, 4,8, that "the origin of friendly relations with others lies in our relations to ourselves." Thus too with regard to principles we have something greater than science, namely understanding.

Secondly, we may speak of charity in respect of its specific nature, namely as denoting man's friendship with God in the first place, and, consequently, with the things of God, among which things is man himself who has charity. Hence, among these other things which he loves out of charity because they pertain to God, he loves also himself out of charity.

Reply to Objection 1. Gregory speaks there of charity under the general notion of friendship: and the Second Objection is to be taken in the same sense.

Reply to Objection 3. Those who love themselves are to be blamed, in so far as they love themselves as regards their sensitive nature, which they humor. This is not to love oneself truly according to one's rational nature, so as to desire for oneself the good things which pertain to the perfection of reason: and in this way chiefly it is through charity that a man loves himself.

ARTICLE 6. WHETHER WE OUGHT TO LOVE SINNERS OUT OF CHARITY?

Objection 1. It would seem that we ought not to love sinners out of charity. For it is written (Psalm 118:113): "I have hated the unjust." But David had perfect charity. Therefore sinners should be hated rather than loved, out of charity.

Objection 2. Further, "love is proved by deeds" as Gregory says in a homily for Pentecost (In Evang. xxx). But good men do no works of the unjust: on the contrary, they do such as would appear to be works of hate, according to Psalm 100:8: "In the morning I put to death all the wicked of the land": and God commanded (Exodus 22:18): "Wizards thou shalt not suffer to live." Therefore sinners should not be loved out of charity.

Objection 3. Further, it is part of friendship that one should desire and wish good things for one's friends. Now the saints, out of charity, desire evil things for the wicked, according to Psalm 9:18: "May the wicked be turned into hell [Douay and A.V.: 'The wicked shall be,' etc. See Reply to this Objection.]." Therefore sinners should not be loved out of charity.

Objection 4. Further, it is proper to friends to rejoice in, and will the same things. Now charity does not make us will what sinners will, nor to rejoice in what gives them joy, but rather the contrary. Therefore sinners should not be loved out of charity.

Objection 5. Further, it is proper to friends to associate together, according to Ethic. viii. But we ought not to associate with sinners, according to 2 Corinthians 6:17: "Go ye out from among them." Therefore we should not love sinners out of charity.

On the contrary, Augustine says (De Doctr. Christ. i, 30) that "when it is said: 'Thou shalt love thy neighbor,' it is evident that we ought to look upon every man as our neighbor." Now sinners do not cease to be men, for sin does not destroy nature. Therefore we ought to love sinners out of charity.

I answer that, Two things may be considered in the sinner: his nature and his guilt. According to his nature, which he has from God, he has a capacity for happiness, on the fellowship of which charity is based, as stated above (3; 23, 1,5), wherefore we ought to love sinners, out of charity, in respect of their nature.

On the other hand their guilt is opposed to God, and is an obstacle to happiness. Wherefore, in respect of their guilt whereby they are opposed to God, all sinners are to be hated, even one's father or mother or kindred, according to

Luke 12:26. For it is our duty to hate, in the sinner, his being a sinner, and to love in him, his being a man capable of bliss; and this is to love him truly, out of charity, for God's sake.

Reply to Objection 1. The prophet hated the unjust, as such, and the object of his hate was their injustice, which was their evil. Such hatred is perfect, of which he himself says (Psalm 138:22): "I have hated them with a perfect hatred." Now hatred of a person's evil is equivalent to love of his good. Hence also this perfect hatred belongs to charity.

Reply to Objection 2. As the Philosopher observes (Ethic. ix, 3), when our friends fall into sin, we ought not to deny them the amenities of friendship, so long as there is hope of their mending their ways, and we ought to help them more readily to regain virtue than to recover money, had they lost it, for as much as virtue is more akin than money to friendship. When, however, they fall into very great wickedness, and become incurable, we ought no longer to show them friendliness. It is for this reason that both Divine and human laws command such like sinners to be put to death, because there is greater likelihood of their harming others than of their mending their ways. Nevertheless the judge puts this into effect, not out of hatred for the sinners, but out of the love of charity, by reason of which he prefers the public good to the life of the individual. Moreover the death inflicted by the judge profits the sinner, if he be converted, unto the expiation of his crime; and, if he be not converted, it profits so as to put an end to the sin, because the sinner is thus deprived of the power to sin any more.

Reply to Objection 3. Such like imprecations which we come across in Holy Writ, may be understood in three ways: first, by way of prediction, not by way of wish, so that the sense is: "May the wicked be," that is, "The wicked shall be, turned into hell." Secondly, by way of wish, yet so that the desire of the wisher is not referred to the man's punishment, but to the justice of the punisher, according to Psalm 57:11: "The just shall rejoice when he shall see the revenge," since, according to Wisdom 1:13, not even God "hath pleasure in the destruction of the wicked [Vulgate: 'living']" when He punishes them, but He rejoices in His justice, according to Psalm 10:8: "The Lord is just and hath loved justice." Thirdly, so that this desire is referred to the removal of the sin, and not to the punishment itself, to the effect, namely, that the sin be destroyed, but that the man may live.

Reply to Objection 4. We love sinners out of charity, not so as to will what they will, or to rejoice in what gives them joy, but so as to make them will what we will, and rejoice in what rejoices us. Hence it is written (Jeremiah 15:19): "They shall be turned to thee, and thou shalt not to be turned to them."

Reply to Objection 5. The weak should avoid associating with sinners, on account of the danger in which they stand of being perverted by them. But it is commendable for the perfect, of whose perversion there is no fear, to associate with sinners that they may convert them. For thus did Our Lord eat and drink with sinners as related by Matthew 9:11-13. Yet all should avoid the society of sinners, as regards fellowship in sin; in this sense it is written (2 Corinthians 6:17): "Go out from among them . . . and touch not the unclean thing," i.e. by consenting to sin.

ARTICLE 7. WHETHER SINNERS LOVE THEMSELVES?

Objection 1. It would seem that sinners love themselves. For that which is the principle of sin, is most of all in the sinner. Now love of self is the principle of sin, since Augustine says (De Civ. Dei xiv, 28) that it "builds up the city of Babylon." Therefore sinners most of all love themselves.

Objection 2. Further, sin does not destroy nature. Now it is in keeping with nature that every man should love himself: wherefore even irrational creatures naturally desire their own good, for instance, the preservation of their being, and so forth. Therefore sinners love themselves.

Objection 3. Further, good is beloved by all, as Dionysius states (Div. Nom. iv). Now many sinners reckon themselves to be good. Therefore many sinners love themselves.

On the contrary, It is written (Psalm 10:6): "He that loveth iniquity, hateth his own soul."

I answer that, Love of self is common to all, in one way; in another way it is proper to the good; in a third way, it is proper to the wicked. For it is common to all for each one to love what he thinks himself to be. Now a man is said to be a thing in two ways: first, in respect of his substance and nature, and in this way all think themselves to be what they are, that is, composed of a soul and body. In this way too, all men, both good and wicked, love themselves, in so far as they love their own preservation.

Secondly, a man is said to be something in respect of some predominance, as the sovereign of a city is spoken of as being the city, and so, what the sovereign does, the city is said to do. In this way, all do not think themselves to be what they are. For the reasoning mind is the predominant part of man, while the sensitive and corporeal nature takes the second place, the former of which the Apostle calls the "inward man," and the latter, the "outward man" (2 Corinthians 4:16). Now the good look upon their rational nature or the inward man as being the chief thing in them, wherefore in this way they think themselves to be what they are. On the other hand, the wicked reckon their sensitive and corporeal nature, or the outward man, to hold the first place. Wherefore, since they know not themselves aright, they do not love themselves aright, but love what they think themselves to be. But the good know themselves truly, and therefore truly love themselves.

The Philosopher proves this from five things that are proper to friendship. For in the first place, every friend wishes his friend to be and to live; secondly, he desires good things for him; thirdly, he does good things to him; fourthly, he takes pleasure in his company; fifthly, he is of one mind with him, rejoicing and sorrowing in almost the same things. In this way the good love themselves, as to the inward man, because they wish the preservation thereof in its integrity, they desire good things for him, namely spiritual goods, indeed they do their best to obtain them, and they take pleasure in entering into their own hearts, because they find there good thoughts in the present, the memory of past good, and the hope of future good, all of which are sources of pleasure. Likewise they experience no clashing of wills, since their whole soul tends to one thing.

On the other hand, the wicked have no wish to be preserved in the integrity of the inward man, nor do they desire spiritual goods for him, nor do they work for that end, nor do they take pleasure in their own company by entering into their own hearts, because whatever they find there, present, past and future, is evil and horrible; nor do they agree with themselves, on account of the gnawings of conscience, according to Psalm 49:21: "I will reprove thee and set before thy face."

In the same manner it may be shown that the wicked love themselves, as regards the corruption of the outward man, whereas the good do not love themselves thus.

Reply to Objection 1. The love of self which is the principle of sin is that which is proper to the wicked, and reaches "to the contempt of God," as stated in the passage quoted, because the wicked so desire external goods as to despise spiritual goods.

Reply to Objection 2. Although natural love is not altogether forfeited by wicked men, yet it is perverted in them, as explained above.

Reply to Objection 3. The wicked have some share of self-love, in so far as they think themselves good. Yet such love of self is not true but apparent: and even this is not possible in those who are very wicked.

ARTICLE 8. WHETHER CHARITY REQUIRES THAT WE SHOULD LOVE OUR ENEMIES?

Objection 1. It would seem that charity does not require us to love our enemies. For Augustine says (Enchiridion lxxiii) that "this great good," namely, the love of our enemies, is "not so universal in its application, as the object of our petition when we say: Forgive us our trespasses." Now no one is forgiven sin without charity, because, according to Proverbs 10:12, "charity covereth all sins." Therefore charity does not require that we should love our enemies.

Objection 2. Further, charity does not do away with nature. Now everything, even an irrational being, naturally hates its contrary, as a lamb hates a wolf, and water fire. Therefore charity does not make us love our enemies.

Objection 3. Further, charity "doth nothing perversely" (1 Corinthians 13:4). Now it seems perverse to love one's enemies, as it would be to hate one's friends: hence Joab upbraided David by saying (2 Samuel 19:6): "Thou lovest them that hate thee, and thou hatest them that love thee." Therefore charity does not make us love our enemies.

On the contrary, Our Lord said (Matthew 4:44): "Love your enemies."

I answer that, Love of one's enemies may be understood in three ways. First, as though we were to love our enemies as such: this is perverse, and contrary to charity, since it implies love of that which is evil in another.

Secondly love of one's enemies may mean that we love them as to their nature, but in general: and in this sense charity requires that we should love our enemies, namely, that in loving God and our neighbor, we should not exclude our enemies from the love given to our neighbor in general.

Thirdly, love of one's enemies may be considered as specially directed to them, namely, that we should have a special movement of love towards our enemies. Charity does not require this absolutely, because it does not require that we should have a special movement of love to every individual man, since this would be impossible. Nevertheless charity does require this, in respect of our being prepared in mind, namely, that we should be ready to love our enemies individually, if the necessity were to occur. That man should actually do so, and love his enemy for God's sake, without it being necessary for him to do so, belongs to the perfection of charity. For since man loves his neighbor, out of charity, for God's sake, the more he loves God, the more does he put enmities aside and show love towards his neighbor: thus if we loved a certain man very much, we would love his children though they were unfriendly towards us. This is the sense in which Augustine speaks in the passage quoted in the First Objection, the Reply to which is therefore evident.

Reply to Objection 2. Everything naturally hates its contrary as such. Now our enemies are contrary to us, as enemies, wherefore this itself should be hateful to us, for their enmity should displease us. They are not, however, contrary to us, as men and capable of happiness: and it is as such that we are bound to love them.

Reply to Objection 3. It is wrong to love one's enemies as such: charity does not do this, as stated above.

QUESTION 26. THE ORDER OF CHARITY

ARTICLE 2. WHETHER GOD OUGHT TO BE LOVED MORE THAN OUR NEIGHBOR?

Objection 1. It would seem that God ought not to be loved more than our neighbor. For it is written (1 John 4:20): "He that loveth not his brother whom he seeth, how can he love God, Whom he seeth not?" Whence it seems to follow that the more a thing is visible the more lovable it is, since loving begins with seeing, according to Ethic. ix, 5,12. Now God is less visible than our neighbor. Therefore He is less lovable, out of charity, than our neighbor.

Objection 2. Further, likeness causes love, according to Sirach 13:19: "Every beast loveth its like." Now man bears more likeness to his neighbor than to God. Therefore man loves his neighbor, out of charity, more than he loves God.

Objection 3. Further, what charity loves in a neighbor, is God, according to Augustine (De Doctr. Christ. i, 22,27). Now God is not greater in Himself than He is in our neighbor. Therefore He is not more to be loved in Himself than in our neighbor. Therefore we ought not to love God more than our neighbor.

On the contrary, A thing ought to be loved more, if others ought to be hated on its account. Now we ought to hate our neighbor for God's sake, if, to wit, he leads us astray from God, according to Luke 14:26: "If any man come to Me and hate not his father, and mother, and wife, end children, and brethren, and sisters . . . he cannot be My disciple." Therefore we ought to love God, out of charity, more than our neighbor.

I answer that, Each kind of friendship regards chiefly the subject in which we chiefly find the good on the fellowship of which that friendship is based: thus civil friendship regards chiefly the ruler of the city, on whom the entire common good of the city depends; hence to him before all, the citizens owe fidelity and obedience. Now the friendship of charity is based on the fellowship of happiness, which consists essentially in God, as the First Principle, whence it flows to all who are capable of happiness.

Therefore God ought to be loved chiefly and before all out of charity: for He is loved as the cause of happiness, whereas our neighbor is loved as receiving together with us a share of happiness from Him.

Reply to Objection 1. A thing is a cause of love in two ways: first, as being the reason for loving. In this way good is the cause of love, since each thing is loved according to its measure of goodness. Secondly, a thing causes love, as being a way to acquire love. It is in this way that seeing is the cause of loving, not as though a thing were lovable according as it is visible, but because by seeing a thing we are led to love it. Hence it does not follow that what is more visible is more lovable, but that as an object of love we meet with it before others: and that is the sense of the Apostle's argument. For, since our neighbor is more visible to us, he is the first lovable object we meet with, because "the soul learns, from those things it knows, to love what it knows not," as Gregory says in a homily (In Evang. xi). Hence it can be argued that, if any man loves not his neighbor, neither does he love God, not because his neighbor is more lovable, but because he is the first thing to demand our love: and God is more lovable by reason of His greater goodness.

Reply to Objection 2. The likeness we have to God precedes and causes the likeness we have to our neighbor: because from the very fact that we share along with our neighbor in something received from God, we become like to our neighbor. Hence by reason of this likeness we ought to love God more than we love our neighbor.

Reply to Objection 3. Considered in His substance, God is equally in all, in whomsoever He may be, for He is not lessened by being in anything. And yet our neighbor does not possess God's goodness equally with God, for God has it essentially, and our neighbor by participation.

ARTICLE 3. WHETHER OUT OF CHARITY, MAN IS BOUND TO LOVE GOD MORE THAN HIMSELF?

Objection 1. It would seem that man is not bound, out of charity, to love God more than himself. For the Philosopher says (Ethic. ix, 8) that "a man's friendly relations with others arise from his friendly relations with himself." Now the cause is stronger than its effect. Therefore man's friendship towards himself is greater than his friendship for anyone else. Therefore he ought to love himself more than God.

Objection 2. Further, one loves a thing in so far as it is one's own good. Now the reason for loving a thing is more loved than the thing itself which is loved for that reason, even as the principles which are the reason for knowing a thing are more known. Therefore man loves himself more than any other good loved by him. Therefore he does not love God more than himself.

Objection 3. Further, a man loves God as much as he loves to enjoy God. But a man loves himself as much as he loves to enjoy God; since this is the highest good a man can wish for himself. Therefore man is not bound, out of charity, to love God more than himself.

On the contrary, Augustine says (De Doctr. Christ. i, 22): "If thou oughtest to love thyself, not for thy own sake, but for the sake of Him in Whom is the rightest end of thy love, let no other man take offense if him also thou lovest for God's sake." Now "the cause of a thing being such is yet more so." Therefore man ought to love God more than himself.

I answer that, The good we receive from God is twofold, the good of nature, and the good of grace. Now the fellowship of natural goods bestowed on us by God is the foundation of natural love, in virtue of which not only man, so long as his nature remains unimpaired, loves God above all things and more than himself, but also every single creature, each in its own way, i.e. either by an intellectual, or by a rational, or by an animal, or at least by a natural love, as stones do, for instance, and other things bereft of knowledge, because each part naturally loves the common good of the whole more than its own particular good. This is evidenced by its operation, since the principal inclination of each part is towards common action conducive to the good of the whole. It may also be seen in civic virtues whereby sometimes the citizens suffer damage even to their own property and persons for the sake of the common good. Wherefore much more is this realized with regard to the friendship of charity which is based on the fellowship of the gifts of grace.

Therefore man ought, out of charity, to love God, Who is the common good of all, more than himself: since happiness is in God as in the universal and fountain principle of all who are able to have a share of that happiness.

Reply to Objection 1. The Philosopher is speaking of friendly relations towards another person in whom the good, which is the object of friendship, resides in some restricted way; and not of friendly relations with another in whom the aforesaid good resides in totality.

Reply to Objection 2. The part does indeed love the good of the whole, as becomes a part, not however so as to refer the good of the whole to itself, but rather itself to the good of the whole.

Reply to Objection 3. That a man wishes to enjoy God pertains to that love of God which is love of desire. Now we love God with the love of friendship more than with the love of desire, because the Divine good is greater in itself, than our share of good in enjoying Him. Hence, out of charity, man simply loves God more than himself.

ARTICLE 4. WHETHER OUR OF CHARITY, MAN OUGHT TO LOVE HIMSELF MORE THAN HIS NEIGHBOR?

Objection 1. It would seem that a man ought not, out of charity, to love himself more than his neighbor. For the principal object of charity is God, as stated above (2; 25, 1,12). Now sometimes our neighbor is more closely united to God than we are ourselves. Therefore we ought to love such a one more than ourselves.

Objection 2. Further, the more we love a person, the more we avoid injuring him. Now a man, out of charity, submits to injury for his neighbor's sake, according to Proverbs 12:26: "He that neglecteth a loss for the sake of a friend, is just." Therefore a man ought, out of charity, to love his neighbor more than himself.

Objection 3. Further, it is written (1 Corinthians 13:5) "charity seeketh not its own." Now the thing we love most is the one whose good we seek most. Therefore a man does not, out of charity, love himself more than his neighbor.

On the contrary, It is written (Leviticus 19:18, Matthew 22:39): "Thou shalt love thy neighbor (Leviticus 19:18: 'friend') as thyself." Whence it seems to follow that man's love for himself is the model of his love for another.

But the model exceeds the copy. Therefore, out of charity, a man ought to love himself more than his neighbor.

I answer that, There are two things in man, his spiritual nature and his corporeal nature. And a man is said to love himself by reason of his loving himself with regard to his spiritual nature, as stated above (Question 25, Article 7): so that accordingly, a man ought, out of charity, to love himself more than he loves any other person.

This is evident from the very reason for loving: since, as stated above (25, 1,12), God is loved as the principle of good, on which the love of charity is founded; while man, out of charity, loves himself by reason of his being a partaker of the aforesaid good, and loves his neighbor by reason of his fellowship in that good. Now fellowship is a reason for love according to a certain union in relation to God. Wherefore just as unity surpasses union, the fact that man himself has a share of the Divine good, is a more potent reason for loving than that another should be a partner with him in that share. Therefore man, out of charity, ought to love himself more than his neighbor: in sign whereof, a man ought not to give way to any evil of sin, which counteracts his share of happiness, not even that he may free his neighbor from sin.

Reply to Objection 1. The love of charity takes its quantity not only from its object which is God, but also from the lover, who is the man that has charity, even as the quantity of any action depends in some way on the subject. Wherefore, though a better neighbor is nearer to God, yet because he is not as near to the man who has charity, as this man is to himself, it does not follow that a man is bound to love his neighbor more than himself.

Reply to Objection 2. A man ought to bear bodily injury for his friend's sake, and precisely in so doing he loves himself more as regards his spiritual mind, because it pertains to the perfection of virtue, which is a good of the mind. On spiritual matters, however, man ought not to suffer injury by sinning, in order to free his neighbor from sin, as stated above.

Reply to Objection 3. As Augustine says in his Rule (Ep. ccxi), the saying, "'charity seeks not her own,' means that it prefers the common to the private good." Now the common good is always more lovable to the individual than his private good, even as the good of the whole is more lovable to the part, than the latter's own partial good, as stated above (Article 3).

ARTICLE 6. WHETHER WE OUGHT TO LOVE ONE NEIGHBOR MORE THAN ANOTHER?

Objection 1. It would seem that we ought not to love one neighbor more than another. For Augustine says (De Doctr. Christ. i, 28): "One ought to love all men equally. Since, however, one cannot do good to all, we ought to consider those chiefly who by reason of place, time or any other circumstance, by a kind of chance, are more closely united to us." Therefore one neighbor ought not to be loved more than another.

Objection 2. Further, where there is one and the same reason for loving several, there should be no inequality of love. Now there is one and the same reason for loving all one's neighbors, which reason is God, as Augustine states (De Doctr. Christ. i, 27). Therefore we ought to love all our neighbors equally.

Objection 3. Further, to love a man is to wish him good things, as the Philosopher states (Rhet. ii, 4). Now to all our neighbors we wish an equal good, viz. everlasting life. Therefore we ought to love all our neighbors equally.

On the contrary, One's obligation to love a person is proportionate to the gravity of the sin one commits in acting against that love. Now it is a more grievous sin to act against the love of certain neighbors, than against the love of others. Hence the commandment (Leviticus 10:9), "He that curseth his father or mother, dying let him die," which does not apply to those who cursed others than the above. Therefore we ought to love some neighbors more than others.

I answer that, There have been two opinions on this question: for some have said that we ought, out of charity, to love all our neighbors equally, as regards our affection, but not as regards the outward effect. They held that the order of love is to be understood as applying to outward favors, which we ought to confer on those who are connected with us in preference to those who are unconnected, and not to the inward affection, which ought to be given equally to all including our enemies.

But this is unreasonable. For the affection of charity, which is the inclination of grace, is not less orderly than the natural appetite, which is the inclination of nature, for both inclinations flow from Divine wisdom. Now we observe in the physical order that the natural inclination in each thing is proportionate to the act or movement that is becoming to the nature of that thing: thus in earth the inclination of gravity is greater than in water, because it is becoming to earth to be beneath water. Consequently the inclination also of grace which is the effect of charity, must needs be proportionate to those actions which have to be performed outwardly, so that, to wit, the affection of our charity be more intense towards those to whom we ought to behave with greater kindness.

We must, therefore, say that, even as regards the affection we ought to love one neighbor more than another. The reason is that, since the principle of love is God, and the person who loves, it must needs be that the affection of love increases in proportion to the nearness to one or the other of those principles. For as we stated above (Article 1), wherever we find a principle, order depends on relation to that principle.

Reply to Objection 1. Love can be unequal in two ways: first on the part of the good we wish our friend. In this respect we love all men equally out of charity: because we wish them all one same generic good, namely everlasting happiness. Secondly love is said to be greater through its action being more intense: and in this way we ought not to love all equally.

Or we may reply that we have unequal love for certain persons in two ways: first, through our loving some and not loving others. As regards beneficence we are bound to observe this inequality, because we cannot do good to all: but as regards benevolence, love ought not to be thus unequal. The other inequality arises from our loving some more than others: and Augustine does not mean to exclude the latter inequality, but the former, as is evident from what he says of beneficence.

Reply to Objection 2. Our neighbors are not all equally related to God; some are nearer to Him, by reason of their greater goodness, and those we ought, out of charity, to love more than those who are not so near to Him.

Reply to Objection 3. This argument considers the quantity of love on the part of the good which we wish our friends.

ARTICLE 7. WHETHER WE OUGHT TO LOVE THOSE WHO ARE BETTER MORE THOSE WHO ARE MORE CLOSELY UNITED US?

Objection 1. It would seem that we ought to love those who are better more than those who are more closely united to us. For that which is in no way hateful seems more lovable than that which is hateful for some reason: just as a thing is all the whiter for having less black mixed with it. Now those who are connected with us are hateful for some reason, according to Luke 14:26: "If any man come to Me, and hate not his father," etc. On the other hand good men are not hateful for any reason. Therefore it seems that we ought to love those who are better more than those who are more closely connected with us.

Objection 2. Further, by charity above all, man is likened to God. But God loves more the better man. Therefore man also, out of charity, ought to love the better man more than one who is more closely united to him.

Objection 3. Further, in every friendship that ought to be loved most which has most to do with the foundation of that friendship: for, by natural friendship we love most those who are connected with us by nature, our parents for instance, or our children. Now the friendship of charity is founded upon the fellowship of happiness, which has more to do with better men than with those who are more closely united to us. Therefore, out of charity, we ought to love better men more than those who are more closely connected with us.

On the contrary, It is written (1 Timothy 5:8): "If any man have not care of his own and especially of those of his house, he hath denied the faith, and is worse than an infidel." Now the inward affection of charity ought to correspond to the outward effect. Therefore charity regards those who are nearer to us before those who are better.

I answer that, Every act should be proportionate both to its object and to the agent. But from its object it takes its species, while, from the power of the agent it takes the mode of its intensity: thus movement has its species from the term to which it tends, while the intensity of its speed arises from the disposition of the thing moved and the power of the mover. Accordingly love takes its species from its object, but its intensity is due to the lover.

Now the object of charity's love is God, and man is the lover. Therefore the specific diversity of the love which is in accordance with charity, as regards the love of our neighbor, depends on his relation to God, so that, out of charity, we should wish a greater good to one who is nearer to God; for though the good which charity wishes to all, viz. everlasting happiness, is one in itself, yet it has various degrees according to various shares of happiness, and it belongs to charity to wish God's justice to be maintained, in accordance with which better men have a fuller share of happiness. And this regards the species of love; for there are different species of love according to the different goods that we wish for those whom we love.

On the other hand, the intensity of love is measured with regard to the man who loves, and accordingly man loves those who are more closely united to him, with more intense affection as to the good he wishes for them, than he loves those who are better as to the greater good he wishes for them.

Again a further difference must be observed here: for some neighbors are connected with us by their natural origin, a connection which cannot be severed, since that origin makes them to be what they are. But the goodness of virtue, wherein some are close to God, can come and go, increase and decrease, as was shown above (24, 4,10,11). Hence it is possible for one, out of charity, to wish this man who is more closely united to one, to be better than another, and so reach a higher degree of happiness.

Moreover there is yet another reason for which, out of charity, we love more those who are more nearly connected with us, since we love them in more ways. For, towards those who are not connected with us we have no other friendship than charity, whereas for those who are connected with us, we have certain other friendships, according to the way in which they are connected. Now since the good on which every other friendship of the virtuous is based, is directed, as to its end, to the good on which charity is based, it follows that charity commands each act of another friendship, even as the art which is about the end commands the art which is about the means. Consequently this very act of loving someone because he is akin or connected with us, or because he is a fellow-countryman or for any like reason that is referable to the end of charity, can be commanded by charity, so that, out of charity both eliciting and commanding, we love in more ways those who are more nearly connected with us.

Reply to Objection 1. We are commanded to hate, in our kindred, not their kinship, but only the fact of their being an obstacle between us and God. In this respect they are not akin but hostile to us, according to Micah 7:6: "A men's enemies are they of his own household."

Reply to Objection 2. Charity conforms man to God proportionately, by making man comport himself towards what is his, as God does towards what is His. For we may, out of charity, will certain things as becoming to us which God does not will, because it becomes Him not to will them, as stated above (I-II, 19, 10), when we were treating of the goodness of the will.

Reply to Objection 3. Charity elicits the act of love not only as regards the object, but also as regards the lover, as stated above. The result is that the man who is more nearly united to us is more loved.

ARTICLE 13. WHETHER THE ORDER OF CHARITY ENDURES IN HEAVEN?

Objection 1. It would seem that the order of charity does not endure in heaven. For Augustine says (De Vera Relig. xlviii): "Perfect charity consists in loving greater goods more, and lesser goods less." Now charity will be perfect in heaven. Therefore a man will love those who are better more than either himself or those who are connected with him.

Objection 2. Further, we love more him to whom we wish a greater good. Now each one in heaven wishes a greater good for those who have more good, else his will would not be conformed in all things to God's will: and there to be better is to have more good. Therefore in heaven each one loves more those who are better, and consequently he loves others more than himself, and one who is not connected with him, more than one who is.

Objection 3. Further, in heaven love will be entirely for God's sake, for then will be fulfilled the words of 1 Corinthians 15:28: "That God may be all in all." Therefore he who is nearer God will be loved more, so that a man will love a better man more than himself, and one who is not connected with him, more than one who is.

On the contrary, Nature is not done away, but perfected, by glory. Now the order of charity given above (A2,3,4) is derived from nature: since all things naturally love themselves more than others. Therefore this order of charity will endure in heaven.

I answer that, The order of charity must needs remain in heaven, as regards the love of God above all things. For this will be realized simply when man shall enjoy God perfectly. But, as regards the order between man himself and other men, a distinction would seem to be necessary, because, as we stated above (A7,9), the degrees of love may be distinguished either in respect of the good which a man desires for another, or according to the intensity of love itself. On the first way a man will love better men more than himself, and those who are less good, less than himself: because, by reason of the perfect conformity of the human to the Divine will, each of the blessed will desire everyone to have what is due to him according to Divine justice. Nor will that be a time for advancing by means of merit to a yet greater reward, as happens now while it is possible for a man to desire both the virtue and the reward of a better man, whereas then the will of each one will rest within the limits determined by God. But in the second way a man will love himself more than even his better neighbors, because the intensity of the act of love arises on the part of the person who loves, as stated above (A7,9). Moreover it is for this that the gift of charity is bestowed by God on each one, namely, that he may first of all direct his mind to God, and this pertains to a man's love for himself, and that, in the second place, he may wish other things to be directed to God, and even work for that end according to his capacity.

As to the order to be observed among our neighbors, a man will simply love those who are better, according to the love of charity. Because the entire life of the blessed consists in directing their minds to God, wherefore the entire ordering of their love will be ruled with respect to God, so that each one will love more and reckon to be nearer to himself those who are nearer to God. For then one man will no longer succor another, as he needs to in the present life, wherein each man has to succor those who are closely connected with him rather than those who are not, no matter what be the nature of their distress: hence it is that in this life, a man, by the inclination of charity, loves more those who are more closely united to him, for he is under a greater obligation to bestow on them the effect of charity. It will however be possible in heaven for a man to love in several ways one who is connected with him, since the causes of virtuous love will not be banished from the mind of the blessed. Yet all these reasons are incomparably surpassed by that which is taken from nighness to God.

Reply to Objection 1. This argument should be granted as to those who are connected together; but as regards man himself, he ought to love himself so much the more than others, as his charity is more perfect, since perfect charity directs man to God perfectly, and this belongs to love of oneself, as stated above.

Reply to Objection 2. This argument considers the order of charity in respect of the degree of good one wills the person one loves.

Reply to Objection 3. God will be to each one the entire reason of his love, for God is man's entire good. For if we make the impossible supposition that God were not man's good, He would not be man's reason for loving. Hence it is that in the order of love man should love himself more than all else after God.

QUESTION 28. JOY

ARTICLE 1. WHETHER JOY IS EFFECTED IN US BY CHARITY?

Objection 1. It would seem that joy is not effected in us by charity. For the absence of what we love causes sorrow rather than joy. But God, Whom we love by charity, is absent from us, so long as we are in this state of life, since "while we are in the body, we are absent from the Lord" (2 Corinthians 5:6). Therefore charity causes sorrow in us rather than joy.

Objection 2. Further, it is chiefly through charity that we merit happiness. Now mourning, which pertains to sorrow, is reckoned among those things whereby we merit happiness, according to Matthew 5:5: "Blessed are they that mourn, for they shall be comforted." Therefore sorrow, rather than joy, is an effect of charity.

Objection 3. Further, charity is a virtue distinct from hope, as shown above (Question 17, Article 6). Now joy is the effect of hope, according to Romans 12:12: "Rejoicing in hope." Therefore it is not the effect of charity.

On the contrary, It is written (Romans 5:5): "The charity of God is poured forth in our hearts by the Holy Ghost, Who is given to us." But joy is caused in us by the Holy Ghost according to Romans 14:17: "The kingdom of God is not meat and drink, but justice and peace, and joy in the Holy Ghost." Therefore charity is a cause of joy.

I answer that, As stated above (I-II, 25, 1,2,3), when we were treating of the passions, joy and sorrow proceed from love, but in contrary ways. For joy is caused by love, either through the presence of the thing loved, or because the proper good of the thing loved exists and endures in it; and the latter is the case chiefly in the love of benevolence, whereby a man rejoices in the well-being of his friend, though he be absent. On the other hand sorrow arises from love, either through the absence of the thing loved, or because the loved object to which we wish well, is deprived of its good or afflicted with some evil. Now charity is love of God, Whose good is unchangeable, since He is His goodness, and from the very fact that He is loved, He is in those who love Him by His most excellent effect, according to 1 John 4:16: "He that abideth in charity, abideth in God, and God in him." Therefore spiritual joy, which is about God, is caused by charity.

Reply to Objection 1. So long as we are in the body, we are said to be "absent from the Lord," in comparison with that presence whereby He is present to some by the vision of "sight"; wherefore the Apostle goes on to say (2 Corinthians 5:6): "For we walk by faith and not by sight." Nevertheless, even in this life, He is present to those who love Him, by the indwelling of His grace.

Reply to Objection 2. The mourning that merits happiness, is about those things that are contrary to happiness. Wherefore it amounts to the same that charity causes this mourning, and this spiritual joy about God, since to rejoice in a certain good amounts to the same as to grieve for things that are contrary to it.

Reply to Objection 3. There can be spiritual joy about God in two ways. First, when we rejoice in the Divine good considered in itself; secondly, when we rejoice in the Divine good as participated by us. The former joy is the better, and proceeds from charity chiefly: while the latter joy proceeds from hope also, whereby we look forward to enjoy the Divine good, although this enjoyment itself, whether perfect or imperfect, is obtained according to the measure of one's charity.

QUESTION 33. FRATERNAL CORRECTION

ARTICLE 1. WHETHER FRATERNAL CORRECTION IS AN ACT OF CHARITY?

Objection 1. It would seem that fraternal correction is not an act of charity. For a gloss on Matthew 18:15, "If thy brother shall offend against thee," says that "a man should reprove his brother out of zeal for justice." But justice is a distinct virtue from charity. Therefore fraternal correction is an act, not of charity, but of justice.

Objection 2. Further, fraternal correction is given by secret admonition. Now admonition is a kind of counsel, which is an act of prudence, for a prudent man is one who is of good counsel (Ethic. vi, 5). Therefore fraternal correction is an act, not of charity, but of prudence.

Objection 3. Further, contrary acts do not belong to the same virtue. Now it is an act of charity to bear with a sinner, according to Galatians 6:2: "Bear ye one another's burdens, and so you shall fulfil the law of Christ," which is the law of charity. Therefore it seems that the correction of a sinning brother, which is contrary to bearing with him, is not an act of charity.

On the contrary, To correct the wrongdoer is a spiritual almsdeed. But almsdeeds are works of charity, as stated above (Question 32, Article 1). Therefore fraternal correction is an act of charity.

I answer that, The correction of the wrongdoer is a remedy which should be employed against a man's sin. Now a man's sin may be considered in two ways, first as being harmful to the sinner, secondly as conducing to the harm of others, by hurting or scandalizing them, or by being detrimental to the common good, the justice of which is disturbed by that man's sin.

Consequently the correction of a wrongdoer is twofold, one which applies a remedy to the sin considered as an evil of the sinner himself. This is fraternal correction properly so called, which is directed to the amendment of the sinner. Now to do away with anyone's evil is the same as to procure his good: and to procure a person's good is an act of charity, whereby we wish and do our friend well. Consequently fraternal correction also is an act of charity, because thereby we drive out our brother's evil, viz. sin, the removal of which pertains to charity rather than the removal of an external loss, or of a bodily injury, in so much as the contrary good of virtue is more akin to charity than the good of the body or of external things. Therefore fraternal correction is an act of charity rather than the healing of a bodily infirmity, or the relieving of an external bodily need. There is another correction which applies a remedy to the sin of the wrongdoer, considered as hurtful to others, and especially to the common good. This correction is an act of justice, whose concern it is to safeguard the rectitude of justice between one man and another.

Reply to Objection 1. This gloss speaks of the second correction which is an act of justice. Or if it speaks of the first correction, then it takes justice as denoting a general virtue, as we shall state further on (58, 5), in which sense again all "sin is iniquity" (1 John 3:4), through being contrary to justice.

Reply to Objection 2. According to the Philosopher (Ethic. vi, 12), prudence regulates whatever is directed to the end, about which things counsel and choice are concerned. Nevertheless when, guided by prudence, we perform some action aright which is directed to the end of some virtue, such as temperance or fortitude, that action belongs chiefly to the virtue to whose end it is directed. Since, then, the admonition which is given in fraternal correction is directed to the removal of a brother's sin, which removal pertains to charity, it is evident that this admonition is chiefly an act of charity, which virtue commands it, so to speak, but secondarily an act of prudence, which executes and directs the action.

Reply to Objection 3. Fraternal correction is not opposed to forbearance with the weak, on the contrary it results from it. For a man bears with a sinner, in so far as he is not disturbed against him, and retains his goodwill towards him: the result being that he strives to make him do better.

QUESTION 37. DISCORD, WHICH IS CONTRARY TO PEACE

ARTICLE 1. WHETHER DISCORD IS A SIN?

Objection 1. It would seem that discord is not a sin. For to disaccord with man is to sever oneself from another's will. But this does not seem to be a sin, because God's will alone, and not our neighbor's, is the rule of our own will. Therefore discord is not a sin.

Objection 2. Further, whoever induces another to sin, sins also himself. But it appears not to be a sin to incite others to discord, for it is written (Acts 23:6) that Paul, knowing that the one part were Sadducees, and the other Pharisees, cried out in the council: "Men brethren, I am a Pharisee, the son of Pharisees, concerning the hope and resurrection of the dead I am called in question. And when he had so said, there arose a dissension between the Pharisees and the Sadducees." Therefore discord is not a sin.

Objection 3. Further, sin, especially mortal sin, is not to be found in a holy man. But discord is to be found even among holy men, for it is written (Acts 15:39): "There arose a dissension" between Paul and Barnabas, "so that they departed one from another." Therefore discord is not a sin. and least of all a mortal sin.

On the contrary, "Dissensions," that is, discords, are reckoned among the works of the flesh (Galatians 5:20), of which it is said afterwards (Galatians 5:21) that "they who do such things shall not obtain the kingdom of God." Now nothing, save mortal sin, excludes man from the kingdom of God. Therefore discord is a mortal sin.

I answer that, Discord is opposed to concord. Now, as stated above (29, 1,3) concord results from charity, in as much as charity directs many hearts together to one thing, which is chiefly the Divine good, secondarily, the good of our neighbor. Wherefore discord is a sin, in so far as it is opposed to this concord.

But it must be observed that this concord is destroyed by discord in two ways: first, directly; secondly, accidentally. Now, human acts and movements are said to be direct when they are according to one's intention. Wherefore a man directly disaccords with his neighbor, when he knowingly and intentionally dissents from the Divine good and his neighbor's good, to which he ought to consent. This is a mortal sin in respect of its genus, because it is contrary to charity, although the first movements of such discord are venial sins by reason of their being imperfect acts.

The accidental in human acts is that which occurs beside the intention. Hence when several intend a good pertaining to God's honor, or our neighbor's profit, while one deems a certain thing good, and another thinks contrariwise, the discord is in this case accidentally contrary to the Divine good or that of our neighbor. Such like discord is neither sinful nor against charity, unless it be accompanied by an error about things necessary to salvation, or by undue obstinacy, since it has also been stated above (29, 1,3, ad 2) that the concord which is an effect of charity, is union of wills not of opinions. It follows from this that discord is sometimes the sin of one party only, for instance, when one wills a good which the other knowingly resists; while sometimes it implies sin in both parties, as when each dissents from the other's good, and loves his own.

Reply to Objection 1. One man's will considered in itself is not the rule of another man's will; but in so far as our neighbor's will adheres to God's will, it becomes in consequence, a rule regulated according to its proper measure. Wherefore it is a sin to disaccord with such a will, because by that very fact one disaccords with the Divine rule.

Reply to Objection 2. Just as a man's will that adheres to God is a right rule, to disaccord with which is a sin, so too a man's will that is opposed to God is a perverse rule, to disaccord with which is good. Hence to cause a discord, whereby a good concord resulting from charity is destroyed, is a grave sin: wherefore it is written (Proverbs 6:16): "Six things there are, which the Lord hateth, and the seventh His soul detesteth," which seventh is stated (Proverbs 6:19) to be "him that soweth discord among brethren." On the other hand, to arouse a discord whereby an evil concord (i.e. concord in an evil will) is destroyed, is praiseworthy. On this way Paul was to be commended for sowing discord among those who concorded together in evil, because Our Lord also said of Himself (Matthew 10:34): "I came not to send peace, but the sword."

Reply to Objection 3. The discord between Paul and Barnabas was accidental and not direct: because each intended some good, yet the one thought one thing good, while the other thought something else, which was owing to human deficiency: for that controversy was not about things necessary to salvation. Moreover all this was ordained by Divine providence, on account of the good which would ensue.

QUESTION 40. WAR

ARTICLE 1. WHETHER IT IS ALWAYS SINFUL TO WAGE WAR?

Objection 1. It would seem that it is always sinful to wage war. Because punishment is not inflicted except for sin. Now those who wage war are threatened by Our Lord with punishment, according to Matthew 26:52: "All that take the sword shall perish with the sword." Therefore all wars are unlawful.

Objection 2. Further, whatever is contrary to a Divine precept is a sin. But war is contrary to a Divine precept, for it is written (Matthew 5:39): "But I say to you not to resist evil"; and (Romans 12:19): "Not revenging yourselves, my dearly beloved, but give place unto wrath." Therefore war is always sinful.

Objection 3. Further, nothing, except sin, is contrary to an act of virtue. But war is contrary to peace. Therefore war is always a sin.

Objection 4. Further, the exercise of a lawful thing is itself lawful, as is evident in scientific exercises. But warlike exercises which take place in tournaments are forbidden by the Church, since those who are slain in these trials are deprived of ecclesiastical burial. Therefore it seems that war is a sin in itself.

On the contrary, Augustine says in a sermon on the son of the centurion [Ep. ad Marcel. cxxxviii]: "If the Christian Religion forbade war altogether, those who sought salutary advice in the Gospel would rather have been counselled to cast aside their arms, and to give up soldiering altogether. On the contrary, they were told: 'Do violence to no man . . . and be content with your pay' [Luke 3:14. If he commanded them to be content with their pay, he did not forbid soldiering."

I answer that, In order for a war to be just, three things are necessary. First, the authority of the sovereign by whose command the war is to be waged. For it is not the business of a private individual to declare war, because he can seek for redress of his rights from the tribunal of his superior. Moreover it is not the business of a private individual to summon together the people, which has to be done in wartime. And as the care of the common weal is committed to those who are in authority, it is their business to watch over the common weal of the city, kingdom or province subject to them. And just as it is lawful for them to have recourse to the sword in defending that common weal against internal disturbances, when they punish evil-doers, according to the words of the Apostle (Romans 13:4): "He beareth not the sword in vain: for he is God's minister, an avenger to execute wrath upon him that doth evil"; so too, it is their business to have recourse to the sword of war in defending the common weal against external enemies. Hence it is said to those who are in authority (Psalm 81:4): "Rescue the poor: and deliver the needy out of the hand of the sinner"; and for this reason Augustine says (Contra Faust. xxii, 75): "The natural order conducive to peace among mortals demands that the power to declare and counsel war should be in the hands of those who hold the supreme authority."

Secondly, a just cause is required, namely that those who are attacked, should be attacked because they deserve it on account of some fault. Wherefore Augustine says (QQ. in Hept., qu. x, super Jos.): "A just war is wont to be described as one that avenges wrongs, when a nation or city has to be punished, for refusing to make amends for the wrongs inflicted by its subjects, or to restore what it has seized unjustly."

Thirdly, it is necessary that the belligerents should have a rightful intention, so that they intend the advancement of good, or the avoidance of evil. Hence Augustine says (De Verb. Dom. [The words quoted are to be found not in St. Augustine's works, but Can. Apud. Caus. xxiii, qu. 1): "True religion looks upon as peaceful those wars that are waged not for motives of aggrandizement, or cruelty, but with the object of securing peace, of punishing evil-doers, and of uplifting the good." For it may happen that the war is declared by the legitimate authority, and for a just cause, and yet be rendered unlawful through a wicked intention. Hence Augustine says (Contra Faust. xxii, 74): "The passion for inflicting harm, the cruel thirst for vengeance, an unpacific and relentless spirit, the fever of revolt, the lust of power, and such like things, all these are rightly condemned in war."

Reply to Objection 1. As Augustine says (Contra Faust. xxii, 70): "To take the sword is to arm oneself in order to take the life of anyone, without the command or permission of superior or lawful authority." On the other hand, to have recourse to the sword (as a private person) by the authority of the sovereign or judge, or (as a public person) through zeal for justice, and by the authority, so to speak, of God, is not to "take the sword," but to use it as commissioned by another, wherefore it does not deserve punishment. And yet even those who make sinful use of the sword are not always slain with the sword, yet they always perish with their own sword, because, unless they repent, they are punished eternally for their sinful use of the sword.

Reply to Objection 2. Such like precepts, as Augustine observes (De Serm. Dom. in Monte i, 19), should always be borne in readiness of mind, so that we be ready to obey them, and, if necessary, to refrain from resistance or self-defense. Nevertheless it is necessary sometimes for a man to act otherwise for the common good, or for the good of those with whom he is fighting. Hence Augustine says (Ep. ad Marcellin. cxxxviii): "Those whom we have to punish with a kindly severity, it is necessary to handle in many ways against their will. For when we are stripping a man of the lawlessness of sin, it is good for him to be vanquished, since nothing is more hopeless than the happiness of sinners, whence arises a guilty impunity, and an evil will, like an internal enemy."

Reply to Objection 3. Those who wage war justly aim at peace, and so they are not opposed to peace, except to the evil peace, which Our Lord "came not to send upon earth" (Matthew 10:34). Hence Augustine says (Ep. ad Bonif. clxxxix): "We do not seek peace in order to be at war, but we go to war that we may have peace. Be peaceful, therefore, in warring, so that you may vanquish those whom you war against, and bring them to the prosperity of peace."

Reply to Objection 4. Manly exercises in warlike feats of arms are not all forbidden, but those which are inordinate and perilous, and end in slaying or plundering. On olden times warlike exercises presented no such danger, and hence they were called "exercises of arms" or "bloodless wars," as Jerome states in an epistle [Reference incorrect: cf. Veget., De Re Milit. i].

QUESTION 47. PRUDENCE, CONSIDERED IN ITSELF

ARTICLE 8. WHETHER COMMAND IS THE CHIEF ACT OF PRUDENCE?

Objection 1. It would seem that command is not the chief act of prudence. For command regards the good to be ensued. Now Augustine (De Trin. xiv, 9) states that it is an act of prudence "to avoid ambushes." Therefore command is not the chief act of prudence.

Objection 2. Further, the Philosopher says (Ethic. vi, 5) that "the prudent man takes good counsel." Now "to take counsel" and "to command" seem to be different acts, as appears from what has been said above (I-II, 57, 6). Therefore command is not the chief act of prudence.

Objection 3. Further, it seems to belong to the will to command and to rule, since the will has the end for its object, and moves the other powers of the soul. Now prudence is not in the will, but in the reason. Therefore command is not an act of prudence.

On the contrary, The Philosopher says (Ethic. vi, 10) that "prudence commands."

I answer that, Prudence is "right reason applied to action," as stated above (Article 2). Hence that which is the chief act of reason in regard to action must needs be the chief act of prudence. Now there are three such acts. The first is "to take counsel," which belongs to discovery, for counsel is an act of inquiry, as stated above (I-II, 14, 1). The second act is "to judge of what one has discovered," and this is an act of the speculative reason. But the practical reason, which is directed to action, goes further, and its third act is "to command," which act consists in applying to action the things counselled and judged. And since this act approaches nearer to the end of the practical reason, it follows that it is the chief act of the practical reason, and consequently of prudence.

In confirmation of this we find that the perfection of art consists in judging and not in commanding: wherefore he who sins voluntarily against his craft is reputed a better craftsman than he who does so involuntarily, because the former seems to do so from right judgment, and the latter from a defective judgment. On the other hand it is the reverse in prudence, as stated in Ethic. vi, 5, for it is more imprudent to sin voluntarily, since this is to be lacking in the chief act of prudence, viz. command, than to sin involuntarily.

Reply to Objection 1. The act of command extends both to the ensuing of good and to the avoidance of evil. Nevertheless Augustine ascribes "the avoidance of ambushes" to prudence, not as its chief act, but as an act of prudence that does not continue in heaven.

Reply to Objection 2. Good counsel is required in order that the good things discovered may be applied to action: wherefore command belongs to prudence which takes good counsel.

Reply to Objection 3. Simply to move belongs to the will: but command denotes motion together with a kind of ordering, wherefore it is an act of the reason, as stated above (I-II, 17, 1).

ARTICLE 10. DOES PRUDENCE EXTEND TO THE GOVERNING OF MANY?

Objection 1. It would seem that prudence does not extend to the governing of many, but only to the government of oneself. For the Philosopher says (Ethic. v, 1) that virtue directed to the common good is justice. But prudence differs from justice. Therefore prudence is not directed to the common good.

Objection 2. Further, he seems to be prudent, who seeks and does good for himself. Now those who seek the common good often neglect their own. Therefore they are not prudent.

Objection 3. Further, prudence is specifically distinct from temperance and fortitude. But temperance and fortitude seem to be related only to a man's own good. Therefore the same applies to prudence.

On the contrary, Our Lord said (Matthew 24:45): "Who, thinkest thou, is a faithful and prudent [Douay: 'wise'] servant whom his lord hath appointed over his family?"

I answer that, According to the Philosopher (Ethic. vi, 8) some have held that prudence does not extend to the common good, but only to the good of the individual, and this because they thought that man is not bound to seek other than his own good. But this opinion is opposed to charity, which "seeketh not her own" (1 Corinthians 13:5): wherefore the Apostle says of himself (1 Corinthians 10:33): "Not seeking that which is profitable to myself, but to many, that they may be saved." Moreover it is contrary to right reason, which judges the common good to be better than the good of the individual.

Accordingly, since it belongs to prudence rightly to counsel, judge, and command concerning the means of obtaining a due end, it is evident that prudence regards not only the private good of the individual, but also the common good of the multitude.

Reply to Objection 1. The Philosopher is speaking there of moral virtue. Now just as every moral virtue that is directed to the common good is called "legal" justice, so the prudence that is directed to the common good is called "political" prudence, for the latter stands in the same relation to legal justice, as prudence simply so called to moral virtue.

Reply to Objection 2. He that seeks the good of the many, seeks in consequence his own good, for two reasons. First, because the individual good is impossible without the common good of the family, city, or kingdom. Hence Valerius Maximus says [Fact. et Dict. Memor. iv, 6 of the ancient Romans that "they would rather be poor in a rich empire than rich in a poor empire." Secondly, because, since man is a part of the home and city, he must needs consider what is good for him by being prudent about the good of the many. For the good disposition of parts depends on their relation to the whole; thus Augustine says (Confess. iii, 8) that "any part which does not harmonize with its whole, is offensive."

Reply to Objection 3. Even temperance and fortitude can be directed to the common good, hence there are precepts of law concerning them as stated in Ethic. v, 1: more so, however, prudence and justice, since these belong to the rational faculty which directly regards the universal, just as the sensitive part regards singulars.

ARTICLE 11. WHETHER PRUDENCE ABOUT ONE'S OWN GOOD IS SPECIFICALLY THE SAME AS THAT WHICH EXTENDS TO THE COMMON GOOD?

Objection 1. It seems that prudence about one's own good is the same specifically as that which extends to the common good. For the Philosopher says (Ethic. vi, 8) that "political prudence, and prudence are the same habit, yet their essence is not the same."

Objection 2. Further, the Philosopher says (Polit. iii, 2) that "virtue is the same in a good man and in a good ruler." Now political prudence is chiefly in the ruler, in whom it is architectonic, as it were. Since then prudence is a virtue of a good man, it seems that prudence and political prudence are the same habit.

Objection 3. Further, a habit is not diversified in species or essence by things which are subordinate to one another. But the particular good, which belongs to prudence simply so called, is subordinate to the common good, which belongs to political prudence. Therefore prudence and political prudence differ neither specifically nor essentially.

On the contrary, "Political prudence," which is directed to the common good of the city, "domestic economy" which is of such things as relate to the common good of the household or family, and "monastic economy" which is concerned with things affecting the good of one person, are all distinct sciences. Therefore in like manner there are different kinds of prudence, corresponding to the above differences of matter.

I answer that, As stated above (5; 54, 2, ad 1), the species of habits differ according to the difference of object considered in its formal aspect. Now the formal aspect of all things directed to the end, is taken from the end itself, as shown above (I-II, Prolog.; I-II, 102, 1), wherefore the species of habits differ by their relation to different ends. Again the individual good, the good of the family, and the good of the city and kingdom are different ends. Wherefore there must needs be different species of prudence corresponding to these different ends, so that one is "prudence" simply so called, which is directed to one's own good; another, "domestic prudence" which is directed to the common good of the home; and a third, "political prudence," which is directed to the common good of the city or kingdom.

Reply to Objection 1. The Philosopher means, not that political prudence is substantially the same habit as any kind of prudence, but that it is the same as the prudence which is directed to the common good. This is called "prudence" in respect of the common notion of prudence, i.e. as being right reason applied to action, while it is called "political," as being directed to the common good.

Reply to Objection 2. As the Philosopher declares (Polit. iii, 2), "it belongs to a good man to be able to rule well and to obey well," wherefore the virtue of a good man includes also that of a good ruler. Yet the virtue of the ruler and of the subject differs specifically, even as the virtue of a man and of a woman, as stated by the same authority (Polit. iii, 2).

Reply to Objection 3. Even different ends, one of which is subordinate to the other, diversify the species of a habit, thus for instance, habits directed to riding, soldiering, and civic life, differ specifically although their ends are subordinate to one another. On like manner, though the good of the individual is subordinate to the good of the many, that does not prevent this difference from making the habits differ specifically; but it follows that the habit which is directed to the last end is above the other habits and commands them.

ARTICLE 12. WHETHER PRUDENCE IS IN SUBJECTS, OR ONLY IN THEIR RULERS?

Objection 1. It would seem that prudence is not in subjects but only in their rulers. For the Philosopher says (Polit. iii, 2) that "prudence alone is the virtue proper to a ruler, while other virtues are common to subjects and rulers, and the prudence of the subject is not a virtue but a true opinion."

Objection 2. Further, it is stated in Polit. i, 5 that "a slave is not competent to take counsel." But prudence makes a man take good counsel (Ethic. vi, 5). Therefore prudence is not befitting slaves or subjects.

Objection 3. Further, prudence exercises command, as stated above (Article 8). But command is not in the competency of slaves or subjects but only of rulers. Therefore prudence is not in subjects but only in rulers.

On the contrary, The Philosopher says (Ethic. vi, 8) that there are two kinds of political prudence, one of which is "legislative" and belongs to rulers, while the other "retains the common name political," and is about "individual actions." Now it belongs also to subjects to perform these individual actions. Therefore prudence is not only in rulers but also in subjects.

I answer that, Prudence is in the reason. Now ruling and governing belong properly to the reason; and therefore it is proper to a man to reason and be prudent in so far as he has a share in ruling and governing. But it is evident that the subject as subject, and the slave as slave, are not competent to rule and govern, but rather to be ruled and governed. Therefore prudence is not the virtue of a slave as slave, nor of a subject as subject.

Since, however, every man, for as much as he is rational, has a share in ruling according to the judgment of reason, he is proportionately competent to have prudence. Wherefore it is manifest that prudence is in the ruler "after the manner of a mastercraft" (Ethic. vi, 8), but in the subjects, "after the manner of a handicraft."

Reply to Objection 1. The saying of the Philosopher is to be understood strictly, namely, that prudence is not the virtue of a subject as such.

Reply to Objection 2. A slave is not capable of taking counsel, in so far as he is a slave (for thus he is the instrument of his master), but he does take counsel in so far as he is a rational animal.

Reply to Objection 3. By prudence a man commands not only others, but also himself, in so far as the reason is said to command the lower powers.

ARTICLE 15. WHETHER PRUDENCE IS IN US BY NATURE?

Objection 1. It would seem that prudence is in us by nature. The Philosopher says that things connected with prudence "seem to be natural," namely "synesis, gnome" [Cf. I-II, 57, 6] and the like, but not those which are connected with speculative wisdom. Now things belonging to the same genus have the same kind of origin. Therefore prudence also is in us from nature.

Objection 2. Further, the changes of age are according to nature. Now prudence results from age, according to Job 12:12: "In the ancient is wisdom, and in length of days prudence." Therefore prudence is natural.

Objection 3. Further, prudence is more consistent with human nature than with that of dumb animals. Now there are instances of a certain natural prudence in dumb animals, according to the Philosopher (De Hist. Anim. viii, 1). Therefore prudence is natural.

On the contrary, The Philosopher says (Ethic. ii, 1) that "intellectual virtue is both originated and fostered by teaching; it therefore demands experience and time." Now prudence is an intellectual virtue, as stated above (Article 4). Therefore prudence is in us, not by nature, but by teaching and experience.

I answer that, As shown above (Article 3), prudence includes knowledge both of universals, and of the singular matters of action to which prudence applies the universal principles. Accordingly, as regards the knowledge of universals, the same is to be said of prudence as of speculative science, because the primary universal principles of either are known naturally, as shown above (Article 6): except that the common principles of prudence are more connatural to man; for as the Philosopher remarks (Ethic. x, 7) "the life which is according to the speculative reason is better than that which is according to man": whereas the secondary universal principles, whether of the speculative or of the practical reason, are not inherited from nature, but are acquired by discovery through experience, or through teaching.

On the other hand, as regards the knowledge of particulars which are the matter of action, we must make a further distinction, because this matter of action is either an end or the means to an end. Now the right ends of human life are fixed; wherefore there can be a natural inclination in respect of these ends; thus it has been stated above (I-II, 51, 1; I-II, 63, 1) that some, from a natural inclination, have certain virtues whereby they are inclined to right ends; and consequently they also have naturally a right judgment about such like ends.

But the means to the end, in human concerns, far from being fixed, are of manifold variety according to the variety of persons and affairs. Wherefore since the inclination of nature is ever to something fixed, the knowledge of those means cannot be in man naturally, although, by reason of his natural disposition, one man has a greater aptitude than another in discerning them, just as it happens with regard to the conclusions of speculative sciences. Since then prudence is not about the ends, but about the means, as stated above (6; I-II, 57, 5), it follows that prudence is not from nature.

Reply to Objection 1. The Philosopher is speaking there of things relating to prudence, in so far as they are directed to ends. Wherefore he had said before (Ethic. vi, 5,11) that "they are the principles of the ou heneka" ['for the sake of which'], namely, the end; and so he does not mention euboulia among them, because it takes counsel about the means.

Reply to Objection 2. Prudence is rather in the old, not only because their natural disposition calms the movement of the sensitive passions, but also because of their long experience.

Reply to Objection 3. Even in dumb animals there are fixed ways of obtaining an end, wherefore we observe that all the animals of a same species act in like manner. But this is impossible in man, on account of his reason, which takes cognizance of universals, and consequently extends to an infinity of singulars.

QUESTION 49. EACH QUASI-INTEGRAL PART OF PRUDENCE

ARTICLE 3. WHETHER DOCILITY SHOULD BE ACCOUNTED A PART OF PRUDENCE?

Objection 1. It would seem that docility should not be accounted a part of prudence. For that which is a necessary condition of every intellectual virtue, should not be appropriated to one of them. But docility is requisite for every intellectual virtue. Therefore it should not be accounted a part of prudence.

Objection 2. Further, that which pertains to a human virtue is in our power, since it is for things that are in our power that we are praised or blamed. Now it is not in our power to be docile, for this is befitting to some through their natural disposition. Therefore it is not a part of prudence.

Objection 3. Further, docility is in the disciple: whereas prudence, since it makes precepts, seems rather to belong to teachers, who are also called "preceptors." Therefore docility is not a part of prudence.

On the contrary, Macrobius [In Somn. Scip. i, 8] following the opinion of Plotinus places docility among the parts of prudence.

I answer that, As stated above (2, ad 1; 47, 3) prudence is concerned with particular matters of action, and since such matters are of infinite variety, no one man can consider them all sufficiently; nor can this be done quickly, for it requires length of time. Hence in matters of prudence man stands in very great need of being taught by others, especially by old folk who have acquired a sane understanding of the ends in practical matters. Wherefore the Philosopher says (Ethic. vi, 11): "It is right to pay no less attention to the undemonstrated assertions and opinions of such persons as are experienced, older than we are, and prudent, than to their demonstrations, for their experience gives them an insight into principles." Thus it is written (Proverbs 3:5): "Lean not on thy own prudence," and (Sirach 6:35): "Stand in the multitude of the ancients" (i.e. the old men), "that are wise, and join thyself from thy heart to their wisdom." Now it is a mark of docility to be ready to be taught: and consequently docility is fittingly reckoned a part of prudence

Reply to Objection 1. Although docility is useful for every intellectual virtue, yet it belongs to prudence chiefly, for the reason given above.

Reply to Objection 2. Man has a natural aptitude for docility even as for other things connected with prudence. Yet his own efforts count for much towards the attainment of perfect docility: and he must carefully, frequently and reverently apply his mind to the teachings of the learned, neither neglecting them through laziness, nor despising them through pride.

Reply to Objection 3. By prudence man makes precepts not only for others, but also for himself, as stated above (47, 12, ad 3). Hence as stated (Ethic. vi, 11), even in subjects, there is place for prudence; to which docility pertains. And yet even the learned should be docile in some respects, since no man is altogether self-sufficient in matters of prudence, as stated above.

ARTICLE 7. WHETHER CIRCUMSPECTION CAN BE A PART OF PRUDENCE?

Objection 1. It would seem that circumspection cannot be a part of prudence. For circumspection seems to signify looking at one's surroundings. But these are of infinite number, and cannot be considered by the reason wherein is prudence. Therefore circumspection should not be reckoned a part of prudence.

Objection 2. Further, circumstances seem to be the concern of moral virtues rather than of prudence. But circumspection seems to denote nothing but attention to circumstances. Therefore circumspection apparently belongs to the moral virtues rather than to prudence.

Objection 3. Further, whoever can see things afar off can much more see things that are near. Now foresight enables a man to look on distant things. Therefore there is no need to account circumspection a part of prudence in addition to foresight.

On the contrary stands the authority of Macrobius, quoted above (Article 48).

I answer that, As stated above (Article 6), it belongs to prudence chiefly to direct something aright to an end; and this is not done aright unless both the end be good, and the means good and suitable.

Since, however, prudence, as stated above (Question 47, Article 3) is about singular matters of action, which contain many combinations of circumstances, it happens that a thing is good in itself and suitable to the end, and nevertheless becomes evil or unsuitable to the end, by reason of some combination of circumstances. Thus to show signs of love to someone seems, considered in itself, to be a fitting way to arouse love in his heart, yet if pride or suspicion of flattery arise in his heart, it will no longer be a means suitable to the end. Hence the need of circumspection in prudence, viz. of comparing the means with the circumstances.

Reply to Objection 1. Though the number of possible circumstances be infinite, the number of actual circumstances is not; and the judgment of reason in matters of action is influenced by things which are few in number

Reply to Objection 2. Circumstances are the concern of prudence, because prudence has to fix them; on the other hand they are the concern of moral virtues, in so far as moral virtues are perfected by the fixing of circumstances.

Reply to Objection 3. Just as it belongs to foresight to look on that which is by its nature suitable to an end, so it belongs to circumspection to consider whether it be suitable to the end in view of the circumstances. Now each of these presents a difficulty of its own, and therefore each is reckoned a distinct part of prudence.

QUESTION 57. RIGHT

ARTICLE 1. WHETHER RIGHT IS THE OBJECT OF JUSTICE?

Objection 1. It would seem that right is not the object of justice. For the jurist Celsus says [Digest. i, 1; De Just. et Jure 1] that "right is the art of goodness and equality." Now art is not the object of justice, but is by itself an intellectual virtue. Therefore right is not the object of justice.

Objection 2. Further, "Law," according to Isidore (Etym. v, 3), "is a kind of right." Now law is the object not of justice but of prudence, wherefore the Philosopher [Ethic. vi, 8] reckons "legislative" as one of the parts of prudence. Therefore right is not the object of justice.

Objection 3. Further, justice, before all, subjects man to God: for Augustine says (De Moribus Eccl. xv) that "justice is love serving God alone, and consequently governing aright all things subject to man." Now right [jus] does not pertain to Divine things, but only to human affairs, for Isidore says (Etym. v, 2) that "'fas' is the Divine law, and 'jus,' the human law." Therefore right is not the object of justice.

On the contrary, Isidore says (Etym. v, 2) that "'jus' [right] is so called because it is just." Now the "just" is the object of justice, for the Philosopher declares (Ethic. v, 1) that "all are agreed in giving the name of justice to the habit which makes men capable of doing just actions."

I answer that, It is proper to justice, as compared with the other virtues, to direct man in his relations with others: because it denotes a kind of equality, as its very name implies; indeed we are wont to say that things are adjusted when they are made equal, for equality is in reference of one thing to some other. On the other hand the other virtues perfect man in those matters only which befit him in relation to himself. Accordingly that which is right in the works of the other virtues, and to which the intention of the virtue tends as to its proper object, depends on its relation to the agent only, whereas the right in a work of justice, besides its relation to the agent, is set up by its relation to others. Because a man's work is said to be just when it is related to some other by way of some kind of equality, for instance the payment of the wage due for a service rendered. And so a thing is said to be just, as having the rectitude of justice, when it is the term of an act of justice, without taking into account the way in which it is done by the agent: whereas in the other virtues nothing is declared to be right unless it is done in a certain way by the agent. For this reason justice has its own special proper object over and above the other virtues, and this object is called the just, which is the same as "right." Hence it is evident that right is the object of justice.

Reply to Objection 1. It is usual for words to be distorted from their original signification so as to mean something else: thus the word "medicine" was first employed to signify a remedy used for curing a sick person, and then it was drawn to signify the art by which this is done. On like manner the word "jus" [right] was first of all used to denote the just thing itself, but afterwards it was transferred to designate the art whereby it is known what is just, and further to denote the place where justice is administered, thus a man is said to appear "in jure" [In English we speak of a court of law, a barrister at law, etc.], and yet further, we say even that a man, who has the office of exercising justice, administers the jus even if his sentence be unjust.

Reply to Objection 2. Just as there pre-exists in the mind of the craftsman an expression of the things to be made externally by his craft, which expression is called the rule of his craft, so too there pre-exists in the mind an expression of the particular just work which the reason determines, and which is a kind of rule of prudence. If this rule be expressed in writing it is called a "law," which according to Isidore (Etym. v, 1) is "a written decree": and so law is not the same as right, but an expression of right.

Reply to Objection 3. Since justice implies equality, and since we cannot offer God an equal return, it follows that we cannot make Him a perfectly just repayment. For this reason the Divine law is not properly called "jus" but "fas," because, to wit, God is satisfied if we accomplish what we can. Nevertheless justice tends to make man repay God as much as he can, by subjecting his mind to Him entirely.

ARTICLE 2. WHETHER RIGHT IS FITTINGLY DIVIDED INTO NATURAL RIGHT AND POSITIVE RIGHT?

Objection 1. It would seem that right is not fittingly divided into natural right and positive right. For that which is natural is unchangeable, and is the same for all. Now nothing of the kind is to be found in human affairs, since all the rules of human right fail in certain cases, nor do they obtain force everywhere. Therefore there is no such thing as natural right.

Objection 2. Further, a thing is called "positive" when it proceeds from the human will. But a thing is not just, simply because it proceeds from the human will, else a man's will could not be unjust. Since then the "just" and the "right" are the same, it seems that there is no positive right.

Objection 3. Further, Divine right is not natural right, since it transcends human nature. In like manner, neither is it positive right, since it is based not on human, but on Divine authority. Therefore right is unfittingly divided into natural and positive.

On the contrary, The Philosopher says (Ethic. v, 7) that "political justice is partly natural and partly legal," i.e. established by law.

I answer that, As stated above (Article 1) the "right" or the "just" is a work that is adjusted to another person according to some kind of equality. Now a thing can be adjusted to a man in two ways: first by its very nature, as when a man gives so much that he may receive equal value in return, and this is called "natural right." In another way a thing is adjusted or commensurated to another person, by agreement, or by common consent, when, to wit, a man deems himself satisfied, if he receive so much. This can be done in two ways: first by private agreement, as that which is confirmed by an agreement between private individuals; secondly, by public agreement, as when the whole community agrees that something should be deemed as though it were adjusted and commensurated to another person, or when this is decreed by the prince who is placed over the people, and acts in its stead, and this is called "positive right."

Reply to Objection 1. That which is natural to one whose nature is unchangeable, must needs be such always and everywhere. But man's nature is changeable, wherefore that which is natural to man may sometimes fail. Thus the restitution of a deposit to the depositor is in accordance with natural equality, and if human nature were always right, this would always have to be observed; but since it happens sometimes that man's will is unrighteous there are cases in which a deposit should not be restored, lest a man of unrighteous will make evil use of the thing deposited: as when a madman or an enemy of the common weal demands the return of his weapons.

Reply to Objection 2. The human will can, by common agreement, make a thing to be just provided it be not, of itself, contrary to natural justice, and it is in such matters that positive right has its place. Hence the Philosopher says (Ethic. v, 7) that "in the case of the legal just, it does not matter in the first instance whether it takes one form or another, it only matters when once it is laid down." If, however, a thing is, of itself, contrary to natural right, the human will cannot make it just, for instance by decreeing that it is lawful to steal or to commit adultery. Hence it is written (Isaiah 10:1): "Woe to them that make wicked laws."

Reply to Objection 3. The Divine right is that which is promulgated by God. Such things are partly those that are naturally just, yet their justice is hidden to man, and partly are made just by God's decree. Hence also Divine right may be divided in respect of these two things, even as human right is. For the Divine law commands certain things because they are good, and forbids others, because they are evil, while others are good because they are prescribed, and others evil because they are forbidden.

ARTICLE 3. WHETHER THE RIGHT OF NATIONS IS THE SAME AS THE NATURAL RIGHT?

Objection 1. It would seem that the right of nations is the same as the natural right. For all men do not agree save in that which is natural to them. Now all men agree in the right of nations; since the jurist [Ulpian: Digest. i, 1; De Just. et Jure i] "the right of nations is that which is in use among all nations." Therefore the right of nations is the natural right.

Objection 2. Further, slavery among men is natural, for some are naturally slaves according to the Philosopher (Polit. i, 2). Now "slavery belongs to the right of nations," as Isidore states (Etym. v, 4). Therefore the right of nations is a natural right.

Objection 3. Further, right as stated above (Article 2) is divided into natural and positive. Now the right of nations is not a positive right, since all nations never agreed to decree anything by common agreement. Therefore the right of nations is a natural right.

On the contrary, Isidore says (Etym. v, 4) that "right is either natural, or civil, or right of nations," and consequently the right of nations is distinct from natural right.

I answer that, As stated above (Article 2), the natural right or just is that which by its very nature is adjusted to or commensurate with another person. Now this may happen in two ways; first, according as it is considered absolutely: thus a male by its very nature is commensurate with the female to beget offspring by her, and a parent is commensurate with the offspring to nourish it. Secondly a thing is naturally commensurate with another person, not according as it is considered absolutely, but according to something resultant from it, for instance the possession of property. For if a particular piece of land be considered absolutely, it contains no reason why it should belong to one man more than to another, but if it be considered in respect of its adaptability to cultivation, and the unmolested use of the land, it has a certain commensuration to be the property of one and not of another man, as the Philosopher shows (Polit. ii, 2).

Now it belongs not only to man but also to other animals to apprehend a thing absolutely: wherefore the right which we call natural, is common to us and other animals according to the first kind of commensuration. But the right of nations falls short of natural right in this sense, as the jurist [Digest. i, 1; De Just. et Jure i] says because "the latter is common to all animals, while the former is common to men only." On the other hand to consider a thing by comparing it with what results from it, is proper to reason, wherefore this same is natural to man in respect of natural reason which dictates it. Hence the jurist

Gaius says (Digest. i, 1; De Just. et Jure i, 9): "whatever natural reason decrees among all men, is observed by all equally, and is called the right of nations." This suffices for the Reply to the First Objection.

Reply to Objection 2. Considered absolutely, the fact that this particular man should be a slave rather than another man, is based, not on natural reason, but on some resultant utility, in that it is useful to this man to be ruled by a wiser man, and to the latter to be helped by the former, as the Philosopher states (Polit. i, 2). Wherefore slavery which belongs to the right of nations is natural in the second way, but not in the first.

Reply to Objection 3. Since natural reason dictates matters which are according to the right of nations, as implying a proximate equality, it follows that they need no special institution, for they are instituted by natural reason itself, as stated by the authority quoted above

ARTICLE 4. WHETHER PATERNAL RIGHT AND RIGHT OF DOMINION SHOULD BE DISTINGUISHED AS SPECIAL SPECIES?

Objection 1. It would seem that "paternal right" and "right of dominion" should not be distinguished as special species. For it belongs to justice to render to each one what is his, as Ambrose states (De Offic. i, 24). Now right is the object of justice, as stated above (Article 1). Therefore right belongs to each one equally; and we ought not to distinguish the rights of fathers and masters as distinct species.

Objection 2. Further, the law is an expression of what is just, as stated above (1, ad 2). Now a law looks to the common good of a city or kingdom, as stated above (I-II, 90, 2), but not to the private good of an individual or even of one household. Therefore there is no need for a special right of dominion or paternal right, since the master and the father pertain to a household, as stated in Polit. i, 2.

Objection 3. Further, there are many other differences of degrees among men, for instance some are soldiers, some are priests, some are princes. Therefore some special kind of right should be allotted to them.

On the contrary, The Philosopher (Ethic. v, 6) distinguishes right of dominion, paternal right and so on as species distinct from civil right.

I answer that, Right or just depends on commensuration with another person. Now "another" has a twofold signification. First, it may denote something that is other simply, as that which is altogether distinct; as, for example, two men neither of whom is subject to the other, and both of whom are subjects of the ruler of the city; and between these according to the Philosopher (Ethic. v, 6) there is the "just" simply. Secondly a thing is said to be other from something else, not simply, but as belonging in some way to that something else: and in this way, as regards human affairs, a son belongs to his father, since he is part of him somewhat, as stated in Ethic. viii, 12, and a slave belongs to his master, because he is his instrument, as stated in Polit. i, 2 [Cf. Ethic. viii, 11]. Hence a father is not compared to his son as to another simply, and so between them there is not the just simply, but a kind of just, called "paternal." In like manner neither is there the just simply, between master and servant, but that which is called "dominative." A wife, though she is something belonging to the husband, since she stands related to him as to her own body, as the Apostle declares (Ephesians 5:28), is nevertheless more distinct from her husband, than a son from his father, or a slave from his master: for she is received into a kind of social life, that of matrimony, wherefore according to the Philosopher (Ethic. v, 6) there is more scope for justice between husband and wife than between father and son, or master and slave, because, as husband and wife have an immediate relation to the community of the household, as stated in Polit. i, 2,5, it follows that between them there is "domestic justice" rather than "civic."

Reply to Objection 1. It belongs to justice to render to each one his right, the distinction between individuals being presupposed: for if a man gives himself his due, this is not strictly called "just." And since what belongs to the son is his father's, and what belongs to the slave is his master's, it follows that properly speaking there is not justice of father to son, or of master to slave.

Reply to Objection 2. A son, as such, belongs to his father, and a slave, as such, belongs to his master; yet each, considered as a man, is something having separate existence and distinct from others. Hence in so far as each of them is a man, there is justice towards them in a way: and for this reason too there are certain laws regulating the relations of father to his son, and of a master to his slave; but in so far as each is something belonging to another, the perfect idea of "right" or "just" is wanting to them.

Reply to Objection 3. All other differences between one person and another in a city have an immediate relation to the community of the city and to its ruler, wherefore there is just towards them in the perfect sense of justice. This "just" however is distinguished according to various offices, hence when we speak of "military," or "magisterial," or "priestly" right, it is not as though such rights fell short of the simply right, as when we speak of "paternal" right, or right of "dominion," but for the reason that something proper is due to each class of person in respect of his particular office.

QUESTION 58. JUSTICE

ARTICLE 1. WHETHER JUSTICE IS FITTINGLY DEFINED AS BEING THE PERPETUAL AND CONSTANT WILL TO RENDER TO EACH ONE HIS RIGHT?

Objection 1. It would seem that lawyers have unfittingly defined justice as being "the perpetual and constant will to render to each one his right" [Digest. i, 1; De Just. et Jure 10]. For, according to the Philosopher (Ethic. v, 1), justice is a habit which makes a man "capable of doing what is just, and of being just in action and in intention." Now "will" denotes a power, or also an act. Therefore justice is unfittingly defined as being a will.

Objection 2. Further, rectitude of the will is not the will; else if the will were its own rectitude, it would follow that no will is unrighteous. Yet, according to Anselm (De Veritate xii), justice is rectitude. Therefore justice is not the will.

Objection 3. Further, no will is perpetual save God's. If therefore justice is a perpetual will, in God alone will there be justice.

Objection 4. Further, whatever is perpetual is constant, since it is unchangeable. Therefore it is needless in defining justice, to say that it is both "perpetual" and "constant."

Objection 5. Further, it belongs to the sovereign to give each one his right. Therefore, if justice gives each one his right, it follows that it is in none but the sovereign: which is absurd.

Objection 6. Further, Augustine says (De Moribus Eccl. xv) that "justice is love serving God alone." Therefore it does not render to each one his right.

I answer that, The aforesaid definition of justice is fitting if understood aright. For since every virtue is a habit that is the principle of a good act, a virtue must needs be defined by means of the good act bearing on the matter proper to that virtue. Now the proper matter of justice consists of those things that belong to our intercourse with other men, as shall be shown further on (2). Hence the act of justice in relation to its proper matter and object is indicated in the words, "Rendering to each one his right," since, as Isidore says (Etym. x), "a man is said to be just because he respects the rights [jus] of others."

Now in order that an act bearing upon any matter whatever be virtuous, it requires to be voluntary, stable, and firm, because the Philosopher says (Ethic. ii, 4) that in order for an act to be virtuous it needs first of all to be done "knowingly," secondly to be done "by choice," and "for a due end," thirdly to be done "immovably." Now the first of these is included in the second, since "what is done through ignorance is involuntary" (Ethic. iii, 1). Hence the definition of justice mentions first the "will," in order to show that the act of justice must be voluntary; and mention is made afterwards of its "constancy" and "perpetuity" in order to indicate the firmness of the act.

Accordingly, this is a complete definition of justice; save that the act is mentioned instead of the habit, which takes its species from that act, because habit implies relation to act. And if anyone would reduce it to the proper form of a definition, he might say that "justice is a habit whereby a man renders to each one his due by a constant and perpetual will": and this is about the same definition as that given by the Philosopher (Ethic. v, 5) who says that "justice is a habit whereby a man is said to be capable of doing just actions in accordance with his choice."

Reply to Objection 1. Will here denotes the act, not the power: and it is customary among writers to define habits by their acts: thus Augustine says (Tract. in Joan. xl) that "faith is to believe what one sees not."

Reply to Objection 2. Justice is the same as rectitude, not essentially but causally; for it is a habit which rectifies the deed and the will.

Reply to Objection 3. The will may be called perpetual in two ways. First on the part of the will's act which endures forever, and thus God's will alone is perpetual. Secondly on the part of the subject, because, to wit, a man wills to do a certain thing always, and this is a necessary condition of justice. For it does not satisfy the conditions of justice that one wish to observe justice in some particular matter for the time being, because one could scarcely find a man willing to act unjustly in every case; and it is requisite that one should have the will to observe justice at all times and in all cases.

Reply to Objection 4. Since "perpetual" does not imply perpetuity of the act of the will, it is not superfluous to add "constant": for while the "perpetual will" denotes the purpose of observing justice always, "constant" signifies a firm perseverance in this purpose.

Reply to Objection 5. A judge renders to each one what belongs to him, by way of command and direction, because a judge is the "personification of justice," and "the sovereign is its guardian" (Ethic. v, 4). On the other hand, the subjects render to each one what belongs to him, by way of execution.

Reply to Objection 6. Just as love of God includes love of our neighbor, as stated above (Question 25, Article 1), so too the service of God includes rendering to each one his due.

ARTICLE 3. WHETHER JUSTICE IS A VIRTUE?

Objection 1. It would seem that justice is not a virtue. For it is written (Luke 17:10): "When you shall have done all these things that are commanded you, say: We are unprofitable servants; we have done that which we ought to do." Now it is not unprofitable to do a virtuous deed: for Ambrose says (De Officiis ii, 6): "We look to a profit that is estimated not by pecuniary gain but by the acquisition of godliness." Therefore to do what one ought to do, is not a virtuous deed. And yet it is an act of justice. Therefore justice is not a virtue.

Objection 2. Further, that which is done of necessity, is not meritorious. But to render to a man what belongs to him, as justice requires, is of necessity. Therefore it is not meritorious. Yet it is by virtuous actions that we gain merit. Therefore justice is not a virtue.

Objection 3. Further, every moral virtue is about matters of action. Now those things which are wrought externally are not things concerning behavior but concerning handicraft, according to the Philosopher (Metaph. ix) [Didot ed., viii, 8]. Therefore since it belongs to justice to produce externally a deed that is just in itself, it seems that justice is not a moral virtue.

On the contrary, Gregory says (Moral. ii, 49) that "the entire structure of good works is built on four virtues," viz. temperance, prudence, fortitude and justice

I answer that, A human virtue is one "which renders a human act and man himself good" [Ethic. ii, 6], and this can be applied to justice. For a man's act is made good through attaining the rule of reason, which is the rule whereby human acts are regulated. Hence, since justice regulates human operations, it is evident that it renders man's operations good, and, as Tully declares (De Officiis i, 7), good men are so called chiefly from their justice, wherefore, as he says again (De Officiis i, 7) "the luster of virtue appears above all in justice."

Reply to Objection 1. When a man does what he ought, he brings no gain to the person to whom he does what he ought, but only abstains from doing him a harm. He does however profit himself, in so far as he does what he ought, spontaneously and readily, and this is to act virtuously. Hence it is written (Wisdom 8:7) that Divine wisdom "teacheth temperance, and prudence, and justice, and fortitude, which are such things as men (i.e. virtuous men) can have nothing more profitable in life."

Reply to Objection 2. Necessity is twofold. One arises from "constraint," and this removes merit, since it runs counter to the will. The other arises from the obligation of a "command," or from the necessity of obtaining an end, when, to wit, a man is unable to achieve the end of virtue without doing some particular thing. The latter necessity does not remove merit, when a man does voluntarily that which is necessary in this way. It does however exclude the credit of supererogation, according to 1 Corinthians 9:16, "If I preach the Gospel, it is no glory to me, for a necessity lieth upon me."

Reply to Objection 3. Justice is concerned about external things, not by making them, which pertains to art, but by using them in our dealings with other men.

ARTICLE 5. WHETHER JUSTICE IS A GENERAL VIRTUE?

Objection 1. It would seem that justice is not a general virtue. For justice is specified with the other virtues, according to Wisdom 8:7, "She teacheth temperance and prudence, and justice, and fortitude." Now the "general" is not specified or reckoned together with the species contained under the same "general." Therefore justice is not a general virtue.

Objection 2. Further, as justice is accounted a cardinal virtue, so are temperance and fortitude. Now neither temperance nor fortitude is reckoned to be a general virtue. Therefore neither should justice in any way be reckoned a general virtue.

Objection 3. Further, justice is always towards others, as stated above (Article 2). But a sin committed against one's neighbor cannot be a general sin, because it is condivided with sin committed against oneself. Therefore neither is justice a general virtue.

On the contrary, The Philosopher says (Ethic. v, 1) that "justice is every virtue."

I answer that, Justice, as stated above (Article 2) directs man in his relations with other men. Now this may happen in two ways: first as regards his relation with individuals, secondly as regards his relations with others in general, in so far as a man who serves a community, serves all those who are included in that community. Accordingly justice in its proper acceptation can be directed to another in both these senses. Now it is evident that all who are included in a community, stand in relation to that community as parts to a whole; while a part, as such, belongs to a whole, so that whatever is the good of a part can be directed to the good of the whole. It follows therefore that the good of any virtue, whether such virtue direct man in relation to himself, or in relation to certain other individual persons, is referable to the common good, to which justice directs: so that all acts of virtue can pertain to justice, in so far as it directs man to the common good. It is in this sense that justice is called a general virtue. And since it belongs to the law to direct to the common good, as stated above (I-II, 90, 2), it follows that the justice which is in this way styled general, is called "legal justice," because thereby man is in harmony with the law which directs the acts of all the virtues to the common good.

Reply to Objection 1. Justice is specified or enumerated with the other virtues, not as a general but as a special virtue, as we shall state further on (A07,12).

Reply to Objection 2. Temperance and fortitude are in the sensitive appetite, viz. in the desiring and spirited. Now these powers are appetitive of certain particular goods, even as the senses are cognitive of particulars. On the other hand justice is in the intellective appetite as its subject, which can have the universal good as its object, knowledge whereof belongs to the intellect. Hence justice can be a general virtue rather than temperance or fortitude.

Reply to Objection 3. Things referable to oneself are referable to another, especially in regard to the common good. Wherefore legal justice, in so far as it directs to the common good, may be called a general virtue: and in like manner injustice may be called a general sin; hence it is written (1 John 3:4) that all "sin is iniquity."

ARTICLE 6. WHETHER JUSTICE, AS A GENERAL VIRTUE, IS ESSENTIALLY THE SAME AS ALL VIRTUE?

Objection 1. It would seem that justice, as a general virtue, is essentially the same as all virtue. For the Philosopher says (Ethic. v, 1) that "virtue and legal justice are the same as all virtue, but differ in their mode of being." Now things that differ merely in their mode of being or logically do not differ essentially. Therefore justice is essentially the same as every virtue.

Objection 2. Further, every virtue that is not essentially the same as all virtue is a part of virtue. Now the aforesaid justice, according to the Philosopher (Ethic. v. 1) "is not a part but the whole of virtue." Therefore the aforesaid justice is essentially the same as all virtue.

Objection 3. Further, the essence of a virtue does not change through that virtue directing its act to some higher end even as the habit of temperance remains essentially the same even though its act be directed to a Divine good. Now it belongs to legal justice that the acts of all the virtues are directed to a higher end, namely the common good of the multitude, which transcends the good of one single individual. Therefore it seems that legal justice is essentially all virtue.

Objection 4. Further, every good of a part can be directed to the good of the whole, so that if it be not thus directed it would seem without use or purpose. But that which is in accordance with virtue cannot be so. Therefore it seems that there can be no act of any virtue, that does not belong to general justice, which directs to the common good; and so it seems that general justice is essentially the same as all virtue.

On the contrary, The Philosopher says (Ethic. v, 1) that "many are able to be virtuous in matters affecting themselves, but are unable to be virtuous in matters relating to others," and (Polit. iii, 2) that "the virtue of the good man is not strictly the same as the virtue of the good citizen." Now the virtue of a good citizen is general justice, whereby a man is directed to the common good. Therefore general justice is not the same as virtue in general, and it is possible to have one without the other.

I answer that, A thing is said to be "general" in two ways. First, by "predication": thus "animal" is general in relation to man and horse and the like: and in this sense that which is general must needs be essentially the same as the things in relation to which it is general, for the reason that the genus belongs to the essence of the species, and forms part of its definition. Secondly a thing is said to be general "virtually"; thus a universal cause is general in relation to all its effects, the sun, for instance, in relation to all bodies that are illumined, or transmuted by its power; and in this sense there is no need for that which is "general" to be essentially the same as those things in relation to which it is general, since cause and effect are not essentially the same. Now it is in the latter sense that, according to what has been said (5), legal justice is said to be a general virtue, in as much, to wit, as it directs the acts of the other virtues to its own end, and this is to move all the other virtues by its command; for just as charity may be called a general virtue in so far as it directs the acts of all the virtues to the Divine good, so too is legal justice, in so far as it directs the acts of all the virtues to the common good. Accordingly, just as charity which regards the Divine good as its proper object, is a special virtue in respect of its essence, so too legal justice is a special virtue in respect of its essence, in so far as it regards the common good as its proper object. And thus it is in the sovereign principally and by way of a mastercraft, while it is secondarily and administratively in his subjects.

However the name of legal justice can be given to every virtue, in so far as every virtue is directed to the common good by the aforesaid legal justice, which though special essentially is nevertheless virtually general. Speaking in this way, legal justice is essentially the same as all virtue, but differs therefrom logically: and it is in this sense that the Philosopher speaks.

Wherefore the Replies to the First and Second Objections are manifest.

Reply to Objection 3. This argument again takes legal justice for the virtue commanded by legal justice.

Reply to Objection 4. Every virtue strictly speaking directs its act to that virtue's proper end: that it should happen to be directed to a further end either always or sometimes, does not belong to that virtue considered strictly, for it needs some higher virtue to direct it to that end. Consequently there must be one supreme virtue essentially distinct from every other virtue, which directs all the virtues to the common good; and this virtue is legal justice.

ARTICLE 7. WHETHER THERE IS A PARTICULAR BESIDES A GENERAL JUSTICE?

Objection 1. It would seem that there is not a particular besides a general justice. For there is nothing superfluous in the virtues, as neither is there in nature. Now general justice directs man sufficiently in all his relations with other men. Therefore there is no need for a particular justice.

Objection 2. Further, the species of a virtue does not vary according to "one" and "many." But legal justice directs one man to another in matters relating to the multitude, as shown above (A5,6). Therefore there is not another species of justice directing one man to another in matters relating to the individual.

Objection 3. Further, between the individual and the general public stands the household community. Consequently, if in addition to general justice there is a particular justice corresponding to the individual, for the same reason there should be a domestic justice directing man to the common good of a household: and yet this is not the case. Therefore neither should there be a particular besides a legal justice.

On the contrary, Chrysostom in his commentary on Matthew 5:6, "Blessed are they that hunger and thirst after justice," says (Hom. xv in Matth.): "By justice He signifies either the general virtue, or the particular virtue which is opposed to covetousness."

I answer that, As stated above (Article 6), legal justice is not essentially the same as every virtue, and besides legal justice which directs man immediately to the common good, there is a need for other virtues to direct him immediately in matters relating to particular goods: and these virtues may be relative to himself or to another individual person. Accordingly, just as in addition to legal justice there is a need for particular virtues to direct man in relation to himself, such as temperance and fortitude, so too besides legal justice there is need for particular justice to direct man in his relations to other individuals.

Reply to Objection 1. Legal justice does indeed direct man sufficiently in his relations towards others. As regards the common good it does so immediately, but as to the good of the individual, it does so mediately. Wherefore there is need for particular justice to direct a man immediately to the good of another individual.

Reply to Objection 2. The common good of the realm and the particular good of the individual differ not only in respect of the "many" and the "few," but also under a formal aspect. For the aspect of the "common" good differs from the aspect of the "individual" good, even as the aspect of "whole" differs from that of "part." Wherefore the Philosopher says (Polit. i, 1) that "they are wrong who maintain that the city and the home and the like differ only as many and few and not specifically."

Reply to Objection 3. The household community, according to the Philosopher (Polit. i, 2), differs in respect of a threefold fellowship; namely "of husband and wife, father and son, master and slave," in each of which one person is, as it were, part of the other. Wherefore between such persons there is not justice simply, but a species of justice, viz. "domestic" justice, as stated in Ethic. v, 6.

ARTICLE 8. WHETHER PARTICULAR JUSTICE HAS A SPECIAL MATTER?

Objection 1. It would seem that particular justice has no special matter. Because a gloss on Genesis 2:14, "The fourth river is Euphrates," says: "Euphrates signifies 'fruitful'; nor is it stated through what country it flows, because justice pertains to all the parts of the soul." Now this would not be the case, if justice had a special matter, since every special matter belongs to a special power. Therefore particular justice has no special matter.

Objection 2. Further, Augustine says (QQ. lxxxiii, qu. 61) that "the soul has four virtues whereby, in this life, it lives spiritually, viz. temperance, prudence, fortitude and justice;" and he says that "the fourth is justice, which pervades all the virtues." Therefore particular justice, which is one of the four cardinal virtues, has no special matter.

Objection 3. Further, justice directs man sufficiently in matters relating to others. Now a man can be directed to others in all matters relating to this life. Therefore the matter of justice is general and not special.

On the contrary, The Philosopher reckons (Ethic. v, 2) particular justice to be specially about those things which belong to social life.

I answer that, Whatever can be rectified by reason is the matter of moral virtue, for this is defined in reference to right reason, according to the Philosopher (Ethic. ii, 6). Now the reason can rectify not only the internal passions of the soul, but also external actions, and also those external things of which man can make use. And yet it is in respect of external actions and external things by means of which men can communicate with one another, that the relation of one man to another is to be considered; whereas it is in respect of internal passions that we consider man's rectitude in himself. Consequently, since justice is directed to others, it is not about the entire matter of moral virtue, but only about external actions and things, under a certain special aspect of the object, in so far as one man is related to another through them.

Reply to Objection 1. It is true that justice belongs essentially to one part of the soul, where it resides as in its subject; and this is the will which moves by its command all the other parts of the soul; and accordingly justice belongs to all the parts of the soul, not directly but by a kind of diffusion.

Reply to Objection 2. As stated above (I-II, 61, 3,4), the cardinal virtues may be taken in two ways: first as special virtues, each having a determinate matter; secondly, as certain general modes of virtue. On this latter sense

Augustine speaks in the passage quoted: for he says that "prudence is knowledge of what we should seek and avoid, temperance is the curb on the lust for fleeting pleasures, fortitude is strength of mind in bearing with passing trials, justice is the love of God and our neighbor which pervades the other virtues, that is to say, is the common principle of the entire order between one man and another."

Reply to Objection 3. A man's internal passions which are a part of moral matter, are not in themselves directed to another man, which belongs to the specific nature of justice; yet their effects, i.e. external actions, are capable of being directed to another man. Consequently it does not follow that the matter of justice is general.

ARTICLE 12. WHETHER JUSTICE STANDS FOREMOST AMONG ALL MORAL VIRTUES?

Objection 1. It would seem that justice does not stand foremost among all the moral virtues. Because it belongs to justice to render to each one what is his, whereas it belongs to liberality to give of one's own, and this is more virtuous. Therefore liberality is a greater virtue than justice.

Objection 2. Further, nothing is adorned by a less excellent thing than itself. Now magnanimity is the ornament both of justice and of all the virtues, according to Ethic. iv, 3. Therefore magnanimity is more excellent than justice.

Objection 3. Further, virtue is about that which is "difficult" and "good," as stated in Ethic. ii, 3. But fortitude is about more difficult things than justice is, since it is about dangers of death, according to Ethic. iii, 6. Therefore fortitude is more excellent than justice.

On the contrary, Tully says (De Offic. i, 7): "Justice is the most resplendent of the virtues, and gives its name to a good man."

I answer that, If we speak of legal justice, it is evident that it stands foremost among all the moral virtues, for as much as the common good transcends the individual good of one person. In this sense the Philosopher declares (Ethic. v, 1) that "the most excellent of the virtues would seem to be justice, and more glorious than either the evening or the morning star." But, even if we speak of particular justice, it excels the other moral virtues for two reasons. The first reason may be taken from the subject, because justice is in the more excellent part of the soul, viz. the rational appetite or will, whereas the other moral virtues are in the sensitive appetite, whereunto appertain the passions which are the matter of the other moral virtues. The second reason is taken from the object, because the other virtues are commendable in respect of the sole good of the virtuous person himself, whereas justice is praiseworthy in respect of the virtuous person being well disposed towards another, so that justice is somewhat the good of another person, as stated in Ethic. v, 1. Hence the Philosopher says (Rhet. i, 9): "The greatest virtues must needs be those which are most profitable to other persons, because virtue is a faculty of doing good to others. For this reason the greatest honors are accorded the brave and the just, since bravery is useful to others in warfare, and justice is useful to others both in warfare and in time of peace."

Reply to Objection 1. Although the liberal man gives of his own, yet he does so in so far as he takes into consideration the good of his own virtue, while the just man gives to another what is his, through consideration of the common good. Moreover justice is observed towards all, whereas liberality cannot extend to all. Again liberality which gives of a man's own is based on justice, whereby one renders to each man what is his.

Reply to Objection 2. When magnanimity is added to justice it increases the latter's goodness; and yet without justice it would not even be a virtue.

Reply to Objection 3. Although fortitude is about the most difficult things, it is not about the best, for it is only useful in warfare, whereas justice is useful both in war and in peace, as stated above.

QUESTION 60. JUDGMENT

ARTICLE 2. WHETHER IT IS LAWFUL TO JUDGE?

Objection 1. It would seem unlawful to judge. For nothing is punished except what is unlawful. Now those who judge are threatened with punishment, which those who judge not will escape, according to Matthew 7:1, "Judge not, and ye shall not be judged." Therefore it is unlawful to judge.

Objection 2. Further, it is written (Romans 14:4): "Who art thou that judgest another man's servant. To his own lord he standeth or falleth." Now God is the Lord of all. Therefore to no man is it lawful to judge.

Objection 3. Further, no man is sinless, according to 1 John 1:8, "If we say that we have no sin, we deceive ourselves." Now it is unlawful for a sinner to judge, according to Romans 2:1, "Thou art inexcusable, O man, whosoever thou art, that judgest; for wherein thou judgest another, thou condemnest thyself, for thou dost the same things which thou judgest." Therefore to no man is it lawful to judge.

On the contrary, It is written (Deuteronomy 16:18): "Thou shalt appoint judges and magistrates in all thy gates . . . that they may judge the people with just judgment."

I answer that, Judgment is lawful in so far as it is an act of justice. Now it follows from what has been stated above (1, ad 1,3) that three conditions are requisite for a judgment to be an act of justice: first, that it proceed from the inclination of justice; secondly, that it come from one who is in authority; thirdly, that it be pronounced according to the right ruling of prudence. If any one of these be lacking, the judgment will be faulty and unlawful. First, when it is contrary to the rectitude of justice, and then it is called "perverted" or "unjust": secondly, when a man judges about matters wherein he has no authority, and this is called judgment "by usurpation": thirdly, when the reason lacks certainty, as when a man, without any solid motive, forms a judgment on some doubtful or hidden matter, and then it is called judgment by "suspicion" or "rash" judgment.

Reply to Objection 1. In these words our Lord forbids rash judgment which is about the inward intention, or other uncertain things, as Augustine states (De Serm. Dom. in Monte ii, 18). Or else He forbids judgment about Divine things, which we ought not to judge, but simply believe, since they are above us, as Hilary declares in his commentary on Matthew 5. Or again according to Chrysostom [Hom. xvii in Matth. in the Opus Imperfectum falsely ascribed to St. John of the Cross], He forbids the judgment which proceeds not from benevolence but from bitterness of heart.

Reply to Objection 2. A judge is appointed as God's servant; wherefore it is written (Deuteronomy 1:16): "Judge that which is just," and further on (Deuteronomy 1:17), "because it is the judgment of God."

Reply to Objection 3. Those who stand guilty of grievous sins should not judge those who are guilty of the same or lesser sins, as Chrysostom [Hom. xxiv] says on the words of Matthew 7:1, "Judge not." Above all does this hold when such sins are public, because there would be an occasion of scandal arising in the hearts of others. If however they are not public but hidden, and there be an urgent necessity for the judge to pronounce judgment, because it is his duty, he can reprove or judge with humility and fear. Hence Augustine says (De Serm. Dom. in Monte ii, 19): "If we find that we are guilty of the same sin as another man, we should groan together with him, and invite him to strive against it together with us." And yet it is not through acting thus that a man condemns himself so as to deserve to be condemned once again, but when, in condemning another, he shows himself to be equally deserving of condemnation on account of another or a like sin.

ARTICLE 4. WHETHER DOUBTS SHOULD BE INTERPRETED FOR THE BEST?

Objection 1. It would seem that doubts should not be interpreted for the best. Because we should judge from what happens for the most part. But it happens for the most part that evil is done, since "the number of fools is infinite" (Ecclesiastes 1:15), "for the imagination and thought of man's heart are prone to evil from his youth" (Genesis 8:21). Therefore doubts should be interpreted for the worst rather than for the best.

Objection 2. Further, Augustine says (De Doctr. Christ. i, 27) that "he leads a godly and just life who is sound in his estimate of things, and turns neither to this side nor to that." Now he who interprets a doubtful point for the best, turns to one side. Therefore this should not be done.

Objection 3. Further, man should love his neighbor as himself. Now with regard to himself, a man should interpret doubtful matters for the worst, according to Job 9:28, "I feared all my works." Therefore it seems that doubtful matters affecting one's neighbor should be interpreted for the worst.

On the contrary, A gloss on Romans 14:3, "He that eateth not, let him not judge him that eateth," says: "Doubts should be interpreted in the best sense."

I answer that, As stated above (3, ad 2), things from the very fact that a man thinks ill of another without sufficient cause, he injures and despises him. Now no man ought to despise or in any way injure another man without urgent cause: and, consequently, unless we have evident indications of a person's wickedness, we ought to deem him good, by interpreting for the best whatever is doubtful about him.

Reply to Objection 1. He who interprets doubtful matters for the best, may happen to be deceived more often than not; yet it is better to err frequently through thinking well of a wicked man, than to err less frequently through having an evil opinion of a good man, because in the latter case an injury is inflicted, but not in the former.

Reply to Objection 2. It is one thing to judge of things and another to judge of men. For when we judge of things, there is no question of the good or evil of the thing about which we are judging, since it will take no harm no matter what kind of judgment we form about it; but there is question of the good of the person who judges, if he judge truly, and of his evil if he judge falsely because "the true is the good of the intellect, and the false is its evil," as stated in Ethic. vi, 2, wherefore everyone should strive to make his judgment accord with things as they are. On the other hand when we judge of men, the good and evil in our judgment is considered chiefly on the part of the person about whom judgment is being formed; for he is deemed worthy of honor from the very fact that he is judged to be good, and deserving of contempt if he is judged to be evil. For this reason we ought, in this kind of judgment, to aim at judging a man good, unless there is evident proof of the contrary. And though we may judge falsely, our judgment in thinking well of another pertains to our good feeling and not to the evil of the intellect, even as neither does it pertain to the intellect's perfection to know the truth of contingent singulars in themselves.

Reply to Objection 3. One may interpret something for the worst or for the best in two ways. First, by a kind of supposition; and thus, when we have to apply a remedy to some evil, whether our own or another's, in order for the remedy to be applied with greater certainty of a cure, it is expedient to take the worst for granted, since if a remedy be efficacious against a worse evil, much more is it efficacious against a lesser evil. Secondly we may interpret something for the best or for the worst, by deciding or determining, and in this case when judging of things we should try to interpret each thing according as it is, and when judging of persons, to interpret things for the best as stated above.

ARTICLE 5. WHETHER WE SHOULD ALWAYS JUDGE ACCORDING TO THE WRITTEN LAW?

Objection 1. It would seem that we ought not always to judge according to the written law. For we ought always to avoid judging unjustly. But written laws sometimes contain injustice, according to Isaiah 10:1, "Woe to them that make wicked laws, and when they write, write injustice." Therefore we ought not always to judge according to the written law.

Objection 2. Further, judgment has to be formed about individual happenings. But no written law can cover each and every individual happening, as the Philosopher declares (Ethic. v, 10). Therefore it seems that we are not always bound to judge according to the written law.

Objection 3. Further, a law is written in order that the lawgiver's intention may be made clear. But it happens sometimes that even if the lawgiver himself were present he would judge otherwise. Therefore we ought not always to judge according to the written law.

On the contrary, Augustine says (De Vera Relig. xxxi): "In these earthly laws, though men judge about them when they are making them, when once they are established and passed, the judges may judge no longer of them, but according to them."

I answer that, As stated above (Article 1), judgment is nothing else but a decision or determination of what is just. Now a thing becomes just in two ways: first by the very nature of the case, and this is called "natural right," secondly by some agreement between men, and this is called "positive right," as stated above (Question 57, Article 2). Now laws are written for the purpose of manifesting both these rights, but in different ways. For the written law does indeed contain natural right, but it does not establish it, for the latter derives its force, not from the law but from nature: whereas the written law both contains positive right, and establishes it by giving it force of authority.

Hence it is necessary to judge according to the written law, else judgment would fall short either of the natural or of the positive right.

Reply to Objection 1. Just as the written law does not give force to the natural right, so neither can it diminish or annul its force, because neither can man's will change nature. Hence if the written law contains anything contrary to the natural right, it is unjust and has no binding force. For positive right has no place except where "it matters not," according to the natural right, "whether a thing be done in one way or in another"; as stated above (57, 2, ad 2). Wherefore such documents are to be called, not laws, but rather corruptions of law, as stated above (I-II, 95, 2): and consequently judgment should not be delivered according to them.

Reply to Objection 2. Even as unjust laws by their very nature are, either always or for the most part, contrary to the natural right, so too laws that are rightly established, fail in some cases, when if they were observed they would be contrary to the natural right. Wherefore in such cases judgment should be delivered, not according to the letter of the law, but according to equity which the lawgiver has in view. Hence the jurist says [Digest. i, 3; De leg. senatusque consult. 25]: "By no reason of law, or favor of equity, is it allowable for us to interpret harshly, and render burdensome, those useful measures which have been enacted for the welfare of man." In such cases even the lawgiver himself would decide otherwise; and if he had foreseen the case, he might have provided for it by law.

This suffices for the Reply to the Third Objection.

QUESTION 64. MURDER

ARTICLE 2. WHETHER IT IS LAWFUL TO KILL SINNERS?

Objection 1. It would seem unlawful to kill men who have sinned. For our Lord in the parable (Matthew 13) forbade the uprooting of the cockle which denotes wicked men according to a gloss. Now whatever is forbidden by God is a sin. Therefore it is a sin to kill a sinner.

Objection 2. Further, human justice is conformed to Divine justice. Now according to Divine justice sinners are kept back for repentance, according to Ezekiel 33:11, "I desire not the death of the wicked, but that the wicked turn from his way and live." Therefore it seems altogether unjust to kill sinners.

Objection 3. Further, it is not lawful, for any good end whatever, to do that which is evil in itself, according to Augustine (Contra Mendac. vii) and the Philosopher (Ethic. ii, 6). Now to kill a man is evil in itself, since we are bound to have charity towards all men, and "we wish our friends to live and to exist," according to Ethic. ix, 4. Therefore it is nowise lawful to kill a man who has sinned.

On the contrary, It is written (Exodus 22:18): "Wizards thou shalt not suffer to live"; and (Psalm 100:8): "In the morning I put to death all the wicked of the land."

I answer that, As stated above (Article 1), it is lawful to kill dumb animals, in so far as they are naturally directed to man's use, as the imperfect is directed to the perfect. Now every part is directed to the whole, as imperfect to perfect, wherefore every part is naturally for the sake of the whole. For this reason we observe that if the health of the whole body demands the excision of a member, through its being decayed or infectious to the other members, it will be both praiseworthy and advantageous to have it cut away. Now every individual person is compared to the whole community, as part to whole. Therefore if a man be dangerous and infectious to the community, on account of some sin, it is praiseworthy and advantageous that he be killed in order to safeguard the common good, since "a little leaven corrupteth the whole lump" (1 Corinthians 5:6).

Reply to Objection 1. Our Lord commanded them to forbear from uprooting the cockle in order to spare the wheat, i.e. the good. This occurs when the wicked cannot be slain without the good being killed with them, either because the wicked lie hidden among the good, or because they have many followers, so that they cannot be killed without danger to the good, as Augustine says (Contra Parmen. iii, 2). Wherefore our Lord teaches that we should rather allow the wicked to live, and that vengeance is to be delayed until the last judgment, rather than that the good be put to death together with the wicked. When, however, the good incur no danger, but rather are protected and saved by the slaying of the wicked, then the latter may be lawfully put to death.

Reply to Objection 2. According to the order of His wisdom, God sometimes slays sinners forthwith in order to deliver the good, whereas sometimes He allows them time to repent, according as He knows what is expedient for His elect. This also does human justice imitate according to its powers; for it puts to death those who are dangerous to others, while it allows time for repentance to those who sin without grievously harming others.

Reply to Objection 3. By sinning man departs from the order of reason, and consequently falls away from the dignity of his manhood, in so far as he is naturally free, and exists for himself, and he falls into the slavish state of the beasts, by being disposed of according as he is useful to others. This is expressed in Psalm 48:21: "Man, when he was in honor, did not understand; he hath been compared to senseless beasts, and made like to them," and Proverbs 11:29: "The fool shall serve the wise." Hence, although it be evil in itself to kill a man so long as he preserve his dignity, yet it may be good to kill a man who has sinned, even as it is to kill a beast. For a bad man is worse than a beast, and is more harmful, as the Philosopher states (Polit. i, 1 and Ethic. vii, 6).

ARTICLE 3. WHETHER IT IS LAWFUL FOR A PRIVATE INDIVIDUAL TO KILL A MAN WHO HAS SINNED?

Objection 1. It would seem lawful for a private individual to kill a man who has sinned. For nothing unlawful is commanded in the Divine law. Yet, on account of the sin of the molten calf, Moses commanded (Exodus 32:27): "Let every man kill his brother, and friend, and neighbor." Therefore it is lawful for private individuals to kill a sinner.

Objection 2. Further, as stated above (2, ad 3), man, on account of sin, is compared to the beasts. Now it is lawful for any private individual to kill a wild beast, especially if it be harmful. Therefore for the same reason, it is lawful for any private individual to kill a man who has sinned.

Objection 3. Further, a man, though a private individual, deserves praise for doing what is useful for the common good. Now the slaying of evildoers is useful for the common good, as stated above (Article 2). Therefore it is deserving of praise if even private individuals kill evil-doers.

On the contrary, Augustine says (De Civ. Dei i) [Can. Quicumque percutit, caus. xxiii, qu. 8]: "A man who, without exercising public authority, kills an evil-doer, shall be judged guilty of murder, and all the more, since he has dared to usurp a power which God has not given him."

I answer that, As stated above (Article 2), it is lawful to kill an evildoer in so far as it is directed to the welfare of the whole community, so that it belongs to him alone who has charge of the community's welfare. Thus it belongs to a physician to cut off a decayed limb, when he has been entrusted with the care of the health of the whole body. Now the care of the common good is entrusted to persons of rank having public authority: wherefore they alone, and not private individuals, can lawfully put evildoers to death.

Reply to Objection 1. The person by whose authority a thing is done really does the thing as Dionysius declares (Coel. Hier. iii). Hence according to Augustine (De Civ. Dei i, 21), "He slays not who owes his service to one who commands him, even as a sword is merely the instrument to him that wields it." Wherefore those who, at the Lord's command, slew their neighbors and friends, would seem not to have done this themselves, but rather He by whose authority they acted thus: just as a soldier slays the foe by the authority of his sovereign, and the executioner slays the robber by the authority of the judge.

Reply to Objection 2. A beast is by nature distinct from man, wherefore in the case of a wild beast there is no need for an authority to kill it; whereas, in the case of domestic animals, such authority is required, not for their sake, but on account of the owner's loss. On the other hand a man who has sinned is not by nature distinct from good men; hence a public authority is requisite in order to condemn him to death for the common good.

Reply to Objection 3. It is lawful for any private individual to do anything for the common good, provided it harm nobody: but if it be harmful to some other, it cannot be done, except by virtue of the judgment of the person to whom it pertains to decide what is to be taken from the parts for the welfare of the whole.

ARTICLE 5. WHETHER IT IS LAWFUL TO KILL ONESELF?

Objection 1. It would seem lawful for a man to kill himself. For murder is a sin in so far as it is contrary to justice. But no man can do an injustice to himself, as is proved in Ethic. v, 11. Therefore no man sins by killing himself.

Objection 2. Further, it is lawful, for one who exercises public authority, to kill evil-doers. Now he who exercises public authority is sometimes an evil-doer. Therefore he may lawfully kill himself.

Objection 3. Further, it is lawful for a man to suffer spontaneously a lesser danger that he may avoid a greater: thus it is lawful for a man to cut off a decayed limb even from himself, that he may save his whole body. Now sometimes a man, by killing himself, avoids a greater evil, for example an unhappy life, or the shame of sin. Therefore a man may kill himself.

Objection 4. Further, Samson killed himself, as related in Judges 16, and yet he is numbered among the saints (Hebrews 11). Therefore it is lawful for a man to kill himself.

Objection 5. Further, it is related (2 Maccabees 14:42) that a certain Razias killed himself, "choosing to die nobly rather than to fall into the hands of the wicked, and to suffer abuses unbecoming his noble birth." Now nothing that is done nobly and bravely is unlawful. Therefore suicide is not unlawful.

On the contrary, Augustine says (De Civ. Dei i, 20): "Hence it follows that the words 'Thou shalt not kill' refer to the killing of a man—not another man; therefore, not even thyself. For he who kills himself, kills nothing else than a man."

I answer that, It is altogether unlawful to kill oneself, for three reasons. First, because everything naturally loves itself, the result being that everything naturally keeps itself in being, and resists corruptions so far as it can. Wherefore suicide is contrary to the inclination of nature, and to charity whereby every man should love himself. Hence suicide is always a mortal sin, as being contrary to the natural law and to charity. Secondly, because every part, as such, belongs to the whole. Now every man is part of the community, and so, as such, he belongs to the community. Hence by killing himself he injures the community, as the Philosopher declares (Ethic. v, 11). Thirdly, because life is God's gift to man, and is subject to His power, Who kills and makes to live. Hence whoever takes his own life, sins against God, even as he who kills another's slave, sins against that slave's master, and as he who usurps to himself judgment of a matter not entrusted to him. For it belongs to God alone to pronounce sentence of death and life, according to Deuteronomy 32:39, "I will kill and I will make to live."

Reply to Objection 1. Murder is a sin, not only because it is contrary to justice, but also because it is opposed to charity which a man should have towards himself: in this respect suicide is a sin in relation to oneself. On relation to the community and to God, it is sinful, by reason also of its opposition to justice.

Reply to Objection 2. One who exercises public authority may lawfully put to death an evil-doer, since he can pass judgment on him. But no man is judge of himself. Wherefore it is not lawful for one who exercises public authority to put himself to death for any sin whatever: although he may lawfully commit himself to the judgment of others.

Reply to Objection 3. Man is made master of himself through his free-will: wherefore he can lawfully dispose of himself as to those matters which pertain to this life which is ruled by man's free-will. But the passage from this life to another and happier one is subject not to man's free-will but to the power of God. Hence it is not lawful for man to take his own life that he may pass to a happier life, nor that he may escape any unhappiness whatsoever of the present life, because the ultimate and most fearsome evil of this life is death, as the Philosopher states (Ethic. iii, 6). Therefore to bring death upon oneself in order to escape the other afflictions of this life, is to adopt a greater evil in order to avoid a lesser. In like manner it is unlawful to take one's own life on account of one's having committed a sin, both because by so doing one does oneself a very great injury, by depriving oneself of the time needful for repentance, and because it is not lawful to slay an evildoer except by the sentence of the public authority. Again it is unlawful for a woman to kill herself lest she be violated, because she ought not to commit on herself the very great sin of suicide, to avoid the lesser sin of another. For she commits no sin in being violated by force, provided she does not consent, since "without consent of the mind there is no stain on the body," as the Blessed Lucy declared. Now it is evident that fornication and adultery are less grievous sins than taking a man's, especially one's own, life: since the latter is most grievous, because one injures oneself, to whom one owes the greatest love. Moreover it is most dangerous since no time is left wherein to expiate it by repentance. Again it is not lawful for anyone to take his own life for fear he should consent to sin, because "evil must not be done that good may come" (Romans 3:8) or that evil may be avoided especially if the evil be of small account and an uncertain event, for it is uncertain whether one will at some future time consent to a sin, since God is able to deliver man from sin under any temptation whatever.

Reply to Objection 4. As Augustine says (De Civ. Dei i, 21), "not even Samson is to be excused that he crushed himself together with his enemies under the ruins of the house, except the Holy Ghost, Who had wrought many wonders through him, had secretly commanded him to do this." He assigns the same reason in the case of certain holy women, who at the time of persecution took their own lives, and who are commemorated by the Church.

Reply to Objection 5. It belongs to fortitude that a man does not shrink from being slain by another, for the sake of the good of virtue, and that he may avoid sin. But that a man take his own life in order to avoid penal evils has indeed an appearance of fortitude (for which reason some, among whom was Razias, have killed themselves thinking to act from fortitude), yet it is not true fortitude, but rather a weakness of soul unable to bear penal evils, as the Philosopher (Ethic. iii, 7) and Augustine (De Civ. Dei 22,23) declare.

ARTICLE 6. WHETHER IT IS LAWFUL TO KILL THE INNOCENT?

Objection 1. It would seem that in some cases it is lawful to kill the innocent. The fear of God is never manifested by sin, since on the contrary "the fear of the Lord driveth out sin" (Sirach 1:27). Now Abraham was commended in that he feared the Lord, since he was willing to slay his innocent son. Therefore one may, without sin, kill an innocent person.

Objection 2. Further, among those sins that are committed against one's neighbor, the more grievous seem to be those whereby a more grievous injury is inflicted on the person sinned against. Now to be killed is a greater injury to a sinful than to an innocent person, because the latter, by death, passes forthwith from the unhappiness of this life to the glory of heaven. Since then it is lawful in certain cases to kill a sinful man, much more is it lawful to slay an innocent or a righteous person.

Objection 3. Further, what is done in keeping with the order of justice is not a sin. But sometimes a man is forced, according to the order of justice, to slay an innocent person: for instance, when a judge, who is bound to judge according to the evidence, condemns to death a man whom he knows to be innocent but who is convicted by false witnesses; and again the executioner, who in obedience to the judge puts to death the man who has been unjustly sentenced.

On the contrary, It is written (Exodus 23:7): "The innocent and just person thou shalt not put to death."

I answer that, An individual man may be considered in two ways: first, in himself; secondly, in relation to something else. If we consider a man in himself, it is unlawful to kill any man, since in every man though he be sinful, we ought to love the nature which God has made, and which is destroyed by slaying him. Nevertheless, as stated above (Article 2) the slaying of a sinner becomes lawful in relation to the common good, which is corrupted by sin. On the other hand the life of righteous men preserves and forwards the common good, since they are the chief part of the community. Therefore it is in no way lawful to slay the innocent.

Reply to Objection 1. God is Lord of death and life, for by His decree both the sinful and the righteous die. Hence he who at God's command kills an innocent man does not sin, as neither does God Whose behest he executes: indeed his obedience to God's commands is a proof that he fears Him.

Reply to Objection 2. In weighing the gravity of a sin we must consider the essential rather than the accidental. Wherefore he who kills a just man, sins more grievously than he who slays a sinful man: first, because he injures one whom he should love more, and so acts more in opposition to charity: secondly, because he inflicts an injury on a man who is less deserving of one, and so acts more in opposition to justice: thirdly, because he deprives the community of a greater good: fourthly, because he despises God more, according to Luke 10:16, "He that despiseth you despiseth Me." On the other hand it is accidental to the slaying that the just man whose life is taken be received by God into glory.

Reply to Objection 3. If the judge knows that man who has been convicted by false witnesses, is innocent he must, like Daniel, examine the witnesses with great care, so as to find a motive for acquitting the innocent: but if he cannot do this he should remit him for judgment by a higher tribunal. If even this is impossible, he does not sin if he pronounce sentence in accordance with the evidence, for it is not he that puts the innocent man to death, but they who stated him to be guilty. He that carries out the sentence of the judge who has condemned an innocent man, if the sentence contains an inexcusable error, he should not obey, else there would be an excuse for the executions of the martyrs: if however it contain no manifest injustice, he does not has no right to discuss the judgment of his superior; nor is it he who slays the innocent man, but the judge whose minister he is.

ARTICLE 7. WHETHER IT IS LAWFUL TO KILL A MAN IN SELF-DEFENSE?

Objection 1. It would seem that nobody may lawfully kill a man in self-defense. For Augustine says to Publicola (Ep. xlvii): "I do not agree with the opinion that one may kill a man lest one be killed by him; unless one be a soldier, exercise a public office, so that one does it not for oneself but for others, having the power to do so, provided it be in keeping with one's person." Now he who kills a man in self-defense, kills him lest he be killed by him. Therefore this would seem to be unlawful.

Objection 2. Further, he says (De Lib. Arb. i, 5) [the speaker is Evodius not Augustine]: "How are they free from sin in sight of Divine providence, who are guilty of taking a man's life for the sake of these contemptible things?" Now among contemptible things he reckons "those which men may forfeit unwillingly," as appears from the context (De Lib. Arb. i, 5): and the chief of these is the life of the body. Therefore it is unlawful for any man to take another's life for the sake of the life of his own body.

Objection 3. Further, Pope Nicolas [Nicolas I, Dist. 1, can. De his clericis] says in the Decretals: "Concerning the clerics about whom you have consulted Us, those, namely, who have killed a pagan in self-defense, as to whether, after making amends by repenting, they may return to their former state, or rise to a higher degree; know that in no case is it lawful for them to kill any man under any circumstances whatever." Now clerics and laymen are alike bound to observe the moral precepts. Therefore neither is it lawful for laymen to kill anyone in self-defense.

Objection 4. Further, murder is a more grievous sin than fornication or adultery. Now nobody may lawfully commit simple fornication or adultery or any other mortal sin in order to save his own life; since the spiritual life is to be preferred to the life of the body. Therefore no man may lawfully take another's life in self-defense in order to save his own life.

Objection 5. Further, if the tree be evil, so is the fruit, according to Matthew 7:17. Now self-defense itself seems to be unlawful, according to Romans 12:19: "Not defending [Douay: 'revenging'] yourselves, my dearly beloved." Therefore its result, which is the slaying of a man, is also unlawful.

On the contrary, It is written (Exodus 22:2): "If a thief be found breaking into a house or undermining it, and be wounded so as to die; he that slew him shall not be guilty of blood." Now it is much more lawful to defend one's life than one's house. Therefore neither is a man guilty of murder if he kill another in defense of his own life.

I answer that, Nothing hinders one act from having two effects, only one of which is intended, while the other is beside the intention. Now moral acts take their species according to what is intended, and not according to what is beside the intention, since this is accidental as explained above (43, 3; I-II, 12, 1). Accordingly the act of self-defense may have two effects, one is the saving of one's life, the other is the slaying of the aggressor. Therefore this act, since one's intention is to save one's own life, is not unlawful, seeing that it is natural to everything to keep itself in "being," as far as possible. And yet, though proceeding from a good intention, an act may be rendered unlawful, if it be out of proportion to the end. Wherefore if a man, in self-defense, uses more than necessary violence, it will be unlawful: whereas if he repel force with moderation his defense will be lawful, because according to the jurists [Cap. Significasti, De Homicid. volunt. vel casual.], "it is lawful to repel force by force, provided one does not exceed the limits of a blameless defense." Nor is it necessary for salvation that a man omit the act of moderate self-defense in order to avoid killing the other man, since one is bound to take more care of one's own life than of another's. But as it is unlawful to take a man's life, except for the public authority acting for the common good, as stated above (Article 3), it is not lawful for a man to intend killing a man in self-defense, except for such as have public authority, who while intending to kill a man in self-defense, refer this to the public good, as in the case of a soldier fighting against the foe, and in the minister of the judge struggling with robbers, although even these sin if they be moved by private animosity.

Reply to Objection 1. The words quoted from Augustine refer to the case when one man intends to kill another to save himself from death. The passage quoted in the Second Objection is to be understood in the same sense. Hence he says pointedly, "for the sake of these things," whereby he indicates the intention. This suffices for the Reply to the Second Objection.

Reply to Objection 3. Irregularity results from the act though sinless of taking a man's life, as appears in the case of a judge who justly condemns a man to death. For this reason a cleric, though he kill a man in self-defense, is irregular, albeit he intends not to kill him, but to defend himself.

Reply to Objection 4. The act of fornication or adultery is not necessarily directed to the preservation of one's own life, as is the act whence sometimes results the taking of a man's life.

Reply to Objection 5. The defense forbidden in this passage is that which comes from revengeful spite. Hence a gloss says: "Not defending yourselves—that is, not striking your enemy back."

QUESTION 66. THEFT AND ROBBERY

ARTICLE 1. WHETHER IT IS NATURAL FOR MAN TO POSSESS EXTERNAL THINGS?

Objection 1. It would seem that it is not natural for man to possess external things. For no man should ascribe to himself that which is God's. Now the dominion over all creatures is proper to God, according to Psalm 23:1, "The earth is the Lord's," etc. Therefore it is not natural for man to possess external things.

Objection 2. Further, Basil in expounding the words of the rich man (Luke 12:18), "I will gather all things that are grown to me, and my goods," says [Hom. in Luc. xii, 18]: "Tell me: which are thine? where did you take them from and bring them into being?" Now whatever man possesses naturally, he can fittingly call his own. Therefore man does not naturally possess external things.

Objection 3. Further, according to Ambrose (De Trin. i [De Fide, ad Gratianum, i, 1) "dominion denotes power." But man has no power over external things, since he can work no change in their nature. Therefore the possession of external things is not natural to man.

On the contrary, It is written (Psalm 8:8): "Thou hast subjected all things under his feet."

I answer that, External things can be considered in two ways. First, as regards their nature, and this is not subject to the power of man, but only to the power of God Whose mere will all things obey. Secondly, as regards their use, and in this way, man has a natural dominion over external things, because, by his reason and will, he is able to use them for his own profit, as they were made on his account: for the imperfect is always for the sake of the perfect, as stated above (Question 64, Article 1). It is by this argument that the Philosopher proves (Polit. i, 3) that the possession of external things is natural to man. Moreover, this natural dominion of man over other creatures, which is competent to man in respect of his reason wherein God's image resides, is shown forth in man's creation (Genesis 1:26) by the words: "Let us make man to our image and likeness: and let him have dominion over the fishes of the sea," etc.

Reply to Objection 1. God has sovereign dominion over all things: and He, according to His providence, directed certain things to the sustenance of man's body. For this reason man has a natural dominion over things, as regards the power to make use of them.

Reply to Objection 2. The rich man is reproved for deeming external things to belong to him principally, as though he had not received them from another, namely from God.

Reply to Objection 3. This argument considers the dominion over external things as regards their nature. Such a dominion belongs to God alone, as stated above.

ARTICLE 2. WHETHER IT IS LAWFUL FOR A MAN TO POSSESS A THING AS HIS OWN?

Objection 1. It would seem unlawful for a man to possess a thing as his own. For whatever is contrary to the natural law is unlawful. Now according to the natural law all things are common property: and the possession of property is contrary to this community of goods. Therefore it is unlawful for any man to appropriate any external thing to himself.

Objection 2. Further, Basil in expounding the words of the rich man quoted above (1, Objection 2), says: "The rich who deem as their own property the common goods they have seized upon, are like to those who by going beforehand to the play prevent others from coming, and appropriate to themselves what is intended for common use." Now it would be unlawful to prevent others from obtaining possession of common goods. Therefore it is unlawful to appropriate to oneself what belongs to the community.

Objection 3. Further, Ambrose says [Serm. lxiv, de temp.], and his words are quoted in the Decretals [Dist. xlvii., Can. Sicut hi.]: "Let no man call his own that which is common property": and by "common" he means external things, as is clear from the context. Therefore it seems unlawful for a man to appropriate an external thing to himself.

On the contrary, Augustine says (De Haeres., haer. 40): "The 'Apostolici' are those who with extreme arrogance have given themselves that name, because they do not admit into their communion persons who are married or possess anything of their own, such as both monks and clerics who in considerable number are to be found in the Catholic Church." Now the reason why these people are heretics was because severing themselves from the Church, they think that those who enjoy the use of the above things, which they themselves lack, have no hope of salvation. Therefore it is erroneous to maintain that it is unlawful for a man to possess property.

I answer that, Two things are competent to man in respect of exterior things. One is the power to procure and dispense them, and in this regard it is lawful for man to possess property. Moreover this is necessary to human life for three reasons. First because every man is more careful to procure what is for himself alone than that which is common to many or to all: since each one would shirk the labor and leave to another that which concerns the community, as happens where there is a great number of servants. Secondly, because human affairs are conducted in more orderly fashion if each man is charged with taking care of some particular thing himself, whereas there would be confusion if everyone had to look after any one thing indeterminately. Thirdly, because a more peaceful state is ensured to man if each one is contented with his own. Hence it is to be observed that quarrels arise more frequently where there is no division of the things possessed.

The second thing that is competent to man with regard to external things is their use. On this respect man ought to possess external things, not as his own, but as common, so that, to wit, he is ready to communicate them to others in their need. Hence the Apostle says (1 Timothy 6:17-18): "Charge the rich of this world . . . to give easily, to communicate to others," etc.

Reply to Objection 1. Community of goods is ascribed to the natural law, not that the natural law dictates that all things should be possessed in common and that nothing should be possessed as one's own: but because the division of possessions is not according to the natural law, but rather arose from human agreement which belongs to positive law, as stated above (57, 2,3). Hence the ownership of possessions is not contrary to the natural law, but an addition thereto devised by human reason.

Reply to Objection 2. A man would not act unlawfully if by going beforehand to the play he prepared the way for others: but he acts unlawfully if by so doing he hinders others from going. On like manner a rich man does not act unlawfully if he anticipates someone in taking possession of something which at first was common property, and gives others a share: but he sins if he excludes others indiscriminately from using it. Hence Basil says (Hom. in Luc. xii, 18): "Why are you rich while another is poor, unless it be that you may have the merit of a good stewardship, and he the reward of patience?"

Reply to Objection 3. When Ambrose says: "Let no man call his own that which is common," he is speaking of ownership as regards use, wherefore he adds: "He who spends too much is a robber."

ARTICLE 7. WHETHER IT IS LAWFUL TO STEAL THROUGH STRESS OF NEED?

Objection 1. It would seem unlawful to steal through stress of need. For penance is not imposed except on one who has sinned. Now it is stated (Extra, De furtis, Cap. Si quis): "If anyone, through stress of hunger or nakedness, steal food, clothing or beast, he shall do penance for three weeks." Therefore it is not lawful to steal through stress of need.

Objection 2. Further, the Philosopher says (Ethic. ii, 6) that "there are some actions whose very name implies wickedness," and among these he reckons theft. Now that which is wicked in itself may not be done for a good end. Therefore a man cannot lawfully steal in order to remedy a need.

Objection 3. Further, a man should love his neighbor as himself. Now, according to Augustine (Contra Mendac. vii), it is unlawful to steal in order to succor one's neighbor by giving him an alms. Therefore neither is it lawful to steal in order to remedy one's own needs.

On the contrary, In cases of need all things are common property, so that there would seem to be no sin in taking another's property, for need has made it common.

I answer that, Things which are of human right cannot derogate from natural right or Divine right. Now according to the natural order established by Divine Providence, inferior things are ordained for the purpose of succoring man's needs by their means. Wherefore the division and appropriation of things which are based on human law, do not preclude the fact that man's needs have to be remedied by means of these very things. Hence whatever certain people have in superabundance is due, by natural law, to the purpose of succoring the poor. For this reason Ambrose [Loc. cit., 2, Objection 3] says, and his words are embodied in the Decretals (Dist. xlvii, can. Sicut ii): "It is the hungry man's bread that you withhold, the naked man's cloak that you store away, the money that you bury in the earth is the price of the poor man's ransom and freedom."

Since, however, there are many who are in need, while it is impossible for all to be succored by means of the same thing, each one is entrusted with the stewardship of his own things, so that out of them he may come to the aid of those who are in need. Nevertheless, if the need be so manifest and urgent, that it is evident that the present need must be remedied by whatever means be at hand (for instance when a person is in some imminent danger, and there is no other possible remedy), then it is lawful for a man to succor his own need by means of another's property, by taking it either openly or secretly: nor is this properly speaking theft or robbery.

Reply to Objection 1. This decretal considers cases where there is no urgent need.

Reply to Objection 2. It is not theft, properly speaking, to take secretly and use another's property in a case of extreme need: because that which he takes for the support of his life becomes his own property by reason of that need.

Reply to Objection 3. In a case of a like need a man may also take secretly another's property in order to succor his neighbor in need.

QUESTION 78. THE SIN OF USURY

ARTICLE 1. WHETHER IT IS A SIN TO TAKE USURY FOR MONEY LENT?

Objection 1. It would seem that it is not a sin to take usury for money lent. For no man sins through following the example of Christ. But Our Lord said of Himself (Luke 19:23): "At My coming I might have exacted it," i.e. the money lent, "with usury." Therefore it is not a sin to take usury for lending money.

Objection 2. Further, according to Psalm 18:8, "The law of the Lord is unspotted," because, to wit, it forbids sin. Now usury of a kind is allowed in the Divine law, according to Deuteronomy 23:19-20: "Thou shalt not fenerate to thy brother money, nor corn, nor any other thing, but to the stranger": nay more, it is even promised as a reward for the observance of the Law, according to Deuteronomy 28:12: "Thou shalt fenerate* to many nations, and shalt not borrow of any one." ['Faeneraberis'—'Thou shalt lend upon usury.' The Douay version has simply 'lend.' The objection lays stress on the word 'faeneraberis': hence the necessity of rendering it by 'fenerate.'] Therefore it is not a sin to take usury.

Objection 3. Further, in human affairs justice is determined by civil laws. Now civil law allows usury to be taken. Therefore it seems to be lawful.

Objection 4. Further, the counsels are not binding under sin. But, among other counsels we find (Luke 6:35): "Lend, hoping for nothing thereby." Therefore it is not a sin to take usury.

Objection 5. Further, it does not seem to be in itself sinful to accept a price for doing what one is not bound to do. But one who has money is not bound in every case to lend it to his neighbor. Therefore it is lawful for him sometimes to accept a price for lending it.

Objection 6. Further, silver made into coins does not differ specifically from silver made into a vessel. But it is lawful to accept a price for the loan of a silver vessel. Therefore it is also lawful to accept a price for the loan of a silver coin. Therefore usury is not in itself a sin.

Objection 7. Further, anyone may lawfully accept a thing which its owner freely gives him. Now he who accepts the loan, freely gives the usury. Therefore he who lends may lawfully take the usury.

On the contrary, It is written (Exodus 22:25): "If thou lend money to any of thy people that is poor, that dwelleth with thee, thou shalt not be hard upon them as an extortioner, nor oppress them with usuries."

I answer that, To take usury for money lent is unjust in itself, because this is to sell what does not exist, and this evidently leads to inequality which is contrary to justice. In order to make this evident, we must observe that there are certain things the use of which consists in their consumption: thus we consume wine when we use it for drink and we consume wheat when we use it for food. Wherefore in such like things the use of the thing must not be reckoned apart from the thing itself, and whoever is granted the use of the thing, is granted the thing itself and for this reason, to lend things of this kind is to transfer the ownership. Accordingly if a man wanted to sell wine separately from the use of the wine, he would be selling the same thing twice, or he would be selling what does not exist, wherefore he would evidently commit a sin of injustice. In like manner he commits an injustice who lends wine or wheat, and asks for double payment, viz. one, the return of the thing in equal measure, the other, the price of the use, which is called usury.

On the other hand, there are things the use of which does not consist in their consumption: thus to use a house is to dwell in it, not to destroy it. Wherefore in such things both may be granted: for instance, one man may hand over to another the ownership of his house while reserving to himself the use of it for a time, or vice versa, he may grant the use of the house, while retaining the ownership. For this reason a man may lawfully make a charge for the use of his house, and, besides this, revendicate the house from the person to whom he has granted its use, as happens in renting and letting a house.

Now money, according to the Philosopher (Ethic. v, 5; Polit. i, 3) was invented chiefly for the purpose of exchange: and consequently the proper and principal use of money is its consumption or alienation whereby it is sunk in exchange. Hence it is by its very nature unlawful to take payment for the use of money lent, which payment is known as usury: and just as a man is bound to restore other ill-gotten goods, so is he bound to restore the money which he has taken in usury.

Reply to Objection 1. In this passage usury must be taken figuratively for the increase of spiritual goods which God exacts from us, for He wishes us ever to advance in the goods which we receive from Him: and this is for our own profit not for His.

Reply to Objection 2. The Jews were forbidden to take usury from their brethren, i.e. from other Jews. By this we are given to understand that to take usury from any man is evil simply, because we ought to treat every man as our neighbor and brother, especially in the state of the Gospel, whereto all are called. Hence it is said without any distinction in Psalm 14:5: "He that hath not put out his money to usury," and (Ezekiel 18:8): "Who hath not taken usury [Vulgate: 'If a man . . . hath not lent upon money, nor taken any increase . . . he is just.']." They were permitted, however, to take usury from foreigners, not as though it were lawful, but in order to avoid a greater evil, lest, to wit, through avarice to which they were prone according to Isaiah 56:11, they should take usury from the Jews who were worshippers of God.

Where we find it promised to them as a reward, "Thou shalt fenerate to many nations," etc., fenerating is to be taken in a broad sense for lending, as in Sirach 29:10, where we read: "Many have refused to fenerate, not out of wickedness," i.e. they would not lend. Accordingly the Jews are promised in reward an abundance of wealth, so that they would be able to lend to others.

Reply to Objection 3. Human laws leave certain things unpunished, on account of the condition of those who are imperfect, and who would be deprived of many advantages, if all sins were strictly forbidden and punishments appointed for them. Wherefore human law has permitted usury, not that it looks upon usury as harmonizing with justice, but lest the advantage of many should be hindered. Hence it is that in civil law [Inst. II, iv, de Usufructu] it is stated that "those things according to natural reason and civil law which are consumed by being used, do not admit of usufruct," and that "the senate did not (nor could it) appoint a usufruct to such things, but established a quasi-usufruct," namely by permitting usury. Moreover the Philosopher, led by natural reason, says (Polit. i, 3) that "to make money by usury is exceedingly unnatural."

Reply to Objection 4. A man is not always bound to lend, and for this reason it is placed among the counsels. Yet it is a matter of precept not to seek profit by lending: although it may be called a matter of counsel in comparison with the maxims of the Pharisees, who deemed some kinds of usury to be lawful, just as love of one's enemies is a matter of counsel. Or again, He speaks here not of the hope of usurious gain, but of the hope which is put in man. For we ought not to lend or do any good deed through hope in man, but only through hope in God.

Reply to Objection 5. He that is not bound to lend, may accept repayment for what he has done, but he must not exact more. Now he is repaid according to equality of justice if he is repaid as much as he lent. Wherefore if he exacts more for the usufruct of a thing which has no other use but the consumption of its substance, he exacts a price of something non-existent: and so his exaction is unjust.

Reply to Objection 6. The principal use of a silver vessel is not its consumption, and so one may lawfully sell its use while retaining one's ownership of it. On the other hand the principal use of silver money is sinking it in exchange, so that it is not lawful to sell its use and at the same time expect the restitution of the amount lent. It must be observed, however, that the secondary use of silver vessels may be an exchange, and such use may not be lawfully sold. On like manner there may be some secondary use of silver money; for instance, a man might lend coins for show, or to be used as security.

Reply to Objection 7. He who gives usury does not give it voluntarily simply, but under a certain necessity, in so far as he needs to borrow money which the owner is unwilling to lend without usury.

QUESTION 104. OBEDIENCE

ARTICLE 5. WHETHER SUBJECTS ARE BOUND TO OBEY THEIR SUPERIORS IN ALL THINGS?

Objection 1. It seems that subjects are bound to obey their superiors in all things. For the Apostle says (Colossians 3:20): "Children, obey your parents in all things," and farther on (Colossians 3:22): "Servants, obey in all things your masters according to the flesh." Therefore in like manner other subjects are bound to obey their superiors in all things.

Objection 2. Further, superiors stand between God and their subjects, according to Deuteronomy 5:5, "I was the mediator and stood between the Lord and you at that time, to show you His words." Now there is no going from extreme to extreme, except through that which stands between. Therefore the commands of a superior must be esteemed the commands of God, wherefore the Apostle says (Galatians 4:14): "You . . . received me as an angel of God, even as Christ Jesus" and (1 Thessalonians 2:13): "When you had received of us the word of the hearing of God, you received it, not as the word of men, but, as it is indeed, the word of God." Therefore as man is bound to obey God in all things, so is he bound to obey his superiors.

Objection 3. Further, just as religious in making their profession take vows of chastity and poverty, so do they also vow obedience. Now a religious is bound to observe chastity and poverty in all things. Therefore he is also bound to obey in all things.

On the contrary, It is written (Acts 5:29): "We ought to obey God rather than men." Now sometimes the things commanded by a superior are against God. Therefore superiors are not to be obeyed in all things.

I answer that, As stated above (A1,4), he who obeys is moved at the bidding of the person who commands him, by a certain necessity of justice, even as a natural thing is moved through the power of its mover by a natural necessity. That a natural thing be not moved by its mover, may happen in two ways. First, on account of a hindrance arising from the stronger power of some other mover; thus wood is not burnt by fire if a stronger force of water intervene. Secondly, through lack of order in the movable with regard to its mover, since, though it is subject to the latter's action in one respect, yet it is not subject thereto in every respect. Thus, a humor is sometimes subject to the action of heat, as regards being heated, but not as regards being dried up or consumed. In like manner there are two reasons, for which a subject may not be bound to obey his superior in all things. First on account of the command of a higher power. For as a gloss says on Romans 13:2, "They that resist [Vulgate: 'He that resisteth'] the power, resist the ordinance of God" (cf. St. Augustine, De Verb. Dom. viii). "If a commissioner issue an order, are you to comply, if it is contrary to the bidding of the proconsul? Again if the proconsul command one thing, and the emperor another, will you hesitate, to disregard the former and serve the latter? Therefore if the emperor commands one thing and God another, you must disregard the former and obey God." Secondly, a subject is not bound to obey his superior if the latter command him to do something wherein he is not subject to him. For Seneca says (De Beneficiis iii): "It is wrong to suppose that slavery falls upon the whole man: for the better part of him is excepted." His body is subjected and assigned to his master but his soul is his own. Consequently in matters touching the internal movement of the will man is not bound to obey his fellow-man, but God alone.

Nevertheless man is bound to obey his fellow-man in things that have to be done externally by means of the body: and yet, since by nature all men are equal, he is not bound to obey another man in matters touching the nature of the body, for instance in those relating to the support of his body or the begetting of his children. Wherefore servants are not bound to obey their masters, nor children their parents, in the question of contracting marriage or of remaining in the state of virginity or the like. But in matters concerning the disposal of actions and human affairs, a subject is bound to obey his superior within the sphere of his authority; for instance a soldier must obey his general in matters relating to war, a servant his master in matters touching the execution of the duties of his service, a son his father in matters relating to the conduct of his life and the care of the household; and so forth.

Reply to Objection 1. When the Apostle says "in all things," he refers to matters within the sphere of a father's or master's authority.

Reply to Objection 2. Man is subject to God simply as regards all things, both internal and external, wherefore he is bound to obey Him in all things. On the other hand, inferiors are not subject to their superiors in all things, but only in certain things and in a particular way, in respect of which the superior stands between God and his subjects, whereas in respect of other matters the subject is immediately under God, by Whom he is taught either by the natural or by the written law.

Reply to Objection 3. Religious profess obedience as to the regular mode of life, in respect of which they are subject to their superiors: wherefore they are bound to obey in those matters only which may belong to the regular mode of life, and this obedience suffices for salvation. If they be willing to obey even in other matters, this will belong to the superabundance of perfection; provided, however, such things be not contrary to God or to the rule they profess, for obedience in this case would be unlawful.

Accordingly we may distinguish a threefold obedience; one, sufficient for salvation, and consisting in obeying when one is bound to obey: secondly, perfect obedience, which obeys in all things lawful: thirdly, indiscreet obedience, which obeys even in matters unlawful.

ARTICLE 6. WHETHER CHRISTIANS ARE BOUND TO OBEY THE SECULAR POWERS?

Objection 1. It seems that Christians are not bound to obey the secular power. For a gloss on Matthew 17:25, "Then the children are free," says: "If in every kingdom the children of the king who holds sway over that kingdom are free, then the children of that King, under Whose sway are all kingdoms, should be free in every kingdom." Now Christians, by their faith in Christ, are made children of God, according to John 1:12: "He gave them power to be made the sons of God, to them that believe in His name." Therefore they are not bound to obey the secular power.

Objection 2. Further, it is written (Romans 7:4): "You . . . are become dead to the law by the body of Christ," and the law mentioned here is the divine law of the Old Testament. Now human law whereby men are subject to the secular power is of less account than the divine law of the Old Testament. Much more, therefore, since they have become members of Christ's body, are men freed from the law of subjection, whereby they were under the power of secular princes.

Objection 3. Further, men are not bound to obey robbers, who oppress them with violence. Now, Augustine says (De Civ. Dei iv): "Without justice, what else is a kingdom but a huge robbery?" Since therefore the authority of secular princes is frequently exercised with injustice, or owes its origin to some unjust usurpation, it seems that Christians ought not to obey secular princes.

On the contrary, It is written (Titus 3:1): "Admonish them to be subject to princes and powers," and (1 Peter 2:13-14): "Be ye subject . . . to every human creature for God's sake: whether it be to the king as excelling, or to governors as sent by him."

I answer that, Faith in Christ is the origin and cause of justice, according to Romans 3:22, "The justice of God by faith of Jesus Christ:" wherefore faith in Christ does not void the order of justice, but strengthens it." Now the order of justice requires that subjects obey their superiors, else the stability of human affairs would cease. Hence faith in Christ does not excuse the faithful from the obligation of obeying secular princes.

Reply to Objection 1. As stated above (Article 5), subjection whereby one man is bound to another regards the body; not the soul, which retains its liberty. Now, in this state of life we are freed by the grace of Christ from defects of the soul, but not from defects of the body, as the Apostle declares by saying of himself (Romans 7:23) that in his mind he served the law of God, but in his flesh the law of sin. Wherefore those that are made children of God by grace are free from the spiritual bondage of sin, but not from the bodily bondage, whereby they are held bound to earthly masters, as a gloss observes on 1 Timothy 6:1, "Whosoever are servants under the yoke," etc.

Reply to Objection 2. The Old Law was a figure of the New Testament, and therefore it had to cease on the advent of truth. And the comparison with human law does not stand because thereby one man is subject to another. Yet man is bound by divine law to obey his fellow-man.

Reply to Objection 3. Man is bound to obey secular princes in so far as this is required by order of justice. Wherefore if the prince's authority is not just but usurped, or if he commands what is unjust, his subjects are not bound to obey him, except perhaps accidentally, in order to avoid scandal or danger.

QUESTION 108. VENGEANCE

ARTICLE 1. WHETHER VENGEANCE IS LAWFUL?

Objection 1. It seems that vengeance is not lawful. For whoever usurps what is God's sins. But vengeance belongs to God, for it is written (Deuteronomy 32:35, Romans 12:19): "Revenge to Me, and I will repay." Therefore all vengeance is unlawful.

Objection 2. Further, he that takes vengeance on a man does not bear with him. But we ought to bear with the wicked, for a gloss on Canticles 2:2, "As the lily among the thorns," says: "He is not a good man that cannot bear with a wicked one." Therefore we should not take vengeance on the wicked.

Objection 3. Further, vengeance is taken by inflicting punishment, which is the cause of servile fear. But the New Law is not a law of fear, but of love, as Augustine states (Contra Adamant. xvii). Therefore at least in the New Testament all vengeance is unlawful.

Objection 4. Further, a man is said to avenge himself when he takes revenge for wrongs inflicted on himself. But, seemingly, it is unlawful even for a judge to punish those who have wronged him: for Chrysostom [Cf. Opus Imperfectum, Hom. v in Matth., falsely ascribed to St. Chrysostom] says: "Let us learn after Christ's example to bear our own wrongs with magnanimity, yet not to suffer God's wrongs, not even by listening to them." Therefore vengeance seems to be unlawful.

Objection 5. Further, the sin of a multitude is more harmful than the sin of only one: for it is written (Sirach 26:5-7): "Of three things my heart hath been afraid . . . the accusation of a city, and the gathering together of the people, and a false calumny." But vengeance should not be taken on the sin of a multitude, for a gloss on Matthew 13:29-30, "Lest perhaps . . . you root up the wheat . . . suffer both to grow," says that "a multitude should not be excommunicated, nor should the sovereign." Neither therefore is any other vengeance lawful.

On the contrary, We should look to God for nothing save what is good and lawful. But we are to look to God for vengeance on His enemies: for it is written (Luke 18:7): "Will not God revenge His elect who cry to Him day and night?" as if to say: "He will indeed." Therefore vengeance is not essentially evil and unlawful.

I answer that, Vengeance consists in the infliction of a penal evil on one who has sinned. Accordingly, in the matter of vengeance, we must consider the mind of the avenger. For if his intention is directed chiefly to the evil of the person on whom he takes vengeance and rests there, then his vengeance is altogether unlawful: because to take pleasure in another's evil belongs to hatred, which is contrary to the charity whereby we are bound to love all men. Nor is it an excuse that he intends the evil of one who has unjustly inflicted evil on him, as neither is a man excused for hating one that hates him: for a man may not sin against another just because the latter has already sinned against him, since this is to be overcome by evil, which was forbidden by the Apostle, who says (Romans 12:21): "Be not overcome by evil, but overcome evil by good."

If, however, the avenger's intention be directed chiefly to some good, to be obtained by means of the punishment of the person who has sinned (for instance that the sinner may amend, or at least that he may be restrained and others be not disturbed, that justice may be upheld, and God honored), then vengeance may be lawful, provided other due circumstances be observed.

Reply to Objection 1. He who takes vengeance on the wicked in keeping with his rank and position does not usurp what belongs to God but makes use of the power granted him by God. For it is written (Romans 13:4) of the earthly prince that "he is God's minister, an avenger to execute wrath upon him that doeth evil." If, however, a man takes vengeance outside the order of divine appointment, he usurps what is God's and therefore sins.

Reply to Objection 2. The good bear with the wicked by enduring patiently, and in due manner, the wrongs they themselves receive from them; but they do not bear with them as to endure the wrongs they inflict on God and their neighbor. For Chrysostom [Cf. Opus Imperfectum, Hom. v in Matth., falsely ascribed to St. Chrysostom] says: "It is praiseworthy to be patient under our own wrongs, but to overlook God's wrongs is most wicked."

Reply to Objection 3. The law of the Gospel is the law of love, and therefore those who do good out of love, and who alone properly belong to the Gospel, ought not to be terrorized by means of punishment, but only those who are not moved by love to do good, and who, though they belong to the Church outwardly, do not belong to it in merit.

Reply to Objection 4. Sometimes a wrong done to a person reflects on God and the Church: and then it is the duty of that person to avenge the wrong. For example, Elias made fire descend on those who were come to seize him (2 Kings 1); likewise Eliseus cursed the boys that mocked him (2 Kings 2); and Pope Sylverius excommunicated those who sent him into exile (XXIII, Q. iv, Cap. Guilisarius). But in so far as the wrong inflicted on a man affects his person, he should bear it patiently if this be expedient. For these precepts of patience are to be understood as referring to preparedness of the mind, as Augustine states (De Serm. Dom. in Monte i).

Reply to Objection 5. When the whole multitude sins, vengeance must be taken on them, either in respect of the whole multitude—thus the Egyptians were drowned in the Red Sea while they were pursuing the children of Israel (Exodus 14), and the people of Sodom were entirely destroyed (Genesis 19)—or as regards part of the multitude, as may be seen in the punishment of those who worshipped the calf.

Sometimes, however, if there is hope of many making amends, the severity of vengeance should be brought to bear on a few of the principals, whose punishment fills the rest with fear; thus the Lord (Numbers 25) commanded the princes of the people to be hanged for the sin of the multitude.

On the other hand, if it is not the whole but only a part of the multitude that has sinned, then if the guilty can be separated from the innocent, vengeance should be wrought on them: provided, however, that this can be done without scandal to others; else the multitude should be spared and severity foregone. The same applies to the sovereign, whom the multitude follow. For his sin should be borne with, if it cannot be punished without scandal to the multitude: unless indeed his sin were such, that it would do more harm to the multitude, either spiritually or temporally, than would the scandal that was feared to arise from his punishment.

QUESTION 110. THE VICES OPPOSED TO TRUTH, AND FIRST OF LYING

ARTICLE 3. WHETHER EVERY LIE IS A SIN?

Objection 1. It seems that not every lie is a sin. For it is evident that the evangelists did not sin in the writing of the Gospel. Yet they seem to have told something false: since their accounts of the words of Christ and of others often differ from one another: wherefore seemingly one of them must have given an untrue account. Therefore not every lie is a sin.

Objection 2. Further, no one is rewarded by God for sin. But the midwives of Egypt were rewarded by God for a lie, for it is stated that "God built them houses" (Exodus 1:21). Therefore a lie is not a sin.

Objection 3. Further, the deeds of holy men are related in Sacred Writ that they may be a model of human life. But we read of certain very holy men that they lied. Thus (Genesis 12 and 20) we are told that Abraham said of his wife that she was his sister. Jacob also lied when he said that he was Esau, and yet he received a blessing (Genesis 27:27-29). Again, Judith is commended (Judith 15:10-11) although she lied to Holofernes. Therefore not every lie is a sin.

Objection 4. Further, one ought to choose the lesser evil in order to avoid the greater: even so a physician cuts off a limb, lest the whole body perish. Yet less harm is done by raising a false opinion in a person's mind, than by someone slaying or being slain. Therefore a man may lawfully lie, to save another from committing murder, or another from being killed.

Objection 5. Further, it is a lie not to fulfill what one has promised. Yet one is not bound to keep all one's promises: for Isidore says (Synonym. ii): "Break your faith when you have promised ill." Therefore not every lie is a sin.

Objection 6. Further, apparently a lie is a sin because thereby we deceive our neighbor: wherefore Augustine says (Lib. De Mend. xxi): "Whoever thinks that there is any kind of lie that is not a sin deceives himself shamefully, since he deems himself an honest man when he deceives others." Yet not every lie is a cause of deception, since no one is deceived by a jocose lie; seeing that lies of this kind are told, not with the intention of being believed, but merely for the sake of giving pleasure. Hence again we find hyperbolical expressions in Holy Writ. Therefore not every lie is a sin.

On the contrary, It is written (Sirach 7:14): "Be not willing to make any manner of lie."

I answer that, An action that is naturally evil in respect of its genus can by no means be good and lawful, since in order for an action to be good it must be right in every respect: because good results from a complete cause, while evil results from any single defect, as Dionysius asserts (Div. Nom. iv). Now a lie is evil in respect of its genus, since it is an action bearing on undue matter. For as words are naturally signs of intellectual acts, it is unnatural and undue for anyone to signify by words something that is not in his mind. Hence the Philosopher says (Ethic. iv, 7) that "lying is in itself evil and to be shunned, while truthfulness is good and worthy of praise." Therefore every lie is a sin, as also Augustine declares (Contra Mend. i).

Reply to Objection 1. It is unlawful to hold that any false assertion is contained either in the Gospel or in any canonical Scripture, or that the writers thereof have told untruths, because faith would be deprived of its certitude which is based on the authority of Holy Writ. That the words of certain people are variously reported in the Gospel and other sacred writings does not constitute a lie. Hence Augustine says (De Consens. Evang. ii): "He that has the wit to understand that in order to know the truth it is necessary to get at the sense, will conclude that he must not be the least troubled, no matter by what words that sense is expressed." Hence it is evident, as he adds (De Consens. Evang. ii), that "we must not judge that someone is lying, if several persons fail to describe in the same way and in the same words a thing which they remember to have seen or heard."

Reply to Objection 2. The midwives were rewarded, not for their lie, but for their fear of God, and for their good-will, which latter led them to tell a lie. Hence it is expressly stated (Exodus 2:21): "And because the midwives feared God, He built them houses." But the subsequent lie was not meritorious.

Reply to Objection 3. In Holy Writ, as Augustine observes (Lib. De Mend. v), the deeds of certain persons are related as examples of perfect virtue: and we must not believe that such persons were liars. If, however, any of their statements appear to be untruthful, we must understand such statements to have been figurative and prophetic. Hence Augustine says (Lib. De Mend. v): "We must believe that whatever is related of those who, in prophetical times, are mentioned as being worthy of credit, was done and said by them prophetically." As to Abraham "when he said that Sara was his sister, he wished to hide the truth, not to tell a lie, for she is called his sister since she was the daughter of his father," Augustine says (QQ. Super. Gen. xxvi; Contra Mend. x; Contra Faust. xxii). Wherefore Abraham himself said (Genesis 20:12): "She is truly my sister, the daughter of my father, and not the daughter of my mother," being related to him on his father's side. Jacob's assertion that he was Esau, Isaac's first-born, was spoken in a mystical sense, because, to wit, the latter's birthright was due to him by right: and he made use of this mode of speech being moved by the spirit of prophecy, in order to signify a mystery, namely, that the younger people, i.e. the Gentiles, should supplant the first-born, i.e. the Jews.

Some, however, are commended in the Scriptures, not on account of perfect virtue, but for a certain virtuous disposition, seeing that it was owing to some praiseworthy sentiment that they were moved to do certain undue things. It is thus that Judith is praised, not for lying to Holofernes, but for her desire to save the people, to which end she exposed herself to danger. And yet one might also say that her words contain truth in some mystical sense.

Reply to Objection 4. A lie is sinful not only because it injures one's neighbor, but also on account of its inordinateness, as stated above in this Article. Now it is not allowed to make use of anything inordinate in order to ward off injury or defects from another: as neither is it lawful to steal in order to give an alms, except perhaps in a case of necessity when all things are common. Therefore it is not lawful to tell a lie in order to deliver another from any danger whatever. Nevertheless it is lawful to hide the truth prudently, by keeping it back, as Augustine says (Contra Mend. x).

Reply to Objection 5. A man does not lie, so long as he has a mind to do what he promises, because he does not speak contrary to what he has in mind: but if he does not keep his promise, he seems to act without faith in changing his mind. He may, however, be excused for two reasons. First, if he has promised something evidently unlawful, because he sinned in promise, and did well to change his mind. Secondly, if circumstances have changed with regard to persons and the business in hand. For, as Seneca states (De Benef. iv), for a man to be bound to keep a promise, it is necessary for everything to remain unchanged: otherwise neither did he lie in promising—since he promised what he had in his mind, due circumstances being taken for granted—nor was he faithless in not keeping his promise, because circumstances are no longer the same. Hence the Apostle, though he did not go to Corinth, whither he had promised to go (2 Corinthians 1), did not lie, because obstacles had arisen which prevented him.

Reply to Objection 6. An action may be considered in two ways. First, in itself, secondly, with regard to the agent. Accordingly a jocose lie, from the very genus of the action, is of a nature to deceive; although in the intention of the speaker it is not told to deceive, nor does it deceive by the way it is told. Nor is there any similarity in the hyperbolical or any kind of figurative expressions, with which we meet in Holy Writ: because, as Augustine says (Lib. De Mend. v), "it is not a lie to do or say a thing figuratively: because every statement must be referred to the thing stated: and when a thing is done or said figuratively, it states what those to whom it is tendered understand it to signify."

ARTICLE 4. WHETHER EVERY LIE IS A MORTAL SIN?

Objection 1. It seems that every lie is a mortal sin. For it is written (Psalm 6:7): "Thou wilt destroy all that speak a lie," and (Wisdom 1:11): "The mouth that belieth killeth the soul." Now mortal sin alone causes destruction and death of the soul. Therefore every lie is a mortal sin.

Objection 2. Further, whatever is against a precept of the decalogue is a mortal sin. Now lying is against this precept of the decalogue: "Thou shalt not bear false witness." Therefore every lie is a mortal sin.

Objection 3. Further, Augustine says (De Doctr. Christ. i, 36): "Every liar breaks his faith in lying, since forsooth he wishes the person to whom he lies to have faith in him, and yet he does not keep faith with him, when he lies to him: and whoever breaks his faith is guilty of iniquity." Now no one is said to break his faith or "to be guilty of iniquity," for a venial sin. Therefore no lie is a venial sin.

Objection 4. Further, the eternal reward is not lost save for a mortal sin. Now, for a lie the eternal reward was lost, being exchanged for a temporal meed. For Gregory says (Moral. xviii) that "we learn from the reward of the midwives what the sin of lying deserves: since the reward which they deserved for their kindness, and which they might have received in eternal life, dwindled into a temporal meed on account of the lie of which they were guilty." Therefore even an officious lie, such as was that of the midwives, which seemingly is the least of lies, is a mortal sin.

Objection 5. Further, Augustine says (Lib. De Mend. xvii) that "it is a precept of perfection, not only not to lie at all, but not even to wish to lie." Now it is a mortal sin to act against a precept. Therefore every lie of the perfect is a mortal sin: and consequently so also is a lie told by anyone else, otherwise the perfect would be worse off than others.

On the contrary, Augustine says on Psalm 5:7, "Thou wilt destroy," etc.: "There are two kinds of lie, that are not grievously sinful yet are not devoid of sin, when we lie either in joking, or for the sake of our neighbor's good." But every mortal sin is grievous. Therefore jocose and officious lies are not mortal sins.

I answer that, A mortal sin is, properly speaking, one that is contrary to charity whereby the soul lives in union with God, as stated above (24, 12; 35, 3). Now a lie may be contrary to charity in three ways: first, in itself; secondly, in respect of the evil intended; thirdly, accidentally.

A lie may be in itself contrary to charity by reason of its false signification. For if this be about divine things, it is contrary to the charity of God, whose truth one hides or corrupts by such a lie; so that a lie of this kind is opposed not only to the virtue of charity, but also to the virtues of faith and religion: wherefore it is a most grievous and a mortal sin. If, however, the false signification be about something the knowledge of which affects a man's good, for instance if it pertain to the perfection of science or to moral conduct, a lie of this description inflicts an injury on one's neighbor, since it causes him to have a false opinion, wherefore it is contrary to charity, as regards the love of our neighbor, and consequently is a mortal sin. On the other hand, if the false opinion engendered by the lie be about some matter the knowledge of which is of no consequence, then the lie in question does no harm to one's neighbor; for instance, if a person be deceived as to some contingent particulars that do not concern him. Wherefore a lie of this kind, considered in itself, is not a mortal sin.

As regards the end in view, a lie may be contrary to charity, through being told with the purpose of injuring God, and this is always a mortal sin, for it is opposed to religion; or in order to injure one's neighbor, in his person, his possessions or his good name, and this also is a mortal sin, since it is a mortal sin to injure one's neighbor, and one sins mortally if one has merely the intention of committing a mortal sin. But if the end intended be not contrary to charity, neither will the lie, considered under this aspect, be a mortal sin, as in the case of a jocose lie, where some little pleasure is intended, or in an officious lie, where the good also of one's neighbor is intended. Accidentally a lie may be contrary to charity by reason of scandal or any other injury resulting therefrom: and thus again it will be a mortal sin, for instance if a man were not deterred through scandal from lying publicly.

Reply to Objection 1. The passages quoted refer to the mischievous lie, as a gloss explains the words of Psalm 5:7, "Thou wilt destroy all that speak a lie."

Reply to Objection 2. Since all the precepts of the decalogue are directed to the love of God and our neighbor, as stated above (44, 1, ad 3; I-II, 100, 5, ad 1), a lie is contrary to a precept of the decalogue, in so far as it is contrary to the love of God and our neighbor. Hence it is expressly forbidden to bear false witness against our neighbor.

Reply to Objection 3. Even a venial sin can be called "iniquity" in a broad sense, in so far as it is beside the equity of justice; wherefore it is written (1 John 3:4): "Every sin is iniquity [Vulgate: 'And sin is iniquity.']." It is in this sense that Augustine is speaking.

Reply to Objection 4. The lie of the midwives may be considered in two ways. First as regards their feeling of kindliness towards the Jews, and their reverence and fear of God, for which their virtuous disposition is commended. For this an eternal reward is due. Wherefore Jerome (in his exposition of Isaiah

65:21, 'And they shall build houses') explains that God "built them spiritual houses." Secondly, it may be considered with regard to the external act of lying. For thereby they could merit, not indeed eternal reward, but perhaps some temporal meed, the deserving of which was not inconsistent with the deformity of their lie, though this was inconsistent with their meriting an eternal reward. It is in this sense that we must understand the words of Gregory, and not that they merited by that lie to lose the eternal reward as though they had already merited it by their preceding kindliness, as the objection understands the words to mean.

Reply to Objection 5. Some say that for the perfect every lie is a mortal sin. But this assertion is unreasonable. For no circumstance causes a sin to be infinitely more grievous unless it transfers it to another species. Now a circumstance of person does not transfer a sin to another species, except perhaps by reason of something annexed to that person, for instance if it be against his vow: and this cannot apply to an officious or jocose lie. Wherefore an officious or a jocose lie is not a mortal sin in perfect men, except perhaps accidentally on account of scandal. We may take in this sense the saying of Augustine that "it is a precept of perfection not only not to lie at all, but not even to wish to lie": although Augustine says this not positively but dubiously, for he begins by saying: "Unless perhaps it is a precept," etc. Nor does it matter that they are placed in a position to safeguard the truth: because they are bound to safeguard the truth by virtue of their office in judging or teaching, and if they lie in these matters their lie will be a mortal sin: but it does not follow that they sin mortally when they lie in other matters.

QUESTION 120. "EPIKEIA" OR EQUITY

ARTICLE 1. WHETHER "EPIKEIA" IS A VIRTUE?

Objection 1. It seems that "epikeia" is not a virtue. For no virtue does away with another virtue. Yet "epikeia" does away with another virtue, since it sets aside that which is just according to law, and seemingly is opposed to severity. Therefore "epikeia" is not a virtue.

Objection 2. Further, Augustine says (De Vera Relig. xxxi): "With regard to these earthly laws, although men pass judgment on them when they make them, yet, when once they are made and established, the judge must pronounce judgment not on them but according to them." But seemingly "epikeia" pronounces judgment on the law, when it deems that the law should not be observed in some particular case. Therefore "epikeia" is a vice rather than a virtue.

Objection 3. Further, apparently it belongs to "epikeia" to consider the intention of the lawgiver, as the Philosopher states (Ethic. v, 10). But it belongs to the sovereign alone to interpret the intention of the lawgiver, wherefore the Emperor says in the Codex of Laws and Constitutions, under Law i: "It is fitting and lawful that We alone should interpret between equity and law." Therefore the act of "epikeia" is unlawful: and consequently "epikeia" is not a virtue.

On the contrary, The Philosopher (Ethic. v, 10) states it to be a virtue.

I answer that, As stated above (I-II, 96, 6), when we were treating of laws, since human actions, with which laws are concerned, are composed of contingent singulars and are innumerable in their diversity, it was not possible to lay down rules of law that would apply to every single case. Legislators in framing laws attend to what commonly happens: although if the law be applied to certain cases it will frustrate the equality of justice and be injurious to the common good, which the law has in view. Thus the law requires deposits to be restored, because in the majority of cases this is just. Yet it happens sometimes to be injurious—for instance, if a madman were to put his sword in deposit, and demand its delivery while in a state of madness, or if a man were to seek the return of his deposit in order to fight against his country. On these and like cases it is bad to follow the law, and it is good to set aside the letter of the law and to follow the dictates of justice and the common good. This is the object of "epikeia" which we call equity. Therefore it is evident that "epikeia" is a virtue.

Reply to Objection 1. "Epikeia" does not set aside that which is just in itself but that which is just as by law established. Nor is it opposed to severity, which follows the letter of the law when it ought to be followed. To follow the letter of the law when it ought not to be followed is sinful. Hence it is written in the Codex of Laws and Constitutions under Law v: "Without doubt he transgresses the law who by adhering to the letter of the law strives to defeat the intention of the lawgiver."

Reply to Objection 2. It would be passing judgment on a law to say that it was not well made; but to say that the letter of the law is not to be observed in some particular case is passing judgment not on the law, but on some particular contingency.

Reply to Objection 3. Interpretation is admissible in doubtful cases where it is not allowed to set aside the letter of the law without the interpretation of the sovereign. But when the case is manifest there is need, not of interpretation, but of execution.

QUESTION 123. FORTITUDE

ARTICLE 5. WHETHER FORTITUDE IS PROPERLY ABOUT DANGERS OF DEATH IN BATTLE?

Objection 1. It seems that fortitude is not properly about dangers of death in battle. For martyrs above all are commended for their fortitude. But martyrs are not commended in connection with battle. Therefore fortitude is not properly about dangers of death in battle.

Objection 2. Further, Ambrose says (De Offic. i) that "fortitude is applicable both to warlike and to civil matters": and Tully (De Offic. i), under the heading, "That it pertains to fortitude to excel in battle rather than in civil life," says: "Although not a few think that the business of war is of greater importance than the affairs of civil life, this opinion must be qualified: and if we wish to judge the matter truly, there are many things in civil life that are more important and more glorious than those connected with war." Now greater fortitude is about greater things. Therefore fortitude is not properly concerned with death in battle.

Objection 3. Further, war is directed to the preservation of a country's temporal peace: for Augustine says (De Civ. Dei xix) that "wars are waged in order to insure peace." Now it does not seem that one ought to expose oneself to the danger of death for the temporal peace of one's country, since this same peace is the occasion of much license in morals. Therefore it seems that the virtue of fortitude is not about the danger of death in battle.

On the contrary, The Philosopher says (Ethic. iii) that fortitude is chiefly about death in battle.

I answer that, As stated above (Article 4), fortitude strengthens a man's mind against the greatest danger, which is that of death. Now fortitude is a virtue; and it is essential to virtue ever to tend to good; wherefore it is in order to pursue some good that man does not fly from the danger of death. But the dangers of death arising out of sickness, storms at sea, attacks from robbers, and the like, do not seem to come on a man through his pursuing some good. on the other hand, the dangers of death which occur in battle come to man directly on account of some good, because, to wit, he is defending the common good by a just fight. Now a just fight is of two kinds. First, there is the general combat, for instance, of those who fight in battle; secondly, there is the private combat, as when a judge or even private individual does not refrain from giving a just judgment through fear of the impending sword, or any other danger though it threaten death. Hence it belongs to fortitude to strengthen the mind against dangers of death, not only such as arise in a general battle, but also such as occur in singular combat, which may be called by the general name of battle. Accordingly it must be granted that fortitude is properly about dangers of death occurring in battle.

Moreover, a brave man behaves well in face of danger of any other kind of death; especially since man may be in danger of any kind of death on account of virtue: thus may a man not fail to attend on a sick friend through fear of deadly infection, or not refuse to undertake a journey with some godly object in view through fear of shipwreck or robbers.

Reply to Objection 1. Martyrs face the fight that is waged against their own person, and this for the sake of the sovereign good which is God; wherefore their fortitude is praised above all. Nor is it outside the genus of fortitude that regards warlike actions, for which reason they are said to have been valiant in battle. [Office of Martyrs, ex. Heb. xi. 34.]

Reply to Objection 2. Personal and civil business is differentiated from the business of war that regards general wars. However, personal and civil affairs admit of dangers of death arising out of certain conflicts which are private wars, and so with regard to these also there may be fortitude properly so called.

Reply to Objection 3. The peace of the city is good in itself, nor does it become evil because certain persons make evil use of it. For there are many others who make good use of it; and many evils prevented by it, such as murders and sacrileges, are much greater than those which are occasioned by it, and which belong chiefly to the sins of the flesh.

ARTICLE 6. WHETHER ENDURANCE IS THE CHIEF ACT OF FORTITUDE?

Objection 1. It seems that endurance is not the chief act of fortitude. For virtue "is about the difficult and the good" (Ethic. ii, 3). Now it is more difficult to attack than to endure. Therefore endurance is not the chief act of fortitude.

Objection 2. Further, to be able to act on another seems to argue greater power than not to be changed by another. Now to attack is to act on another, and to endure is to persevere unchangeably. Since then fortitude denotes perfection of power, it seems that it belongs to fortitude to attack rather than to endure.

Objection 3. Further, one contrary is more distant from the other than its mere negation. Now to endure is merely not to fear, whereas to attack denotes a movement contrary to that of fear, since it implies pursuit. Since then fortitude above all withdraws the mind from fear, it seems that it regards attack rather than endurance.

On the contrary, The Philosopher says (Ethic. iii, 9) that "certain persons are" said to be brave chiefly because they endure affliction.

I answer that, As stated above (Article 3), and according to the Philosopher (Ethic. iii, 9), "fortitude is more concerned to allay fear, than to moderate daring." For it is more difficult to allay fear than to moderate daring, since the danger which is the object of daring and fear, tends by its very nature to check daring, but to increase fear. Now to attack belongs to fortitude in so far as the latter moderates daring, whereas to endure follows the repression of fear. Therefore the principal act of fortitude is endurance, that is to stand immovable in the midst of dangers rather than to attack them.

Reply to Objection 1. Endurance is more difficult than aggression, for three reasons. First, because endurance seemingly implies that one is being attacked by a stronger person, whereas aggression denotes that one is attacking as though one were the stronger party; and it is more difficult to contend with a stronger than with a weaker. Secondly, because he that endures already feels the presence of danger, whereas the aggressor looks upon danger as something to come; and it is more difficult to be unmoved by the present than by the future. Thirdly, because endurance implies length of time, whereas aggression is consistent with sudden movements; and it is more difficult to remain unmoved for a long time, than to be moved suddenly to something arduous. Hence the Philosopher says (Ethic. iii, 8) that "some hurry to meet danger, yet fly when the danger is present; this is not the behavior of a brave man."

Reply to Objection 2. Endurance denotes indeed a passion of the body, but an action of the soul cleaving most resolutely [fortissime] to good, the result being that it does not yield to the threatening passion of the body. Now virtue concerns the soul rather than the body.

Reply to Objection 3. He that endures fears not, though he is confronted with the cause of fear, whereas this cause is not present to the aggressor.

ARTICLE 7. WHETHER THE BRAVE MAN ACTS FOR THE SAKE OF THE GOOD OF HIS HABIT?

Objection 1. It seems that the brave man does not act for the sake of the good of his habit. For in matters of action the end, though first in intention, is last in execution. Now the act of fortitude, in the order of execution, follows the habit of fortitude. Therefore it is impossible for the brave man to act for the sake of the good of his habit.

Objection 2. Further, Augustine says (De Trin. xiii): "We love virtues for the sake of happiness, and yet some make bold to counsel us to be virtuous," namely by saying that we should desire virtue for its own sake, "without loving happiness. If they succeed in their endeavor, we shall surely cease to love virtue itself, since we shall no longer love that for the sake of which alone we love virtue." But fortitude is a virtue. Therefore the act of fortitude is directed not to fortitude but to happiness.

Objection 3. Further, Augustine says (De Morib. Eccl. xv) that "fortitude is love ready to bear all things for God's sake." Now God is not the habit of fortitude, but something better, since the end must needs be better than what is directed to the end. Therefore the brave man does not act for the sake of the good of his habit.

On the contrary, The Philosopher says (Ethic. iii, 7) that "to the brave man fortitude itself is a good": and such is his end.

I answer that, An end is twofold: proximate and ultimate. Now the proximate end of every agent is to introduce a likeness of that agent's form into something else: thus the end of fire in heating is to introduce the likeness of its heat into some passive matter, and the end of the builder is to introduce into matter the likeness of his art. Whatever good ensues from this, if it be intended, may be called the remote end of the agent. Now just as in things made, external matter is fashioned by art, so in things done, human deeds are fashioned by prudence. Accordingly we must conclude that the brave man intends as his proximate end to reproduce in action a likeness of his habit, for he intends to act in accordance with his habit: but his remote end is happiness or God.

This suffices for the Replies to the Objections: for the First Objection proceeds as though the very essence of a habit were its end, instead of the likeness of the habit in act, as stated. The other two objections consider the ultimate end.

ARTICLE 8. WHETHER THE BRAVE MAN DELIGHTS IN HIS ACT?

Objection 1. It seems that the brave man delights in his act. For "delight is the unhindered action of a connatural habit" (Ethic. x, 4,6,8). Now the brave deed proceeds from a habit which acts after the manner of nature. Therefore the brave man takes pleasure in his act.

Objection 2. Further, Ambrose, commenting on Galatians 5:22, "But the fruit of the Spirit is charity, joy, peace," says that deeds of virtue are called "fruits because they refresh man's mind with a holy and pure delight." Now the brave man performs acts of virtue. Therefore he takes pleasure in his act.

Objection 3. Further, the weaker is overcome by the stronger. Now the brave man has a stronger love for the good of virtue than for his own body, which he exposes to the danger of death. Therefore the delight in the good of virtue banishes the pain of the body; and consequently the brave man does all things with pleasure.

On the contrary, The Philosopher says (*Ethic.* iii, 9) that "the brave man seems to have no delight in his act."

I answer that, As stated above (I-II, 31, 3,4,5) where we were treating of the passions, pleasure is twofold; one is bodily, resulting from bodily contact, the other is spiritual, resulting from an apprehension of the soul. It is the latter which properly results from deeds of virtue, since in them we consider the good of reason. Now the principal act of fortitude is to endure, not only certain things that are unpleasant as apprehended by the soul—for instance, the loss of bodily life, which the virtuous man loves not only as a natural good, but also as being necessary for acts of virtue, and things connected with them—but also to endure things unpleasant in respect of bodily contact, such as wounds and blows. Hence the brave man, on one side, has something that affords him delight, namely as regards spiritual pleasure, in the act itself of virtue and the end thereof: while, on the other hand, he has cause for both spiritual sorrow, in the thought of losing his life, and for bodily pain. Hence we read (2 Maccabees 6:30) that Eleazar said: "I suffer grievous pains in body: but in soul am well content to suffer these things because I fear Thee."

Now the sensible pain of the body makes one insensible to the spiritual delight of virtue, without the copious assistance of God's grace, which has more strength to raise the soul to the Divine things in which it delights, than bodily pains have to afflict it. Thus the Blessed Tiburtius, while walking barefoot on the burning coal, said that he felt as though he were walking on roses.

Yet the virtue of fortitude prevents the reason from being entirely overcome by bodily pain. And the delight of virtue overcomes spiritual sorrow, inasmuch as a man prefers the good of virtue to the life of the body and to whatever appertains thereto. Hence the Philosopher says (*Ethic.* ii, 3; iii, 9) that "it is not necessary for a brave man to delight so as to perceive his delight, but it suffices for him not to be sad."

Reply to Objection 1. The vehemence of the action or passion of one power hinders the action of another power: wherefore the pain in his senses hinders the mind of the brave man from feeling delight in its proper operation.

Reply to Objection 2. Deeds of virtue are delightful chiefly on account of their end; yet they can be painful by their nature, and this is principally the case with fortitude. Hence the Philosopher says (*Ethic.* iii, 9) that "to perform deeds with pleasure does not happen in all virtues, except in so far as one attains the end."

Reply to Objection 3. In the brave man spiritual sorrow is overcome by the delight of virtue. Yet since bodily pain is more sensible, and the sensitive apprehension is more in evidence to man, it follows that spiritual pleasure in the end of virtue fades away, so to speak, in the presence of great bodily pain.

ARTICLE 10. WHETHER THE BRAVE MAN MAKES USE OF ANGER IN HIS ACTION?

Objection 1. It seems that the brave man does not use anger in his action. For no one should employ as an instrument of his action that which he cannot use at will. Now man cannot use anger at will, so as to take it up and lay it aside when he will. For, as the Philosopher says (De Memoria ii), when a bodily passion is in movement, it does not rest at once just as one wishes. Therefore a brave man should not employ anger for his action.

Objection 2. Further, if a man is competent to do a thing by himself, he should not seek the assistance of something weaker and more imperfect. Now the reason is competent to achieve by itself deeds of fortitude, wherein anger is impotent: wherefore Seneca says (De Ira i): "Reason by itself suffices not only to make us prepared for action but also to accomplish it. On fact is there greater folly than for reason to seek help from anger? the steadfast from the unstaid, the trusty from the untrustworthy, the healthy from the sick?" Therefore a brave man should not make use of anger.

Objection 3. Further, just as people are more earnest in doing deeds of fortitude on account of anger, so are they on account of sorrow or desire; wherefore the Philosopher says (Ethic. iii, 8) that wild beasts are incited to face danger through sorrow or pain, and adulterous persons dare many things for the sake of desire. Now fortitude employs neither sorrow nor desire for its action. Therefore in like manner it should not employ anger.

On the contrary, The Philosopher says (Ethic. iii, 8) that "anger helps the brave."

I answer that, As stated above (I-II, 24, 2), concerning anger and the other passions there was a difference of opinion between the Peripatetics and the Stoics. For the Stoics excluded anger and all other passions of the soul from the mind of a wise or good man: whereas the Peripatetics, of whom Aristotle was the chief, ascribed to virtuous men both anger and the other passions of the soul albeit modified by reason. And possibly they differed not in reality but in their way of speaking. For the Peripatetics, as stated above (I-II, 24, 2), gave the name of passions to all the movements of the sensitive appetite, however they may comport themselves. And since the sensitive appetite is moved by the command of reason, so that it may cooperate by rendering action more prompt, they held that virtuous persons should employ both anger and the other passions of the soul, modified according to the dictate of reason. On the other hand, the Stoics gave the name of passions to certain immoderate emotions of the sensitive appetite, wherefore they called them sicknesses or diseases, and for this reason severed them altogether from virtue.

Accordingly the brave man employs moderate anger for his action, but not immoderate anger.

Reply to Objection 1. Anger that is moderated in accordance with reason is subject to the command of reason: so that man uses it at his will, which would not be the case were it immoderate.

Reply to Objection 2. Reason employs anger for its action, not as seeking its assistance, but because it uses the sensitive appetite as an instrument, just as it uses the members of the body. Nor is it unbecoming for the instrument to be more imperfect than the principal agent, even as the hammer is more imperfect than the smith. Moreover, Seneca was a follower of the Stoics, and the above words were aimed by him directly at Aristotle.

Reply to Objection 3. Whereas fortitude, as stated above (Article 6), has two acts, namely endurance and aggression, it employs anger, not for the act of endurance, because the reason by itself performs this act, but for the act of aggression, for which it employs anger rather than the other passions, since it belongs to anger to strike at the cause of sorrow, so that it directly cooperates with fortitude in attacking. On the other hand, sorrow by its very nature gives way to the thing that hurts; though accidentally it helps in aggression, either as being the cause of anger, as stated above (I-II, 47, 3), or as making a person expose himself to danger in order to escape from sorrow. On like manner desire, by its very nature, tends to a pleasurable good, to which it is directly contrary to withstand danger: yet accidentally sometimes it helps one to attack, in so far as one prefers to risk dangers rather than lack pleasure. Hence the Philosopher says (Ethic. iii, 5): "Of all the cases in which fortitude arises from a passion, the most natural is when a man is brave through anger, making his choice and acting for a purpose," i.e. for a due end; "this is true fortitude."

QUESTION 129. MAGNANIMITY

ARTICLE 3. WHETHER MAGNANIMITY IS A VIRTUE?

Objection 1. It seems that magnanimity is not a virtue. For every moral virtue observes the mean. But magnanimity observes not the mean but the greater extreme: because the "magnanimous man deems himself worthy of the greatest things" (Ethic. iv, 3). Therefore magnanimity is not a virtue.

Objection 2. Further, he that has one virtue has them all, as stated above (I-II, 65, 1). But one may have a virtue without having magnanimity: since the Philosopher says (Ethic. iv, 3) that "whosoever is worthy of little things and deems himself worthy of them, is temperate, but he is not magnanimous." Therefore magnanimity is not a virtue.

Objection 3. Further, "Virtue is a good quality of the mind," as stated above (I-II, 55, 4). But magnanimity implies certain dispositions of the body: for the Philosopher says (Ethic. iv, 3) of "a magnanimous man that his gait is slow, his voice deep, and his utterance calm." Therefore magnanimity is not a virtue.

Objection 4. Further, no virtue is opposed to another virtue. But magnanimity is opposed to humility, since "the magnanimous deems himself worthy of great things, and despises others," according to Ethic. iv, 3. Therefore magnanimity is not a virtue.

Objection 5. Further, the properties of every virtue are praiseworthy. But magnanimity has certain properties that call for blame. For, in the first place, the magnanimous is unmindful of favors; secondly, he is remiss and slow of action; thirdly, he employs irony [Cf. 113] towards many; fourthly, he is unable to associate with others; fifthly, because he holds to the barren things rather than to those that are fruitful. Therefore magnanimity is not a virtue.

On the contrary, It is written in praise of certain men (2 Maccabees 15:18): "Nicanor hearing of the valor of Judas' companions, and the greatness of courage [animi magnitudinem] with which they fought for their country, was afraid to try the matter by the sword." Now, only deeds of virtue are worthy of praise. Therefore magnanimity which consists in greatness of courage is a virtue.

I answer that, The essence of human virtue consists in safeguarding the good of reason in human affairs, for this is man's proper good. Now among external human things honors take precedence of all others, as stated above (1; I-II, 11, 2, Objection 3). Therefore magnanimity, which observes the mode of reason in great honors, is a virtue.

Reply to Objection 1. As the Philosopher again says (Ethic. iv, 3), "the magnanimous in point of quantity goes to extremes," in so far as he tends to what is greatest, "but in the matter of becomingness, he follows the mean," because he tends to the greatest things according to reason, for "he deems himself worthy in accordance with his worth" (Ethic. iv, 3), since his aims do not surpass his deserts.

Reply to Objection 2. The mutual connection of the virtues does not apply to their acts, as though everyone were competent to practice the acts of all the virtues. Wherefore the act of magnanimity is not becoming to every virtuous man, but only to great men. On the other hand, as regards the principles of virtue, namely prudence and grace, all virtues are connected together, since their habits reside together in the soul, either in act or by way of a proximate disposition thereto. Thus it is possible for one to whom the act of magnanimity is not competent, to have the habit of magnanimity, whereby he is disposed to practice that act if it were competent to him according to his state.

Reply to Objection 3. The movements of the body are differentiated according to the different apprehensions and emotions of the soul. And so it happens that to magnanimity there accrue certain fixed accidents by way of bodily movements. For quickness of movement results from a man being intent on many things which he is in a hurry to accomplish, whereas the magnanimous is intent only on great things; these are few and require great attention, wherefore they call for slow movement. Likewise shrill and rapid speaking is chiefly competent to those who are quick to quarrel about anything, and this becomes not the magnanimous who are busy only about great things. And just as these dispositions of bodily movements are competent to the magnanimous man according to the mode of his emotions, so too in those who are naturally disposed to magnanimity these conditions are found naturally.

Reply to Objection 4. There is in man something great which he possesses through the gift of God; and something defective which accrues to him through the weakness of nature. Accordingly magnanimity makes a man deem himself worthy of great things in consideration of the gifts he holds from God: thus if his soul is endowed with great virtue, magnanimity makes him tend to perfect works of virtue; and the same is to be said of the use of any other good, such as science or external fortune. On the other hand, humility makes a man think little of himself in consideration of his own deficiency, and magnanimity makes him despise others in so far as they fall away from God's gifts: since he does not think so much of others as to do anything wrong for their sake. Yet humility makes us honor others and esteem them better than ourselves, in so far as we see some of God's gifts in them. Hence it is written of the just man (Psalm 14:4): "In his sight a vile person is contemned [Douay: 'The malignant is brought to nothing, but he glorifieth,' etc.]," which indicates the contempt of magnanimity, "but he honoreth them that fear the Lord," which points to the reverential bearing of humility. It is therefore evident that magnanimity and humility are not contrary to one another, although they seem to tend in contrary directions, because they proceed according to different considerations.

Reply to Objection 5. These properties in so far as they belong to a magnanimous man call not for blame, but for very great praise. For in the first place, when it is said that the magnanimous is not mindful of those from whom he has received favors, this points to the fact that he takes no pleasure in accepting favors from others unless he repay them with yet greater favor; this belongs to the perfection of gratitude, in the act of which he wishes to excel, even as in the acts of other virtues. Again, in the second place, it is said that he is remiss and slow of action, not that he is lacking in doing what becomes him, but because he does not busy himself with all kinds of works, but only with great works, such as are becoming to him. He is also said, in the third place, to employ irony, not as opposed to truth, and so as either to say of himself vile things that are not true, or deny of himself great things that are true, but because he does not disclose all his greatness, especially to the large number of those who are beneath him, since, as also the Philosopher says (Ethic. iv, 3), "it belongs to a magnanimous man to be great towards persons of dignity and affluence, and unassuming towards the middle class." In the fourth place, it is said that he cannot associate with others: this means that he is not at home with others than his friends: because he altogether shuns flattery and hypocrisy, which belong to littleness of mind. But he associates with all, both great and little, according as he ought, as stated above (ad 1). It is also said, fifthly, that he prefers to have barren things, not indeed any, but good, i.e. virtuous; for in all things he prefers the virtuous to the useful, as being greater: since the useful is sought in order to supply a defect which is inconsistent with magnanimity.

QUESTION 130. PRESUMPTION

ARTICLE 1. WHETHER PRESUMPTION IS A SIN?

Objection 1. It seems that presumption is not a sin. For the Apostle says: "Forgetting the things that are behind, I stretch forth [Vulgate: 'and stretching forth'] myself to those that are before." But it seems to savor of presumption that one should tend to what is above oneself. Therefore presumption is not a sin.

Objection 2. Further, the Philosopher says (Ethic. i, 7) "we should not listen to those who would persuade us to relish human things because we are men, or mortal things because we are mortal, but we should relish those that make us immortal"; and (Metaph. i) "that man should pursue divine things as far as possible." Now divine and immortal things are seemingly far above man. Since then presumption consists essentially in tending to what is above oneself, it seems that presumption is something praiseworthy, rather than a sin.

Objection 3. Further, the Apostle says (2 Corinthians 3:5): "Not that we are sufficient to think anything of ourselves, as of ourselves." If then presumption, by which one strives at that for which one is not sufficient, be a sin, it seems that man cannot lawfully even think of anything good: which is absurd. Therefore presumption is not a sin.

On the contrary, It is written (Sirach 37:3): "O wicked presumption, whence camest thou?" and a gloss answers: "From a creature's evil will." Now all that comes of the root of an evil will is a sin. Therefore presumption is a sin.

I answer that, Since whatever is according to nature, is ordered by the Divine Reason, which human reason ought to imitate, whatever is done in accordance with human reason in opposition to the order established in general throughout natural things is vicious and sinful. Now it is established throughout all natural things, that every action is commensurate with the power of the agent, nor does any natural agent strive to do what exceeds its ability. Hence it is vicious and sinful, as being contrary to the natural order, that any one should assume to do what is above his power: and this is what is meant by presumption, as its very name shows. Wherefore it is evident that presumption is a sin.

Reply to Objection 1. Nothing hinders that which is above the active power of a natural thing, and yet not above the passive power of that same thing: thus the air is possessed of a passive power by reason of which it can be so changed as to obtain the action and movement of fire, which surpass the active power of air. Thus too it would be sinful and presumptuous for a man while in a state of imperfect virtue to attempt the immediate accomplishment of what belongs to perfect virtue. But it is not presumptuous or sinful for a man to endeavor to advance towards perfect virtue. On this way the Apostle stretched himself forth to the things that were before him, namely continually advancing forward.

Reply to Objection 2. Divine and immortal things surpass man according to the order of nature. Yet man is possessed of a natural power, namely the intellect, whereby he can be united to immortal and Divine things. On this respect the Philosopher says that "man ought to pursue immortal and divine things," not that he should do what it becomes God to do, but that he should be united to Him in intellect and will.

Reply to Objection 3. As the Philosopher says (Ethic. iii, 3), "what we can do by the help of others we can do by ourselves in a sense." Hence since we can think and do good by the help of God, this is not altogether above our ability. Hence it is not presumptuous for a man to attempt the accomplishment of a virtuous deed: but it would be presumptuous if one were to make the attempt without confidence in God's assistance.

ARTICLE 2. WHETHER PRESUMPTION IS OPPOSED TO MAGNANIMITY BY EXCESS?

Objection 1. It seems that presumption is not opposed to magnanimity by excess. For presumption is accounted a species of the sin against the Holy Ghost, as stated above (14, 2; 21, 1). But the sin against the Holy Ghost is not opposed to magnanimity, but to charity. Neither therefore is presumption opposed to magnanimity.

Objection 2. Further, it belongs to magnanimity that one should deem oneself worthy of great things. But a man is said to be presumptuous even if he deem himself worthy of small things, if they surpass his ability. Therefore presumption is not directly opposed to magnanimity.

Objection 3. Further, the magnanimous man looks upon external goods as little things. Now according to the Philosopher (Ethic. iv, 3), "on account of external fortune the presumptuous disdain and wrong others, because they deem external goods as something great." Therefore presumption is opposed to magnanimity, not by excess, but only by deficiency.

On the contrary, The Philosopher says (Ethic. ii, 7; iv, 3) that the "vain man," i.e. a vaporer or a wind-bag, which with us denotes a presumptuous man, "is opposed to the magnanimous man by excess."

I answer that, As stated above (129, 3, ad 1), magnanimity observes the means, not as regards the quantity of that to which it tends, but in proportion to our own ability: for it does not tend to anything greater than is becoming to us.

Now the presumptuous man, as regards that to which he tends, does not exceed the magnanimous, but sometimes falls far short of him: but he does exceed in proportion to his own ability, whereas the magnanimous man does not exceed his. It is in this way that presumption is opposed to magnanimity by excess.

Reply to Objection 1. It is not every presumption that is accounted a sin against the Holy Ghost, but that by which one contemns the Divine justice through inordinate confidence in the Divine mercy. The latter kind of presumption, by reason of its matter, inasmuch, to wit, as it implies contempt of something Divine, is opposed to charity, or rather to the gift of fear, whereby we revere God. Nevertheless, in so far as this contempt exceeds the proportion to one's own ability, it can be opposed to magnanimity.

Reply to Objection 2. Presumption, like magnanimity, seems to tend to something great. For we are not, as a rule, wont to call a man presumptuous for going beyond his powers in something small. If, however, such a man be called presumptuous, this kind of presumption is not opposed to magnanimity, but to that virtue which is about ordinary honor, as stated above (Question 129, Article 2).

Reply to Objection 3. No one attempts what is above his ability, except in so far as he deems his ability greater than it is. In this one may err in two ways. First only as regards quantity, as when a man thinks he has greater virtue, or knowledge, or the like, than he has. Secondly, as regards the kind of thing, as when he thinks himself great, and worthy of great things, by reason of something that does not make him so, for instance by reason of riches or goods of fortune. For, as the Philosopher says (Ethic. iv, 3), "those who have these things without virtue, neither justly deem themselves worthy of great things, nor are rightly called magnanimous."

Again, the thing to which a man sometimes tends in excess of his ability, is sometimes in very truth something great, simply as in the case of Peter, whose intent was to suffer for Christ, which exceeded his power; while sometimes it is something great, not simply, but only in the opinion of fools, such as wearing costly clothes, despising and wronging others. This savors of an excess of magnanimity, not in any truth, but in people's opinion. Hence Seneca says (De Quat. Virtut.) that "when magnanimity exceeds its measure, it makes a man high-handed, proud, haughty restless, and bent on excelling in all things, whether in words or in deeds, without any considerations of virtue." Thus it is evident that the presumptuous man sometimes falls short of the magnanimous in reality, although in appearance he surpasses him.

QUESTION 131. AMBITION

ARTICLE 1. WHETHER AMBITION IS A SIN?

Objection 1. It seems that ambition is not a sin. For ambition denotes the desire of honor. Now honor is in itself a good thing, and the greatest of external goods: wherefore those who care not for honor are reproved. Therefore ambition is not a sin; rather is it something deserving of praise, in so far as a good is laudably desired.

Objection 2. Further, anyone may, without sin, desire what is due to him as a reward. Now honor is the reward of virtue, as the Philosopher states (Ethic. i, 12; iv, 3; viii, 14). Therefore ambition of honor is not a sin.

Objection 3. Further, that which heartens a man to do good and disheartens him from doing evil, is not a sin. Now honor heartens men to do good and to avoid evil; thus the Philosopher says (Ethic. iii, 8) that "with the bravest men, cowards are held in dishonor, and the brave in honor": and Tully says (De Tusc. Quaest. i) that "honor fosters the arts." Therefore ambition is not a sin.

On the contrary, It is written (1 Corinthians 13:5) that "charity is not ambitious, seeketh not her own." Now nothing is contrary to charity, except sin. Therefore ambition is a sin.

I answer that, As stated above (103, 1 and 2), honor denotes reverence shown to a person in witness of his excellence. Now two things have to be considered with regard to man's honor. The first is that a man has not from himself the thing in which he excels, for this is, as it were, something Divine in him, wherefore on this count honor is due principally, not to him but to God. The second point that calls for observation is that the thing in which man excels is given to him by God, that he may profit others thereby: wherefore a man ought so far to be pleased that others bear witness to his excellence, as this enables him to profit others.

Now the desire of honor may be inordinate in three ways. First, when a man desires recognition of an excellence which he has not: this is to desire more than his share of honor. Secondly, when a man desires honor for himself without referring it to God. Thirdly, when a man's appetite rests in honor itself, without referring it to the profit of others. Since then ambition denotes inordinate desire of honor, it is evident that it is always a sin.

Reply to Objection 1. The desire for good should be regulated according to reason, and if it exceed this rule it will be sinful. In this way it is sinful to desire honor in disaccord with the order of reason. Now those are reproved who care not for honor in accordance with reason's dictate that they should avoid what is contrary to honor.

Reply to Objection 2. Honor is not the reward of virtue, as regards the virtuous man, in this sense that he should seek for it as his reward: since the reward he seeks is happiness, which is the end of virtue. But it is said to be the reward of virtue as regards others, who have nothing greater than honor whereby to reward the virtuous; which honor derives greatness from the very fact that it bears witness to virtue. Hence it is evident that it is not an adequate reward, as stated in Ethic. iv, 3.

Reply to Objection 3. Just as some are heartened to do good and disheartened from doing evil, by the desire of honor, if this be desired in due measure; so, if it be desired inordinately, it may become to man an occasion of doing many evil things, as when a man cares not by what means he obtains honor. Wherefore Sallust says (Catilin.) that "the good as well as the wicked covet honors for themselves, but the one," i.e. the good, "go about it in the right way," whereas "the other," i.e. the wicked, "through lack of the good arts, make use of deceit and falsehood." Yet they who, merely for the sake of honor, either do good or avoid evil, are not virtuous, according to the Philosopher (Ethic. iii, 8), where he says that they who do brave things for the sake of honor are not truly brave.

ARTICLE 2. WHETHER AMBITION IS OPPOSED TO MAGNANIMITY BY EXCESS?

Objection 1. It seems that ambition is not opposed to magnanimity by excess. For one mean has only one extreme opposed to it on the one side. Now presumption is opposed to magnanimity by excess as stated above (Question 130, Article 2). Therefore ambition is not opposed to it by excess.

Objection 2. Further, magnanimity is about honors; whereas ambition seems to regard positions of dignity: for it is written (2 Maccabees 4:7) that

"Jason ambitiously sought the high priesthood." Therefore ambition is not opposed to magnanimity.

Objection 3. Further, ambition seems to regard outward show: for it is written (Acts 25:27) that "Agrippa and Berenice . . . with great pomp [ambitione]. . . . had entered into the hall of audience" ['Praetorium.' The Vulgate has 'auditorium,' but the meaning is the same], and (2 Chronicles 16:14) that when Asa died they "burned spices and . . . ointments over his body" with very great pomp [ambitione]. But magnanimity is not about outward show. Therefore ambition is not opposed to magnanimity.

On the contrary, Tully says (De Offic. i) that "the more a man exceeds in magnanimity, the more he desires himself alone to dominate others." But this pertains to ambition. Therefore ambition denotes an excess of magnanimity.

I answer that, As stated above (Article 1), ambition signifies inordinate love of honor. Now magnanimity is about honors and makes use of them in a becoming manner. Wherefore it is evident that ambition is opposed to magnanimity as the inordinate to that which is well ordered.

Reply to Objection 1. Magnanimity regards two things. It regards one as its end, in so far as it is some great deed that the magnanimous man attempts in proportion to his ability. On this way presumption is opposed to magnanimity by excess: because the presumptuous man attempts great deeds beyond his ability. The other thing that magnanimity regards is its matter, viz. honor, of which it makes right use: and in this way ambition is opposed to magnanimity by excess. Nor is it impossible for one mean to be exceeded in various respects.

Reply to Objection 2. Honor is due to those who are in a position of dignity, on account of a certain excellence of their estate: and accordingly inordinate desire for positions of dignity pertains to ambition. For if a man were to have an inordinate desire for a position of dignity, not for the sake of honor, but for the sake of a right use of a dignity exceeding his ability, he would not be ambitious but presumptuous.

Reply to Objection 3. The very solemnity of outward worship is a kind of honor, wherefore in such cases honor is wont to be shown. This is signified by the words of James 2:2-3: "If there shall come into your assembly a man having a golden ring, in fine apparel . . . and you . . . shall say to him: Sit thou here well," etc. Wherefore ambition does not regard outward worship, except in so far as this is a kind of honor.

QUESTION 132. VAINGLORY

ARTICLE 1. WHETHER THE DESIRE OF GLORY IS A SIN?

Objection 1. It seems that the desire of glory is not a sin. For no one sins in being likened to God: in fact we are commanded (Ephesians 5:1): "Be ye . . . followers of God, as most dear children." Now by seeking glory man seems to imitate God, Who seeks glory from men: wherefore it is written (Isaiah 43:6-7): "Bring My sons from afar, and My daughters from the ends of the earth. And every one that calleth on My name, I have created him for My glory." Therefore the desire for glory is not a sin.

Objection 2. Further, that which incites a man to do good is apparently not a sin. Now the desire of glory incites men to do good. For Tully says (De Tusc. Quaest. i) that "glory inflames every man to strive his utmost": and in Holy Writ glory is promised for good works, according to Romans 2:7: "To them, indeed, who according to patience in good work . . . glory and honor" [Vulgate: 'Who will render to every man according to his works, to them indeed who . . . seek glory and honor and incorruption, eternal life.']. Therefore the desire for glory is not a sin.

Objection 3. Further, Tully says (De Invent. Rhet. ii) that glory is "consistent good report about a person, together with praise": and this comes to the same as what Augustine says (Contra Maximin. iii), viz. that glory is, "as it were, clear knowledge with praise." Now it is no sin to desire praiseworthy renown: indeed, it seems itself to call for praise, according to Sirach 41:15, "Take care of a good name," and Romans 12:17, "Providing good things not only in the sight of God, but also in the sight of all men." Therefore the desire of vainglory is not a sin.

On the contrary, Augustine says (De Civ. Dei v): "He is better advised who acknowledges that even the love of praise is sinful."

I answer that, Glory signifies a certain clarity, wherefore Augustine says (Tract. lxxxii, c, cxiv in Joan.) that to be "glorified is the same as to be clarified." Now clarity and comeliness imply a certain display: wherefore the word glory properly denotes the display of something as regards its seeming comely in the sight of men, whether it be a bodily or a spiritual good. Since, however, that which is clear simply can be seen by many, and by those who are far away, it follows that the word glory properly denotes that somebody's good is known and approved by many, according to the saying of Sallust (Catilin.) [The quotation is from Livy: Hist., Lib. XXII C, 39: "I must not boast while I am addressing one man].

But if we take the word glory in a broader sense, it not only consists in the knowledge of many, but also in the knowledge of few, or of one, or of oneself alone, as when one considers one's own good as being worthy of praise. Now it is not a sin to know and approve one's own good: for it is written (1 Corinthians 2:12): "Now we have received not the spirit of this world, but the Spirit that is of God that we may know the things that are given us from God." Likewise it is not a sin to be willing to approve one's own good works: for it is written (Matthew 5:16): "Let your light shine before men." Hence the desire for glory does not, of itself, denote a sin: but the desire for empty or vain glory denotes a sin: for it is sinful to desire anything vain, according to Psalm 4:3, "Why do you love vanity, and seek after lying?"

Now glory may be called vain in three ways. First, on the part of the thing for which one seeks glory: as when a man seeks glory for that which is unworthy of glory, for instance when he seeks it for something frail and perishable: secondly, on the part of him from whom he seeks glory, for instance a man whose judgment is uncertain: thirdly, on the part of the man himself who seeks glory, for that he does not refer the desire of his own glory to a due end, such as God's honor, or the spiritual welfare of his neighbor.

Reply to Objection 1. As Augustine says on John 13:13, "You call Me Master and Lord; and you say well" (Tract. lviii in Joan.): "Self-complacency is fraught with danger of one who has to beware of pride. But He Who is above all, however much He may praise Himself, does not uplift Himself. For knowledge of God is our need, not His: nor does any man know Him unless he be taught of Him Who knows." It is therefore evident that God seeks glory, not for His own sake, but for ours. On like manner a man may rightly seek his own glory for the good of others, according to Matthew 5:16, "That they may see your good works, and glorify your Father Who is in heaven."

Reply to Objection 2. That which we receive from God is not vain but true glory: it is this glory that is promised as a reward for good works, and of which it is written (2 Corinthians 10:17-18): "He that glorieth let him glory in the Lord, for not he who commendeth himself is approved, but he whom God commendeth." It is true that some are heartened to do works of virtue, through desire for human glory, as also through the desire for other earthly goods. Yet he is not truly virtuous who does virtuous deeds for the sake of human glory, as Augustine proves (De Civ. Dei v).

Reply to Objection 3. It is requisite for man's perfection that he should know himself; but not that he should be known by others, wherefore it is not to be desired in itself. It may, however, be desired as being useful for something, either in order that God may be glorified by men, or that men may become better by reason of the good they know to be in another man, or in order that man, knowing by the testimony of others' praise the good which is in him, may himself strive to persevere therein and to become better. On this sense it is praiseworthy that a man should "take care of his good name," and that he should "provide good things in the sight of God and men": but not that he should take an empty pleasure in human praise.

ARTICLE 2. WHETHER VAINGLORY IS OPPOSED TO MAGNANIMITY?

Objection 1. It seems that vainglory is not opposed to magnanimity. For, as stated above (Article 1), vainglory consists in glorying in things that are not, which pertains to falsehood; or in earthly and perishable things, which pertains to covetousness; or in the testimony of men, whose judgment is uncertain, which pertains to imprudence. Now these vices are not contrary to magnanimity. Therefore vainglory is not opposed to magnanimity.

Objection 2. Further, vainglory is not, like pusillanimity, opposed to magnanimity by way of deficiency, for this seems inconsistent with vainglory. Nor is it opposed to it by way of excess, for in this way presumption and ambition are opposed to magnanimity, as stated above (130, 2; 131, 2): and these differ from vainglory. Therefore vainglory is not opposed to magnanimity.

Objection 3. Further, a gloss on Philippians 2:3, "Let nothing be done through contention, neither by vainglory," says: "Some among them were given to dissension and restlessness, contending with one another for the sake of vainglory." But contention [Cf. 38] is not opposed to magnanimity. Neither therefore is vainglory.

On the contrary, Tully says (De Offic. i) under the heading, "Magnanimity consists in two things: We should beware of the desire for glory, since it enslaves the mind, which a magnanimous man should ever strive to keep untrammeled." Therefore it is opposed to magnanimity.

I answer that, As stated above (103, 1, ad 3), glory is an effect of honor and praise: because from the fact that a man is praised, or shown any kind of reverence, he acquires charity in the knowledge of others. And since magnanimity is about honor, as stated above (129, 1 and 2), it follows that it also is about glory: seeing that as a man uses honor moderately, so too does he use glory in moderation. Wherefore inordinate desire of glory is directly opposed to magnanimity.

Reply to Objection 1. To think so much of little things as to glory in them is itself opposed to magnanimity. Wherefore it is said of the magnanimous man (Ethic. iv) that honor is of little account to him. In like manner he thinks little of other things that are sought for honor's sake, such as power and wealth. Likewise it is inconsistent with magnanimity to glory in things that are not; wherefore it is said of the magnanimous man (Ethic. iv) that he cares more for truth than for opinion. Again it is incompatible with magnanimity for a man to glory in the testimony of human praise, as though he deemed this something great; wherefore it is said of the magnanimous man (Ethic. iv), that he cares not to be praised. And so, when a man looks upon little things as though they were great, nothing hinders this from being contrary to magnanimity, as well as to other virtues.

Reply to Objection 2. He that is desirous of vainglory does in truth fall short of being magnanimous, because he glories in what the magnanimous man thinks little of, as stated in the preceding Reply. But if we consider his estimate, he is opposed to the magnanimous man by way of excess, because the glory which he seeks is something great in his estimation, and he tends thereto in excess of his deserts.

Reply to Objection 3. As stated above (127, 2, ad 2), the opposition of vices does not depend on their effects. Nevertheless contention, if done intentionally, is opposed to magnanimity: since no one contends save for what he deems great. Wherefore the Philosopher says (Ethic. iv, 3) that the magnanimous man is not contentious, because nothing is great in his estimation.

QUESTION 133. PUSILLANIMITY

ARTICLE 1. WHETHER PUSILLANIMITY IS A SIN?

Objection 1. It seems that pusillanimity is not a sin. For every sin makes a man evil, just as every virtue makes a man good. But a fainthearted man is not evil, as the Philosopher says (Ethic. iv, 3). Therefore pusillanimity is not a sin.

Objection 2. Further, the Philosopher says (Ethic. iv, 3) that "a fainthearted man is especially one who is worthy of great goods, yet does not deem himself worthy of them." Now no one is worthy of great goods except the virtuous, since as the Philosopher again says (Ethic. iv, 3), "none but the virtuous are truly worthy of honor." Therefore the fainthearted are virtuous: and consequently pusillanimity is not a sin.

Objection 3. Further, "Pride is the beginning of all sin" (Sirach 10:15). But pusillanimity does not proceed from pride, since the proud man sets himself above what he is, while the fainthearted man withdraws from the things he is worthy of. Therefore pusillanimity is not a sin.

Objection 4. Further, the Philosopher says (Ethic. iv, 3) that "he who deems himself less worthy than he is, is said to be fainthearted." Now sometimes holy men deem themselves less worthy than they are; for instance, Moses and Jeremias, who were worthy of the office God chose them for, which they both humbly declined (Exodus 3:11; Jeremiah 1:6). Therefore pusillanimity is not a sin.

On the contrary, Nothing in human conduct is to be avoided save sin. Now pusillanimity is to be avoided: for it is written (Colossians 3:21): "Fathers, provoke not your children to indignation, lest they be discouraged." Therefore pusillanimity is a sin.

I answer that, Whatever is contrary to a natural inclination is a sin, because it is contrary to a law of nature. Now everything has a natural inclination to accomplish an action that is commensurate with its power: as is evident in all natural things, whether animate or inanimate. Now just as presumption makes a man exceed what is proportionate to his power, by striving to do more than he can, so pusillanimity makes a man fall short of what is proportionate to his power, by refusing to tend to that which is commensurate thereto. Wherefore as presumption is a sin, so is pusillanimity. Hence it is that the servant who buried in the earth the money he had received from his master, and did not trade with it through fainthearted fear, was punished by his master (Matthew 25; Luke 19).

Reply to Objection 1. The Philosopher calls those evil who injure their neighbor: and accordingly the fainthearted is said not to be evil, because he injures no one, save accidentally, by omitting to do what might be profitable to others. For Gregory says (Pastoral. i) that if "they who demur to do good to their neighbor in preaching be judged strictly, without doubt their guilt is proportionate to the good they might have done had they been less retiring."

Reply to Objection 2. Nothing hinders a person who has a virtuous habit from sinning venially and without losing the habit, or mortally and with loss of the habit of gratuitous virtue. Hence it is possible for a man, by reason of the virtue which he has, to be worthy of doing certain great things that are worthy of great honor, and yet through not trying to make use of his virtue, he sins sometimes venially, sometimes mortally.

Again it may be replied that the fainthearted is worthy of great things in proportion to his ability for virtue, ability which he derives either from a good natural disposition, or from science, or from external fortune, and if he fails to use those things for virtue, he becomes guilty of pusillanimity.

Reply to Objection 3. Even pusillanimity may in some way be the result of pride: when, to wit, a man clings too much to his own opinion, whereby he thinks himself incompetent for those things for which he is competent. Hence it is written (Proverbs 26:16): "The sluggard is wiser in his own conceit than seven men that speak sentences." For nothing hinders him from depreciating himself in some things, and having a high opinion of himself in others. Wherefore Gregory says (Pastoral. i) of Moses that "perchance he would have been proud, had he undertaken the leadership of a numerous people without misgiving: and again he would have been proud, had he refused to obey the command of his Creator."

Reply to Objection 4. Moses and Jeremias were worthy of the office to which they were appointed by God, but their worthiness was of Divine grace: yet they, considering the insufficiency of their own weakness, demurred; though not obstinately lest they should fall into pride.

ARTICLE 2. WHETHER PUSILLANIMITY IS OPPOSED TO MAGNANIMITY?

Objection 1. It seems that pusillanimity is not opposed to magnanimity. For the Philosopher says (Ethic., 3) that "the fainthearted man knows not himself: for he would desire the good things, of which he is worthy, if he knew himself." Now ignorance of self seems opposed to prudence. Therefore pusillanimity is opposed to prudence.

Objection 2. Further our Lord calls the servant wicked and slothful who through pusillanimity refused to make use of the money. Moreover the Philosopher says (Ethic. iv, 3) that the fainthearted seem to be slothful. Now sloth is opposed to solicitude, which is an act of prudence, as stated above (Question 47, Article 09). Therefore pusillanimity is not opposed to magnanimity.

Objection 3. Further, pusillanimity seems to proceed from inordinate fear: hence it is written (Isaiah 35:4): "Say to the fainthearted: Take courage and fear not." It also seems to proceed from inordinate anger, according to Colossians 3:21, "Fathers, provoke not your children to indignation, lest they be discouraged." Now inordinate fear is opposed to fortitude, and inordinate anger to meekness. Therefore pusillanimity is not opposed to magnanimity.

Objection 4. Further, the vice that is in opposition to a particular virtue is the more grievous according as it is more unlike that virtue. Now pusillanimity is more unlike magnanimity than presumption is. Therefore if pusillanimity is opposed to magnanimity, it follows that it is a more grievous sin than presumption: yet this is contrary to the saying of Sirach 37:3, "O wicked presumption, whence camest thou?" Therefore pusillanimity is not opposed to magnanimity.

On the contrary, Pusillanimity and magnanimity differ as greatness and littleness of soul, as their very names denote. Now great and little are opposites. Therefore pusillanimity is opposed to magnanimity.

I answer that, Pusillanimity may be considered in three ways. First, in itself; and thus it is evident that by its very nature it is opposed to magnanimity, from which it differs as great and little differ in connection with the same subject. For just as the magnanimous man tends to great things out of greatness of soul, so the pusillanimous man shrinks from great things out of littleness of soul. Secondly, it may be considered in reference to its cause, which on the part of the intellect is ignorance of one's own qualification, and on the part of the appetite is the fear of failure in what one falsely deems to exceed one's ability. Thirdly, it may be considered in reference to its effect, which is to shrink from the great things of which one is worthy. But, as stated above (132, 2, ad 3), opposition between vice and virtue depends rather on their respective species than on their cause or effect. Hence pusillanimity is directly opposed to magnanimity.

Reply to Objection 1. This argument considers pusillanimity as proceeding from a cause in the intellect. Yet it cannot be said properly that it is opposed to prudence, even in respect of its cause: because ignorance of this kind does not proceed from indiscretion but from laziness in considering one's own ability, according to Ethic. iv, 3, or in accomplishing what is within one's power.

Reply to Objection 2. This argument considers pusillanimity from the point of view of its effect.

Reply to Objection 3. This argument considers the point of view of cause. Nor is the fear that causes pusillanimity always a fear of the dangers of death: wherefore it does not follow from this standpoint that pusillanimity is opposed to fortitude. As regards anger, if we consider it under the aspect of its proper movement, whereby a man is roused to take vengeance, it does not cause pusillanimity, which disheartens the soul; on the contrary, it takes it away. If, however, we consider the causes of anger, which are injuries inflicted whereby the soul of the man who suffers them is disheartened, it conduces to pusillanimity.

Reply to Objection 4. According to its proper species pusillanimity is a graver sin than presumption, since thereby a man withdraws from good things, which is a very great evil according to Ethic. iv. Presumption, however, is stated to be "wicked" on account of pride whence it proceeds.

QUESTION 141. TEMPERANCE

ARTICLE 4. WHETHER TEMPERANCE IS ONLY ABOUT DESIRES AND PLEASURES OF TOUCH?

Objection 1. It would seem that temperance is not only about desires and pleasures of touch. For Augustine says (De Morib. Eccl. xix) that "the function of temperance is to control and quell the desires which draw us to the things which withdraw us from the laws of God and from the fruit of His goodness"; and a little further on he adds that "it is the duty of temperance to spurn all bodily allurements and popular praise." Now we are withdrawn from God's laws not only by the desire for pleasures of touch, but also by the desire for pleasures of the other senses, for these, too, belong to the bodily allurements, and again by the desire for riches or for worldly glory: wherefore it is written (1 Timothy 6:10). "Desire ['Cupiditas,' which is the Douay version following the Greek philargyria renders 'desire of money'] is the root of all evils." Therefore temperance is not only about desires of pleasures of touch.

Objection 2. Further, the Philosopher says (Ethic. iv, 3) that "one who is worthy of small things and deems himself worthy of them is temperate, but he is not magnificent." Now honors, whether small or great, of which he is speaking there, are an object of pleasure, not of touch, but in the soul's apprehension. Therefore temperance is not only about desires for pleasures of touch.

Objection 3. Further, things that are of the same genus would seem to pertain to the matter of a particular virtue under one same aspect. Now all pleasures of sense are apparently of the same genus. Therefore they all equally belong to the matter of temperance.

Objection 4. Further, spiritual pleasures are greater than the pleasures of the body, as stated above (I-II, 31, 5) in the treatise on the passions. Now sometimes men forsake God's laws and the state of virtue through desire for spiritual pleasures, for instance, through curiosity in matters of knowledge: wherefore the devil promised man knowledge, saying (Genesis 3:5): "Ye shall be as Gods, knowing good and evil." Therefore temperance is not only about pleasures of touch.

Objection 5. Further, if pleasures of touch were the proper matter of temperance, it would follow that temperance is about all pleasures of touch. But it is not about all, for instance, about those which occur in games. Therefore pleasures of touch are not the proper matter of temperance.

On the contrary, The Philosopher says (Ethic. iii, 10) that "temperance is properly about desires of pleasures of touch."

I answer that, As stated above (Article 3), temperance is about desires and pleasures in the same way as fortitude is about fear and daring. Now fortitude is about fear and daring with respect to the greatest evils whereby nature itself is dissolved; and such are dangers of death. Wherefore in like manner temperance must needs be about desires for the greatest pleasures. And since pleasure results from a natural operation, it is so much the greater according as it results from a more natural operation. Now to animals the most natural operations are those which preserve the nature of the individual by means of meat and drink, and the nature of the species by the union of the sexes. Hence temperance is properly about pleasures of meat and drink and sexual pleasures. Now these pleasures result from the sense of touch. Wherefore it follows that temperance is about pleasures of touch.

Reply to Objection 1. In the passage quoted Augustine apparently takes temperance, not as a special virtue having a determinate matter, but as concerned with the moderation of reason, in any matter whatever: and this is a general condition of every virtue. However, we may also reply that if a man can control the greatest pleasures, much more can he control lesser ones. Wherefore it belongs chiefly and properly to temperance to moderate desires and pleasures of touch, and secondarily other pleasures.

Reply to Objection 2. The Philosopher takes temperance as denoting moderation in external things, when, to wit, a man tends to that which is proportionate to him, but not as denoting moderation in the soul's emotions, which pertains to the virtue of temperance.

Reply to Objection 3. The pleasures of the other senses play a different part in man and in other animals. For in other animals pleasures do not result from the other senses save in relation to sensibles of touch: thus the lion is pleased to see the stag, or to hear its voice, in relation to his food. On the other hand man derives pleasure from the other senses, not only for this reason, but also on account of the becomingness of the sensible object. Wherefore temperance is about the pleasures of the other senses, in relation to pleasures of touch, not principally but consequently: while in so far as the sensible objects of the other senses are pleasant on account of their becomingness, as when a man is pleased at a well-harmonized sound, this pleasure has nothing to do with the preservation of nature. Hence these passions are not of such importance that temperance can be referred to them antonomastically.

Reply to Objection 4. Although spiritual pleasures are by their nature greater than bodily pleasures, they are not so perceptible to the senses, and consequently they do not so strongly affect the sensitive appetite, against whose impulse the good of reason is safeguarded by moral virtue. We may also reply that spiritual pleasures, strictly speaking, are in accordance with reason, wherefore they need no control, save accidentally, in so far as one spiritual pleasure is a hindrance to another greater and more binding.

Reply to Objection 5. Not all pleasures of touch regard the preservation of nature, and consequently it does not follow that temperance is about all pleasures of touch.

QUESTION 153. LUST

ARTICLE 2. WHETHER NO VENEREAL ACT CAN BE WITHOUT SIN?

Objection 1. It would seem that no venereal act can be without sin. For nothing but sin would seem to hinder virtue. Now every venereal act is a great hindrance to virtue. For Augustine says (Soliloq. i, 10): "I consider that nothing so casts down the manly mind from its height as the fondling of a woman, and those bodily contacts." Therefore, seemingly, no venereal act is without sin.

Objection 2. Further, any excess that makes one forsake the good of reason is sinful, because virtue is corrupted by "excess" and "deficiency" as stated in Ethic. ii, 2. Now in every venereal act there is excess of pleasure, since it so absorbs the mind, that "it is incompatible with the act of understanding," as the Philosopher observes (Ethic. vii, 11); and as Jerome [Origen, Hom. vi in Num.; Cf. Jerome, Ep. cxxiii ad Ageruch.] states, rendered the hearts of the prophets, for the moment, insensible to the spirit of prophecy. Therefore no venereal act can be without sin.

Objection 3. Further, the cause is more powerful than its effect. Now original sin is transmitted to children by desire, without which no venereal act is possible, as Augustine declares (De Nup. et Concup. i, 24). Therefore no venereal act can be without sin.

On the contrary, Augustine says (De Bono Conjug. xxv): "This is a sufficient answer to heretics, if only they will understand that no sin is committed in that which is against neither nature, nor morals, nor a commandment": and he refers to the act of sexual intercourse between the patriarchs of old and their several wives. Therefore not every venereal act is a sin.

I answer that, A sin, in human acts, is that which is against the order of reason. Now the order of reason consists in its ordering everything to its end in a fitting manner. Wherefore it is no sin if one, by the dictate of reason, makes use of certain things in a fitting manner and order for the end to which they are adapted, provided this end be something truly good. Now just as the preservation of the bodily nature of one individual is a true good, so, too, is the preservation of the nature of the human species a very great good. And just as the use of food is directed to the preservation of life in the individual, so is the use of venereal acts directed to the preservation of the whole human race. Hence Augustine says (De Bono Conjug. xvi): "What food is to a man's well-being, such is sexual intercourse to the welfare of the whole human race." Wherefore just as the use of food can be without sin, if it be taken in due manner and order, as required for the welfare of the body, so also the use of venereal acts can be without sin, provided they be performed in due manner and order, in keeping with the end of human procreation.

Reply to Objection 1. A thing may be a hindrance to virtue in two ways. First, as regards the ordinary degree of virtue, and as to this nothing but sin is an obstacle to virtue. Secondly, as regards the perfect degree of virtue, and as to this virtue may be hindered by that which is not a sin, but a lesser good. In this way sexual intercourse casts down the mind not from virtue, but from the height, i.e. the perfection of virtue. Hence Augustine says (De Bono Conjug.

viii): "Just as that was good which Martha did when busy about serving holy men, yet better still that which Mary did in hearing the word of God: so, too, we praise the good of Susanna's conjugal chastity, yet we prefer the good of the widow Anna, and much more that of the Virgin Mary."

Reply to Objection 2. As stated above (152, 2, ad 2; I-II, 64, 2), the mean of virtue depends not on quantity but on conformity with right reason: and consequently the exceeding pleasure attaching to a venereal act directed according to reason, is not opposed to the mean of virtue. Moreover, virtue is not concerned with the amount of pleasure experienced by the external sense, as this depends on the disposition of the body; what matters is how much the interior appetite is affected by that pleasure. Nor does it follow that the act in question is contrary to virtue, from the fact that the free act of reason in considering spiritual things is incompatible with the aforesaid pleasure. For it is not contrary to virtue, if the act of reason be sometimes interrupted for something that is done in accordance with reason, else it would be against virtue for a person to set himself to sleep. That venereal desire and pleasure are not subject to the command and moderation of reason, is due to the punishment of the first sin, inasmuch as the reason, for rebelling against God, deserved that its body should rebel against it, as Augustine says (De Civ. Dei xiii, 13).

Reply to Objection 3. As Augustine says (De Civ. Dei xiii, 13), "the child, shackled with original sin, is born of fleshly desire (which is not imputed as sin to the regenerate) as of a daughter of sin." Hence it does not follow that the act in question is a sin, but that it contains something penal resulting from the first sin.

QUESTION 154. THE PARTS OF LUST

ARTICLE 1. WHETHER SIX SPECIES ARE FITTINGLY ASSIGNED TO LUST?

Objection 1. It would seem that six species are unfittingly assigned to lust, namely, "simple fornication, adultery, incest, seduction, rape, and the unnatural vice." For diversity of matter does not diversify the species. Now the aforesaid division is made with regard to diversity of matter, according as the woman with whom a man has intercourse is married or a virgin, or of some other condition. Therefore it seems that the species of lust are diversified in this way.

Objection 2. Further, seemingly the species of one vice are not differentiated by things that belong to another vice. Now adultery does not differ from simple fornication, save in the point of a man having intercourse with one who is another's, so that he commits an injustice. Therefore it seems that adultery should not be reckoned a species of lust.

Objection 3. Further, just as a man may happen to have intercourse with a woman who is bound to another man by marriage, so may it happen that a man has intercourse with a woman who is bound to God by vow. Therefore sacrilege should be reckoned a species of lust, even as adultery is.

Objection 4. Further, a married man sins not only if he be with another woman, but also if he use his own wife inordinately. But the latter sin is comprised under lust. Therefore it should be reckoned among the species thereof.

Objection 5. Further, the Apostle says (2 Corinthians 12:21): "Lest again, when I come, God humble me among you, and I mourn many of them that sinned before, and have not done penance for the uncleanness and fornication and lasciviousness that they have committed." Therefore it seems that also uncleanness and lasciviousness should be reckoned species of lust, as well as fornication.

Objection 6. Further, the thing divided is not to be reckoned among its parts. But lust is reckoned together with the aforesaid: for it is written (Galatians 5:19): "The works of the flesh are manifest, which are fornication, uncleanness, immodesty, lust [Douay: 'luxury']." Therefore it seems that fornication is unfittingly reckoned a species of lust.

On the contrary, The aforesaid division is given in the Decretals 36, qu. i [Append. Grat. ad can. Lex illa].

I answer that As stated above (Question 153, Article 3), the sin of lust consists in seeking venereal pleasure not in accordance with right reason. This may happen in two ways. First, in respect of the matter wherein this pleasure is sought; secondly, when, whereas there is due matter, other due circumstances are not observed. And since a circumstance, as such, does not specify a moral act, whose species is derived from its object which is also its matter, it follows that the species of lust must be assigned with respect to its matter or object.

Now this same matter may be discordant with right reason in two ways. First, because it is inconsistent with the end of the venereal act. In this way, as hindering the begetting of children, there is the "vice against nature," which attaches to every venereal act from which generation cannot follow; and, as hindering the due upbringing and advancement of the child when born, there is "simple fornication," which is the union of an unmarried man with an unmarried woman. Secondly, the matter wherein the venereal act is consummated may be discordant with right reason in relation to other persons; and this in two ways. First, with regard to the woman, with whom a man has connection, by reason of due honor not being paid to her; and thus there is "incest," which consists in the misuse of a woman who is related by consanguinity or affinity. Secondly, with regard to the person under whose authority the woman is placed: and if she be under the authority of a husband, it is "adultery," if under the authority of her father, it is "seduction," in the absence of violence, and "rape" if violence be employed.

These species are differentiated on the part of the woman rather than of the man, because in the venereal act the woman is passive and is by way of matter, whereas the man is by way of agent; and it has been stated above (Objection 1) that the aforesaid species are assigned with regard to a difference of matter.

Reply to Objection 1. The aforesaid diversity of matter is connected with a formal difference of object, which difference results from different modes of opposition to right reason, as stated above.

Reply to Objection 2. As stated above (I-II, 18, 07), nothing hinders the deformities of different vices concurring in the one act, and in this way adultery is comprised under lust and injustice. Nor is this deformity of injustice altogether accidental to lust: since the lust that obeys desire so far as to lead to injustice, is thereby shown to be more grievous.

Reply to Objection 3. Since a woman, by vowing continence, contracts a spiritual marriage with God, the sacrilege that is committed in the violation of such a woman is a spiritual adultery. In like manner, the other kinds of sacrilege pertaining to lustful matter are reduced to other species of lust.

Reply to Objection 4. The sin of a husband with his wife is not connected with undue matter, but with other circumstances, which do not constitute the species of a moral act, as stated above (I-II, 18, 2).

Reply to Objection 5. As a gloss says on this passage, "uncleanness" stands for lust against nature, while "lasciviousness" is a man's abuse of boys, wherefore it would appear to pertain to seduction. We may also reply that "lasciviousness" relates to certain acts circumstantial to the venereal act, for instance kisses, touches, and so forth.

Reply to Objection 6. According to a gloss on this passage "lust" there signifies any kind of excess.

QUESTION 157. CLEMENCY AND MEEKNESS

ARTICLE 2. WHETHER BOTH CLEMENCY AND MEEKNESS ARE VIRTUES?

Objection 1. It would seem that neither clemency nor meekness is a virtue. For no virtue is opposed to another virtue. Yet both of these are apparently opposed to severity, which is a virtue. Therefore neither clemency nor meekness is a virtue.

Objection 2. Further, "Virtue is destroyed by excess and defect" [Ethic. ii, 2]. But both clemency and meekness consist in a certain decrease; for clemency decreases punishment, and meekness decreases anger. Therefore neither clemency nor meekness is a virtue.

Objection 3. Further, meekness or mildness is included (Matthew 5:4) among the beatitudes, and (Galatians 5:23) among the fruits. Now the virtues differ from the beatitudes and fruits. Therefore they are not comprised under virtue.

On the contrary, Seneca says (De Clementia ii, 5): "Every good man is conspicuous for his clemency and meekness." Now it is virtue properly that belongs to a good man, since "virtue it is that makes its possessor good, and renders his works good also" (Ethic. ii, 6). Therefore clemency and meekness are virtues.

I answer that, The nature of moral virtue consists in the subjection of appetite to reason, as the Philosopher declares (Ethic. i, 13). Now this is verified both in clemency and in meekness. For clemency, in mitigating punishment, "is guided by reason," according to Seneca (De Clementia ii, 5), and meekness, likewise, moderates anger according to right reason, as stated in Ethic. iv, 5. Wherefore it is manifest that both clemency and meekness are virtues.

Reply to Objection 1. Meekness is not directly opposed to severity; for meekness is about anger. On the other hand, severity regards the external infliction of punishment, so that accordingly it would seem rather to be opposed to clemency, which also regards external punishing, as stated above (Article 1). Yet they are not really opposed to one another, since they are both according to right reason. For severity is inflexible in the infliction of punishment when right reason requires it; while clemency mitigates punishment also according to right reason, when and where this is requisite. Wherefore they are not opposed to one another as they are not about the same thing.

Reply to Objection 2. According to the Philosopher (Ethic. iv, 5), "the habit that observes the mean in anger is unnamed; so that the virtue is denominated from the diminution of anger, and is designated by the name of meekness." For the virtue is more akin to diminution than to excess, because it is more natural to man to desire vengeance for injuries done to him, than to be lacking in that desire, since "scarcely anyone belittles an injury done to himself," as Sallust observes [Cf. 120]. As to clemency, it mitigates punishment, not in respect of that which is according to right reason, but as regards that which is according to common law, which is the object of legal justice: yet on account of some particular consideration, it mitigates the punishment, deciding, as it were, that a man is not to be punished any further. Hence Seneca says (De Clementia ii, 1): "Clemency grants this, in the first place, that those whom she sets free are declared immune from all further punishment; and remission of punishment due amounts to a pardon." Wherefore it is clear that clemency is related to severity as equity [the Greek 'epieikeia' [Cf. 120]] to legal justice, whereof severity is a part, as regards the infliction of punishment in accordance with the law. Yet clemency differs from equity, as we shall state further on (3, ad 1).

Reply to Objection 3. The beatitudes are acts of virtue: while the fruits are delights in virtuous acts. Wherefore nothing hinders meekness being reckoned both virtue, and beatitude and fruit.

QUESTION 161. HUMILITY

ARTICLE 1. WHETHER HUMILITY IS A VIRTUE?

Objection 1. It would seem that humility is not a virtue. For virtue conveys the notion of a penal evil, according to Psalm 104:18, "They humbled his feet in fetters." Therefore humility is not a virtue.

Objection 2. Further, virtue and vice are mutually opposed. Now humility seemingly denotes a vice, for it is written (Sirach 19:23): "There is one that humbleth himself wickedly." Therefore humility is not a virtue.

Objection 3. Further, no virtue is opposed to another virtue. But humility is apparently opposed to the virtue of magnanimity, which aims at great things, whereas humility shuns them. Therefore it would seem that humility is not a virtue.

Objection 4. Further, virtue is "the disposition of that which is perfect" (Phys. vii, text. 17). But humility seemingly belongs to the imperfect: wherefore it becomes not God to be humble, since He can be subject to none. Therefore it seems that humility is not a virtue.

Objection 5. Further, every moral virtue is about actions and passions, according to Ethic. ii, 3. But humility is not reckoned by the Philosopher among the virtues that are about passions, nor is it comprised under justice which is about actions. Therefore it would seem not to be a virtue.

On the contrary, Origen commenting on Luke 1:48, "He hath regarded the humility of His handmaid," says (Hom. viii in Luc.): "One of the virtues, humility, is particularly commended in Holy Writ; for our Saviour said: 'Learn of Me, because I am meek, and humble of heart.'"

I answer that, As stated above (I-II, 23, 2) when we were treating of the passions, the difficult good has something attractive to the appetite, namely the aspect of good, and likewise something repulsive to the appetite, namely the difficulty of obtaining it. On respect of the former there arises the movement of hope, and in respect of the latter, the movement of despair. Now it has been stated above (I-II, 61, 2) that for those appetitive movements which are a kind of impulse towards an object, there is need of a moderating and restraining moral virtue, while for those which are a kind of recoil, there is need, on the part of the appetite, of a moral virtue to strengthen it and urge it on. Wherefore a twofold virtue is necessary with regard to the difficult good: one, to temper and restrain the mind, lest it tend to high things immoderately; and this belongs to the virtue of humility: and another to strengthen the mind against despair, and urge it on to the pursuit of great things according to right reason; and this is magnanimity. Therefore it is evident that humility is a virtue.

Reply to Objection 1. As Isidore observes (Etym. x), "a humble man is so called because he is, as it were, 'humo acclinis'" [Literally, 'bent to the ground'], i.e. inclined to the lowest place. This may happen in two ways. First, through an extrinsic principle, for instance when one is cast down by another, and thus humility is a punishment. Secondly, through an intrinsic principle: and this may be done sometimes well, for instance when a man, considering his own failings, assumes the lowest place according to his mode: thus Abraham said to the Lord (Genesis 18:27), "I will speak to my Lord, whereas I am dust and ashes." In this way humility is a virtue. Sometimes, however, this may be ill-done, for instance when man, "not understanding his honor, compares himself to senseless beasts, and becomes like to them" (Psalm 48:13).

Reply to Objection 2. As stated (ad 1), humility, in so far as it is a virtue, conveys the notion of a praiseworthy self-abasement to the lowest place. Now this is sometimes done merely as to outward signs and pretense: wherefore this is "false humility," of which Augustine says in a letter (Ep. cxlix) that it is "grievous pride," since to wit, it would seem to aim at excellence of glory. Sometimes, however, this is done by an inward movement of the soul, and in this way, properly speaking, humility is reckoned a virtue, because virtue does not consist in externals, but chiefly in the inward choice of the mind, as the Philosopher states (Ethic. ii, 5).

Reply to Objection 3. Humility restrains the appetite from aiming at great things against right reason: while magnanimity urges the mind to great things in accord with right reason. Hence it is clear that magnanimity is not opposed to humility: indeed they concur in this, that each is according to right reason.

Reply to Objection 4. A thing is said to be perfect in two ways. First absolutely; such a thing contains no defect, neither in its nature nor in respect of anything else, and thus God alone is perfect. To Him humility is fitting, not as regards His Divine nature, but only as regards His assumed nature. Secondly, a thing may be said to be perfect in a restricted sense, for instance in respect of its nature or state or time. Thus a virtuous man is perfect: although in comparison with God his perfection is found wanting, according to the word of

Isaiah 40:17, "All nations are before Him as if they had no being at all." In this way humility may be competent to every man.

Reply to Objection 5. The Philosopher intended to treat of virtues as directed to civic life, wherein the subjection of one man to another is defined according to the ordinance of the law, and consequently is a matter of legal justice. But humility, considered as a special virtue, regards chiefly the subjection of man to God, for Whose sake he humbles himself by subjecting himself to others.

ARTICLE 3. WHETHER ONE OUGHT, BY HUMILITY, TO SUBJECT ONESELF TO ALL MEN?

Objection 1. It would seem that one ought not, by humility, to subject oneself to all men. For, as stated above (2, ad 3), humility consists chiefly in man's subjection to God. Now one ought not to offer to a man that which is due to God, as is the case with all acts of religious worship. Therefore, by humility, one ought not to subject oneself to man.

Objection 2. Further, Augustine says (De Nat. et Gratia xxxiv): "Humility should take the part of truth, not of falsehood." Now some men are of the highest rank, who cannot, without falsehood, subject themselves to their inferiors. Therefore one ought not, by humility, to subject oneself to all men.

Objection 3. Further no one ought to do that which conduces to the detriment of another's spiritual welfare. But if a man subject himself to another by humility, this is detrimental to the person to whom he subjects himself; for the latter might wax proud, or despise the other. Hence Augustine says in his Rule (Ep. ccxi): "Lest through excessive humility the superior lose his authority." Therefore a man ought not, by humility, to subject himself to all.

On the contrary, It is written (Philippians 2:3): "In humility, let each esteem others better than themselves."

I answer that, We may consider two things in man, namely that which is God's, and that which is man's. Whatever pertains to defect is man's: but whatever pertains to man's welfare and perfection is God's, according to the saying of Hosea 13:9, "Destruction is thy own, O Israel; thy help is only in Me." Now humility, as stated above (1, ad 5; 2, ad 3), properly regards the reverence whereby man is subject to God. Wherefore every man, in respect of that which is his own, ought to subject himself to every neighbor, in respect of that which the latter has of God's: but humility does not require a man to subject what he has of God's to that which may seem to be God's in another. For those who have a share of God's gifts know that they have them, according to 1 Corinthians 2:12: "That we may know the things that are given us from God." Wherefore without prejudice to humility they may set the gifts they have received from God above those that others appear to have received from Him; thus the Apostle says (Ephesians 3:5): "(The mystery of Christ) was not known to the sons of men as it is now revealed to His holy apostles." In like manner. humility does not require a man to subject that which he has of his own to that which his neighbor has of man's: otherwise each one would have to esteem himself a greater sinner than anyone else: whereas the Apostle says without prejudice to humility (Galatians 2:15): "We by nature are Jews, and not of the Gentiles, sinners." Nevertheless a man may esteem his neighbor to have some good which he lacks himself, or himself to have some evil which another has not: by reason of which, he may subject himself to him with humility.

Reply to Objection 1. We must not only revere God in Himself, but also that which is His in each one, although not with the same measure of reverence as we revere God. Wherefore we should subject ourselves with humility to all our neighbors for God's sake, according to 1 Peter 2:13, "Be ye subject . . . to every human creature for God's sake"; but to God alone do we owe the worship of latria.

Reply to Objection 2. If we set what our neighbor has of God's above that which we have of our own, we cannot incur falsehood. Wherefore a gloss [St. Augustine, QQ. lxxxiii, qu. 71 on Philippians 2:3, "Esteem others better than themselves," says: "We must not esteem by pretending to esteem; but we should in truth think it possible for another person to have something that is hidden to us and whereby he is better than we are, although our own good whereby we are apparently better than he, be not hidden."

Reply to Objection 3. Humility, like other virtues, resides chiefly inwardly in the soul. Consequently a man, by an inward act of the soul, may subject himself to another, without giving the other man an occasion of detriment to his spiritual welfare. This is what Augustine means in his Rule (Ep. ccxi): "With fear, the superior should prostrate himself at your feet in the sight of God." On the other hand, due moderation must be observed in the outward acts of humility even as of other virtues, lest they conduce to the detriment of others. If, however, a man does as he ought, and others take therefrom an occasion of sin, this is not imputed to the man who acts with humility; since he does not give scandal, although others take it.

QUESTION 182. THE ACTIVE LIFE IN COMPARISON WITH THE CONTEMPLATIVE LIFE

ARTICLE 1. WHETHER THE ACTIVE LIFE IS MORE EXCELLENT THAN THE CONTEMPLATIVE?

Objection 1. It would seem that the active life is more excellent than the contemplative. For "that which belongs to better men would seem to be worthier and better," as the Philosopher says (Top. iii, 1). Now the active life belongs to persons of higher rank, namely prelates, who are placed in a position of honor and power; wherefore Augustine says (De Civ. Dei xix, 19) that "in our actions we must not love honor or power in this life." Therefore it would seem that the active life is more excellent than the contemplative.

Objection 2. Further, in all habits and acts, direction belongs to the more important; thus the military art, being the more important, directs the art of the bridle-maker [Ethic. i, 1. Now it belongs to the active life to direct and command the contemplative, as appears from the words addressed to Moses (Exodus 19:21), "Go down and charge the people, lest they should have a mind to pass the" fixed "limits to see the Lord." Therefore the active life is more excellent than the contemplative.

Objection 3. Further, no man should be taken away from a greater thing in order to be occupied with lesser things: for the Apostle says (1 Corinthians 12:31): "Be zealous for the better gifts." Now some are taken away from the state of the contemplative life to the occupations of the active life, as in the case of those who are transferred to the state of prelacy. Therefore it would seem that the active life is more excellent than the contemplative.

On the contrary, Our Lord said (Luke 10:42): "Mary hath chosen the best part, which shall not be taken away from her." Now Mary figures the contemplative life. Therefore the contemplative life is more excellent than the active.

I answer that, Nothing prevents certain things being more excellent in themselves, whereas they are surpassed by another in some respect. Accordingly we must reply that the contemplative life is simply more excellent than the active: and the Philosopher proves this by eight reasons (Ethic. x, 7,8). The first is, because the contemplative life becomes man according to that which is best in him, namely the intellect, and according to its proper objects, namely things intelligible; whereas the active life is occupied with externals. Hence Rachael, by whom the contemplative life is signified, is interpreted "the vision of the principle," [Or rather, 'One seeing the principle,' if derived from rah and irzn; Cf. Jerome, De Nom. Hebr.] whereas as Gregory says (Moral. vi, 37) the active life is signified by Lia who was blear-eyed. The second reason is because the contemplative life can be more continuous, although not as regards the highest degree of contemplation, as stated above (180, 8, ad 2; 181, 4, ad 3), wherefore Mary, by whom the contemplative life is signified, is described as "sitting" all the time "at the Lord's feet." Thirdly, because the contemplative life is more delightful than the active; wherefore Augustine says (De Verb. Dom. Serm. ciii) that "Martha was troubled, but Mary feasted." Fourthly, because in the contemplative life man is more self-sufficient, since he needs fewer things for that purpose; wherefore it was said (Luke 10:41): "Martha,

Martha, thou art careful and art troubled about many things." Fifthly, because the contemplative life is loved more for its own sake, while the active life is directed to something else. Hence it is written (Psalm 36:4): "One thing I have asked of the Lord, this will I seek after, that I may dwell in the house of the Lord all the days of my life, that I may see the delight of the Lord." Sixthly, because the contemplative life consists in leisure and rest, according to Psalm 45:11, "Be still and see that I am God." Seventhly, because the contemplative life is according to Divine things, whereas active life is according to human things; wherefore Augustine says (De Verb. Dom. Serm. civ): "'In the beginning was the Word': to Him was Mary hearkening: 'The Word was made flesh': Him was Martha serving." Eighthly, because the contemplative life is according to that which is most proper to man, namely his intellect; whereas in the works of the active life the lower powers also, which are common to us and brutes, have their part; wherefore (Psalm 35:7) after the words, "Men and beasts Thou wilt preserve, O Lord," that which is special to man is added (Psalm 35:10): "In Thy light we shall see light."

Our Lord adds a ninth reason (Luke 10:42) when He says: "Mary hath chosen the best part, which shall not be taken away from her," which words Augustine (De Verb. Dom. Serm. ciii) expounds thus: "Not—Thou hast chosen badly but—She has chosen better. Why better? Listen—because it shall not be taken away from her. But the burden of necessity shall at length be taken from thee: whereas the sweetness of truth is eternal."

Yet in a restricted sense and in a particular case one should prefer the active life on account of the needs of the present life. Thus too the Philosopher says (Topic. iii, 2): "It is better to be wise than to be rich, yet for one who is in need, it is better to be rich . . ."

Reply to Objection 1. Not only the active life concerns prelates, they should also excel in the contemplative life; hence Gregory says (Pastor. ii, 1): "A prelate should be foremost in action, more uplifted than others in contemplation."

Reply to Objection 2. The contemplative life consists in a certain liberty of mind. For Gregory says (Hom. iii in Ezech.) that "the contemplative life obtains a certain freedom of mind, for it thinks not of temporal but of eternal things." And Boethius says (De Consol. v, 2): "The soul of man must needs be more free while it continues to gaze on the Divine mind, and less so when it stoops to bodily things." Wherefore it is evident that the active life does not directly command the contemplative life, but prescribes certain works of the active life as dispositions to the contemplative life; which it accordingly serves rather than commands. Gregory refers to this when he says (Hom. iii in Ezech.) that "the active life is bondage, whereas the contemplative life is freedom."

Reply to Objection 3. Sometimes a man is called away from the contemplative life to the works of the active life, on account of some necessity of the present life, yet not so as to be compelled to forsake contemplation altogether. Hence Augustine says (De Civ. Dei xix, 19): "The love of truth seeks a holy leisure, the demands of charity undertake an honest toil," the work namely of the active life. "If no one imposes this burden upon us we must devote ourselves to the research and contemplation of truth, but if it be imposed on us, we must bear it because charity demands it of us. Yet even then we must not altogether forsake the delights of truth, lest we deprive ourselves of its sweetness, and this burden overwhelm us." Hence it is clear that when a person is called from the contemplative life to the active life, this is done by way not of subtraction but of addition.

ARTICLE 3. WHETHER THE CONTEMPLATIVE LIFE IS HINDERED BY THE ACTIVE LIFE?

Objection 1. It would seem that the contemplative life is hindered by the active life. For the contemplative life requires a certain stillness of mind, according to Psalm 45:11, "Be still, and see that I am God"; whereas the active life involves restlessness, according to (Luke 10:41), "Martha, Martha, thou art careful and troubled about many things." Therefore the active life hinders the contemplative.

Objection 2. Further, clearness of vision is a requisite for the contemplative life. Now active life is a hindrance to clear vision; for Gregory says (Hom. xiv in Ezech.) that it "is blear-eyed and fruitful, because the active life, being occupied with work, sees less." Therefore the active life hinders the contemplative.

Objection 3. Further, one contrary hinders the other. Now the active and the contemplative life are apparently contrary to one another, since the active life is busy about many things, while the contemplative life attends to the contemplation of one; wherefore they differ in opposition to one another. Therefore it would seem that the contemplative life is hindered by the active.

On the contrary, Gregory says (Moral. vi, 37): "Those who wish to hold the fortress of contemplation, must first of all train in the camp of action."

I answer that, The active life may be considered from two points of view. First, as regards the attention to and practice of external works: and thus it is evident that the active life hinders the contemplative, in so far as it is impossible for one to be busy with external action, and at the same time give oneself to Divine contemplation. Secondly, active life may be considered as quieting and directing the internal passions of the soul; and from this point of view the active life is a help to the contemplative, since the latter is hindered by the inordinateness of the internal passions. Hence Gregory says (Moral. vi, 37): "Those who wish to hold the fortress of contemplation must first of all train in the camp of action. Thus after careful study they will learn whether they no longer wrong their neighbor, whether they bear with equanimity the wrongs their neighbors do to them, whether their soul is neither overcome with joy in the presence of temporal goods, nor cast down with too great a sorrow when those goods are withdrawn. In this way they will known when they withdraw within themselves, in order to explore spiritual things, whether they no longer carry with them the shadows of the things corporeal, or, if these follow them, whether they prudently drive them away." Hence the work of the active life conduces to the contemplative, by quelling the interior passions which give rise to the phantasms whereby contemplation is hindered.

This suffices for the Replies to the Objections; for these arguments consider the occupation itself of external actions, and not the effect which is the quelling of the passions.

SUPPLEMENT TO THE THIRD PART

QUESTION 41. THE SACRAMENT OF MATRIMONY AS DIRECTED TO AN OFFICE OF NATURE

ARTICLE 1. WHETHER MATRIMONY IS OF NATURAL LAW?

Objection 1. It would seem that matrimony is not natural. Because "the natural law is what nature has taught all animals" [Digest. I, i, de justitia et jure, 1.] But in other animals the sexes are united without matrimony. Therefore matrimony is not of natural law.

Objection 1. Further, that which is of natural law is found in all men with regard to their every state. But matrimony was not in every state of man, for as Tully says (De Inv. Rhet.), "at the beginning men were savages and then no man knew his own children, nor was he bound by any marriage tie," wherein matrimony consists. Therefore it is not natural.

Objection 3. Further, natural things are the same among all. But matrimony is not in the same way among all, since its practice varies according to the various laws. Therefore it is not natural.

Objection 4. Further, those things without which the intention of nature can be maintained would seem not to be natural. But nature intends the preservation of the species by generation which is possible without matrimony, as in the case of fornicators. Therefore matrimony is not natural.

On the contrary, At the commencement of the Digests it is stated: "The union of male and female, which we call matrimony, is of natural law."

Further, the Philosopher (Ethic. viii, 12) says that "man is an animal more inclined by nature to connubial than political society." But "man is naturally a political and gregarious animal," as the same author asserts (Polit. i, 2). Therefore he is naturally inclined to connubial union, and thus the conjugal union or matrimony is natural.

I answer that, A thing is said to be natural in two ways. First, as resulting of necessity from the principles of nature; thus upward movement is natural to fire. In this way matrimony is not natural, nor are any of those things that come to pass at the intervention or motion of the free-will. Secondly, that is said to be natural to which nature inclines although it comes to pass through the intervention of the free-will; thus acts of virtue and the virtues themselves are called natural; and in this way matrimony is natural, because natural reason inclines thereto in two ways. First, in relation to the principal end of matrimony, namely the good of the offspring. For nature intends not only the begetting of offspring, but also its education and development until it reach the perfect state of man as man, and that is the state of virtue. Hence, according to the Philosopher (Ethic. viii, 11,12), we derive three things from our parents, namely "existence," "nourishment," and "education." Now a child cannot be brought up and instructed unless it have certain and definite parents, and this would not be the case unless there were a tie between the man and a definite woman and it is in this that matrimony consists. Secondly, in relation to the secondary end of matrimony, which is the mutual services which married persons render one another in household matters. For just as natural reason dictates that men should live together, since one is not self-sufficient in all things concerning life, for which reason man is described as being naturally inclined to political society, so too among those works that are necessary for human life some are becoming to men, others to women. Wherefore nature inculcates that society of man and woman which consists in matrimony. These two reasons are given by the Philosopher (Ethic. viii, 11,12).

Reply to Objection 1. Man's nature inclines to a thing in two ways. In one way, because that thing is becoming to the generic nature, and this is common to all animals; in another way because it is becoming to the nature of the difference, whereby the human species in so far as it is rational overflows the genus; such is an act of prudence or temperance. And just as the generic nature, though one in all animals, yet is not in all in the same way, so neither does it incline in the same way in all, but in a way befitting each one. Accordingly man's nature inclines to matrimony on the part of the difference, as regards the second reason given above; wherefore the Philosopher (Ethic. viii, 11,12; Polit. i) gives this reason in men over other animals; but as regards the first reason it inclines on the part of the genus; wherefore he says that the begetting of offspring is common to all animals. Yet nature does not incline thereto in the same way in all animals; since there are animals whose offspring are able to seek food immediately after birth, or are sufficiently fed by their mother; and in these there is no tie between male and female; whereas in those whose offspring needs the support of both parents, although for a short time, there is a certain tie, as may be seen in certain birds. In man, however, since the child needs the parents' care for a long time, there is a very great tie between male and female, to which tie even the generic nature inclines.

Reply to Objection 2. The assertion of Tully may be true of some particular nation, provided we understand it as referring to the proximate beginning of that nation when it became a nation distinct from others; for that to which natural reason inclines is not realized in all things, and this statement is not universally true, since Holy Writ states that there has been matrimony from the beginning of the human race.

Reply to Objection 3. According to the Philosopher (Ethic. vii) "human nature is not unchangeable as the Divine nature is." Hence things that are of natural law vary according to the various states and conditions of men; although those which naturally pertain to things Divine nowise vary.

Reply to Objection 4. Nature intends not only being in the offspring, but also perfect being, for which matrimony is necessary, as shown above.

QUESTION 67. THE BILL OF DIVORCE

ARTICLE 1. WHETHER INSEPARABLENESS OF THE WIFE IS OF NATURAL LAW?

Objection 1. It would seem that inseparableness of the wife is not of natural law. For the natural law is the same for all. But no law save Christ's has forbidden the divorcing of a wife. Therefore inseparableness of a wife is not of natural law.

Objection 2. Further, the sacraments are not of the natural law. But the indissolubility of marriage is one of the marriage goods. Therefore it is not of the natural law.

Objection 3. Further, the union of man and woman in marriage is chiefly directed to the begetting, rearing, and instruction of the offspring. But all things are complete by a certain time. Therefore after that time it is lawful to put away a wife without prejudice to the natural law.

Objection 4. Further, the good of the offspring is the principal end of marriage. But the indissolubility of marriage is opposed to the good of the offspring, because, according to philosophers, a certain man cannot beget offspring of a certain woman, and yet he might beget of another, even though she may have had intercourse with another man. Therefore the indissolubility of marriage is against rather than according to the natural law.

On the contrary, Those things which were assigned to nature when it was well established in its beginning belong especially to the law of nature. Now the indissolubility of marriage is one of these things according to Matthew 19:4-6. Therefore it is of natural law.

Further, it is of natural law that man should not oppose himself to God. Yet man would, in a way, oppose himself to God if he were to sunder "what God hath joined together." Since then the indissolubility of marriage is gathered from this passage (Matthew 19:6) it would seem that it is of natural law.

I answer that, By the intention of nature marriage is directed to the rearing of the offspring, not merely for a time, but throughout its whole life. Hence it is of natural law that parents should lay up for their children, and that children should be their parents' heirs (2 Corinthians 12:14). Therefore, since the offspring is the common good of husband and wife, the dictate of the natural law requires the latter to live together forever inseparably: and so the indissolubility of marriage is of natural law.

Reply to Objection 1. Christ's law alone brought mankind "to perfection" [Cf. Hebrews 7:19] by bringing man back to the state of the newness of nature. Wherefore neither Mosaic nor human laws could remove all that was contrary to the law of nature, for this was reserved exclusively to "the law of the spirit of life" [Cf. Romans 8:2].

Reply to Objection 2. Indissolubility belongs to marriage in so far as the latter is a sign of the perpetual union of Christ with the Church, and in so far as it fulfills an office of nature that is directed to the good of the offspring, as stated above. But since divorce is more directly incompatible with the signification of the sacrament than with the good of the offspring, with which it is incompatible consequently, as stated above (65, 2, ad 5), the indissolubility of marriage is implied in the good of the sacrament rather than in the good of the offspring, although it may be connected with both. And in so far as it is connected with the good of the offspring, it is of the natural law, but not as connected with the good of the sacrament.

The Reply to the Third Objection may be gathered from what has been said.

Reply to Objection 4. Marriage is chiefly directed to the common good in respect of its principal end, which is the good of the offspring; although in respect of its secondary end it is directed to the good of the contracting party, in so far as it is by its very nature a remedy for desire. Hence marriage laws consider what is expedient for all rather than what may be suitable for one. Therefore although the indissolubility of marriage hinder the good of the offspring with regard to some individual, it is proportionate with the good of the offspring absolutely speaking: and for this reason the argument does not prove.

APPENDIX II: PURGATORY

ARTICLE 1. WHETHER THERE IS A PURGATORY AFTER THIS LIFE?

Objection 1. It would seem that there is not a Purgatory after this life. For it is said (Apocalypse 14:13): "Blessed are the dead who die in the Lord. From henceforth now, saith the Spirit, that they may rest from their labors." Therefore after this life no cleansing labor awaits those who die in the Lord, nor those who do not die in the Lord, since they cannot be cleansed. Therefore there is no Purgatory after this life.

Objection 2. Further, as charity is to an eternal reward, so is mortal sin to eternal punishment. Now those who die in mortal sin are forthwith consigned to eternal punishment. Therefore those who die in charity go at once to their reward; and consequently no Purgatory awaits them after this life.

Objection 3. Further, God Who is supremely merciful is more inclined to reward good than to punish evil. Now just as those who are in the state of charity, do certain evil things which are not deserving of eternal punishment, so those who are in mortal sin, at times perform actions, generically good, which are not deserving of an eternal reward. Therefore since these good actions are not rewarded after this life in those who will be damned, neither should those evil actions be punished after this life. Hence the same conclusion follows.

On the contrary, It is said (2 Maccabees 12:46): "It is a holy and wholesome thought to pray for the dead, that they may be loosed from sins." Now there is no need to pray for the dead who are in heaven, for they are in no need; nor again for those who are in hell, because they cannot be loosed from sins. Therefore after this life, there are some not yet loosed from sins, who can be loosed therefrom; and the like have charity, without which sins cannot be loosed, for "charity covereth all sins" [Proverbs 10:12]. Hence they will not be consigned to everlasting death, since "he that liveth and believeth in Me, shall not die for ever" [John 11:26]: nor will they obtain glory without being cleansed, because nothing unclean shall obtain it, as stated in the last chapter of the Apocalypse (verse 14). Therefore some kind of cleansing remains after this life.

Further, Gregory of Nyssa [De iis qui in fide dormiunt] says: "If one who loves and believes in Christ," has failed to wash away his sins in this life, "he is set free after death by the fire of Purgatory." Therefore there remains some kind of cleansing after this life.

I answer that, From the conclusions we have drawn above (III, 86, 4-5; Supplement, 12, 1) it is sufficiently clear that there is a Purgatory after this life. For if the debt of punishment is not paid in full after the stain of sin has been washed away by contrition, nor again are venial sins always removed when mortal sins are remitted, and if justice demands that sin be set in order by due punishment, it follows that one who after contrition for his fault and after being absolved, dies before making due satisfaction, is punished after this life. Wherefore those who deny Purgatory speak against the justice of God: for which reason such a statement is erroneous and contrary to faith. Hence Gregory of Nyssa, after the words quoted above, adds: "This we preach, holding to the teaching of truth, and this is our belief; this the universal Church holds, by praying for the dead that they may be loosed from sins." This cannot be understood except as referring to Purgatory: and whosoever resists the authority of the Church, incurs the note of heresy.

Reply to Objection 1. The authority quoted is speaking of the labor of working for merit, and not of the labor of suffering to be cleansed.

Reply to Objection 2. Evil has not a perfect cause, but results from each single defect: whereas good arises from one perfect cause, as Dionysius asserts [Div. Nom. iv, 4]. Hence each defect is an obstacle to the perfection of good; while not every good hinders some consummation of evil, since there is never evil without some good. Consequently venial sin prevents one who has charity from obtaining the perfect good, namely eternal life, until he be cleansed; whereas mortal sin cannot be hindered by some conjoined good from bringing a man forthwith to the extreme of evils.

Reply to Objection 3. He that falls into mortal sin, deadens all the good he has done before, and what he does, while in mortal sin, is dead: since by offending God he deserves to lose all the good he has from God. Wherefore no reward after this life awaits him who dies in mortal sin, whereas sometimes punishment awaits him who dies in charity, which does not always wash away the sin which it finds, but only that which is contrary to it.

DE DIVINIS MORIBUS
(THE WAYS OF GOD)

TRANSLATED BY RAISSA MARITAIN & MARGARET SUMNER

"Be perfect as your heavenly Father is perfect" (Mat 5:48). Holy Scripture never orders and never counsels us to do the impossible. By these words, then, the Lord Jesus does not command us to accomplish the very works and ways of God, that no one can attain in perfection.

But he invites us to model ourselves on them, as much as is possible, by applying ourselves to imitate them. We can do this with the help of grace and we should do so. And, as the Bishop John said, nothing is more suitable to man than to imitate his Creator, and to carry out according to the measure of his possibility, the designs of God.

GOD IS UNCHANGEABLE

Among the ways of God, there is a primary perfection which is that He never changes. He himself declares it by the Prophet: "I am God and I do not change" (Malachy 3:6), and by Saint James: "Every best gift, and every perfect gift, is from above, coming down from the Father of lights, with whom there is no change nor shadow of alteration" (1:17). Created things bear in themselves a trace of this changelessness, in that they are unchangeable in their essence. And if sometimes he sends his angels, and sometimes does not send them; if at time he withdraws his grace and at times confers it, if now he punishes sins, and now cloaks them, the change is in creatures, in no way in the Creator.

In short, the changeless of his decrees, in regard to the good and the bad will confirm itself at the last day, when he will give forever to he good a recompense superior to their merits, and will inflict forever on the bad a punishment that is less than the gravity of their faults.

Let us strive therefore to acquire stability of spirit, in order that, broken by adversity or tempted by prosperity, we never depart from the right way, and that we may say with Job: "My justification, which I have begun to hold, I will not forsake; for my heart does not reproach me in all my life" (27:6). and with Saint Paul: "For I am sure that neither death, nor life, nor angels, nor principalities, nor powers, nor things present, nor things to come, etc., shall be able to separate us from the love of God" (Romans 8).

But, alas, how inconstant we are in holy meditations, in lawful affections, in steadfastness of conscience, in a right will. Ah, how suddenly we pass from good to bad, from hope to a groundless fear, and from fear to hope, from joy to unreasonable grief, and from sadness to vain joy, from silence to loquaciousness, from gravity to trifling, from charity to rancor or to envy, from fervor to tepidity, from humility to vain-glory or to pride, from gentleness to anger, from joy and spiritual love to carnal love and pleasure.

In this way we never remain one single instant in the same state, if it be not, alas, that we are constant in inconstancy, in infidelity, in ingratitude, in spiritual defects, in imperfection, in negligence, in frivolity, and in ill-regulated thoughts and affections. Even the motions that trouble our exterior senses and our limbs reveal our interior instability.

Nevertheless we should work without ceasing to acquire constancy of soul, in order to conduct ourselves in all circumstances with equanimity, maturity and sweetness.

GOOD IS PLEASING TO GOD

Among the ways of God there is another perfection, it is that all good is pleasing to him by nature, always and everywhere, whether it be in the angels or in the other creatures: qualities of the body, like beauty, strength, grace, sweetness, and the fullness of natural maturity; qualities of the soul, such as perspicacity of the spirit, tenacity of memory, subtlety of the intelligence, rectitude of the will, vigor of free-will; natural gifts, such as to read well, to sing well, to preach well, to be eloquent, sober continent, to have well regulated habits; finally, the gifts of grace, which please God above everything, like faith, hope, charity, humility, patience, obedience, mercy, temperance, justice, prudence and knowledge.

Similarly all evil displeases him everywhere and always and in whatever it exists. As justice is the enemy of injustice and impurity of purity,—equally so the malice of man is contrary to the goodness of God, because it diminishes or even completely destroys the divine good that grace brings to nature.

All that is good should please us also, always and everywhere and in every creature. We should protect and support good with solicitude and resist boldly those who combat it.

We should detest evil with all our heart and lay ourselves out to prevent it because it is injurious to God and harmful to one's neighbor; and even more because it endangers man's fate.

But, alas, oftener it is the opposite that takes place. For if we feel sad because someone is praised, and is beloved on account of his humility, his piety, his sermons, his devotion etc., and if we try to diminish his merits,—how do we show ourselves if not as beings whom good does not please?

And when we are conversing with slanderers and laugh with them, when we delight in these frivolities and other faults of the same order,—what do we do, if not certify that evil things do not displease us?

We also should tend towards this perfection, in order that no matter how grievously a man has injured us, we never hate his nature; and that, wishing him every kind of good, whatever be the corporal and spiritual help he expects from us, we should be always ready to grant it to him at once.

But there is in God a just hatred that we also should partake of; for it is necessary that the love we have for man should not extend to loving his sin, no more than we should detest human nature because we detest its vices. Let us know, everywhere, how to hate evil and love the very being of things.

THE JUSTICE OF GOD

Among the ways of God there is another perfection, which is that the malice of one person never damages, in the judgement of God, the good that is in another. Thus the fall of Lucifer did not harm the Archangel Michael; and the perfidy of Judas did not lessen the charity of the blessed Peter.

But we, miserable as we are, if a monk is guilty of some excess, we reproach the whole convent and the entire Order and even every monk without exception, with the fault of a single one.

If one of our enemies offends us, we pursue a great number of innocent people with our hatred, all his descendants, his friends and associates. That is something that the Law of God forbids. "The soul that sins, the same shall die, the son shall not bear the iniquity of the father, and the father shall not bear the iniquity of the son; the justice of the just shall be upon him, and he wickedness of the wicked shall be upon him." (Ezechiel 18:20). "For everyone shall bear his own burden" (Galatians 6:5).

And how often does it not happen, when our soul is troubled, that we blame God himself, who certainly does not deserve it—for then we no longer wish to sing nor study, nor read nor pray.

THE RECTITUDE OF GOD

Among the ways of God there is another perfection, which is that he never omits nor puts aside mercy for justice, or justice for mercy. In fact, he never judges nor condemns without mercy, and when he pardons justice is never wounded.

Whereas we, unfortunates, if we try to practice justice, mercy dies out in our soul, and if we open our hearts to mercy, it is at this moment that justice is buried.

But Scripture recommends justice and mercy both at the same time: "May mercy and truth never abandon you" (Proverbs 3). And the Psalmist said: "I will sing of mercy and of justice before you, O Lord" (100 [101]:1).

THE LONGANIMITY OF GOD

Among the ways of God there is another perfection. Whereas, at time, all the saints and all creatures cry vengeance against the sinner, as is written in the Apocalypse (6:10): "And they cried in a loud voice, 'How long will it be, O Master, holy and true, before you judge our cause and avenge our blood among the inhabitants of the earth?'" God, however, with patience and mercy awaits the sinner until his death in order to have pity upon him, if he will, even in this last moment, regret his evil ways and turn towards him. For the Lord infinitely good cannot rejoice at the loss of the living.

But we, in our impatience, before the grave is dug for the sinner, cursing him and crying out for justice, would like to see him swallowed up on the very instant. We reproach God for bearing so long with the evil that the wicked cause the just to suffer, and we do not wish to consider the good that his wisdom expects to draw even from the malice of the impious.

For, in his forbearance with the wicked the Lord is equally good and also equally worthy of praise as though he had preserved the world from sin, had it pleased him to act thus,—or delivered it completely from evil.

It would have been easy, as a fact, to fling the wicked into the depths of Hell; but where above all his power is manifest is in the mercy which bears him to have pity on the sinner, and to forgive him.

THE BOUNTY OF GOD

Among the ways of God there is another perfection, he communicates to creatures all the good that in its essence is communicable and that they have the capacity to receive, and this continuously, as soon as they allow him to give, even though he sees that his gifts do not fructify in them.

He united human nature and the divine nature in the person of the Word, the greatest work of all. And, without mentioning his other spiritual gifts, he has made the human soul capable of receiving the Trinity within itself, and he nourishes it with the flesh and blood of his beloved Son.

He withheld nothing that could be given, and this is the property of Divine Goodness. That which he possesses by his nature, God communicated to creatures by grace; bliss to the angels, without their having known misery; power to the choir of Apostles, in such a way that all that they should bind or unbind on earth, should be bound or unbound in Heaven; the prevision of things to come to the Choir of Prophets; strength to the Choir of Martyrs; constancy to the Choir of Confessors, and to the Choir of Virgins continence amid the seductions of the flesh.

She shares also with some in particular the blessings that he has by his nature. He gave magnanimity to Abraham, meekness to Moses, who was the gentlest of men, the stewardship of Egypt to Joseph, to Sampson strength, To Eli zeal for justice, to Job and to Tobit patience, to Elisha power to raise the dead, to Daniel wisdom in judgements, to Samuel faithfulness, to David mercy towards his persecutors, to Solomon prudence, to John the Baptist love of holiness and truth, to Peter charity, to John chastity, to blessed Paul zeal for souls and the understanding of things above, to the Blessed Virgin humility. Each one distinguished himself in the exercise of his special gift, while possessing also the other virtues.

And we, not only should we make a mutual gift of our eyes, that they may see for others, of our ears that hear penitents, of our mouth that it be ready to preach and to counsel, of our feet that they may be the servants of our neighbor, and of our heart that it may meditate his salvation,—but also all that we can do outwardly by our works, inwardly by our desires, all that we are in body and in soul, we should give generously to each of those who are in Purgatory and to those who are now alive and who soon will be gone, in order that the will of God be accomplished in them now and always.

GOD ALLOWS HIMSELF TO BE EASILY APPEASED

Among the ways of God there is another perfection, which inclines him to forgive immediately the gravest and most numerous offenses, if we make a firm resolution to turn from them and truly to amend.

Even more, he forgets them in return for a single lamentation of a contrite heart, as the Scripture says. And, if we remain in this good-will, he does not meditate vengeance for our sins later on, nor does he meditate reproaching us with them in order to dismay us, nor charging us with them in order to love us less, nor driving us away from him in withdrawing his intimacy.

But we who should walk in the footprints of God, it is with difficulty that we agree to forgive, from the heart, a single small offense to one who implores our forgiveness. If it happens that we do not forgive, we almost never forget; we rejoice in the embarrassment of our debtor; we have small pity for him in adversity, or else we love him less than we did before. If we do not reproach him it is certain, however, that we exclude him from our intimacy, and even in times of trial we refuse him our counsel and our support.

We should, on the contrary, forget the offenses of our enemy, even though he neither repents nor amends, in imitation of Christ, who prayed for those who crucified him, and who, far from repenting, mocked him.

Nothing makes us more like God, said Saint John Chrysostom, than to allow ourselves to be easily appeased and to be pitiful to the wayward and to those who harm us. For the height of perfection is to love our enemies, and to pray for them as did the Lord Jesus.

THE MERCY OF GOD

Among the was of God there is another perfection; he exacts nothing that is beyond our strength in fasting, prayers, watchings, almsgiving, bodily mortifications and regular discipline etc.

And, if we fail in great and difficult works—to efface our sins he contents himself with the most humble things, such as tears that come from the heart.

It is thus he considered the tears of Ezechiah, and revoking the sentence of death that he had pronounced upon him by the Prophet, he granted him fifteen more years of life.

He listened, with the same mercy, to the tears of blessed Peter, when at the cock-crow, he wept bitterly over the enormous fault of his denial.

If it happens that some one cannot weep, a single word, coming from a contrite heart, suffices for God. It is thus that to the robber who said to him, "Lord, remember me when you come into your kingdom," Jesus replied: "This day you shall be with me in Paradise."

And if some one lost in the use of his tongue, God would accept fully the lamentations of his heart, according as it is written: "At whatever hour the sinner laments I will forget all his iniquities."

Finally, if illness deprived a man of the use of all his members, and even of the power to groan, before this extreme weakness God would even be contented with a good and sincere will, in order to forgive the most grievous offenses.

Do not let us then exact more from whomsoever it be, secular or religious, even though by reason of his vocation he is bound to greater perfection, if he has done faithfully what he was capable of doing.

GOD IS PERFECTLY BALANCED IN HIS JUDGMENTS

Among the ways of God there is another perfection; he reproaches no one with their natural defects of body or of soul, such as blindness, deafness, deformity of the members, stupidity, lack of intelligence, of mind, of memory, of reason and natural pusillanimity. For defects of this kind God does not disdain and does not reject any man.

But he gravely charges us with the spiritual defects that are easy for each one to rise above with the help of grace, such as to take pride in the greatness of certain gifts, to desire superfluous things, to be sad at the progress of the just, to rejoice at their afflictions, to detest good works or to obstruct them, to vilify one's neighbor, to lessen his good reputation, to hold obstinately to one's preferences, never to renounce one's own opinion, to apply one's self to please man, to hate reprimand, to love adulation, to seek extraneous consolations, to cherish carnal affections.

In the same way we should never be contemptuous to those who are deprived of health, strength, beauty, eloquence, charm in conversation,—gifts that no one holds from himself. Let us give thanks to God for those who possess these gifts. Let us be patient with the others, and let us try, according to our strength, to supply all they lack.

THE GENEROSITY OF GOD

Among the ways of God there is another perfection, which leads him to grant his grace with extreme liberality according to the calling of each one—as is said in the Gospel: "And he gave to one five talents, and to another two and to a third a single one, to each according to his capacity" (Matthew 25:25).

Also, the more the heart of man is dilated by love of God and of his neighbor, the more his meditations, his fervent prayers, his humility and his generosity will have opened his soul to grace—the more elevated and greater is the grace that God the All Powerful will bestow upon him. And in the measure, even, that he seeks to conserve it and to use it for the praise of God and the common utility, in the same measure he disposes himself to receive a more abundant infusion of grace in this world and of glory in Paradise.

Let us then dilate our hearts and prepare them by frequent aspirations in order that God who is "rich in mercy to all who invoke him" may shower his grace upon us according to his munificence.

But let him who is charged to dispense spiritual goods by preaching and by counsels, watch with the greatest care that he does not give holy things to the dogs, and does not throw pearls before swine.

"Day to day utters speech and night to night shows knowledge" (Ps 18 [19]:3); which signifies that the most perfect things must be given to the perfect and less perfect to the imperfect, as is the duty of a faithful steward. It is thus, indeed, that Saint Paul announced Jesus to the imperfect, even Jesus crucified, but the mystery of wisdom contained therein he disclosed only to the perfect (1 Cor 2).

THE DISCRETION OF GOD

Among the ways of God there is another perfection: "He exacts much from him to whom he has given much, and even more from him to whom he has given more" (Luke 12:48).

From him whom God has loaded with temporal goods, he requires more abundant almsgiving; and from him who has received as his share health and strength, more fasting and watchings, meditations, pilgrimages and good works.

From him to whom he has remitted a greater number of sins, or graver sins, and from him whom he has preserved from them, he awaits a more generous love and more worthy fruits of penitence.

From him to whom he grants superior virtues, more perfect natural gifts of the spirit, of the intelligence, of the memory, of the will, and to whom he provides more numerous and more uplifted spiritual gifts, such as devotion, peace of conscience, spiritual joy, a firm and universal confidence, wisdom in discourse, persevering search for perfection, diligence in well-doing, purity of intention, zeal for souls, fervor in prayer, God lawfully requires greater acts of thanksgiving.

And from him whom God in his benevolence admits more often, and in a more intimate manner, to the knowledge of his goodness, of his serenity, of his immensity, of his all-powerfulness, of his liberality, of his charity, of his wisdom, of his mercy, of his justice, of his truth, of his faithfulness, of his patience, of his humility, of his suavity and his nobility, he expects praise more abundant, more frequent and more fervent.

From him whom he illumines in the quest for and knowledge of a higher perfection, in order that he shall practice it effectively and make more and more progress in it, God claims more; it is necessary as a result, that such a one by his words, his example, his prayers and his desires, bring, as much as he is able, to the knowledge and practice of perfection, those whom he judges capable of it.

Let us watch therefore, in order that on the day of reckoning we may be able to render to God with interest each of the gifts he confides to us lest he should order them to be taken away from us, and to throw us miserably into exterior darkness, with the lazy servant who had enveloped and hidden in a cloth the talent given him by the Lord.

THE JUST JUDGMENT OF GOD

Among the ways of God there is another perfection, which is that he does not judge human acts on their exterior appearance, but he discerns all in his immense and ineffable wisdom, according to the intentions of the heart. And it is according to the intention which gave birth to them that he accords to our works grave punishment or excellent recompense.

Neither, then, let us judge anyone on the testimony of our senses alone, on that which we see or hear.

That men show us an affable or a severe face, that they speak to us with sweetness or with rudeness, that they make us gifts or not, in every circumstance let us be attentive no only to what they do, but to the intention that prompts them, and let us conduct ourselves accordingly.

For it is more useful to us to bear rude words from a veritable friend who proposes our amendment, than to listen to the sweet and flattering discourses of those who do not truly love us, and whose only aim is to please us. "Wounds made by those who love us" said Solomon, "are better than lying kisses from those who hate us."

THE VERACITY OF GOD

Among the ways of God there is another perfection: He is true in his promises.

According to his own testimony, it is easier for heaven and earth to pass away than that a single one of his words should change or cease to be true.

For the Lord Jesus never speaks in vain, as we others do, but each one of the words he has pronounced in time were said, in his wisdom, from all eternity.

And as he accomplished, in coming among us, the hidden predictions of the Prophets touching his incarnation, his nativity, his passion, his resurrection, his ascension and the mission of the Holy Spirit, he will in the same way bring to pass the general resurrection that he has promised—and the future judgment.

He will hold to what he has promised to the poor, when at the last day he will place them upon twelve thrones, to judge the twelve tribes of Israel, and to that which he promised to those who weep when he himself will console them as a mother consoles her children.

He will hold to what he promised to the humble, when he will exalt them, in the same measure that hey had been abased and disdained, and to what he promised to the proud, when he will humble them as much as they had glorified themselves.

And he will keep the promise that he made to the oppressed when, at the command of his Father, he will trample under his feet the neck of the oppressor.

"For God is faithful in all his words, and what he has promised he is powerful to accomplish."

Let us also be true and, first of all, let us keep faithfully the baptismal promises that our god-fathers have made in our name, and which oblige us to persevere in the Catholic Faith, to renounce the Devil and all his works, and to keep the ten commandments, keeping also, in the same way, the vows we may have made spontaneously later on: vows of obedience, of continence, of abstinence, of religion etc.

Let us be true in our dealings with our neighbor. That our speech be yes, yes; no, no; that is to say that our heart be always in accord with our lips.

Let us be faithful in our promises, and if we owe anything, no matter what, to a living person or to a dead one, let us free ourselves of our debt without delay. For God demands the truth, and punishes severely those who despise it.

Alas, alas, how odious to men is this most excellent truth by which salvation comes to all. "He who hates the truth, hates Christ." They hate truth, they betray it. And not only he betrays the truth who proffers lies for truth, said Saint John Chrysostom, but he who does not speak it freely also betrays it, for it must be freely spoken; also he who does not defend it boldly, for it must be boldly defended.

GOD IS NO RESPECTER OF PERSONS

Among the ways of God there is another perfection: He is no respecter of persons (Acts 10).

Under the ancient Law, as a fact, it is not the illustrious and the mighty, but obscure men like Moses, Joshua, Gideon, that he established judges of his people.

Later he chose men of humble origin to reign, like Saul, son of Cis, and David, the least among his brothers, who tended sheep.

When he founded his Church, it was not nobles and men of great learning, but simple fishermen whom he constituted princes over the whole earth, confiding to them the government of the Church. As said the Apostle, "But the foolish things of the world has God chosen, that he may confound the wise" (1 Cor 1).

Today it is the same, in dispensing his favors God does not consider men's power, nor strength, nor riches, nor bodily beauty. "But that man is pleasing to God, no matter from what nation, who fears him and performs works of justice" (Acts 10).

It is not only men who are handsome, rich, illustrious, that the Lord calls to eternal life. It is also the poor, the blind, the lame, the weak, that he urges to enter in, and it is above all people of humble condition who progress in the Church of God and abound in spiritual grace.

At the last judgment he will take no account of the person of kings and princes. He will judge with perfect equity the great and the lowly, and he will glorify them uniquely according to the degree of their humility and of their charity.

Let us then keep ourselves from the respecting of persons. One must, as said Saint Gregory, honor man, because he is man and made in the image and likeness of God, and not for anything that surrounds him, like riches, precious clothing, power, a noble name, and a multitude of friends and relations, for in the Scriptures the respecting of persons is considered a great imperfection.

May one never hear, then, a preacher in his sermons praise the life of the rich and great, who have their consolation on his earth, nor blame without reason the life of the poor and afflicted who suffer here below.

God grant that a confessor never listen more willingly to a person who enjoys the advantages of fortune, of social rank, of youth or of beauty, or from whom he expects some personal profit, rather than to an old man, a poor man, an infirm, a man of the people, who might have greater need. He should not give more time and effort to the one than to the other. Or, if he occupies himself with the former, let it be only because they are more exposed to sin than others, and because they can drag a greater number into evil-doing.

And neither may it please God that those who distribute alms be respecters of persons. Let the alms be more abundant there where misery is the greatest; and let those who are progressing in virtue be aided more amply.

Nevertheless in all circumstances one must act according to the teaching of the Apostle (Rom 13) "Render to each man his due, to one who fears, fear, to one to whom honor is due, honor." To one who loves, love, to one who is friendly, friendliness according the degree of holiness, and according to the dignity of each one.

THE CARE OF GOD FOR CREATURES

Among the ways of God there is another perfection; it is that he takes care of all creatures. Two sparrows sell for only a penny, even so not one is forgotten by him. He maintains all the living in their being and supplies unceasingly all their necessities. He takes care of all inert matter, the herbs and the trees that nourish themselves by it, and of all the animals, great and small, who dwell upon the earth, in the air or in the waters.

But above all he takes care of men, created in his image and likeness. He made them members of his beloved Son and temples of the Holy Spirit. He has sent to each one an angel to watch over him. He gives life to them in the precious flesh and blood of his only Son. He provided for the necessities of all, and admirably too for the temporal needs of sinners, his enemies, still more abundantly than for the needs of his friends.

He takes care of the souls in Purgatory in permitting that they be rescued by the desires of the Church triumphant, by the prayers of the Church militant, and by the oblations of priests, even when they offer them unworthily, and therefore would, themselves, deserve to be condemned.

And while prayers, almsgiving, fasting and pilgrimages, accomplished without charity, are insufficient to efface the sins of those who practice these devotions, it is, however, permitted piously to believe that such works, offered for the souls in Purgatory, may obtain for them, by an effect of divine goodness, some relief and even the remission of their sufferings, on account of the merits that they had here below.

Finally, God takes great care of the holy angels, whom he has established in such bliss, and whom he has forever preserved from all experience of evil.

Let us also care for creatures, using each one according to the order willed by God, lest at the day of judgment they testify against us.

Let us care for all men, assuming intimately their joys and griefs, seeking to restrain them from wrong doing, and to comfort them in the Lord, by our desires, our prayers and our good examples.

Let us care for the souls in Purgatory, applying ourselves frequently to relieving their sufferings by works of mercy.

Let us care for the angels in order that they shall not, by our fault, be deprived of the joy they should receive from the progress that, thanks to their good care and to their protection, we make in virtue.

And last and above everything, let us take tender care of God himself, doing everywhere and always what he most desires us to do and that for which he has particularly destined us.

NOTHING CAN DISTURB THE SERENITY OF GOD

Among the ways of God there is another perfection: Nothing can perturb him. And though Scripture often speaks of his anger and his fury, it only wishes by this to show him taking vengeance on sin, or justly retiring his grace from his creature.

But he himself is entirely serene. He has no contrary. His simplicity is so perfect, he possesses in his own nature such a felicity, so great a joyfulness, that no perturbations can ever touch him.

We must therefore as much as possible flee all that unbalances us, for grace cannot dwell in a soul that is agitated.

But to keep inner peace one must occupy one's self vehemently with God. It is necessary that love strong as death accomplish in us the work of death, in order that seeing the actions of those who approach us, we do not see them, and that hearing words which could harm us or which are said against us, we do not hear them, and that our heart be not occupied with these things. We should, in imitation of David, be like the blind, the deaf and the dumb, and like men without feeling. "But I as a deaf man heard not, and as a dumb man not opening his mouth" (Ps 37 [38]:14).

Let us then give ourselves up faithfully and with fervor to the things of God, and leave each one to his own conscience, to the judgment of his superiors, and to the ultimate justice of God, who said "Vengeance belongs to me and I will render it to men according to their works in the appointed time."

Let us keep ourselves even more from troubling others, lest they in turn trouble us also, as often happens, and that our conscience be tormented.

For God the All-Powerful, who loves justice, will not leave unpunished at the last day actions which, in causing confusion, will have contributed to diminishing here below the number of holy meditations, of right desires, of prayers and of other good works, and thus harmed Catholicity in heaven or on earth or in purgatory.

THE DISINTERESTEDNESS OF GOD

Among the ways of God there is another perfection, which is that in all that he has done and arranged he has entirely ignored all thought of his own interest; he has considered, uniquely, the abundance of his eternal and immense goodness, and ordered all for the greatest good of the angelic and the human creatures.

In the creation and the preservation of the heavens, and of all that hey enclose, it is not his own advantage that he has proposed to himself, but rather than of men and of angels.

Whatever he ordains among his creatures, fair weather or tempests, famine or abundance, health or epidemics, all that he does for men, that he confers, that he retires his grace, that he makes them vigorous or weak, poor or rich, that he makes them to live or die, that he permits the good or the bad to reign, to succor or to afflict the poor, to judge with equity or to offend justice,—he does all, he orders all, he permits all, because of his infinite goodness, and in view of the common good of men.

In like manner in all our desires, prayers, fasting, almsgiving, in all our acts, in all our words, in all that we bear from God, let our intentions be pure.

Without aiming at our interest, without seeking to please men, without fear of displeasing them, without even fixing our intention on what we might receive of grace in the present time, and of glory in the time to come, we should only consider the admirable goodness of God, act purely and above all for it, and in the second place for the salvation of our neighbor.

The more our intention be pure and strongly directed towards God, the less we dwell upon our own advantages and even upon those of other men,—the more our works will be agreeable to God and profitable to all. But, alas, how much they will lose in value before God, and for the universality of creatures, if we see in them any other thing than the pure goodness of the Lord.

"He will separate the grain from the straw with his fan," says the Gospel (Matthew 3). His wisdom will separate the pure from the impure; he will gather up the wheat alone in his barns, and he will burn the straw; that is to say he will reward in heaven and will allow to serve for the good of all, only that which has, with a pure intention, been done or omitted or suffered for him alone. "The Lord will reward me according to my justice," said David, " and will repay me according to the cleanness of my hands, as my hands shall have been pure before his eyes" (Ps 17 [18]).

GOD HAS DONE ALL THINGS WELL

Among the ways of God there is another perfection, in virtue of which he has done all his works in an excellent manner.

For the works of heaven and of the earth, of angels and of men, and of all the other creatures, is so perfect that it would be impossible conceive it better ordained.

Supremely perfect above all is the work of the Redemption; that non other, in heaven nor on earth, would have been able to accomplish but God.

"He carried wisdom to its summit when he conquered the Devil through that wood by means of which the Devil had triumphed,"—that is in hiding until the end the divine power under the fragility of humanity. "Because if the demons had recognized him," says the Apostle (1 Cor 2), "never would they have crucified the Lord of glory," that is to say they would not have incited the Jews to crucify him.

And all that God does today, be it that he chastises sins, be it that he cloaks them on account of repentance, be it that he confers his graces on the elect, be it that he retires his graces from them, that he acts towards the faithful soul no familiarly, now as a stranger, that the air be cold or warm, that it rain, that it blow, that the road be dry or humid, that the fruits of the earth abound or perish—it would not be possible that all this could be better at the given moment, because the immense wisdom of God by an extreme charity and benignity produces each thing at the very time it is needed.

He will also accomplish very perfectly the work of remuneration, when he will attribute to each sin, and to each member which will have been the instrument of the iniquity, its just punishment according to the quantity and the gravity of the fault committed and when he will recompense with justice each act of good-will, each word, each example, according to the intensity of the supernatural love that produced them.

We should then take every car, we also, to accomplish as well as possible each of our actions, doing them by the virtue of our Lord Jesus-Christ, with all the desire of the Church triumphant and militant, and in the name of our Creator, as though our salvation and the interest of God and of the universality of creatures depended upon a single act that we do, as if we should never again do a like act, or never again do anything at all.

For each time that an extraneous thought introduces itself into our actions, a turning of the should toward something else, the spirit relaxes in its present work. For example, when we are praying, if at this moment we suggest to ourselves that we must write, or undertake some other work, our attention to prayer lessens, and we soon leave what we had begun.

THE BENEVOLENCE OF GOD

Among the ways of God there is another perfection, which leads him to judge no man according to his malice or his justice in the past or future, but according to the present state of his soul.

It is thus that he did not condemn Paul on account of is previous malice, nor save Judas on account of his past justice.

But we, miserable creatures, whatever be the progress that some one makes in virtue or in holiness, we do not omit to remind ourselves often of his past injustice. On the other hand, if the just man happens to turn aside form the way of justice in some one point, though it be one single time,—even if he repents of it, we no longer remember his holiness.

Similarly, God never punishes twice for the same fault, if a first chastisement suffices and if the fault be corrected following the punishment.

Yet we, miserable creatures that we are, we would inflict, if it were in our power, one hundred most terrible punishments for one single injury that is done us.

THE SOUL SHOULD MODEL ITSELF ON GOD

The faithful soul should make its effort to model itself as much as is possible on the divine ways of which we have been speaking.

For the more it has been modeled on its Creator in this world, the more it will be like him in the life to come, and the more it is like him,—the greater will be its bliss, the more it will give glory to God and will be useful to every creature.

From this moment on it behooves the faithful to exult in joy, for it will possess these ways of God in life eternal, "when we shall be like him and see him as he is."

Made in the USA
Monee, IL
03 November 2020